THE 50 GREATEST PLAYERS IN CINCINNATI REDS HISTORY

ALSO AVAILABLE IN THE 50 GREATEST PLAYERS SERIES

The 50 Greatest Players in Boston Celtics History
The 50 Greatest Players in Boston Red Sox History
The 50 Greatest Players in Braves History
The 50 Greatest Players in Buffalo Bills History
The 50 Greatest Players in Chicago Bears History
The 50 Greatest Players in Cincinnati Bengals History
The 50 Greatest Players in Cleveland Browns History
The 50 Greatest Players in Dallas Cowboys History
The 50 Greatest Players in Denver Broncos History
The 50 Greatest Players in Detroit Tigers History
The 50 Greatest Players in Green Bay Packers History
The 50 Greatest Players in Houston Astros History
The 50 Greatest Players in Kansas City Chiefs History
The 50 Greatest Players in Minnesota Vikings History
The 50 Greatest Players in New England Patriots History
The 50 Greatest Players in New York Giants History
The 50 Greatest Players in New York Yankees History
The 50 Greatest Players in Philadelphia Eagles History
The 50 Greatest Players in Philadelphia Phillies History
The 50 Greatest Players in Pittsburgh Pirates History
The 50 Greatest Players in Pittsburgh Steelers History
The 50 Greatest Players in San Francisco 49ers History
The 50 Greatest Players in St. Louis Cardinals History

THE 50 GREATEST PLAYERS IN CINCINNATI REDS HISTORY

ROBERT W. COHEN

ESSEX, CONNECTICUT

An imprint of The Globe Pequot Publishing Group, Inc.
64 South Main Street
Essex, CT 06426
LyonsPress.com

Distributed by NATIONAL BOOK NETWORK

British Library Cataloguing in Publication Information available

Library of Congress Cataloging-in-Publication Data available

ISBN 978-1-4930-8591-0 (cloth)
ISBN 978-1-4930-8592-7 (electronic)

CONTENTS

ACKNOWLEDGMENTS

I would like to thank Kate Yeakley of RMYauctions.com, George Kitrinos, Keith Allison, Dirk Hansen, Mike Morbeck, and Hayden Schiff, each of whom generously contributed to the photographic content of this work.

INTRODUCTION

The origins of the Cincinnati Reds can be traced back to a Cincinnati Red Stockings team that competed in the newly formed National League from 1876 to 1880, before being expelled from the circuit for serving beer at games and allowing its park to be used on Sundays. Incensed over the Red Stockings' expulsion from the NL, *Cincinnati Enquirer* sports editor O. P. Caylor formed a new independent team of the same name that became a charter member of the American Association (AA), a rival league that began play in 1882.

Owned and operated by former Red Stockings president Justus Thorner and managed by catcher/first baseman Pop Snyder, the latest version of the Cincinnati ballclub, which spent most of its formative years playing its home games at League Park, excelled in the AA's inaugural season, winning the league championship by posting a record of 55–25 behind the superb pitching of 40-game winner Will White. Continuing to perform well the next seven seasons after clothing firm executive and theatrical producer Aaron S. Stern assumed control of the team, the Red Stockings, who shortened their name to the Reds during this period, compiled a winning record each year under the guidance of four different managers.

Choosing to leave the American Association and join the National League in 1890, the Reds experienced little success the next six seasons, never finishing any higher than fourth, as Tom Loftus (1890–1891), Charles Comiskey (1892–1894), and Buck Ewing (1895) took turns managing the ballclub. Nevertheless, future Hall of Fame second baseman Bid McPhee distinguished himself with his outstanding all-around play.

Although the Reds posted a winning record five straight times under Ewing from 1895 to 1899, their failure to seriously contend for the NL flag prompted team president and owner John T. Brush to relieve him of his duties following the conclusion of the 1899 campaign. The Reds subsequently took a step backward under managers Bob Allen (1900), Bid McPhee (1901–1902), and Joe Kelley (1902–1903) the next four years, finishing above .500 just once, while moving into a newly constructed stadium called the Palace of the Fans in 1902 after a fire demolished their previous home.

Purchased that same year by a group headed by Garry Herrmann, who served as a member of Cincinnati's school board and president of the city's Water Works Commission, the Reds experienced a brief resurgence under player-manager Kelley in 1904 and 1905, posting back-to-back winning records, with star outfielder Cy Seymour setting a single-season franchise record that still stands by compiling a league-leading batting average of .377 in the second of those campaigns. However, following the release of Kelley at the end of 1905, the Reds entered one of the darkest periods in franchise history, finishing with a winning mark just three times between 1906 and 1918 under seven different managers. Meanwhile, with the Reds struggling on the playing field, they christened Redland Field as their new home in 1912 after the Palace of the Fans suffered its own devastating fire in 1911. A steel-and-concrete ballpark located on the corner of Findlay and Western Avenues on the city's west side, Redland Field (later renamed Crosley Field after new team owner Powel Crosley Jr. in 1934) remained home to the Reds until they moved into Riverfront Stadium 58 years later.

Finally emerging from their malaise under new manager Pat Moran in 1919, the Reds captured their first NL pennant by compiling a record of 96–44 during the regular season, before winning the World Series by defeating the Chicago White Sox in eight games. Unfortunately, the "Black Sox" scandal broke one year later, thereby tainting the Reds' triumph in the Fall Classic. Nevertheless, the 1919 Reds possessed an extremely talented roster that included Hall of Fame outfielder Edd Roush, standout third baseman Heinie Groh, solid-hitting, slick-fielding first baseman Jake Daubert, 21-game winner Slim Sallee, and 19-game winners Hod Eller and Dutch Ruether.

Proving to be a one-year wonder, the Reds seriously contended for the NL flag just three times during the 1920s, winning as many as 90 games only once. Yet, even though their lack of offensive firepower consistently relegated them to second-tier status, the Reds annually featured one of the league's best pitching staffs, with Hall of Fame southpaw Eppa Rixey and star right-handers Dolf Luque and Pete Donohue all excelling on the mound for much of the decade.

With the onset of the Great Depression, the Reds entered another period of extended mediocrity, finishing toward the bottom of the NL standings nine straight times from 1929 to 1937, as managers Jack Hendricks (1924–1929), Dan Howley (1930–1932), Donie Bush (1933), Bob O'Farrell (1934), and Chuck Dressen (1934–1937) all attempted to right the ship. The Reds finally began to show signs of life shortly after Powel Crosley Jr. purchased the team in 1934 from Sidney Weil, who had assumed ownership of the club four years earlier. An electronics magnate who, with his brother Lewis, had started WLW radio and the Crosley Broadcasting Corporation in Cincinnati, Crosley made the hiring of longtime baseball executive Larry MacPhail as general manager one of his first moves. MacPhail set about developing the Reds' farm system, which, over the course of the next few seasons, produced star first baseman Frank McCormick, hard-hitting outfielder Ival Goodman, and standout pitcher Johnny Vander Meer. A shrewd judge of talent, MacPhail also acquired via trade Bucky Walters, who proved to be the NL's finest pitcher much of his time in Cincinnati. And with MacPhail retaining the services of star catcher Ernie Lombardi and four-time 20-game winner Paul Derringer, the Reds soon emerged as strong contenders in the senior circuit, finishing six games behind the pennant-winning Cubs in 1938, before capturing the NL flag in each of the next two seasons under manager Bill McKechnie. Unfortunately, the Reds came up short against the Yankees in the 1939 World Series, losing to them in four straight games. But they captured their second world championship the following year by defeating the Detroit Tigers 4–3 in the Fall Classic.

McKechnie continued to manage the Reds for six more years, guiding them to a runner-up finish to St. Louis in 1943 and a pair of third-place finishes in 1941 and 1944, before being handed his walking papers during the latter stages of the 1946 campaign after piloting them to a mark of just 64–86. Continuing to struggle the next seven seasons under four different managers, the Reds failed to finish any higher than fifth, winning as many as 70 games just once.

Following two more losing seasons under new skipper Birdie Tebbetts, the Reds reemerged as contenders for the NL flag in 1956, when their powerful offense (they hit 221 home runs as a team) led them to a total of 91 victories that left them just two games behind the pennant-winning Dodgers in the final standings. While slugging first baseman Ted Kluszewski and hard-hitting outfielders Wally Post and Gus Bell all made a major impact on offense, the arrival in Cincinnati of NL Rookie of the Year Frank Robinson, who went on to become one of the greatest players in the history of the game, contributed more than anything to the Reds' return to prominence.

Meanwhile, three years before the Reds rejoined the NL's elite, they briefly changed their name to the Redlegs in response to the "Second Red Scare" that took place at the height of the Communist movement. The new moniker never caught on, though, prompting them to change their name back to the Reds prior to the start of the 1959 campaign.

The Reds finished near the middle of the pack in the NL standings four straight times from 1957 to 1960 under managers Tebbetts (1957–1958), Jimmy Dykes (1958), Mayo Smith (1959), and Fred Hutchinson (1959–1960), before the latter led them to their fourth league championship in 1961, the same year that longtime baseball executive Bill DeWitt purchased the team from the estate of Powel Crosley, who died suddenly prior to the start of the regular season. Assuming the role of general manager as well, DeWitt engineered trades for veteran third baseman Gene Freese and right-handed pitcher Joey Jay, each of whom made significant contributions to the Reds' successful run to the pennant. While Jay ended up leading the staff with 21 victories, Freese provided solid defense and another productive bat to a lineup that already included league MVP Frank Robinson and speedy young center fielder Vada Pinson, who finished second in the NL batting race to Roberto Clemente with a mark of .343. However, the Reds ran into a buzzsaw in the World Series in the form of the Yankees, who defeated them in five games.

The Reds remained serious contenders for the NL flag the next three years, posting more than 90 victories and finishing fewer than five games off the pace in both 1962 and 1964, before losing their beloved leader when Fred Hutchinson died of cancer. Nevertheless, with the Reds boasting a farm system that produced the likes of Pete Rose, Jim Maloney, Tony Pérez, and Lee May, they continued to perform well under managers Dick Sisler and Dave Bristol the next few years, even after DeWitt made a monumental error in judgment by trading Frank Robinson to the Baltimore Orioles at the end of 1965. One year later, DeWitt sold the Reds to an ownership group headed by *Cincinnati Enquirer* publisher Francis L. Dale, who, after appointing Bob Howsam general manager and team president, negotiated a deal with the city of Cincinnati and Hamilton County in which the two parties agreed to build a new, state-of-the-art stadium on the edge of the Ohio River, thereby averting a potential move of the team to San Diego. The Reds continued to call Crosley Field home until June 30, 1970, when they moved into brand-new Riverfront Stadium (later renamed Cinergy Field), a 52,000-seat multipurpose venue located in downtown Cincinnati that housed both the Reds and the NFL's Cincinnati Bengals for the next three decades. Meanwhile, with MLB adopting a new two-division setup in each league in 1969, the Reds became a member of the NL West, which they spent the next 24 years sharing with the Los Angeles Dodgers, San Francisco Giants, Atlanta Braves, Houston Astros, and San Diego Padres.

After the Reds finished four games behind the first-place Braves in 1969, Bob Howsam replaced Dave Bristol at the helm with the little-known George "Sparky" Anderson, who had spent most of his professional career playing and managing in the minor leagues. Flourishing under Anderson, the Reds finished well over .500 in eight of the next nine seasons, winning in the process five division titles, four pennants, and two World Series, with their powerful offense earning them the nickname "The Big Red Machine."

The Reds began their exceptional run in 1970 by running away with the division title with a record of 102–60. They subsequently advanced to the World Series by sweeping the Pittsburgh Pirates in three straight games in the NLCS. However, despite their potent lineup that included Pete Rose, speedy center fielder Bobby Tolan, and middle-of-the-order sluggers Lee May, Tony Pérez, and NL MVP Johnny Bench, the Reds proved to be no match for the Baltimore Orioles in the Fall Classic, losing to them in five games.

Following a subpar showing in 1971, the Reds completed an eight-player trade with the Houston Astros the following offseason that helped establish them as the NL's preeminent team. Sending Lee May, All-Star second baseman Tommy Helms, and infielder/outfielder Jimmy Stewart to Houston, the Reds received in return pitcher Jack Billingham, infielder Denis Menke, second sacker Joe Morgan, and outfielders Ed Armbrister and César Gerónimo. While Billingham, Menke, and Gerónimo all contributed significantly to the success the Reds experienced the next several years, Morgan proved to be the key to the deal, performing at a Hall of Fame level during his time in Cincinnati.

Still, it took the Reds four more years to reach their ultimate goal. After winning the division title in 1972 and edging out the Pirates 3–2 in the NLCS, the Reds lost a hard-fought seven-game World Series to the Oakland Athletics. NL West champions again in 1973, the Reds subsequently suffered a five-game defeat at the hands of the vastly inferior New York Mets in the NLCS. After minority owner Louis Nippert purchased majority control of the team from Francis Dale at the end of the year, the Reds finished a close second to the Dodgers in 1974, before reclaiming the division title the following year by posting a franchise-best regular-season mark of 108–54. The Reds subsequently swept the Pirates in the NLCS, before defeating the Boston Red Sox in seven games in one of the most memorable World Series ever played. Having exorcised their earlier demons, the Reds dominated their 1976 postseason opposition after laying claim to their second straight division title, sweeping the Phillies in the NLCS and the Yankees in the Fall Classic.

Generally ranked among the greatest teams in the history of the game, the Reds' championship squads of 1975 and 1976 featured lineups that, from top to bottom, had no weaknesses. With Pete Rose and Ken Griffey Sr. manning the top two spots, Joe Morgan, Johnny Bench, Tony Pérez, and George Foster comprising the middle of the order, and César Gerónimo and Dave Concepción preceding the pitcher at the bottom of the lineup, The Big Red Machine applied constant pressure to opposing hurlers. Though often overlooked, the Reds also had a solid pitching staff that included starters Don Gullett, Gary Nolan, Jack Billingham, and Fred Norman, and relievers Rawly Eastwick, Clay Carroll, and Pedro Borbón.

Following their back-to-back championships, the Reds underwent several changes in personnel that brought their period of dominance to an end. After losing Don Gullett to free agency on November 18, 1976, the Reds traded an aging Tony Pérez to the Montreal Expos one month later. Pete Rose signed as a free agent with the Philadelphia Phillies at the end of 1978. Meanwhile, age and injuries began to take their toll on Johnny Bench and Joe Morgan. The Reds added an ace to their pitching staff when they acquired Tom Seaver from the Mets midway through the 1977 campaign. But ownership replaced the man who engineered that trade, Bob Howsam, with longtime front office executive Dick Wagner the following offseason. And after the Reds finished second in the NL West two straight times, Wagner fired manager Sparky Anderson at the end of 1978 and replaced him with former Oakland Athletics and San Diego Padres skipper, John McNamara.

Faring well under McNamara his first year in charge, the Reds edged out Houston for the division title in 1979 by compiling a record of 90–71. However, they exited the postseason tournament quickly, losing to the Pirates in three straight games in the NLCS. After finishing 3.5 games off the pace the following year, the Reds posted the best overall record in baseball during the strike-interrupted 1981 campaign. But with the 108-game season being split into two halves and the Reds finishing second in the division in both halves, they failed to advance to the playoffs. The Reds subsequently slumped to a mark of 61–101 in 1982, costing McNamara his job. Continuing to struggle the next two seasons under managers Russ Nixon and Vern Rapp, the Reds finished well out of contention both years, leading to the hiring of Pete Rose, who assumed the dual role of player-manager during the latter stages of the 1984 campaign.

As the managing carousel continued in Cincinnati, the Reds experienced numerous changes in ownership and upper management as well. After Louis Nippert sold his shares of the team to a group headed by minority owners William and James Williams in 1981, the Williams brothers remained in charge until 1984, when minority owner Marge Schott purchased controlling interest in the ballclub. Prior to relinquishing control of the team, though, the Williams brothers replaced Dick Wagner as GM with Bob Howsam, who, before giving way to Bill Bergesch in 1985, helped return the Reds to respectability by making several wise moves, including trading for veteran slugger Dave Parker.

Performing relatively well under Pete Rose, who officially retired as an active player at the end of 1986 with more career hits (4,256) than anyone else in the history of the game, the Reds finished second in the NL West four straight times from 1985 to 1988. However, they stumbled somewhat in 1989, slumping to fifth place in the division, with Rose receiving a lifetime suspension from MLB commissioner Bart Giamatti during the latter stages of the campaign for "conduct detrimental to baseball" for betting on the game.

Following the banishment of Rose, new Cincinnati GM Murray Cook replaced him with Lou Piniella, who led the Reds to the division title, a six-game win over the Pirates in the NLCS, and a stunning four-game sweep of the heavily favored Oakland Athletics in the World Series his first year in charge. Although the 1990 Reds lacked the offensive firepower of The Big Red Machine, they proved to be an extremely well-balanced team whose lineup featured star center fielder Eric Davis, 1988 NL Rookie of the Year third baseman Chris Sabo, and future Hall of Fame shortstop Barry Larkin. Meanwhile, José Rijo, who earned Series MVP honors by winning both his starts against Oakland, and "Nasty Boys" relievers Rob Dibble, Norm Charlton, and Randy Myers anchored arguably the best bullpen in either league.

Piniella managed the Reds for two more years, failing to lead them back to the playoffs in either of those, before being relieved of his duties following the conclusion of the 1992 campaign. Following a brief 44-game managerial stint by fan favorite Tony Pérez, former New York Mets skipper Davey Johnson assumed control of the team for the next three seasons, during which time further expansion caused MLB to adopt a new three-division alignment in each league that resulted in the Reds being placed in the NL Central, which they spent the next few years sharing with the Chicago Cubs, St. Louis Cardinals, Pittsburgh Pirates, and Houston

Astros (the Milwaukee Brewers joined the division in 1998, and the Astros moved to the AL in 2013).

Posting a winning record under Johnson in both 1994 and 1995, the Reds won the division title in the second of those campaigns and then swept the Dodgers in three straight games in the NLDS. But they subsequently suffered a four-game sweep at the hands of the Braves in the NLCS, prompting general manager Jim Bowden to replace Johnson at the helm with former Reds third baseman Ray Knight, a close personal friend of team owner Marge Schott. Knight lasted less than two full seasons, before the Reds' uninspired play led to his firing and the hiring of Jack McKeon, who piloted the team for the next three-plus years. Meanwhile, Schott, whose racist comments and controversial statements supporting the domestic policies of Adolf Hitler drew her two lengthy suspensions from MLB, agreed to sell her controlling interest in the team to a group headed by Cincinnati businessman Carl Lindner on April 20, 1999.

Although the Reds posted a winning record in two of their three full seasons under McKeon, their failure to advance to the playoffs convinced Jim Bowden to replace him with former All-Star catcher and Kansas City Royals manager Bob Boone at the end of 2000.

Performing miserably under Boone the next three seasons despite the presence in their lineup of Ken Griffey Jr., Sean Casey, and Adam Dunn, the Reds finished well under .500 each year, eliciting the firings of both Bowden and Boone on July 28, 2003.

Yet, despite the team's poor showing in 2003, the season remains a memorable one since it marked the opening of Great American Ball Park, which has now served as home to the Reds for more than two decades. Located at 100 Joe Nuxhall Way, just east of the site on which Riverfront Stadium (Cinergy Field) once stood, Great American Ball Park, which opened at a cost of $290 million and has a seating capacity of 42,271, houses not only the Reds but also the team's Hall of Fame.

Following the dismissals of Bowden and Boone, the Reds continued to struggle the next few seasons under GM's Dan O'Brien and Wayne Krivsky, who failed in their attempts to restore the team to prominence by hiring managers Dave Miley (2003–2005), Jerry Narron (2005–2007), and Pete Mackanin (2007). The Reds experienced a brief resurgence shortly after Cincinnati businessman Bob Castellini purchased a majority share of the team from Carl Lindner in 2006 and replaced Krivsky with former St. Louis Cardinals GM Walt Jocketty, who, in turn, appointed Dusty Baker manager prior to the start of the 2008 campaign. Following two more losing seasons, the Reds, led by NL MVP Joey Votto, won the division title in

2010, nearly earning Baker NL Manager of the Year honors for the fourth time. Unfortunately, they subsequently exited the postseason tournament quickly, losing to the Phillies in three straight games in the NLDS. After finishing well out of contention the following year, the Reds advanced to the playoffs in each of the next two seasons, capturing the division title again in 2012 by posting a regular-season record of 97–65 that represented their best mark in more than three decades. However, they failed to make it out of the first round of the postseason tournament both years, losing to the Giants in five games in the 2012 NLDS, before suffering a 6–2 defeat at the hands of the Pirates in the 2013 NL Wild Card Game.

Returning to the depths of the NL Central after pitching coach Bryan Price replaced Dusty Baker as skipper in 2014, the Reds failed to win more than 68 games in four of the next five seasons, prompting new GM Nick Krall to attempt to rebuild the organization's farm system by dealing slugging outfielder Jay Bruce and star pitchers Johnny Cueto and Aroldis Chapman to other teams for top prospects. Krall also assigned managerial duties to David Bell, who, following a major-league career during which he manned third base for six different teams, spent the next decade managing in the minors and coaching at the big-league level.

Bell's first five years as skipper yielded mixed results, with the Reds posting three winning records and two losing marks and advancing to the playoffs as a wild card during the pandemic-shortened 2020 campaign. But following a disappointing showing in 2024 that saw them finish under .500 for the second time in three years, the Reds fired Bell and replaced him with Terry Francona, who previously led the Cleveland Indians/Guardians to one AL pennant and the Boston Red Sox to two world championships.

Although it has now been more than three decades since the Reds won their last World Series, the presence on their roster of talented young players such as outfielder Spencer Steer, shortstop Elly De La Cruz, and pitcher Hunter Greene appears to have them set up for future success. Their next world championship will be their sixth. The Reds have also won 10 division titles and nine National League pennants, which ranks as the sixth-highest total in the history of the senior circuit.

In addition to the success the Reds have experienced as a team over the years, a significant number of players have attained notable individual honors during their time in Cincinnati. The Reds boast 12 MVP winners, placing them fourth in NL history, behind only the Cardinals, Giants, and Dodgers. They have also featured nine home-run champions and nine batting champions. Meanwhile, a Reds pitcher has led the NL in wins 12 times, strikeouts 11 times, and ERA on nine separate occasions.

Furthermore, eight players have had their number retired by the team and 26 members of the Baseball Hall of Fame spent at least one full season playing for the Reds, 10 of whom had most of their finest seasons as a member of the organization.

FACTORS USED TO DETERMINE RANKINGS

It should come as no surprise that selecting the 50 greatest players ever to perform for a team with the rich history of the Cincinnati Reds presented a difficult and daunting task. Even after narrowing the field down to a mere 50 men, I found myself faced with the challenge of ranking the elite players that remained. Certainly, the names of Frank Robinson, Pete Rose, Johnny Bench, Joe Morgan, Barry Larkin, and Joey Votto would appear at, or near, the top of virtually everyone's list, although the order might vary somewhat from one person to the next. Several other outstanding performers have gained general recognition through the years as being among the greatest players ever to wear a Reds uniform, with Bucky Walters, Tony Pérez, George Foster, Eric Davis, and Dave Concepción heading the list of other Reds icons. But how does one differentiate between the all-around brilliance of Morgan and the offensive dominance of Robinson, or the pitching excellence of Walters and the tremendous slugging of Foster? After initially deciding whom to include on my list, I then needed to determine what criteria I should use to formulate my final rankings.

The first thing I decided to examine was the level of dominance a player attained during his time in Cincinnati. How often did he lead the National League in a major offensive or pitching statistical category? How did he fare in the annual MVP and/or Cy Young voting? How many times did he make the All-Star team?

I also needed to weigh the level of statistical compilation a player achieved while wearing a Reds uniform. Where does a batter rank in team annals in the major offensive categories? How high on the all-time list of Reds hurlers does a pitcher rank in wins, ERA, complete games, innings pitched, shutouts, and saves? Of course, I also needed to consider the era in which the player performed when evaluating his overall numbers. For example, modern-day starting pitchers such as José Rijo and Johnny Cueto were not likely to throw nearly as many complete games or shutouts as Eppa Rixey, who anchored Cincinnati's starting rotation during the 1920s. And Adam Dunn, who slugged home runs at a prodigious pace during the first decade of the 21st century, was likely to reach the seats far more often than Cy Seymour, who starred in the outfield for the Reds some 100 years earlier.

Other important factors I needed to consider were the overall contributions a player made to the success of the team, the degree to which he improved the fortunes of the ballclub during his time in the Queen City, the manner in which he impacted the team, both on and off the field, and the degree to which he added to the Reds' legacy of winning. While the number of pennants the Reds won during a particular player's years with the ballclub certainly factored into the equation, I chose not to deny a top performer his rightful place on the list if his years in Cincinnati happened to coincide with a lack of overall success by the team. As a result, players such as Ted Kluszewski and Sean Casey will figure prominently in these rankings.

There are two other things I should mention. Firstly, I only considered a player's performance during his time in Cincinnati when formulating my rankings. That being the case, the names of Hall of Famers Tom Seaver and Ken Griffey Jr., both of whom had most of their best years while playing for other teams, may appear lower on this list than one might expect. In addition, since several of the rules that governed 19th-century baseball (including permitting batters to dictate the location of pitches until 1887, situating the pitcher's mound only 50 feet from home plate until 1893, and crediting a stolen base to a runner any time he advanced from first to third base on a hit) differed dramatically from those to which we have become accustomed, I elected to include only those players who competed after 1900, which is generally considered to be the beginning of baseball's "modern era." Doing so eliminated from consideration 19th-century standouts such as Bid McPhee and Will White.

Having established the guidelines to be used throughout this book, we are ready to examine the careers of the 50 greatest players in Cincinnati Reds history, starting with number 1 and working our way down to number 50.

1
JOHNNY BENCH

Johnny Bench received stiff competition from Frank Robinson and Pete Rose for the top spot in these rankings, with Robinson and Rose each surpassing the man generally recognized as the greatest catcher in MLB history by a considerably wide margin in several statistical categories. While Bench hit more homers and knocked in more runs than any other player in team annals, Rose compiled a much higher batting average, scored many more runs, and accumulated far more hits, doubles, triples, and walks than his longtime teammate. Meanwhile, Robinson, in addition to holding franchise records for highest career slugging percentage and OPS, hit just 65 fewer homers and knocked in only 367 fewer runs than Bench in more than 2,200 fewer plate appearances. Rose and Robinson also each earned NL MVP honors once during their time in Cincinnati. But Bench won the award twice while serving as the cornerstone of Reds teams that won six division titles, four pennants, and two World Series. The best defender of the three, Bench also won 10 Gold Gloves for his brilliant work behind home plate, which, along with his tremendous offensive production, helped him earn 14 NL All-Star nominations, a number 16 ranking on the *Sporting News*' 1999 list of Baseball's 100 Greatest Players, a berth on MLB's All-Century Team, and a place in the Baseball Hall of Fame. Furthermore, while Robinson and Rose each spent several seasons playing for other teams, Bench remained in Cincinnati his entire career. Factoring everything into the equation, Bench seemed like the best choice for number one on this list, forcing Robinson and Rose to settle for the next two spots.

Born in Oklahoma City, Oklahoma, on December 7, 1947, Johnny Lee Bench moved with his family at the age of five some 60 miles west, to the town of Binger, where he grew up with his younger sister and two older brothers. The son of a former semiprofessional baseball player, Bench developed an affinity for sports early in life, remembering, "When I wasn't playing, I was watching games, just eating and living and breathing sports."

Johnny Bench served as the cornerstone of Reds teams that won six division titles, four pennants, and two World Series.
Courtesy of RMYAuctions.com

Encouraged by his dad, Bench practiced baseball daily and played catcher for several local Little League teams, recalling, "My father said catching was the quickest way to the big leagues because that's what they wanted."

Adding that he first began entertaining thoughts of playing professionally while watching fellow Oklahoma native Mickey Mantle compete in the

World Series, Bench revealed that he said to himself at the time, "You mean, you can be from Oklahoma and play in the major leagues!"

Developing into an excellent all-around athlete during his teenage years, Bench earned All-State honors in both baseball and basketball at Binger High School, setting off a recruiting frenzy as graduation neared. But after briefly considering attending college on a baseball/basketball scholarship, Bench chose to sign with the Reds for $6,000 plus college tuition when they selected him in the second round of the June 1965 MLB Amateur Draft, with the 36th overall pick.

The 17-year-old Bench subsequently began his pro career with Tampa in the Florida State League, failing to distinguish himself on offense, but drawing favorable reviews for his defense. Far more effective at the bat for Class A Peninsula in 1966, Bench earned Carolina League Player of the Year honors by batting .294, hitting 22 homers, and driving in 68 runs, in only 99 games, before being promoted to Triple-A Buffalo during the latter stages of the campaign. Returning to Buffalo in 1967, Bench gained recognition from the *Sporting News* as that publication's Minor League Player of the Year with his excellent all-around play, which earned him a late-season callup to Cincinnati. Although Bench batted just .163 in his 26 games with the parent club, he received a boost in confidence during spring training the following year when an impressed Ted Williams presented him with an autographed baseball that read, "To Johnny Bench, a Hall of Famer for sure."

Though still only 20 years old, Bench ended up laying claim to the starting catcher's job, after which he went on to earn 1968 NL Rookie of the Year honors and the first of his 13 consecutive All-Star nominations by hitting 15 homers, driving in 82 runs, batting .275, posting an OPS of .743, and finishing third in the league with 40 doubles. Bench also garnered Gold Glove honors for the first of 10 straight times by leading all NL receivers in both putouts (942) and assists (102).

While Bench posted better numbers on offense than any other NL catcher in his first full big-league season, he received widespread acclaim for his defense, with Roy Blount Jr. of *Sports Illustrated* writing of his powerful throwing arm, "It is about the size of a good healthy leg, and it works like a recoilless rifle."

Stating confidently, "I can throw out any man alive," Bench also drew praise from Baltimore Orioles GM Harry Dalton, who commented, "Every time Bench throws, everybody in baseball drools."

Bench also did an exceptional job of handling Cincinnati's pitching staff, with the team's hurlers marveling at his ability to call a great game at such a young age and expressing amazement at how quickly he learned the league's hitters. Commenting on his batterymate's ability to get the most out of him, veteran Reds right-hander Jim Maloney stated, "He'll come out on the mound and treat me like a two-year-old, but so help me, I like it. . . . This kid coaches me. . . . When you're in a big sweat and nervous, he can calm you down more ways than I have ever seen."

Ironically, Maloney initially resisted Bench's advice more than any other Reds pitcher, before learning to fully appreciate his knowledge of his craft through an incident that occurred at 1968 spring training. Maloney, an eight-year veteran at the time, had endured numerous injuries through the years that significantly reduced the velocity of his once-blazing fastball. Nevertheless, he continued to "shake off" his young catcher's signals for breaking balls, preferring instead to throw his rather mediocre heater. An exasperated Bench bluntly told Maloney, "Your fastball's not popping," to which the veteran right-hander responded with an expletive. To prove his point, Bench finally called for a fastball. Then, after Maloney released his pitch, the catcher dropped his mitt and casually caught the offering bare-handed. Maloney never again questioned Bench's signal-calling abilities.

Bench followed up his outstanding rookie campaign by hitting 26 homers, driving in 90 runs, scoring 83 times, batting .293, and posting an OPS of .840 in 1969, before leading the Reds to the pennant the following year by topping the senior circuit with 45 homers and 148 RBIs, ranking among the league leaders with 355 total bases and a .587 slugging percentage, batting .293, compiling an OPS of .932, and scoring 97 runs, with his fabulous performance earning him NL MVP and *Sporting News* MLB Player of the Year honors. Bench subsequently suffered through a subpar 1971 season, hitting 27 homers, but driving in only 61 runs and batting just .238. However, he rebounded in 1972 to begin an extremely productive four-year stretch during which he posted the following numbers:

YEAR	HR	RBI	RUNS	AVG	OBP	SLG	OPS
1972	**40**	**125**	87	.270	.379	.541	.920
1973	25	104	83	.253	.345	.429	.774
1974	33	**129**	108	.280	.363	.507	.870
1975	28	110	83	.283	.359	.519	.878

* Please note that any numbers printed in bold throughout this book indicate that the player led the league in that statistical category that year.

In addition to consistently ranking among the NL leaders in home runs, RBIs, and slugging percentage, Bench finished second in the league with 108 runs scored and 38 doubles in 1974. An NL All-Star and Gold Glove Award winner each season, Bench also earned four straight top-10 finishes in the league MVP voting, winning the award for a second time in 1972, when he led the Reds to the pennant despite spending part of the year playing with a growth on his lung that doctors discovered while conducting a routine physical examination during the latter stages of the campaign. Undergoing surgery the following offseason that required doctors to make a 12-inch incision under his right arm and break a rib, Bench had a lesion removed from his lung that proved to be benign. But Bench later said, "They cut the ribs, they cut the bones, they cut the nerves, and, so, I never was the same player afterwards."

Nevertheless, Bench remained the finest all-around catcher in the game, separating himself from his fellow receivers with his tremendous offensive production and superior defensive skills. Big and strong at 6'1" and 200 pounds, the right-handed-hitting Bench possessed outstanding power to all fields, although he pulled almost all his homers to left. One of baseball's most consistent RBI-men, Bench performed especially well in pressure situations, enabling him to knock in more than 100 runs a total of six times over the course of his career.

Meanwhile, in addition to his powerful throwing arm, Bench displayed exceptional quickness in the field, with Cubs manager Leo Durocher exclaiming after watching him tag out a Chicago runner on a high throw to the plate, "I still don't believe it. I have never seen that play executed so precisely."

Capable of holding seven baseballs in one of his huge hands, Bench used a hinged catcher's mitt, rather than the prevalent circular "pillow" style, which made him more effective at fielding bunts and making plays at the plate. One of the first catchers to employ a one-handed catching style, Bench kept his right hand behind his back to protect it from foul tips.

Hampered by back problems in 1976, Bench finished the season with just 16 homers, 74 RBIs, and a .234 batting average, although he managed to post a respectable .348 on-base percentage by drawing 81 bases on balls. But, with the Reds capturing their second consecutive pennant, Bench redeemed himself during the postseason, batting .333 against Philadelphia in the NLCS, before earning World Series MVP honors by homering twice, driving in six runs, and batting .533, in leading his team to a four-game sweep of the Yankees in the Fall Classic.

Asked by a journalist to compare Yankee catcher Thurman Munson (who batted .529 in the Series) to Bench following Cincinnati's win in Game 4, Reds manager Sparky Anderson ruffled a few feathers when he replied, "You don't compare anyone to Johnny Bench. You don't want to embarrass anybody."

Bench had his last big year for the Reds in 1977, hitting 31 homers, knocking in 109 runs, and batting .275, before his body began to break down. Plagued by injuries in each of the next three seasons, Bench garnered as many as 500 plate appearances just once, limiting him to a total of only 69 home runs and 221 RBIs. A part-time player by 1981, Bench spent most of the next three seasons manning either first base or third, before announcing his retirement following the conclusion of the 1983 campaign with career totals of 389 homers, 1,376 RBIs, 1,091 runs scored, 2,048 hits, 381 doubles, 24 triples, and 68 stolen bases, a lifetime batting average of .267, an on-base percentage of .342, and a slugging percentage of .476.

Following his playing days, Bench spent several years broadcasting games on radio and television, while also cohosting with then-Dodgers manager Tommy Lasorda a syndicated TV show called *The Baseball Bunch*, which helped a group of boys and girls learn the finer points of the game. Bench also became a regular public speaker and, after participating in many celebrity golf tournaments during his playing career, joined the senior circuit once he turned 50 years old.

Inducted into the Reds Hall of Fame in 1986, Bench had his #5 retired by the club the same year. Some two decades later, the Reds honored Bench again by erecting a bronze statue of him outside Great American Ball Park that depicts him in full gear, throwing out a runner with his powerful right arm.

Named one of baseball's four greatest living players prior to the 2015 MLB All-Star Game (along with Sandy Koufax and the now deceased Willie Mays and Hank Aaron), Bench, who currently resides in Florida with his two sons from his fourth marriage, has often been called the greatest catcher in the history of the game, with writer Roger Kahn saying on ESPN Classic's SportsCentury tribute to him, "I remember I said to Red Smith, 'I've seen Campy [Roy Campanella] and [Yogi] Berra; this fellow's better than them.' And Red said to me, 'I've seen [Bill] Dickey and Mickey Cochrane, and this fellow is better than them also.' Ergo, Johnny Bench is the best catcher who ever lived."

CAREER HIGHLIGHTS

Best Season

Although Bench also performed brilliantly in 1972, 1974, and 1975, he compiled the best overall numbers of his career in his first MVP campaign of 1970, when he led the NL with 45 homers and 148 RBIs, finished second in the league with 355 total bases, batted .293, posted a slugging percentage of .587 and an OPS of .932, scored 97 runs, and collected 177 hits and 35 doubles.

Memorable Moments/Greatest Performances

Bench helped lead the Reds to a 7–2 win over the Phillies on June 2, 1970, by homering twice, knocking in four runs, and scoring three times.

Bench led the Reds to a 12–5 win over the Cardinals on July 26, 1970, by going 4-for-5 with three home runs and seven RBIs, hitting all his homers off Steve Carlton.

Bench experienced one of his most memorable moments in Game 5 of the 1972 NLCS, when, with the series tied at two games apiece and the Reds trailing Pittsburgh by a score of 3–2 and facing elimination heading into the bottom of the ninth inning, he led off the frame with an opposite field home run off Pirates relief ace Dave Giusti. Following two singles and a pair of flyball outs, the Reds advanced to the World Series when Bob Moose threw a wild pitch while facing pinch-hitter Hal McRae.

Bench continued to be a thorn in the side of Steve Carlton on May 9, 1973, once again homering three times and driving in seven runs against him during a 9–7 win over the Phillies.

Bench contributed to a 12–2 victory over the Braves on July 27, 1973, by hitting a pair of homers and knocking in six runs.

Bench led the Reds to a 10–3 win over the Montreal Expos on August 31, 1974, by driving in seven runs with a homer and double, delivering the game's big blow in the bottom of the sixth inning, when he reached the seats with the bases loaded.

Bench proved to be the difference in a 6–2 win over the Braves on September 12, 1974, knocking in all six runs with a pair of homers, the second of which came with the bases loaded.

Bench contributed to an 11–3 rout of the Cubs on June 14, 1975, by going 5-for-5 with two doubles, a walk, one RBI, and two runs scored.

Bench earned 1976 World Series MVP honors by batting .533 (8-for-15) with two homers, a triple, a double, six RBIs, four runs scored, and an OPS of 1.667 during the Reds' four-game sweep of the Yankees. Particularly outstanding in the Game 4 clincher, Bench led the Reds to a 7–2 win by homering twice and knocking in five runs, with his three-run blast off reliever Dick Tidrow in the top of the ninth inning sealing the victory.

Bench provided most of the offensive firepower during a 5–3 win over the Padres on May 29, 1980, knocking in four runs with three homers off Randy Jones.

Notable Achievements

- Hit more than 20 home runs 11 times, surpassing 30 homers four times and 40 homers twice.
- Knocked in more than 100 runs six times, topping 120 RBIs on three occasions.
- Scored more than 100 runs once.
- Posted slugging percentage over .500 five times.
- Posted OPS over .900 twice.
- Topped 30 doubles five times.
- Drew 100 bases on balls once.
- Hit three home runs in one game three times (vs. Cardinals on July 26, 1970, vs. Phillies on May 9, 1973, and vs. Padres on May 29, 1980).
- Led NL in home runs twice, RBIs three times, total bases once, intentional bases on balls once, and sacrifice flies three times.
- Finished second in NL in home runs once, RBIs once, runs scored once, doubles once, and total bases once.
- Led NL catchers in putouts twice, assists once, double plays turned once, fielding percentage once, and caught stealing percentage three times.
- Holds Reds career records for most home runs (389), RBIs (1,376), and sacrifice flies (90).
- Ranks among Reds career leaders in runs scored (5th), doubles (5th), hits (6th), extra-base hits (3rd), total bases (3rd), bases on balls (5th), intentional bases on balls (2nd), games played (4th), plate appearances (5th), and at-bats (5th).
- Six-time division champion (1970, 1972, 1973, 1975, 1976, and 1979).
- Four-time NL champion (1970, 1972, 1975, and 1976).

- Two-time world champion (1975 and 1976).
- Three-time NL Player of the Week.
- 10-time Gold Glove Award winner (1968, 1969, 1970, 1971, 1972, 1973, 1974, 1975, 1976, and 1977).
- 1968 NL Rookie of the Year.
- 1970 *Sporting News* Major League Player of the Year.
- 1975 Lou Gehrig Memorial Award winner.
- 1976 World Series MVP.
- Two-time Reds team MVP (1970 and 1972).
- Two-time NL MVP (1970 and 1972).
- Finished in top five of NL MVP voting two other times (1974 and 1975).
- 14-time NL All-Star selection (1968, 1969, 1970, 1971, 1972, 1973, 1974, 1975, 1976, 1977, 1978, 1979, 1980, and 1983).
- Seven-time Sporting News NL All-Star selection (1968, 1969, 1970, 1972, 1973, 1974, and 1975).
- Member of Major League Baseball's All-Century Team.
- Number 16 on the *Sporting News'* 1999 list of Baseball's 100 Greatest Players.
- Elected to Baseball Hall of Fame by members of BBWAA in 1989.
- #5 retired by Reds.

2
FRANK ROBINSON

Identified by former Baltimore Orioles teammate Jim Palmer as "the best player I ever saw," Frank Robinson established himself as one of the greatest players in the history of the game over the course of a 21-year major-league career that included stints with five different teams. A member of the Reds from 1956 to 1965, Robinson had many of his finest seasons in Cincinnati, earning six All-Star nominations, one NL MVP award, and five other top-10 finishes in the balloting by surpassing 30 homers seven times, 100 runs scored six times, and 100 RBIs four times, while also batting over .300 on five separate occasions. Continuing to perform at an elite level after leaving the Queen City, Robinson earned six more All-Star selections and his second MVP trophy, becoming in the process the only player in MLB history to win the award in both leagues. An exceptional leader of men, Robinson served as one of the central figures on teams that won five pennants and two world championships, with his total body of work earning him a number 22 ranking on the *Sporting News*' 1999 list of Baseball's 100 Greatest Players and gaining him induction into the Baseball Hall of Fame the first time his name appeared on the ballot. Yet, despite his extraordinary list of accomplishments, which also includes being baseball's first Black manager, Robinson remains one of the most overlooked truly great players in the history of the game, as Mike Schmidt, who grew up in the Cincinnati area rooting for the Reds, suggested when he said, "Of all the players who have ever played this game, Frank Robinson may well be the most underrated."

Born in Beaumont, Texas, on August 31, 1935, Frank Robinson grew up in what was essentially a single-parent household after his father deserted the family during his infancy. Looking back on his childhood, Robinson told *Sports Illustrated*, "I never really knew my own father. But it didn't bother me. My mother, my brothers, and sisters . . . I was always right in the middle of a bunch of bigger boys, and they'd rough me up and give me

Frank Robinson earned NL MVP honors in 1961, when he led the Reds to their first pennant in 21 years.
Courtesy of RMYAuctions.com

information. They were always keeping my feet on the ground, making me see the outlook from other sides."

The youngest of 10 children, Robinson moved at the age of four with his two half-brothers and mother, whose previous two marriages produced her nine other offspring, to California, where the family eventually settled in the Oakland area. Developing a love for sports at an early age, Robinson spent virtually every spare moment of his childhood playing baseball, football, or basketball, joining an American Legion team shortly after he celebrated his 14th birthday. Later emerging as a star athlete at McClymonds High School, Robinson excelled in both baseball and basketball, serving as a teammate of future NBA Hall of Famer Bill Russell on the hardwood.

Offered a contract by Cincinnati super-scout Bobby Mattick immediately upon his graduation from McClymonds High in 1953, Robinson signed with the Reds for $3,500, after which he began his pro career at

Class C Ogden (Utah). Robinson subsequently spent the next three seasons in the minors, performing extremely well on the field even though he experienced a considerable amount of racism in his two years with Columbia of the South Atlantic League. Often persecuted by fans in the circuit's southern-based states, Robinson grew so upset one afternoon that he considered going after one spectator in the stands with a baseball bat. Promoted to the parent club in 1956, Robinson arrived in Cincinnati, in his own words, "quiet and withdrawn," both afraid and unwilling to associate with his teammates.

Expressing himself on the playing field instead after laying claim to the starting left field job, Robinson earned a seventh-place finish in the NL MVP voting and both NL All-Star and Rookie of the Year honors by batting .290, driving in 83 runs, leading the league with 122 runs scored, and finishing second in the circuit with 38 homers and an OPS of .936, with his 38 round-trippers tying the mark previously set by Boston's Wally Berger in 1930 for the most home runs by a first-year player. Posting excellent numbers again in 1957, Robinson garnered All-Star recognition and another top-10 finish in the NL MVP voting by hitting 29 homers, knocking in 75 runs, scoring 97 times, compiling an OPS of .905, and finishing third in the league with a .322 batting average and 197 hits. Plagued by an arm injury in 1958 that forced him to spend much of the next two seasons at first base, Robinson batted just .269. But he still managed to hit 31 homers, drive in 83 runs, score 90 times, and earn his lone Gold Glove nomination for his outstanding play in the outfield, before beginning an exceptional four-year run during which he posted the following numbers:

YEAR	HR	RBIS	RUNS	HITS	AVG	OBP	SLG	OPS
1959	36	125	106	168	.311	.391	.583	.975
1960	31	83	86	138	.297	.407	**.595**	**1.002**
1961	37	124	117	176	.323	.404	**.611**	**1.015**
1962	39	136	**134**	208	.342	**.421**	**.624**	**1.045**

In addition to leading the NL in both slugging percentage and OPS in each of the last three seasons, Robinson consistently placed near the top of the league rankings in batting average, on-base percentage, home runs, RBIs, runs scored, total bases, and doubles, with his league-leading 51 two-baggers in 1962 setting a single-season franchise record that still stands. An NL All-Star in three of those four seasons, Robinson also earned three top-10 finishes in the league MVP voting, winning the award in

1961, when he led the Reds to their first pennant in 21 years after being moved to right field, which remained his primary position for the rest of his career.

Quick-wristed and deceptively strong, the right-handed-hitting Robinson, who stood 6'1" and weighed 185 pounds, drove the ball with power to all fields. A fearless hitter, Robinson dared opposing pitchers to throw inside to him by standing extremely close to home plate and leaning forward in the batter's box. Explaining the attitude he took with him to the plate, Robinson said, "Pitchers did me a favor when they knocked me down. It made me more determined. I wouldn't let that pitcher get me out. They say you can't hit if you're on your back, but I didn't hit on my back. I got up."

An excellent baserunner, Robinson, who swiped more than 20 bags three times, also employed a hard-nosed style on the basepaths, testing the courage of opposing infielders by sliding hard into each base and going into second harder than perhaps any other player in baseball when breaking up the double play. Describing the philosophy that he used while running the bases, Robinson stated, "The baselines belong to the runner, and whenever I was running the bases, I always slid hard. I wanted infielders to have that instant's hesitation about coming across the bag at second, or about standing in there awaiting a throw to make a tag. There are only 27 outs in a ballgame, and it was my job to save one for my team every time I possibly could."

Robinson's aggressive style of play led to one of the more memorable brawls in baseball history, when, during the first game of a doubleheader sweep of the Braves on August 15, 1960, he slid hard into third base while attempting to stretch a double into a triple, prompting Milwaukee third sacker Eddie Mathews to deliver several blows to his forehead that blackened both his eyes. Though bruised and battered, Robinson returned in game two to lead the Reds to a 4–0 victory by homering, doubling, and robbing Mathews of an extra-base hit, earning in the process the respect and admiration of his assailant, who said in the next day's newspaper, "That's the way to get even."

Although quiet and reserved when he first arrived in Cincinnati, Robinson eventually started to display his strong personality and tremendous leadership ability as he grew more comfortable in his new surroundings. Robinson also began to address the subject of civil rights, causing him to receive a series of death threats during the early 1960s. In response, Robinson took to carrying around a gun in self-defense, which resulted in him being arrested at one point during the 1961 campaign after he displayed his weapon to an abusive restaurant employee who refused to serve him.

Following a subpar 1963 campaign in which he hit 21 homers, knocked in 91 runs, scored only 79 times, and batted just .259, Robinson posted excellent numbers in each of the next two seasons. After earning a fourth-place finish in the NL MVP voting in 1964 by hitting 29 homers, driving in 96 runs, stealing 23 bases, batting .306, and ranking among the league leaders with 103 runs scored, 38 doubles, and an OPS of .943, Robinson batted .296 and placed near the top of the league rankings with 33 homers, 113 RBIs, 109 runs scored, and an OPS of .925 the following year. Nevertheless, Reds GM Bill DeWitt, having grown weary of interacting with someone so controversial and outspoken, completed a trade with the Orioles on December 9, 1965, that sent the 30-year-old Robinson to Baltimore for outfielder Dick Simpson and pitchers Milt Pappas and Jack Baldschun, in what turned out to be one of the most lopsided deals in baseball history.

With DeWitt attempting to explain the trading of his team's best player by describing him as "a fading talent increasingly hobbled by leg injuries" and calling him "an old 30," Robinson later said, "My mind went blank when the trade was announced. But when I thought about it, I changed my thinking. . . . I did not feel I had anything to prove, yet I wanted to prove to Bill DeWitt that I was not done at age 30."

Leaving no doubt as to his ability to still compete at an extremely high level, Robinson, who, in his 10 years with the Reds, hit 324 homers, knocked in 1,009 runs, scored 1,043 times, collected 1,673 hits, 318 doubles, and 50 triples, stole 161 bases, batted .303, compiled a .389 on-base percentage, and set franchise records for highest slugging percentage (.554) and OPS (.943), led the Orioles to the world championship his first year in Baltimore by topping the junior circuit in nine different offensive categories, including homers (49), RBIs (122), runs scored (122), batting average (.316), and OPS (1.047), with his fabulous performance earning him AL MVP honors.

In discussing the impact that Robinson made in his first year with his new team, Orioles pitcher Dave McNally later told John Eisenberg of the *Baltimore Sun*, "As good as Frank was, it was how hard he played that really made an impact. . . . The intensity the man had was just incredible."

Injured for parts of the next two seasons, Robinson failed to perform at the same lofty level, although he still managed to earn All-Star honors in 1967 by batting .311, hitting 30 homers, and driving in 94 runs, in only 129 games. Robinson subsequently helped lead the Orioles to three straight pennants and their second world championship by averaging 28 homers and 92 RBIs from 1969 to 1971, while posting batting averages of .308, .306, and .281. Along the way, Robinson gained a measure of revenge against his former team by homering twice and knocking in four runs during Baltimore's five-game victory over the Reds in the 1970 World Series.

With the 36-year-old Robinson finally beginning to show signs of slowing down, the Orioles included him in a six-player trade they completed with the Dodgers following the conclusion of the 1971 campaign. Robinson subsequently split the next five seasons between the Dodgers, Angels, and Indians, spending his last two years in Cleveland assuming the role of player-manager, before retiring as an active player at the end of 1976.

Over the course of his career, Robinson hit 586 homers, knocked in 1,812 runs, scored 1,829 times, collected 2,943 hits, 528 doubles, and 72 triples, stole 204 bases, batted .294, compiled a .389 on-base percentage, and posted a .537 slugging percentage, with his 586 round-trippers representing the fourth-highest total in the history of the game at the time of his retirement (he has since slipped to 10th). A 12-time All-Star, Robinson also earned three *Sporting News* All-Star nominations and six top-five finishes in the MVP voting, winning the award twice.

Relieved of his managerial duties in Cleveland after the Indians got off to a slow start in 1977, Robinson spent most of the next three decades either coaching or managing in the major leagues, serving at various times as skipper of the Giants, Orioles, and Montreal Expos/Washington Nationals, or serving as MLB's director of discipline. Eventually named honorary president of the American League, Robinson continued to hold that post until February 7, 2019, when he died of bone cancer in Los Angeles at the age of 83.

Upon learning of his passing, Reds CEO Bob Castellini issued a statement that read: "Frank Robinson is considered one of the greatest players to ever wear a Cincinnati Reds uniform. His talent and success brought dynamic change to the Reds and to our city. His retired Number 20 and statue gracing the gates of Great American Ball Park stand in tribute and appreciation for the immense contribution Frank made to the Reds. We offer our deepest condolences to Frank's family, friends, and fans."

Former Baltimore Orioles teammate Brooks Robinson also paid tribute to his longtime friend by saying, "Today is a very sad day because I lost not only my teammate, but also a very dear friend. I loved Frank and got to know him so much better after we both retired. I spoke to him a few days ago, and he sounded good. He wanted to be home. I let him know that Connie and I were pulling for him, and that he, [wife] Barbara, and [daughter] Nichelle were in our prayers."

Robinson added, "As a player, I put Frank in a class with Willie Mays, Hank Aaron, and Mickey Mantle. He was the best player I ever played with. When he came here in 1966, he put us over the top. He was a great man, and he will be deeply missed."

Some years earlier, Maury Wills, who competed against Robinson as a member of the Dodgers, commented, "Although he was often overlooked in favor of Willie Mays, Hank Aaron, and Roberto Clemente, Frank Robinson could do everything any one of them could do . . . and some things better."

REDS CAREER HIGHLIGHTS

Best Season

It would be difficult to argue with anyone who suggested that Robinson played his best ball for the Reds during the pennant-winning campaign of 1961, when he earned NL MVP honors by ranking among the league leaders with 37 homers, 124 RBIs, 117 runs scored, a .323 batting average, a .404 on-base percentage, 176 hits, 32 doubles, 333 total bases, and 22 stolen bases, while topping the circuit with a .611 slugging percentage and an OPS of 1.015. Nevertheless, Robinson posted even better numbers the following year, when he earned a fourth-place finish in the MVP balloting by leading the NL with a .421 on-base percentage, a .624 slugging percentage, an OPS of 1.045, 134 runs scored, and 51 doubles, finishing second in the league with a .342 batting average, 208 hits, and 380 total bases, and placing third in the circuit with 39 homers and 136 RBIs.

Memorable Moments/Greatest Performances

Robinson gave the Reds a 5–4 win over the Cardinals on April 30, 1958, when he led off the bottom of the 10th inning with his second solo homer of the game.

Robinson provided further heroics on July 23, 1958, when his two-run homer in the bottom of the 10th inning gave the Reds a 6–5 victory over the Cubs.

Robinson hit for the cycle during a lopsided 16–4 victory over the Dodgers on May 2, 1959, going 4-for-5 with a walk, five RBIs, and two runs scored.

Robinson again feasted on Dodger pitching on July 13, 1959, going 4-for-5 with two homers, a double, three RBIs, and four runs scored during a 13–5 Reds win.

Robinson helped lead the Reds to a 15–13 win over the Phillies on August 14, 1959, by going 5-for-6 with a homer, double, four RBIs, and three runs scored.

Robinson had a huge day at the plate against the Cardinals on August 22, 1959, hitting three homers and knocking in six runs during an 11–4 Reds win.

Robinson led the Reds to a 14–3 rout of the Dodgers on July 9, 1961, by going 4-for-4 with two homers, a double, a walk, seven RBIs, and three runs scored.

Robinson gave the Reds a dramatic 7–3 victory over the Dodgers on August 20, 1962, when he homered with the bases loaded with two men out in the bottom of the 10th inning.

Robinson led an assault on Houston pitching on May 9, 1963, going 5-for-5 with two homers, a double, seven RBIs, and three runs scored during a 13–3 Reds win.

Robinson contributed to a 13–6 win over the Mets on September 14, 1965, by knocking in five runs with a double and a pair of homers, walking once, and scoring three times.

Notable Achievements

- Hit more than 30 home runs seven times.
- Knocked in more than 100 runs four times, topping 120 RBIs on three occasions.
- Scored more than 100 runs six times, surpassing 120 runs scored twice.
- Batted over .300 five times, topping the .320 mark on three occasions.
- Compiled on-base percentage over .400 three times.
- Posted slugging percentage over .500 nine times, topping the .600 mark twice.
- Posted OPS over 1.000 three times, topping the .900 mark five other times.
- Amassed more than 200 hits once.
- Topped 30 doubles six times, collecting more than 50 two-baggers once.
- Stole more than 20 bases three times.
- Hit three home runs in one game vs. Cardinals on August 22, 1959.
- Hit for the cycle vs. Dodgers on May 2, 1959.

- Led NL in runs scored twice, doubles once, extra-base hits once, on-base percentage once, slugging percentage three times, OPS three times, intentional bases on balls four times, and sacrifice flies once.
- Finished second in NL in home runs once, RBIs three times, runs scored once, batting average once, on-base percentage four times, OPS once, hits once, total bases once, and bases on balls once.
- Led NL left fielders in putouts twice and fielding percentage once.
- Led NL right fielders in fielding percentage twice.
- Ranks 10th in MLB history with 586 home runs.
- Holds share of Reds single-season record for most doubles (51 in 1962).
- Holds Reds career records for highest slugging percentage (.554) and highest OPS (.943).
- Ranks among Reds career leaders in home runs (3rd), RBIs (6th), runs scored (6th), on-base percentage (5th), doubles (8th), hits (11th), extra-base hits (5th), total bases (8th), bases on balls (9th), sacrifice flies (8th), games played (10th), plate appearances (10th), and at-bats (10th).
- 1961 NL champion.
- Two-time NL Player of the Month.
- 1958 Gold Glove Award winner.
- 1956 NL Rookie of the Year.
- Only player in MLB history to win MVP award in both leagues.
- Four-time Reds team MVP (1959, 1961, 1962, and 1964).
- 1961 NL MVP.
- Finished in top 10 of NL MVP voting five other times, placing in top five twice.
- Six-time NL All-Star selection (1956, 1957, 1959, 1961, 1962, and 1965).
- Two-time *Sporting News* NL All-Star selection (1961 and 1962).
- Number 22 on the *Sporting News*' 1999 list of Baseball's 100 Greatest Players.
- Elected to Baseball Hall of Fame by members of BBWAA in 1982.
- #20 retired by Reds.

3

PETE ROSE

Major League Baseball's all-time hit king, Pete Rose spent 19 of his 24 big-league seasons in Cincinnati, amassing a total of 3,358 safeties that places him first in team annals by a wide margin. Rose, who also holds franchise records for most runs scored, extra-base hits, doubles, total bases, games played, plate appearances, and official at-bats, batted over .300 14 times, scored more than 100 runs 10 times, and surpassed 200 hits on nine separate occasions as a member of the Reds, earning in the process 13 All-Star nominations, one NL MVP award, and eight other top-10 finishes in the balloting. A three-time NL batting champion, Rose also performed well in the field for the Reds at six different positions, with his superior all-around play making him a huge contributor to teams that won five division titles, four pennants, and two World Series. Yet even though Rose's vast list of accomplishments earned him a berth on MLB's All-Century Team and a prominent place on the *Sporting News*' 1999 list of Baseball's 100 Greatest Players, the sins he committed while managing the Reds during his second tour of duty with the club have left him on the outside looking in when it comes to enshrinement at Cooperstown.

Born in Cincinnati, Ohio, on April 14, 1941, Peter Edward Rose grew up in the city's Anderson Ferry section, just 10 minutes from Crosley Field. Acquiring his fierce competitive spirit from his father, a semipro athlete who boxed and played baseball, softball, and football well into his 40s, Rose eventually emerged as a standout athlete himself at Western Hills High School, where he excelled in baseball and football. However, with Rose failing to display a similar aptitude in the classroom, he had to repeat the ninth grade, making him ineligible to compete on the diamond for Western Hills his senior year. Choosing instead to play in a semipro league, Rose attracted the attention of Reds scout Buddy Bloebaum, who signed him to a contract the day he graduated from high school in 1960, with Rose recalling, "I don't remember ever wanting to be anything but a professional athlete, and it's a good thing I became one because I never prepared for anything else."

Pete Rose amassed more hits during his career than any other player in MLB history.

Originally a second baseman, Rose spent three seasons manning that post at three different levels of the Reds' farm system, batting .277 for Class D Geneva in 1960, .331 for Class D Tampa in 1961, and .330 for Class A Macon in 1962, before joining the parent club prior to the start of the 1963 campaign. But the cocky 22-year-old rookie initially received a cool reception from most of his teammates, who preferred that the popular Don Blasingame remain the team's starting second sacker.

Remembering that only Frank Robinson and Vada Pinson welcomed him with open arms, Rose later told *Sports Illustrated*, "It was different with me because, to be honest with you, I was called in the Reds' office during that year, and I was told I was hanging around with the African American players too much. I hung out with them because Frank Robinson and Vada Pinson treated me like I was one of the guys. You have to understand that the Reds won the pennant in 1961 and came close in 1962 and had a second baseman named Don Blasingame who had a great year. In '63, they thought they could win it again, but the manager [Fred Hutchinson] sticks this brash kid named me in there, but most of the team thought Blasingame should be the second baseman."

Eventually winning over his teammates with his strong all-around play, Rose earned NL Rookie of the Year honors by batting .273, scoring 101 runs, collecting 170 hits, and finishing second among players at his position with 360 putouts. Yet, when asked what he remembered most about his first big-league season, Rose mentioned his entrance into the US Army, saying, "I went to Fort Knox to do my basic training in the offseason, and as a result, I only hit .269 the next year. After that, I went to Venezuela to go hone my skills. I went down there for the winter after the '64 season and really learned how to hit. I think I hit over .300 for 10 or 12 seasons after that. We just worked. We went to the ballpark every day. That was growing up for me. There weren't many 19, 20, or 21-year-old kids that were dominating the big leagues back in those days, but when I came back, I was full of confidence, and I started getting 200 hits a year."

After batting just .269 and scoring only 64 runs in 1964, Rose posted the following numbers over the course of the next 10 seasons:

YEAR	HR	RBI	RUNS	HITS	AVG	SLG	OBP	OPS
1965	11	81	117	**209**	.312	.382	.446	.828
1966	16	70	97	205	.313	.351	.460	.811
1967	12	76	86	176	.301	.364	.444	.808
1968	10	49	94	**210**	**.335**	**.391**	.470	.861
1969	16	82	**120**	218	**.348**	.428	.512	.940
1970	15	52	120	**205**	.316	.385	.470	.855
1971	13	44	86	192	.304	.373	.421	.793
1972	6	57	107	**198**	.307	.382	.417	.799
1973	5	64	115	**230**	**.338**	.401	.437	.838
1974	3	51	**110**	185	.284	.385	.388	.773

Consistently placing near the top of the league rankings in batting average, hits, and runs scored, Rose led the NL in each of those categories multiple times, while also annually ranking among the leaders in doubles, triples, and total bases. Displaying his versatility in the field as well, Rose manned second base in 1965 and 1966, before moving to the outfield in 1967 to make room at second for the slick-fielding Tommy Helms. Rose subsequently spent most of the next eight seasons shuttling back and forth between both corner outfield positions, although he also saw some action in center. Performing well at all three posts, Rose earned Gold Glove honors in 1969 and 1970 by committing a total of only five errors, while also collecting 18 outfield assists. An All-Star in eight of those 10 seasons, Rose also earned seven top-10 finishes in the NL MVP voting, winning the award in 1973, and placing second in the balloting to Bob Gibson in 1968.

The switch-hitting Rose, who stood 5'11" and weighed close to 200 pounds, employed a short, compact swing from both sides of the plate that made him extremely difficult to strike out. Rarely swinging for the fences, Rose never hit more than 16 homers in any single season. But he had enough power to accumulate at least 40 doubles seven times and surpass 10 homers on eight separate occasions. And with Rose hitting mostly out of the leadoff spot in the batting order, he served as the Reds' offensive catalyst, infusing the team with his boundless energy and constant hustle that earned him the nickname "Charlie Hustle."

Known for his aggressive style of play and win-at-all-cost mentality, Rose squeezed more production out of his somewhat limited natural ability than perhaps anyone else who ever played the game. Blessed with neither outstanding running speed, superior power at the plate, nor a powerful throwing arm in the field, Rose once admitted, "I didn't get to the majors on God-given ability. I got there on hustle, and I have had to hustle to stay. That's the only way I know how to play the game."

Further expounding upon the aggressive approach that he took to his craft on another occasion, Rose said, "People say I don't have great tools. They say that I can't throw like Ellis Valentine or run like Tim Raines or hit with power like Mike Schmidt. Who can? I make up for it in other ways, by putting out a little bit more. That's my theory, to go through life hustling. In the big leagues, hustle usually means being in the right place at the right time. It means backing up a base. It means backing up your teammate. It means taking that headfirst slide. It means doing everything you can do to win a baseball game."

Also known for his unbridled enthusiasm and obsession with winning, Rose, said longtime teammate Joe Morgan, "played the game, always, for keeps. Every game was the seventh game of the World Series. He had this unbelievable capacity to literally roar through 162 games as if they were each that one single game."

However, Rose's take-no-prisoners mentality and forceful personality often rubbed opposing teams and their fans the wrong way, causing him to develop a reputation as someone who cared little about the welfare of others. After seriously injuring the Cleveland Indians' promising young catcher Ray Fosse in a collision at home plate in the 1970 All-Star Game, Rose set off a bench-clearing brawl in the 1973 NLCS when he picked a fight with slightly built Mets shortstop Bud Harrelson, causing him to be viewed by many as a bully. Nevertheless, while aggressive and combative on the playing field, Rose proved to be extremely accommodating to reporters and fans, rarely refusing requests for interviews or autographs. And, even though Rose often found himself being portrayed as a selfish player who cared only about money, fame, and his statistics, he always picked up the check at dinner, routinely invited teammates to live with him, and agreed to change positions several times during his career to help his team, as he did again in 1975, when he moved to third base to allow George Foster to start in left field.

Manning the hot corner for the Reds the next four seasons, Rose earned four more All-Star selections and a pair of top-five finishes in the NL MVP voting by batting over .300 each year, while also amassing more than 200 hits, 40 doubles, and 100 runs scored three times each. Particularly outstanding in 1975 and 1976, Rose helped the Reds win back-to-back pennants and world championships by batting .317, posting an OPS of .838, collecting 210 hits, and leading the league with 112 runs scored and 47 doubles in the first of those campaigns, before batting .323, compiling an OPS of .854, and topping the circuit with 215 hits, 42 doubles, and 130 runs scored in the second. Although the Reds failed to advance to the playoffs in either of the next two seasons, Rose made history in 1978, when he set a modern NL record by hitting safely in 44 consecutive games.

A free agent at the end of 1978, Rose chose to sign with the Phillies for four years and $3.2 million when his nasty divorce, hard lifestyle, and alleged association with gamblers left the Reds feeling lukewarm about inking him to a long-term deal. Rose ended up spending five seasons in Philadelphia, earning four more All-Star nominations, before his skills began to diminish. One of the central figures on Phillies teams that won two pennants and one World Series, Rose later received high praise from Steve Carlton, who said, "Pete Rose came over to the Phillies in '79, and he became the catalyst that helped us to put it all together. His example on the field and his leadership helped to bring everybody's play up a notch."

Released by the Phillies following the conclusion of the 1983 campaign, Rose signed with the Montreal Expos, for whom he appeared in 95 games, before returning to Cincinnati on August 16, 1984, when the Reds reacquired him for utility infielder Tom Lawless. Rose subsequently spent the next two-plus seasons assuming the dual role of player-manager, seeing a limited amount of action on the playing field, before unofficially retiring as a player after the Reds dropped him from their 40-man roster on November 11, 1986. In addition to ending his career with more hits (4,256), games played (3,562), plate appearances (15,890), at-bats (14,053), and times on base (5,929) than any other player in major-league history, Rose, who hit 160 homers, knocked in 1,314 runs, collected 135 triples, stole 198 bases, batted .303, compiled an on-base percentage of .375, and posted a slugging percentage of .409, ranks among baseball's all-time leaders with 2,165 runs scored, 746 doubles, and 5,752 total bases. As a member of the Reds, Rose hit 152 homers, knocked in 1,036 runs, scored 1,741 times, collected 3,358 hits, 601 doubles, and 115 triples, stole 146 bases, batted .307, compiled a .379 on-base percentage, and posted a .425 slugging percentage.

Following his retirement as an active player, Rose remained manager in Cincinnati until August 24, 1989, when he voluntarily accepted a permanent place on baseball's ineligible list after an investigation conducted by the commissioner's office determined that he had bet on the sport during his tenure as Reds skipper. Although Rose continued to deny the allegations made against him for the next 15 years, he finally admitted his guilt in his 2004 book entitled *My Prison Without Bars*. Some 10 years later, on June 22, 2015, ESPN concluded its own investigation of Rose, which revealed through records obtained by US federal authorities from one of his associates that he had bet on baseball while still serving the Reds as a player-manager. Long before that, though, in April 1990, Rose pleaded guilty to charges related to income-tax evasion and served five months in the federal penitentiary in Marion, Illinois.

Despite his many transgressions, Rose remained a beloved figure in Cincinnati long after he left baseball, with the Reds inducting him into their Hall of Fame and retiring his #14 jersey in 2016. One year later, the team erected a statue of him outside Great American Ball Park that depicts him sliding headfirst into a base with his body in full flight. Rose lived until September 30, 2024, when he died of unspecified causes at the age of 83.

Upon learning of his passing, Reds principal owner and managing partner Bob Castellini issued a statement that read: "Our hearts are deeply saddened by the news of Pete's passing. He was one of the fiercest competitors the game has ever seen, and every team he played for was better because of him. Pete was a Red through and through. No one loved the game more than Pete, and no one loved Pete more than Reds Country. We must never forget what he accomplished."

REDS CAREER HIGHLIGHTS

Best Season

While Rose's MVP campaign of 1973 is often considered to be the best of his career, he performed just as well in two or three other years, with the 1969 season standing out as arguably his finest. In addition to leading the NL with 120 runs scored and a .348 batting average, Rose hit 16 homers, knocked in 82 runs, and ranked among the league leaders with a .428 on-base percentage, .512 slugging percentage, OPS of .940, 321 total bases, 218 hits, 33 doubles, 11 triples, and 88 walks, establishing in the process career-high marks in eight different offensive categories. Furthermore, Rose earned Gold Glove honors for the first of two straight times for his strong outfield play.

Memorable Moments/Greatest Performances

Rose contributed to a 14–4 rout of the Phillies on July 18, 1964, by going 4-for-4 with a homer, double, walk, six RBIs, and three runs scored.

Rose had five hits in one game an NL record 10 times over the course of his career, accomplishing the feat for the first time on April 30, 1965, when he went 5-for-5 with a homer, double, and two RBIs during a 6–1 win over the Mets.

Rose led the Reds to a 6–4 win over the Cardinals on August 30, 1966, by going 3-for-5 with two homers and three RBIs.

Rose fashioned the first lengthy hitting streak of his career when he hit safely in 25 straight games from May 3 to May 29, 1967, going 41-for-105 (.390), with three homers, two triples, nine doubles, 12 walks, 11 RBIs, and 23 runs scored.

Rose helped lead the Reds to a 7–5 win over the Braves on June 18, 1968, by going a perfect 5-for-5 at the plate with three doubles, one RBI, and two runs scored.

Rose starred in defeat on July 26, 1973, going 5-for-5 with a homer, two RBIs, two runs scored, and three stolen bases during a 6–4 loss to the Braves.

After hitting safely in three of his four previous trips to the plate, Rose gave the Reds a 5–3 win over the Astros on April 20, 1975, when he homered with one man aboard in the bottom of the ninth inning.

Rose performed magnificently for the Reds during the 1975 postseason, batting .357 against Pittsburgh in the NLCS, before earning World Series MVP honors by collecting 10 hits, walking five times, batting .370, and posting an OPS of .966 against Boston.

Rose flexed his muscles on April 29, 1978, when he collected five hits, homered three times, knocked in four runs, and scored four times during a 14–7 win over the Mets.

Rose became a member of the 3,000-hit club on May 5, 1978, when he singled to left field off Montreal starter Steve Rogers during a 4–3 loss to the Expos.

Rose established a 20th-century NL record by hitting safely in 44 straight games from June 14 to July 31, 1978, going 70-for-182 (.385), with 14 doubles, 12 walks, 11 RBIs, and 30 runs scored.

Rose led the Reds to a 7–2 win over the Braves on September 29, 1978, by driving in five runs with a homer and single.

Rose surpassed Ty Cobb as baseball's all-time hit king on September 11, 1985, when his first-inning single off San Diego starter Eric Show during a 2–0 win over the Padres gave him a career total of 4,192 safeties.

Notable Achievements

- Batted over .300 14 times, topping the .330 mark on four occasions.
- Compiled on-base percentage over .400 five times.
- Posted slugging percentage over .500 once.
- Posted OPS over .900 once.
- Scored more than 100 runs 10 times.
- Surpassed 200 hits nine times.
- Finished in double digits in triples three times.
- Topped 30 doubles 13 times, surpassing 40 two-baggers on five occasions.
- Drew more than 100 bases on balls once.
- Hit three home runs in one game vs. Mets on April 29, 1978.
- Led NL in batting average three times, on-base percentage once, runs scored four times, hits six times, doubles four times, games played four times, and at-bats four times.
- Finished second in NL in batting average once, runs scored twice, hits five times, triples twice, doubles twice, and total bases once.
- Led NL second basemen in putouts once.
- Led NL third basemen in fielding percentage once.

- Led NL outfielders in assists twice and fielding percentage twice.
- Led NL left fielders in putouts three times.
- Led NL right fielders in putouts once.
- Holds MLB records for most hits (4,256), games played (3,562), plate appearances (15,890), and at-bats (14,053).
- Ranks among MLB career leaders with 2,165 runs scored (6th), 746 doubles (2nd), and 5,752 total bases (9th).
- Holds 20th-century NL record for longest hitting streak (44 games, from June 14 to July 31, 1978).
- Holds Reds single-season records for most hits (230 in 1973), doubles (51 in 1978), games played (163 in 1974), plate appearances (771 in 1974), and at-bats (680 in 1973).
- Holds franchise career records for most runs scored (1,741), hits (3,358), extra-base hits (868), doubles (601), total bases (4,645), games played (2,722), plate appearances (12,344), and at-bats (10,934).
- Ranks among Reds career leaders with 1,036 RBIs (5th), .307 batting average (tied for 10th), .379 on-base percentage (tied for 9th), 115 triples (4th), 1,210 bases on balls (2nd), and 56 sacrifice flies (7th).
- Five-time division champion (1970, 1972, 1973, 1975, and 1976).
- Four-time NL champion (1970, 1972, 1975, and 1976).
- Two-time world champion (1975 and 1976).
- 1963 NL Rookie of the Year.
- Two-time NL Player of the Week.
- Five-time NL Player of the Month.
- Two-time Gold Glove Award winner (1969 and 1970).
- 1969 Lou Gehrig Memorial Award winner.
- 1976 Roberto Clemente Award winner.
- Five-time Reds team MVP (1966, 1968, 1969, 1973, and 1978).
- 1973 NL MVP.
- Finished in top 10 of NL MVP voting eight other times, placing in top five on four occasions.
- 1975 World Series MVP.
- 13-time NL All-Star selection (1965, 1967, 1968, 1969, 1970, 1971, 1973, 1974, 1975, 1976, 1977, 1978, and 1985).
- Five-time Sporting News NL All-Star selection (1965, 1966, 1968, 1973, and 1978).
- Member of Major League Baseball's All-Century Team.
- Number 25 on the *Sporting News*' 1999 list of Baseball's 100 Greatest Players.
- #14 retired by Reds.

4

JOE MORGAN

Among the handful of greatest second basemen in the history of the game, Joe Morgan manned that post for five different teams over the course of a lengthy big-league career that spanned parts of 22 seasons. Particularly outstanding for the Reds from 1972 to 1979, Morgan served as the offensive catalyst for teams that won five division titles, three pennants, and two World Series by hitting more than 20 homers four times, driving in more than 100 runs once, scoring more than 100 runs six times, batting over .300 twice, and stealing more than 40 bases on six separate occasions. A five-time Gold Glove Award winner, Morgan excelled in the field as well, leading all players at his position in putouts and fielding percentage three times each, with his exceptional all-around play earning him eight All-Star selections, two NL MVP trophies, and two other top-five finishes in the balloting. And following the conclusion of his playing career, Morgan received the additional honors of being included on the *Sporting News*' 1999 list of Baseball's 100 Greatest Players, having his #8 retired by the Reds, and gaining induction into the Baseball Hall of Fame in his first year of eligibility.

Born in Bonham, Texas, on September 19, 1943, Joe Leonard Morgan moved with his family at the age of five to Oakland, California, where his father worked for a tire and rubber company. Looking back on his childhood, Morgan, who grew up with five younger siblings, said, "I had a great childhood. My parents always made sure that I was able to enjoy the fruits of being a child, you know? I didn't have to mature too quickly. I was not expected to know everything at the age of 10 or 12. I could be a kid and enjoy, you know, just enjoy life."

After getting his start in organized sports in the local Babe Ruth League at the age of 13, Morgan went on to star in baseball at Castlemont High School, where he also played basketball and ran track. Failing to receive any college scholarship offers, Morgan spent one season playing baseball at Merritt Community College, before signing with the expansion Houston Colt .45s as an amateur free agent at only 19 years of age on November 1, 1962.

Joe Morgan won back-to-back NL MVP awards as a member of the Reds in 1975 and 1976.

Morgan subsequently spent the next two years advancing through Houston's farm system, performing well enough at every stop to earn brief callups to the parent club at the end of each season. Yet even though Morgan garnered Carolina League All-Star honors by batting .332 in 95 games with the Durham Bulls, he seriously considered quitting due to the racism he encountered as the team's only Black player. Ultimately electing to continue to pursue his dream of playing in the majors, Morgan recalled, "It would be nice to say that I changed my mind because of the example of earlier Black players who had it tougher, like Jackie Robinson. . . . But my decision came from my own sense of shame and embarrassment. When I thought of facing my father and telling him that I had quit—I simply could not go ahead."

Arriving in the big leagues to stay in 1965 after earning Texas League MVP honors the previous year by batting .323, driving in 90 runs, and stealing 47 bases at Double-A San Antonio, Morgan performed well in his first full season, earning a runner-up finish in the NL Rookie of the Year voting by hitting 14 homers, collecting 12 triples, scoring 100 runs, stealing 20 bases, batting .271, compiling an OPS of .791, and leading the league with 97 walks. Morgan followed that up with two more solid seasons, gaining All-Star recognition in 1966 by batting .285, drawing 89 bases on balls, posting an OPS of .801, and finishing second in the league with a .410 on-base percentage, before missing almost all of 1968 with torn ligaments in his knee.

Fully healed by the start of the 1969 campaign, Morgan established himself as one of the league's best middle infielders over the course of the next three seasons, performing especially well in 1970, when he earned his second All-Star nomination by batting .268, compiling an on-base percentage of .383, drawing 102 bases on balls, scoring 102 times, and stealing 42 bases. Nevertheless, after Morgan spent much of the 1971 season feuding with Houston manager Harry Walker, the Astros included him in a trade they completed with the Reds at the end of the year that also sent infielder Denis Menke, pitcher Jack Billingham, and outfielders César Gerónimo and Ed Armbrister to Cincinnati in exchange for first baseman Lee May, second baseman Tommy Helms, and utilityman Jimmy Stewart.

While Reds fans initially voiced their displeasure over having to say goodbye to the slugging May and slick-fielding Helms, Morgan looked forward to a fresh start in Cincinnati, especially after manager Sparky Anderson told him, "I just want you to know that whatever happened in Houston is over. You get a fresh start here."

Morgan also relished the idea of becoming more of a table-setter at the top of the Reds' powerful lineup, saying upon learning of the deal, "Now I can just try to get on base. I set a goal of scoring 100 runs every year, getting 100 walks, and driving in 50 runs. I want to hit .300, too, but I haven't been able to do that yet."

Given a free hand by Anderson, who took note of his superior athletic ability and tremendous baseball acumen, Morgan reached a level of excellence in Cincinnati that he never attained during his time in Houston, compiling the following numbers over the course of the next six seasons:

YEAR	HR	RBI	RUNS	SB	AVG	OBP	SLG	OPS
1972	16	73	**122**	58	.292	**.417**	.435	.851
1973	26	82	116	67	.290	.406	.493	.899
1974	22	67	107	58	.293	**.427**	.494	.921
1975	17	94	107	67	.327	**.466**	.508	**.974**
1976	27	111	113	60	.320	**.444**	**.576**	**1.020**
1977	22	78	113	49	.288	.417	.478	.895

In addition to leading the NL in OPS twice and slugging percentage once, Morgan placed at, or near, the top of the league rankings in on-base percentage, runs scored, stolen bases, and bases on balls each season, leading the league in walks twice, while finishing second in steals on four separate occasions. An NL All-Star each year, Morgan also won five Gold Gloves and earned two *Sporting News* MLB Player of the Year nominations and four top-five finishes in the league MVP voting, winning the award in both 1975 and 1976, when he led the Reds to back-to-back world championships.

Arguably the finest all-around player in the game for much of that period, Morgan drew praise for the totality of his game from Sparky Anderson, who said of his second baseman, "That little man can do everything."

Further expressing his admiration for Morgan following his magnificent 1975 campaign, Anderson stated, "I have never seen anyone, and I mean anyone, play better than Joe has played this year."

Though diminutive in stature, the 5'7," 160-pound Morgan, who spent most of his career hitting either first or second in his team's lineup before being moved down to the number three spot in the batting order midway through the 1975 campaign, possessed good power at the plate, surpassing 20 homers four times after leaving the cavernous Astrodome. A left-handed hitter who flapped his back elbow like a chicken to keep it from dipping while awaiting the pitcher's offering, Morgan also drove the ball well to the outfield gaps, finishing in double digits in triples on three separate occasions. However, Morgan's greatest strengths as a hitter proved to be his tremendous patience and keen batting eye. Consistently working his way deep into the count, Morgan rarely swung at bad pitches, striking out more than 70 times in a season just twice in his career, while drawing more than 100 bases on balls on eight separate occasions. A terror on the basepaths as well, Morgan scored more than 100 runs eight times and stole at least

40 bases nine straight times, topping 50 thefts on five separate occasions as a member of the Reds.

While not as strong defensively during the early stages of his career, Morgan gradually developed into one of the NL's top fielding second basemen, leading all players at his position in putouts three times, assists once, double plays turned once, and fielding percentage three times. In discussing the importance that he placed on being a complete player, Morgan stated, "Growing up in California, my father would take me to the minor league games, the Oakland Oaks. We would see the players, and my father would say, 'Well, he's a good player. He can hit, but he doesn't field very well. He can field, but he doesn't hit.' And my father always impressed upon me to try to be a complete player. So, I think I worked harder on my defense than I did on any other part of the game. . . . I did everything to make myself a complete player."

Taking great pride in the fact that he ultimately accomplished his goal, Morgan later said, "I'm blessed with the ability to do more things than other people can. I'm not the best power hitter in baseball, not the best hitter for average, not the best fielder, not the best base stealer. But when you put all those things together, no player in baseball can do any two of them better than Joe Morgan."

Finally beginning to show signs of aging in 1978, the 34-year-old Morgan batted just .236, although he still managed to hit 13 homers, knock in 75 runs, and score 68 times. Morgan followed that up with another mediocre performance in 1979, hitting just nine homers, driving in only 32 runs, scoring 70 times, and batting .250, before signing with the Astros as a free agent at the end of the year.

Morgan, who, during his time in Cincinnati, hit 152 homers, knocked in 612 runs, scored 816 times, collected 1,155 hits, 220 doubles, and 27 triples, stole 406 bases, batted .288, compiled an on-base percentage of .415, and posted a slugging percentage of .470, ended up spending just one year in Houston, before splitting the next four seasons between the Giants, Phillies, and A's. Choosing to announce his retirement following the conclusion of the 1984 campaign, Morgan ended his playing career with 268 homers, 1,133 RBIs, 1,650 runs scored, 2,517 hits, 449 doubles, 96 triples, 689 stolen bases, 1,865 walks and only 1,015 strikeouts, a .271 batting average, a .392 on-base percentage, and a .427 slugging percentage, with his 1,865 bases on balls representing the fifth-highest total in MLB history. Morgan also amassed the third-most assists (6,967) and the fourth-most putouts (5,742) of any second baseman in the history of the game.

After retiring as an active player, Morgan began a lengthy career in broadcasting during which he served as a television color analyst for the Reds, ABC, NBC, and ESPN, where he partnered with Jon Miller on *Sunday Night Baseball* for more than two decades. Morgan also wrote several books on baseball and worked for many years as a businessman and philanthropist.

Inducted into the Baseball Hall of Fame the first time his name appeared on the ballot in 1990, Morgan said during his acceptance speech, "I take my vote as a salute to the little guy, the one who doesn't hit 500 home runs. I was one of the guys that did all they could to win. I'm proud of my stats, but I don't think I ever got on for Joe Morgan. If I stole a base, it was to help us win a game, and I like to think that's what made me special."

Diagnosed with myelodysplastic syndrome (a form of cancer) in 2015, Morgan received a bone marrow transplant from one of his daughters that allowed him to live another five years, until October 11, 2020, when he died at his home in Danville, California, at the age of 77 from a nerve condition called polyneuropathy.

Upon learning of his passing, Joey Votto discussed what Morgan meant to him and the Reds as a franchise when he stated, "Joe is the greatest second baseman of all time. I don't think there's ever been a better player to put on the Reds uniform. He could do everything. He was the best hitter on the team. He was the best baserunner on the team. He was a Gold Glove defender. He played second base, a premium position. Most importantly, he was loved by his teammates. I think you could ask—when Sparky (Anderson) was alive—I think he believed Joe was the best player on the team and the most important player on the team."

Meanwhile, Johnny Bench said of his former Reds teammate, "He did it all, and he did it all the time. I always thought that Joe was the best player I ever played with, and that takes in a lot of ground."

Bench then added, "Joe wasn't just the best second baseman in baseball history, he was the best player I ever saw, and one of the best people I've ever known. He was a dedicated father and husband, and a day won't go by that I won't think about his wisdom and friendship. He left the world a better, fairer, and more equal place than he found it, and he inspired millions along the way."

REDS CAREER HIGHLIGHTS

Best Season

With Morgan proving to be the finest all-around player in the game in both 1975 and 1976, either of those seasons would make an excellent choice here. We'll go with 1976 since, in addition to leading the NL in on-base percentage (.444), slugging percentage (.576), and OPS (1.020), Morgan placed near the top of the league rankings with 27 homers, 111 RBIs, 113 runs scored, a .320 batting average, 60 stolen bases, and 114 bases on balls, establishing in the process career-high marks in four different offensive categories.

Memorable Moments/Greatest Performances

Morgan led the Reds to a 13–11 win over the Braves on July 31, 1973, by going 4-for-5 with two homers, a double, a walk, a stolen base, and five RBIs.

Morgan helped lead the Reds to a 15–2 rout of the Phillies on August 19, 1974, by knocking in seven runs with a three-run homer in the second inning and a third-inning grand slam.

Morgan drove home Ken Griffey with the decisive run of a 4–3 victory over the Red Sox in Game 7 of the 1975 World Series when he singled to center field off reliever Jim Burton with two men out in the top of the ninth inning.

Morgan contributed to a 9–3 victory over the Giants on August 14, 1977, by homering twice and knocking in five runs, with one of his long balls coming with the bases loaded.

Morgan displayed the totality of his game on April 6, 1978, when he went 3-for-4 with a homer, two doubles, a walk, a stolen base, five RBIs, and three runs scored during an 11–9 win over the Astros.

After hitting safely in three of his five previous trips to the plate, Morgan gave the Reds a 7–6 victory over the Giants on April 8, 1979, when he delivered a game-winning RBI single to right field with a man on third and two men out in the bottom of the 10th inning.

Notable Achievements

- Hit more than 20 home runs four times.
- Knocked in more than 100 runs once.
- Scored more than 100 runs six times.
- Batted over .300 twice.
- Compiled on-base percentage over .400 six times.

- Posted slugging percentage over .500 twice.
- Posted OPS over 1.000 once, finishing with mark over .900 two other times.
- Topped 30 doubles three times.
- Stole more than 40 bases six times.
- Drew more than 100 bases on balls six times.
- Led NL in runs scored once, bases on balls twice, on-base percentage four times, slugging percentage once, OPS twice, and sacrifice flies once.
- Finished second in NL in RBIs once, runs scored twice, on-base percentage once, bases on balls three times, extra-base hits once, and stolen bases four times.
- Led NL second basemen in putouts three times, double plays turned once, and fielding percentage three times.
- Ranks fifth in MLB history with 1,865 bases on balls.
- Holds franchise single-season record for highest on-base percentage (.466 in 1975).
- Holds franchise career record for highest on-base percentage (.415).
- Ranks among Reds career leaders in OPS (5th), runs scored (12th), stolen bases (2nd), bases on balls (6th), and sacrifice flies (9th).
- Five-time division champion (1972, 1973, 1975, 1976, and 1979).
- Three-time NL champion (1972, 1975, and 1976).
- Two-time world champion (1975 and 1976).
- June 29, 1975, NL Player of the Week.
- Three-time NL Player of the Month.
- Five-time Gold Glove Award winner (1973, 1974, 1975, 1976, and 1977).
- Two-time Sporting News Major League Player of the Year (1975 and 1976).
- Three-time Reds team MVP (1974, 1975, and 1976).
- Two-time NL MVP (1975 and 1976).
- Finished in top 10 of NL MVP voting three other times, placing in top five twice.
- Eight-time NL All-Star selection (1972, 1973, 1974, 1975, 1976, 1977, 1978, and 1979).
- Five-time *Sporting News* NL All-Star selection (1972, 1974, 1975, 1976, and 1977).
- Number 60 on the *Sporting News*' 1999 list of Baseball's 100 Greatest Players.
- Elected to Baseball Hall of Fame by members of BBWAA in 1990.
- #8 retired by Reds.

5

BARRY LARKIN

A classic case of "hometown boy made good," Barry Larkin spent parts of 19 seasons starring at shortstop for the team he rooted for as a youth. The NL's finest all-around player at his position for much of his career, Larkin combined power, speed, and outstanding defense to earn 12 NL All-Star selections, nine *Sporting News* NL All-Star nominations, and one league MVP trophy. The first shortstop to surpass 30 home runs and 30 steals in the same season, Larkin topped 20 homers twice, stole more than 30 bases five times, and batted over .300 on nine separate occasions, in leading the Reds to two division titles, one pennant, and one world championship. The winner of nine Silver Sluggers, Larkin, who ranks among the franchise's career leaders in virtually every major offensive category, also won three Gold Gloves, with his superb all-around play gaining him admittance to the Baseball Hall of Fame the third time his name appeared on the ballot and prompting the Reds to retire his #11 jersey.

Born in Cincinnati, Ohio, on April 28, 1964, Barry Louis Larkin grew up with his four siblings in the nearby suburb of Silverton, where he closely followed the daily exploits of The Big Red Machine and his favorite player, Dave Concepción. After deciding at an early age that he would eventually replace Concepción at short for the Reds, Larkin went on to establish himself as a star in multiple sports at the Queens City's Moeller High School, setting a school record by compiling a career batting average of .482 on the diamond, while also excelling as both a running back and defensive back on the gridiron.

Presented with an opportunity to pursue his childhood dream when the Reds selected him in the second round of the June 1982 MLB Amateur Draft, Larkin weighed his options carefully before finally accepting a football scholarship from the University of Michigan, where he also played baseball his freshman year. But after the physicality of football began to take its toll on him, Larkin decided to focus exclusively on further developing his baseball skills, remembering, "I did enjoy football, but the injury factor

Barry Larkin led the Reds to their last world championship in 1990.
Courtesy of George A. Kitrinos

for me, you know, I had so many issues. I don't know how long my career would've been."

Starring at shortstop for Michigan the next three seasons, Larkin led the Wolverines to two College World Series, earning in the process All-America and Big Ten Player of the Year honors twice each.

Recalling the development of Larkin into an elite player, Danny Hall, his position coach at Michigan, stated, "Barry was a star right away, but he was raw. He had a good arm, but his hands and his feet weren't as good. Once we started working with him, he picked it up right away because he was such a hard worker. He started at shortstop from Day 1. . . . Even [head football coach] Bo [Schembechler] knew what Barry's future was once he saw him play as a freshman."

Selected again by the Reds in the June 1985 MLB Draft, this time with the fourth overall pick, Larkin began his professional career at Double-A Vermont, before being promoted to Triple-A Denver, where he earned Triple-A Player of the Year honors in 1986 by batting .329 and posting an OPS of .899. Joining the Reds during the latter stages of the campaign after spending less than two full seasons in the minors, Larkin acquitted himself well in his 34 starts and 41 games with the parent club, batting .283, scoring 27 runs, and going a perfect 8-for-8 in stolen base attempts.

Larkin subsequently struggled at the plate the first few months of the 1987 season while competing for the starting shortstop job with Kurt Stillwell, whom the Reds had drafted second overall in 1983, posting a batting average of just .209 by the All-Star break. But after receiving a pep talk from teammates Dave Parker and Eric Davis, who he recalled "imposed their will on me in a not so nice way," Larkin eventually righted himself and ended up finishing the season with a respectable .244 batting average, 12 homers, and 21 steals, prompting the Reds to trade Stillwell to Kansas City the following offseason.

Playing with a newfound confidence in 1988, Larkin gained All-Star recognition for the first of four straight times by hitting 12 homers, driving in 56 runs, scoring 91 others, stealing 40 bases, batting .296, posting an OPS of .776, and leading all major leaguers with only 24 strikeouts in 652 total plate appearances. However, Larkin also committed a league-high 29 errors in the field, causing him to spend the entire offseason working hard on improving his defense. Sidelined for much of the ensuing campaign by a torn ligament in his elbow, Larkin appeared in only 97 games. Nevertheless, he earned Silver Slugger honors for the second consecutive time by batting .342 and compiling an OPS of .821.

Fully healthy by the start of the 1990 season, Larkin established himself as the finest all-around shortstop in the senior circuit, earning a seventh-place finish in the NL MVP balloting by hitting seven homers, driving in 67 runs, scoring 85 times, stealing 30 bases, and batting .301, while also leading all players at his position in assists and double plays turned. Emerging as the leader of a Reds squad that ended up winning the World Series, Larkin called a team meeting in September during which he criticized his teammates for coasting down the stretch after they built up a big lead in the NL West the first few months of the campaign. Responding to his words, his teammates quickly closed out the division, before defeating the Pirates in the NLCS and sweeping the heavily favored Oakland Athletics in four straight games in the World Series, with Larkin batting .353 during the Fall Classic.

Praising Larkin for his outstanding play at the end of the year, Reds manager Lou Piniella stated, "There's no doubt in my mind that he's the best shortstop in the league now, and don't forget he's young. He's going to get better; he's going to hit some home runs, too."

Despite missing a significant amount of playing time in two of the next three seasons due to injury, Larkin continued to put up excellent numbers on offense, hitting as many as 20 home runs in 1991, compiling batting averages of .302, .304, and .315, and posting an OPS well over .800 each year. Meanwhile, Larkin, who always had great range, developed into one of the league's most consistent defensive shortstops, committing a total of only 42 errors in the field from 1991 to 1993.

After batting .279, scoring 78 runs, and stealing 26 bases during the strike-shortened 1994 campaign, Larkin reached the apex of his career the next two seasons, posting the following numbers:

YEAR	HR	RBI	RUNS	SB	AVG	OBP	SLG	OPS
1995	15	66	98	51	.319	.394	.492	.886
1996	33	89	117	36	.298	.410	.567	.977

By hitting 33 home runs and stealing 36 bases in 1996, Larkin became the first major-league shortstop to reach the 30 mark in both categories in the same season. Performing brilliantly in the field as well, Larkin earned consecutive Gold Gloves by leading all players at his position in putouts once and placing in the top three in fielding percentage twice. An NL All-Star both years, Larkin also earned league MVP honors in the first of those campaigns by leading the Reds to the Central Division title, with his superb all-around play prompting rival shortstop Ozzie Smith to approach him at the All-Star Game, present him with an autographed bat, and say, "The torch is now yours."

Although the right-handed-swinging Larkin, who stood 6 feet and weighed 185 pounds, had the ability to reach the seats, he proved to be much more of a contact hitter who drove the ball well to all fields and rarely struck out. Commenting on his approach at the plate after he left the yard 33 times in 1996, Larkin claimed, "I'm not a home run hitter. I'm a line drive hitter. I hit (33) line drives that went over the fence."

Typically hitting out of either the first, second, or third spot in the Reds' lineup, Larkin did an excellent job of setting the table for middle-of-the order sluggers such as Ron Gant, Reggie Sanders, and Kevin Mitchell and using his exceptional speed on the basepaths.

An outstanding team leader as well, Larkin drew praise for his many contributions to the ballclub at one point during the 1995 campaign from Reds manager Davey Johnson, who said of his star shortstop, "He is the heart and soul of this team."

Expressing similar sentiments, first baseman Hal Morris stated, "The real reason for what we've done is Barry. Everyone talks about how we have talent, but when you've got Barry Larkin, you've got a talented team. It doesn't matter who you put around him."

And after Larkin was named league MVP at the end of the year, teammate Bret Boone said, "If you look at numbers, there are guys who have more homers and RBIs. But it's nice to see people look at 'most valuable.' He was really great on our team. He was our leader."

An extremely unselfish player who always put the team before himself, Larkin also received high praise from Reds pitcher David Wells, who stated, "Barry's just an unbelievable player—and person. He does it all, every day. He makes adjustments as the game goes on and sacrifices his game probably more than anyone we have for the good of the team. That's what's most impressive about him. . . . If you had 25 guys who took Barry's approach on the field, you'd be unbeatable."

Valued greatly by Reds general manager Jim Bowden, Larkin shared a unique relationship with his team's GM, who said, "Barry is such a leader, and we've always had a close relationship. How many (other) GMs in baseball consult with their players? . . . This is Barry Larkin's house. He's as much a part of this organization as anyone else we have, including the owner or the GM or the manager."

Named captain of the Reds prior to the start of the 1997 campaign, Larkin said at the time, "It's been that way ever since the departure of Eric

Davis (after the 1991 season). The only difference is I have a 'C' on my uniform now and it's official."

Unfortunately, Larkin suffered injuries to his calf, heel, and Achilles tendon in his first year as team captain that limited him to just 73 games, although he still managed to compile a batting average of .317 and an OPS of .913. But after having his Achilles tendon surgically repaired and undergoing another operation the following offseason for a perforated disk in his neck, Larkin returned to top form the next two seasons. A Silver Slugger winner in both 1998 and 1999, Larkin hit 17 homers, knocked in 72 runs, scored 93 times, batted .309, and compiled an OPS of .901 in the first of those campaigns, before homering 12 times, driving in 75 runs, scoring 108 others, batting .293, and posting an OPS of .810 in the second.

Although Larkin earned two more All-Star nominations, the 1999 season proved to be his last as a truly elite player. Hampered by injuries for the remainder of his career, Larkin appeared in as many as 120 games just once more over the course of the next five seasons, before announcing his retirement at the end of 2004. Over parts of 19 big-league seasons, Larkin hit 198 homers, knocked in 960 runs, scored 1,329 times, collected 2,340 hits, 441 doubles, and 76 triples, stole 379 bases, batted .295, compiled an on-base percentage of .371, and posted a slugging percentage of .444—numbers that would have been even better had he not been forced to go on the disabled list a total of 14 times.

Following his playing days, Larkin accepted a position as a special assistant to the GM of the Washington Nationals, a post he retained until 2011, when he became an analyst for ESPN's *Baseball Tonight* broadcast. Larkin later rejoined the Reds as both a member of their television broadcast team and a minor-league instructor. During the offseason, Larkin provides private coaching to minor-league players at the Champions Sports Complex he created in Orlando, Florida, several years ago to assist in the social, emotional, and educational development of youth.

Elected to the Baseball Hall of Fame by the members of the BBWAA in 2012, Larkin displayed his humility and selfless attitude upon learning of the results of the voting by saying, "It's the approach to the game I'm most proud of. I considered myself a complementary player. My approach to the game was how do I help this team win as opposed to how do I get my numbers. That, in my opinion, is what I'm most proud of."

After being told by Eric Davis, "You're in the Hall of Fame. There are no complementary players in the Hall of Fame," Larkin received further assurance that he belonged in Cooperstown from former teammate Tom

Browning, who said, "He earned it. . . . Of all the guys I ever played with or against, if I was starting a franchise, he'd be my shortstop."

Dusty Baker also spoke highly of Larkin, saying, "Barry not only was one of the most talented and gifted players, but he was one of the most intelligent on and off the field. He had great speed but had the ability to slow down the game, so he made very few mistakes. He is one of the few players who maximized the ability he was born with. Barry could do it all. He is the six-tool player all the scouts are looking for now, one with all the baseball skills, plus intellect."

Meanwhile, former Reds skipper Davey Johnson, who also managed the Mets, Orioles, Dodgers, and Nationals, stated, "I've had some great players. Yet when people ask who was the best and who did I most enjoy managing, it always came down to Larkin with me. He led by example and was the epitome of a manager's dream."

Further expounding on everything Larkin contributed to the Reds through the years, Jim Bowden said that he "represented everything on and off the field that was right about baseball. A man of high character, Larkin was a leader, teacher, motivator, big brother and, most of all, a winner. . . . Larkin mentored practically every young player during his tenure, from Aaron Boone to Sean Casey to Mike Cameron to Dmitri Young, among others. He knew when to give a teammate a kick in the butt, a pat on the back, a motivational lecture, a lesson on work ethic, or a tip on how to improve his fielding, hitting, throwing mechanics or base running. . . . When a player didn't know how to carry himself as a professional, Larkin taught him. When a player needed to work on his leads and breaks, Larkin was out early to work with him. As Casey once put it to me: Larkin was like having an extra coach and teacher on the field; it was always team first, Larkin second."

CAREER HIGHLIGHTS

Best Season

Although Larkin earned NL MVP honors in 1995 by hitting 15 homers, driving in 66 runs, scoring 98 times, stealing 51 bases, batting .319, and compiling an OPS of .886 for the division-winning Reds, he posted better overall numbers the following year, when, in addition to batting .298 and swiping 36 bags, he established career-high marks in homers (33), RBIs (89), runs scored (117), total bases (293), walks (96), slugging percentage (.567), and OPS (.977).

Memorable Moments/Greatest Performances

Larkin knocked in all three runs the Reds scored during a 3–0 win over the Padres on June 27, 1991, with a pair of homers.

Larkin followed that up by homering three times and driving in six runs during an 8–5 win over the Astros the next evening.

Larkin led the Reds to a 6–5 victory over the Giants on August 4, 1991, by knocking in five runs with a homer and double.

After homering once and hitting safely in three of his five previous trips to the plate, Larkin gave the Reds a 3–2 victory over the Expos on May 29, 1992, when he drove home the winning run from second base with an RBI single with two men out in the bottom of the 11th inning.

Larkin provided the offensive firepower during a 5–3 win over the Phillies on July 23, 1996, knocking in all five runs the Reds scored with a pair of homers.

Larkin again served as the Reds' primary offensive weapon during an 8–0 win over the Arizona Diamondbacks on July 11, 1998, driving in five runs with two homers and a double.

Larkin helped lead the Reds to an 11–5 win over the Padres on June 24, 2000, by going 5-for-5 with two homers and four runs scored.

Larkin gave the Reds a 6–5 victory over the Cardinals on May 6, 2003, when he homered with one man aboard off reliever Kiko Calero in the bottom of the ninth inning.

Notable Achievements

- Batted over .300 nine times, topping the .340 mark once.
- Compiled on-base percentage over .400 twice.
- Posted slugging percentage over .500 three times.
- Posted OPS over .900 three times.
- Hit at least 20 home runs twice, topping 30 homers once.
- Scored more than 100 runs twice.
- Finished in double digits in triples once.
- Topped 30 doubles six times.
- Stole more than 20 bases nine times, surpassing 30 steals five times and 40 steals twice.
- Hit three home runs in one game vs. Astros on June 28, 1991.
- Finished second in NL in triples once and stolen bases once.
- Led NL shortstops in putouts twice, assists once, and double plays turned once.

- Holds share of franchise record for most seasons played (19).
- Ranks among Reds career leaders in home runs (11th), RBIs (7th), runs scored (3rd), hits (2nd), extra-base hits (4th), triples (11th), doubles (3rd), total bases (4th), bases on balls (4th), stolen bases (3rd), sacrifice flies (4th), games played (3rd), plate appearances (4th), and at-bats (4th).
- Two-time division champion (1990 and 1995).
- 1990 NL champion.
- 1990 world champion.
- Four-time NL Player of the Week.
- June 1991 NL Player of the Month.
- 1993 Roberto Clemente Award winner.
- 1994 Lou Gehrig Memorial Award winner.
- Nine-time Silver Slugger Award winner (1988, 1989, 1990, 1991, 1992, 1995, 1996, 1998, and 1999).
- Three-time Gold Glove Award winner (1994, 1995, and 1996).
- Four-time Reds team MVP (1990, 1991, 1995, and 1996).
- 1995 NL MVP.
- Finished seventh in 1990 NL MVP voting.
- 12-time NL All-Star selection (1988, 1989, 1990, 1991, 1993, 1994, 1995, 1996, 1997, 1999, 2000, and 2004).
- Nine-time Sporting News NL All-Star selection (1988, 1990, 1991, 1992, 1994, 1995, 1996, 1998, and 1999).
- Elected to Baseball Hall of Fame by members of BBWAA in 2012.
- #11 retired by Reds.

6

JOEY VOTTO

Perhaps the most beloved player in team annals, Joey Votto spent 17 seasons in Cincinnati earning the affection of the hometown fans with his consistently excellent play and willingness to give back to the community. An outstanding gap-to-gap hitter with good home-run power, the lefty-swinging Votto surpassed 30 homers and 100 RBIs three times each, while also batting over .300 nine times and posting an OPS over 1.000 on four separate occasions. Known for his keen batting eye, Votto, who, in addition to ranking among the Reds' career leaders in virtually every other offensive category, amassed more bases on balls than anyone else in franchise history, led the NL in walks five times and on-base percentage seven times, while serving as the central figure on teams that won two division titles. Outstanding with the glove as well, Votto led all NL first basemen in assists six times and putouts once, with his superb all-around play earning him league MVP honors once, two other top-five finishes in the balloting, and six All-Star nominations.

Born in Toronto, Canada, on September 10, 1983, Joseph Daniel Votto grew up just west of the city, in suburban Etobicoke, Ontario. Despite being raised in a region known for its passionate hockey fans, Votto found himself being drawn to baseball at an early age, recalling, "What drew me to the game originally was that it was something I could do solo . . . an individual game. I'm an introvert. To practice (baseball), you could just throw a ball against a wall—a rubber ball. That's all it takes. Then it was a chance to spend time with my father. I'd play catch with him. He was my first coach when I was seven or eight years old."

Eventually emerging as a three-sport star at Richview Collegiate Institute, Votto excelled in baseball, basketball, and hockey, while also further honing his skills on the diamond as a member of the amateur Etobicoke Rangers. Offered a scholarship to play college baseball for the Coastal Carolina Chanticleers, Votto initially signed a letter of intent, before changing

Joey Votto walked more times than anyone else in franchise history.
Courtesy of Keith Allison

his plans when the Reds selected him in the second round of the June 2002 MLB Amateur Draft, with the 44th overall pick.

Votto subsequently spent most of the next six seasons advancing through Cincinnati's farm system, before finally being promoted to the parent club in September 2007 after hitting 22 homers, driving in 92 runs, and batting .294 at Triple-A Louisville. Making his major-league debut six days shy of his 24th birthday, Votto hit four homers, knocked in 17 runs, and batted .321 over the final month of the campaign, with his strong performance prompting new Reds manager Dusty Baker to name him the team's starting first baseman prior to the start of the 2008 season. Acquitting himself extremely well in his first full big-league season, Votto earned a runner-up finish in the NL Rookie of the Year voting by hitting 24 homers, driving in 84 runs, scoring 69 times, batting .297, and posting an OPS of .874, while also leading all NL first sackers in assists.

Despite his strong play, Votto suffered a tremendous loss during the latter stages of the campaign, when his father died suddenly at only 52 years of age on August 9, 2008. Although Votto threw himself back into work after taking the week of bereavement leave that the league offers, he found it extremely difficult to cope with the loss of his dad, later saying, "Baseball was my refuge. When I came on the field, I did my job, and did the best I could and focused on that. Then I went home, and I was miserable. That was pretty much my routine every day."

Still hurting from the loss of his father several months later, Votto began to experience panic attacks during games early in 2009, causing him to take a one-month leave of absence from the ballclub during which he spent time in the hospital undergoing counseling. Following his discharge, Votto returned to the ballfield, but only after he spoke publicly about his personal issues, saying at the time that he wanted other people in his situation to feel less alone.

Votto ended up posting solid numbers in 2009, finishing the season with 25 homers, 84 RBIs, 82 runs scored, a batting average of .322, and an OPS of .981. Taking his game up a notch in 2010, Votto helped lead the Reds to their first division title in 15 years by topping the circuit with a .424 on-base percentage and a .600 slugging percentage, while also ranking among the leaders with 37 homers, 113 RBIs, 106 runs scored, 328 total bases, 91 walks, and a .324 batting average, with his superior play earning him NL MVP honors and the first of his four straight All-Star nominations.

Sharing his thoughts with reporters after being informed of his selection as league MVP, Votto stated, "I had a really, really difficult time I guess getting over the death of my father. It's still difficult for me sometimes now. It's hard when you lose someone in your life that means so much. It was a difficult 2009 and quite a bit less difficult in 2010, and I think that was definitely a big reason why I was able to stay on the ballfield every day and succeed and make progress and feel better about life."

Continuing to perform at an elite level in 2011, Votto earned a sixth-place finish in the NL MVP balloting by hitting 29 homers, driving in 103 runs, scoring 101 times, collecting a career-high 185 hits, batting .309, compiling an OPS of .947, and leading the league with 40 doubles, 110 walks, and a .416 on-base percentage. Excelling in the field as well, Votto garnered Gold Glove honors by leading all NL first basemen in both putouts and assists. Subsequently forced to miss two months of action in 2012 after undergoing arthroscopic surgery in mid-July to repair a torn meniscus in his left knee, Votto appeared in only 111 games. Nevertheless, he managed to bat .337 and lead the league with 94 walks and a .474 on-base percentage, while also hitting 14 homers, knocking in 56 runs, amassing 44 doubles, and posting an OPS of 1.041.

Fully recovered by the start of the 2013 season, Votto earned another sixth-place finish in the NL MVP voting by hitting 24 homers, driving in 73 runs, scoring 101 times, batting .305, posting an OPS of .926, and leading the league with 135 walks and a .435 on-base percentage, while appearing in every game the Reds played. But Votto ended up missing much of the ensuing campaign with a strained left quadriceps that limited him to just 62 games and 272 total plate appearances. Healthy again in 2015, Votto began an extremely productive three-year stretch during which he posted the following numbers:

YEAR	HR	RBI	RUNS	BB	AVG	OBP	SLG	OPS
2015	29	80	95	**143**	.314	.459	.541	1.000
2016	29	97	101	108	.326	**.434**	.550	.985
2017	36	100	106	**134**	.320	**.454**	.578	**1.032**

In addition to leading the NL in OPS once and topping the circuit in walks and on-base percentage twice each, Votto ranked among the league leaders in homers twice and both batting average and slugging percentage all three seasons. After tying Pete Rose's franchise record by reaching base in 48 consecutive games in 2015, Votto got off to a poor start the following year, with his batting average standing at a season-low .213 on May 31. But he caught fire during the season's second half, becoming the first player since Ichiro Suzuki in 2004 to hit .400 after the All-Star break by compiling a mark of .408 from July 15 to the end of the year. Receiving serious consideration for league MVP honors each year, Votto finished third in the balloting in 2015, before placing seventh and second in the voting the next two seasons.

Although the 6'2", 220-pound Votto did not think of himself as a home-run hitter, once saying that he hit line drives that happened to go over the fence, he had the ability to hit the ball out of any part of the ballpark, displaying almost as much power to left-center as he had to right. Employing a deep crouch in the batter's box, Votto stood at the plate barely moving, seeking to drive the ball hard to all fields. Known for his tremendous patience as a hitter and ability to lay off bad pitches, Votto typically swung at fewer pitches outside the strike zone than any other player in either league.

A self-described "boring introvert" away from the playing field, Votto revealed, "I was always fine being on my own, comfortable in my own company. I'm more naturally introverted. I have a great time with my teammates, and I get along with just about everybody. But I'm more inclined to do things solo. In the off-season, when it's time to play catch, I do exactly what I did when I was eight years old. I go to the playground and find a wall and a ball, and I'll start throwing, first close, then stretching it out. I get everything I need out of that."

Described in a 2021 profile that appeared in *The Athletic* as perhaps "the most interesting man in baseball," Votto has also been described on SB Nation as a "magnificent weirdo" and by various teammates as "his own man," "a genius," and being "on a different wavelength than most people." Yet Votto, who began using social media for the first time during the COVID-19 pandemic to combat feelings of isolation and engage with fans, served as an inspiration to several of his younger teammates and gradually assumed more of a role of leadership on the Reds as his career progressed, with teammate Zack Cozart saying in 2017, "Basically, everything I'm doing this year, I've watched him. That's what I'm trying to implement into what I do. I've said it a thousand times, he's the best hitter in the game. You could poll people, and when they talk about a guy who never gives away at-bats, he would be up at the top with almost everybody, I would think."

Over time, Votto also developed a more outgoing persona, mingling with fans, often showing up unannounced at local hospitals to visit sick children, and contributing time and energy to several charitable causes.

Plagued by sore knees and an aching back, Votto totaled just 27 homers, knocked in only 114 runs, and posted a composite batting average of just .272 from 2018 to 2019, although he led the NL with a .417 on-base percentage in the first of those seasons. Continuing to struggle at the plate during the pandemic-shortened 2020 campaign, Votto hit 11 homers but knocked in only 22 runs and batted just .226 in 54 games. But after going on a weightlifting program and altering his hitting style by straightening his stance somewhat and making a conscious effort to transfer his weight more toward the pitcher, Votto rebounded in 2021 to hit 36 homers, knock in 99 runs, bat .266, and post an OPS of .938, despite missing a month of action with a broken thumb.

Unfortunately, the aging Votto failed to perform at the same level in either of the next two seasons. After being limited to just 91 games,

11 homers, 41 RBIs, and a .205 batting average by a torn left rotator cuff that required season-ending surgery in 2022, Votto appeared in only 65 games and batted just .202 the following year. Feeling that Votto had little left in the tank, the Reds announced on November 4, 2023, that they had decided to decline the $20 million club option on him, making him a free agent.

In making the team's decision known to the public, Reds president of baseball operations Nick Krall issued a statement that read: "For 17 seasons, Joey has been the heart of Reds baseball as a Most Valuable Player, All-Star, and respected clubhouse leader. His contributions to our team and his extraordinary generosity toward those in need, throughout our region and beyond, cannot be measured. . . . At this point of the off-season, based on our current roster and projected plans for 2024, as an organization we cannot commit to the playing time Joey deserves. He forever will be part of the Reds' family, and at the appropriate time we will thank and honor him as one of the greatest baseball players of this or any generation."

Votto, in turn, expressed his gratitude to the Reds and their fans on a short video he posted to his X (formerly Twitter) account the next day by saying: "If this is the last time I'll play as a Cincinnati Red, I want to speak out loud my gratitude. I want to thank the community; I want to thank Cincinnati for being so welcoming. . . . I'm from Toronto, Canada, and when I came down to the US as an 18-year-old, it was an intimidating experience. I grew comfortable and eventually made it to Cincinnati, and that was another intimidating experience. But it blossomed into the best stretch of my entire life. . . . Thank you to all the Reds fans in Cincinnati and elsewhere. I couldn't have loved an experience more. I'm so proud to have been able to play for a team, the oldest Major League team, to have played for a team that was endless gifts coming my way. I'm so humbled. I'm so grateful. It couldn't have happened without all of you, without the Cincinnati community. I'll always be a Cincinnati Red."

Over parts of 17 seasons in Cincinnati, Votto hit 356 homers, knocked in 1,144 runs, scored 1,171 times, collected 2,135 hits, 459 doubles, and 22 triples, stole 80 bases, drew 1,365 bases on balls, batted .294, compiled a .409 on-base percentage, posted a .511 slugging percentage, and amassed a total of 1,758 assists in the field, which places him second only to Eddie Murray all-time among big-league first basemen.

Following his release by the Reds, Votto remained a free agent until March 8, 2024, when he signed a minor-league contract with the Toronto Blue Jays. After failing to appear in a single game with the parent club all year, Votto officially announced his retirement from professional baseball on August 21, 2024.

CAREER HIGHLIGHTS

Best Season

Votto performed magnificently for the Reds in 2011, 2015, 2016, and 2017, hitting at least 29 homers, batting well over .300, and compiling an OPS well in excess of .900 in each of those seasons, while also scoring more than 100 runs three times and knocking in more than 100 runs twice. Nevertheless, Votto's MVP campaign of 2010 would have to be considered the finest of his career. En route to earning his lone *Sporting News* NL All-Star nomination, Votto led the NL in on-base percentage (.424), slugging percentage (.600), and OPS (1.024), finished second in the league in batting average (.324), and placed third in the circuit in home runs (37), RBIs (113), and total bases (328).

Memorable Moments/Greatest Performances

Votto led the Reds to a 9–0 rout of the Cubs on May 7, 2008, by hitting three homers, stealing a base, and driving in four runs.

Votto gave the Reds a 3–2 victory over the Diamondbacks on July 2, 2009, when, with the bases loaded and two men out in the bottom of the 10th inning, he drove home the winning run with his fourth hit of the game.

After collecting three hits, homering twice, and knocking in three runs earlier in the contest, Votto drove home the decisive run of a 12–11 win over the Giants on August 25, 2010, with a two-out RBI single in the top of the 12th inning.

Votto gave the Reds a 5–4 win over the Pirates on September 11, 2010, when he led off the bottom of the 10th inning with an opposite field home run off left-handed reliever Justin Thomas.

Votto contributed to a 10–5 victory over the Orioles on June 25, 2011, by going 3-for-4 with two homers, a walk, five RBIs, and three runs scored.

After hitting a solo home run earlier in the game, Votto gave the Reds a 5–4 win over the Nationals on August 28, 2011, when he led off the bottom of the 14th inning with his second homer of the contest.

Votto led the Reds to a 9–6 victory over the Nationals on May 13, 2012, by going 4-for-5 with three homers, a double, six RBIs, and four runs scored, with his two-out grand slam off Henry Rodríguez in the bottom of the ninth inning ending the game in dramatic fashion.

Votto homered three times in one game for the third time in his career during an 11–2 rout of the Phillies on June 9, 2015, concluding the contest with three hits, four RBIs, and four runs scored.

Votto homered at least once in seven straight games from July 24 to July 30, 2021, reaching the seats a total of nine times.

Votto made a triumphant return to the Reds lineup on June 19, 2023, when, after being out of action for the previous 10 months following surgery on his left shoulder, he knocked in three runs with a solo homer and two-run single during a 5–4 win over Colorado, with his home run in the bottom of the fifth inning eliciting a standing ovation from the hometown fans.

Notable Achievements

- Hit more than 20 home runs nine times, surpassing 30 homers on three occasions.
- Knocked in more than 100 runs three times.
- Scored more than 100 runs five times.
- Batted over .300 nine times, topping the .320 mark on six occasions.
- Compiled on-base percentage over .400 nine times.
- Posted slugging percentage over .500 ten times.
- Posted OPS over 1.000 four times, surpassing the .900 mark six other times.
- Topped 30 doubles 10 times.
- Drew more than 100 bases on balls six times.
- Hit three home runs in one game three times (vs. Cubs on May 7, 2008, vs. Washington Nationals on May 13, 2012, and vs. Phillies on June 9, 2015).
- Led NL in on-base percentage seven times, slugging percentage once, OPS twice, doubles once, and bases on balls five times.
- Finished second in NL in batting average once, on-base percentage once, OPS twice, doubles once, and bases on balls once.
- Led NL first basemen in assists six times and putouts once.
- Ranks second all-time among MLB first basemen with 1,758 career assists.

- Holds franchise single-season record for most bases on balls (143 in 2015).
- Holds franchise career record for most bases on balls (1,365).
- Ranks among Reds career leaders in home runs (2nd), RBIs (3rd), runs scored (4th), hits (5th), extra-base hits (2nd), doubles (2nd), total bases (2nd), on-base percentage (2nd), slugging percentage (6th), OPS (2nd), games played (6th), plate appearances (5th), and at-bats (6th).
- Two-time division champion (2010 and 2012).
- Six-time NL Player of the Week.
- July 2021 NL Player of the Month.
- 2010 NL Hank Aaron Award winner.
- 2011 Gold Glove Award winner.
- Six-time Reds team MVP (2008, 2010, 2011, 2015, 2016, and 2017).
- 2010 NL MVP.
- Finished in top 10 of NL MVP voting five other times, placing second once and third once.
- Six-time NL All-Star selection (2010, 2011, 2012, 2013, 2017, and 2018).
- 2010 *Sporting News* NL All-Star selection.

7

TONY PÉREZ

Called "the best clutch hitter I've ever seen" by his longtime manager, Sparky Anderson, Tony Pérez teamed up with Johnny Bench, Joe Morgan, and Pete Rose to form the nucleus of a Cincinnati Reds club that dominated the National League for much of the 1970s. A member of the Reds for parts of 16 seasons, Pérez helped lead them to five division titles, four pennants, and two world championships by hitting at least 20 homers eight times, driving in more than 100 runs six times, and batting over .300 on three separate occasions. Although sometimes overlooked in favor of Bench, Morgan, and Rose, Pérez stood out as the foremost leader on one of the greatest ballclubs in the history of the game, with his overall contributions to the success the Reds experienced during his time in Cincinnati earning him seven All-Star selections, four top-10 finishes in the NL MVP voting, a place in the Baseball Hall of Fame, and the honor of having his #24 retired by the organization.

Born in the town of Ciego de Ávila in Camagüey, Cuba, on May 14, 1942, Atanasio Pérez Rigal grew up in a two-bedroom row house owned by the sugar mill where his father worked. After spending some time working alongside his dad, Pérez joined the mill's baseball team, later describing his life in those days as being about "school, work, and baseball, and baseball was what you lived for."

Discovered by Reds scout Tony Pacheco while playing shortstop for the Camagüey sugar factory team, Pérez received an offer to turn pro. Inking his deal with the organization's Latin American scout at only 17 years of age, Pérez received no signing bonus, but merely a plane ticket plus $2.50 for an exit visa. After initially being assigned to the Reds' Cuban-based minor-league team, the Havana Sugar Kings, Pérez left for the United States against the wishes of his mother, who feared for her son's well-being in a foreign land.

Still two months shy of his 18th birthday when he arrived in the States, Pérez experienced numerous difficulties in his new surroundings, including growing accustomed to a completely different climate. Recalling his initial

Tony Pérez knocked in more than 100 runs for the Reds six times.

reaction to the cold when he reported to Geneva, New York, in 1960 for minor-league orientation, Pérez said, "I could feel it in my bones, how I missed the heat of my country and the love of my family."

Pérez also had to adjust to a new language and culture after the team moved south to Tampa, Florida, for spring training. Barely able to speak English, Pérez found it hard to fully understand the words of his instructors, remembering, "To hear words like 'cutoff man,' 'go to first,' 'go to third,' simple things like that. . . . I had to learn how to play the game all over again in English."

Even more disturbing, Pérez got his first taste of segregation, later telling *Sports Illustrated*, "The black players and I could not stay with the rest of the team. We also couldn't eat with the white players, and sometimes we would wait in the bus outside a restaurant until the white players finished their meals and brought us hamburgers."

Nevertheless, Pérez's quiet, dignified manner and fierce determination enabled him to eventually overcome every obstacle put before him. After adapting to his new environment, Pérez hit 27 homers and led the New York–Penn League with 132 RBIs and a .348 batting average in just his second pro season. Also performing exceptionally well for the Triple-A San Diego Padres in 1964 after moving from third base to first, Pérez earned Pacific Coast League MVP honors by hitting 34 homers, driving in 107 runs, and batting .309.

Finally promoted to the parent club in late-July 1964 after spending almost five full seasons in the minors, Pérez appeared in only 12 games with the Reds the rest of the year, compiling a batting average of just .080 in 25 official at-bats. But over the season's final two months, the 22-year-old rookie closely observed the aggressive style of play employed by Cincinnati veterans Frank Robinson and Pete Rose, which greatly influenced the way he approached the game throughout his career.

Pérez spent the next two seasons posting relatively modest numbers while platooning at first base with the left-handed-hitting Gordy Coleman, before moving across the diamond to third in 1967 to make room at first for Lee May. Displacing former NL RBI-champ Deron Johnson as the starter at the hot corner, Pérez began an outstanding nine-year run during which he posted the following numbers:

YEAR	HR	RBI	RUNS	HITS	AVG	OBP	SLG	OPS
1967	26	102	78	174	.290	.328	.490	.818
1968	18	92	93	176	.282	.338	.430	.769
1969	37	122	103	185	.294	.357	.526	.883
1970	40	129	107	186	.317	.401	.589	.990
1971	25	91	72	164	.269	.325	.438	.764
1972	21	90	64	146	.283	.349	.497	.846
1973	27	101	73	177	.314	.393	.527	.919
1974	28	101	81	158	.265	.331	.460	.791
1975	20	109	74	144	.282	.350	.466	.816

Although Pérez, who earned six All-Star selections and four top-10 finishes in the NL MVP voting over the course of those nine seasons, never led the league in any major statistical category, he consistently ranked among the leaders in RBIs, finishing second once and third twice. In fact, Pérez knocked in at least 90 runs in 11 consecutive seasons, with only teammate Johnny Bench accumulating more RBIs than the 954 he amassed during the 1970s.

A superb clutch hitter, the right-handed-swinging Pérez, who stood 6'2" and weighed close to 215 pounds, became known for his ability to excel in pressure situations, with Pirates Hall of Famer Willie Stargell saying, "With men in scoring position and the game on the line, Tony's the last guy an opponent wanted to see."

Identifying Pérez as one of the toughest hitters he ever had to face due to his ability to drive the ball with power to right-center field, Tommy John recollected, "He waited on the ball well, and I couldn't throw hard enough to get it by him inside."

Meanwhile, former Reds teammate Pat Corrales spoke of the lack of notoriety Pérez often received, saying, "Pete (Rose) would get his 200 hits, and (Johnny) Bench would do his thing. And Tony would get shoved to the background, driving in his 100 runs every year. You'd see it in the notes at the end of the stories in the paper—'Oh, by the way, Pérez hit a three-run homer to win the game.'"

Fully aware of his ability to deliver big hits, Pérez's teammates deferred to him the honor of being considered the foremost leader of The Big Red Machine, with fellow superstars Johnny Bench, Pete Rose, and Joe Morgan each acquiescing to the man they referred to as "Big Dog." With all four men supremely confident in their ability, they often exchanged friendly barbs as a way of challenging one another. On one particular occasion, the Reds' three other leaders pestered Pérez as he took batting practice, reminding him of the hitting slump he found himself immersed in at the time. In response, Pérez calmly stepped out of the batting cage and suggested to his tormentors, "If the *Big Dog* doesn't hit, the Reds don't win," a proclamation with which none of his teammates found fault.

Commenting on the tremendous impact Pérez made on the other players around him, Rose stated, "He was a fatherly type in the clubhouse, especially to the Spanish ballplayers. They looked up to him, as well as relating to him through his background and language."

While Pérez never received much acclaim for his defense, he did a solid job with the glove, leading all players at his position in double plays turned three times, assists and putouts twice each, and fielding percentage once, while splitting his time between first and third. Moving back to first base in 1972 following the multiplayer trade with the Astros that sent Lee May and Tommy Helms to Houston in exchange for Joe Morgan, versatile infielder Denis Menke, and three other players, Pérez spent his remaining time in Cincinnati manning that post, contributing significantly to teams that won three pennants and two world championships. But with promising young first baseman Dan Driessen waiting in the wings, Reds general manager Bob Howsam foolishly traded the 34-year-old Pérez to the Montreal Expos for two ordinary pitchers (Woodie Fryman and Dale Murray) after he hit 19 homers, knocked in 91 runs, and batted .260 in 1976. Although Driessen performed well in Cincinnati the next several years, he never came close to replacing the leadership that Pérez brought to the Reds, who failed to make it back to the playoffs in either of the next two seasons.

Showing that he still had a lot left after joining the Expos, Pérez hit 19 homers, knocked in 91 runs, and batted .283 in his first year with his new team, before posting solid numbers in each of the next two seasons as well. From Montreal, Pérez moved on to Boston, where he had his last big year, hitting 25 homers, knocking in 105 runs, and batting .275 for the Red Sox in 1980. After assuming a part-time role in Beantown the next two seasons, Pérez joined the Phillies for one year, before returning to Cincinnati, where he spent his final three big-league seasons serving the Reds as a backup first baseman and pinch-hitter. Choosing to announce his retirement following the conclusion of the 1986 campaign, Pérez ended his career with 379 homers, 1,652 RBIs, 1,272 runs scored, 2,732 hits, 505 doubles, 79 triples, a .279 batting average, a .341 on-base percentage, and a .463 slugging percentage. As a member of the Reds, Pérez hit 287 homers, knocked in 1,192 runs, scored 936 times, collected 1,934 hits, 339 doubles, and 56 triples, batted .283, compiled an on-base percentage of .346, and posted a slugging percentage of .474.

Following his playing days, Pérez briefly managed both the Reds and Florida Marlins while anxiously awaiting a call from Cooperstown. Finally elected to the Baseball Hall of Fame by the members of the BBWAA in 2000, Pérez, said Johnny Bench, earned that distinction not only with his exceptional play, but by "casting a net over the entire team with his attitude. He was always up, always had a sense of humor." Pérez later received the additional honors of having his #24 retired by the Reds and having a statue of him erected outside Great American Ball Park.

REDS CAREER HIGHLIGHTS

Best Season

Pérez had a great year for the Reds in 1969, earning his third straight All-Star selection and a top-10 finish in the NL MVP voting by batting .294, compiling an OPS of .883, scoring 103 runs, and placing near the top of the league rankings with 37 homers, 122 RBIs, and 331 total bases. But he posted even better numbers when the Reds won the pennant the following year, earning a third-place finish in the MVP balloting and the first of his two *Sporting News* NL All-Star nominations in 1970 by establishing career-high marks in nine different offensive categories, including homers (40), RBIs (129), runs scored (107), total bases (346), batting average (.317), on-base percentage (.401), and slugging percentage (.589).

Memorable Moments/Greatest Performances

Pérez helped lead the Reds to an 8–7 victory over the Pirates on May 15, 1967, by going 4-for-5 with two doubles, two RBIs, and three runs scored, with his two-out double in the bottom of the 10th inning driving home Pete Rose from first base with the winning run.

Pérez experienced one of his most memorable moments in the 1967 MLB All-Star Game, when he earned game MVP honors by homering off Catfish Hunter in the top of the 15th inning to give the NL a 2–1 win over the AL.

Pérez contributed to a 7–6, 12-inning win over the Pirates on July 23, 1968, by going 5-for-6 with a homer and two RBIs.

Pérez led the Reds to a 6–5 win over the Giants on April 12, 1970, by going 4-for-4 with two homers, a walk, and four RBIs.

Pérez collected three hits, homered twice, and knocked in six runs during a 10–5 win over the Dodgers on August 8, 1970.

Pérez knocked in all five runs the Reds scored during a 5–3 win over the Mets on July 11, 1971, with a pair of homers.

Pérez concluded a 5-for-5 evening with a three-run homer off Charlie Hough in the top of the 10th inning that provided the margin of victory in a 4–1 win over the Dodgers on September 21, 1973.

Pérez capped a five-run rally in the bottom of the ninth inning with a two-run homer off reliever Randy Moffitt that gave the Reds a 14–13 victory over the Giants on July 25, 1974.

Pérez led the Reds to a 6–2 win over the Red Sox in Game 5 of the 1975 World Series by knocking in four runs with a pair of homers off Boston starter Reggie Cleveland.

Pérez again came up big for the Reds in Game 7, delivering a two-out, two-run homer off Bill Lee in the top of the sixth inning in the Series finale.

Pérez gave the Reds an 8–7 win over the Cardinals on June 11, 1976, when he homered off reliever Al Hrabosky with two men aboard in the bottom of the ninth inning.

Pérez put the Reds up 2–0 in the 1976 World Series when he delivered a two-out RBI single to left field off Catfish Hunter in the bottom of the ninth inning that drove home Ken Griffey from second base with the winning run of a 4–3 victory over the Yankees.

Notable Achievements

- Hit at least 20 home runs eight times, surpassing 30 homers twice and 40 homers once.
- Knocked in more than 100 runs six times.
- Scored more than 100 runs twice.
- Batted over .300 three times.
- Compiled on-base percentage over .400 once.
- Posted slugging percentage over .500 three times.
- Posted OPS over .900 twice.
- Topped 30 doubles four times.
- Finished second in NL in RBIs once, slugging percentage once, and total bases once.
- Finished third in NL in home runs once, RBIs twice, runs scored once, and total bases once.
- Led NL first basemen in putouts once, double plays turned once, and fielding percentage once.
- Led NL third basemen in putouts once, assists twice, and double plays turned twice.
- Ranks among Reds career leaders in home runs (4th), RBIs (2nd), runs scored (9th), hits (7th), extra-base hits (6th), doubles (7th), total bases (5th), bases on balls (11th), sacrifice flies (3rd), games played (7th), plate appearances (7th), and at-bats (7th).
- Five-time division champion (1970, 1972, 1973, 1975, and 1976).
- Four-time NL champion (1970, 1972, 1975, and 1976).
- Two-time world champion (1975 and 1976).
- Two-time NL Player of the Week.

- August 1975 NL Player of the Month.
- 1967 Reds team MVP.
- Finished in top 10 of NL MVP voting four times, placing in top five once (third in 1970).
- Seven-time NL All-Star selection (1967, 1968, 1969, 1970, 1974, 1975, and 1976).
- Two-time *Sporting News* NL All-Star selection (1970 and 1973).
- Elected to Baseball Hall of Fame by members of BBWAA in 2000.
- #24 retired by Reds.

8
VADA PINSON

An exceptional all-around player who excelled in every aspect of the game, Vada Pinson spent parts of 11 seasons in Cincinnati, combining with Frank Robinson most of that time to give the Reds one of the most formidable hitting tandems in all of baseball. Despite often being overshadowed by his more celebrated teammate, Pinson proved to be a tremendous force on offense, hitting at least 20 homers six times, surpassing 100 RBIs twice, and scoring more than 100 runs, batting over .300, and collecting more than 200 hits four times each. An outstanding baserunner and superb defender as well, Pinson stole more than 20 bases seven times and led all NL outfielders in putouts on three separate occasions, earning in the process two All-Star nominations and a pair of top-10 finishes in the league MVP voting. Nevertheless, some 50 years after he played his last game, Pinson continues to receive virtually no support for inclusion in the Baseball Hall of Fame.

Born in Memphis, Tennessee, on August 11, 1938, Vada Edward Pinson moved with his family at the age of seven to Oakland, California, where he played the trumpet so well at McClymonds High School that he seriously considered pursuing a career as a musician. However, legendary McClymonds coach George Powles, who had earlier helped develop the athletic skills of Frank Robinson, Curt Flood, and Boston Celtics great Bill Russell, ultimately convinced Pinson to focus more on sports.

Choosing to concentrate solely on baseball, Pinson recalled, "The coaches wanted me to go out for football, but I never could see any sense in carrying all that heavy stuff around on your back. I tried basketball for a while, but all you do there is run up and down the floor. And track, well, that interferes with baseball. And besides, I guess nobody really knew I could run very fast."

Eventually emerging as a star on the diamond, Pinson received an offer to sign with the Reds for $4,000 following his graduation, remembering, "The Reds were the only team after me big. Some others talked to me, but Cincinnati was the only one that offered me any money. And I liked [Reds

Vada Pinson finished second to the great Roberto Clemente in the 1961 NL batting race.
Courtesy of RMYAuctions.com

scout Bobby] Mattick, the way he treated me, and [Frank] Robinson was with Cincinnati; so, when I graduated, I signed up with the Reds."

Pinson subsequently spent two seasons in the minors, performing especially well at Visalia in the California League in 1957, where he batted .367, hit 20 homers, knocked in 97 runs, and collected 209 hits. Invited to spring training the following year, Pinson ended up earning a spot on the parent club's Opening Day roster by making an extremely favorable impression on all those in attendance. In addition to displaying grace in the outfield, good power at the plate, and superb instincts, Pinson recorded a time of 3.3 seconds going from home plate to first base that prompted others to compare him to Mickey Mantle, Willie Mays, and Hank Aaron in terms of his pure speed and athleticism. Meanwhile, Pinson remained so quiet throughout the spring that Reds coach Jimmy Dykes, believing him to be Hispanic, spoke to him in gestures and broken English until the 19-year-old outfielder finally said, "Mr. Dykes, if there is something you want me to do with my stance, please tell me."

The Reds' starting right fielder on Opening Day, Pinson made a huge impact in just his second big-league game, when he delivered the decisive blow of a 4–1 win over the Pirates by homering with the bases loaded. However, Pinson later said, "Probably the worst thing that happened to me was hitting that homer against Pittsburgh. It won the game but didn't do me any good. I started thinking of myself as a slugger."

With Pinson spending far too much time the next few weeks swinging for the fences, he fell into a slump that prompted the Reds to return him to the minors. Recalled later in the year after regaining his stroke with Seattle in the Pacific Coast League, Pinson ended up hitting one homer, driving in eight runs, scoring 20 times, and batting .271 in 27 games with the Reds.

Named Cincinnati's starting center fielder prior to the start of the ensuing campaign, Pinson established himself as one of the league's finest players at that position before long, beginning an outstanding seven-year run during which he posted the following numbers:

YEAR	HR	RBI	RUNS	HITS	AVG	OBP	SLG	OPS
1959	20	84	**131**	205	.316	.371	.509	.880
1960	20	61	107	187	.287	.339	.472	.811
1961	16	87	101	**208**	.343	.379	.504	.883
1962	23	100	107	181	.292	.341	.477	.817
1963	22	106	96	**204**	.313	.347	.514	.861
1964	23	84	99	166	.266	.316	.448	.764
1965	22	94	97	204	.305	.352	.484	.836

In addition to leading the NL in hits twice and runs scored once, Pinson topped the senior circuit in both triples and doubles on multiple occasions, with his league-leading 47 two-baggers in 1959 representing one of the highest single-season totals in team annals. Pinson, who consistently ranked among the league leaders in runs scored, doubles, triples, total bases, and steals, also finished second in the circuit in hits three times and batting average once, with only Roberto Clemente's mark of .351 in 1961 preventing him from winning the batting title. Meanwhile, Pinson led all NL center fielders in putouts and assists three times each, with his excellent all-around play earning him two All-Star selections and five top-20 finishes in the league MVP balloting.

Extremely graceful both at the plate and in the field, the 5'11", 180-pound Pinson, who typically batted either second or third in the Reds lineup, possessed a smooth and compact left-handed swing that he used to drive the ball to all parts of the ballpark. Employing a short stride, Pinson tended to pull inside pitches to right field and hit outside offerings either to center or left. Deceptively strong, Pinson had good gap-to-gap power, which, along with his tremendous running speed, allowed him to annually rank among the NL leaders in extra-base hits.

Commenting on Pinson's ability to turn singles into doubles and doubles into triples, Reds coach Wally Moses marveled, "Sometimes, he'll take that turn at first and keep right on going, and I'll think, 'Boy, you're out. They've got you dead this time.' But he always makes it. Nobody ever throws him out."

In describing Pinson's running style, former *Cincinnati Post* reporter Earl Lawson wrote, "Pinson, one of the most graceful runners ever to put on a baseball uniform, gave the appearance of gliding across the ground, his feet barely touching the surface."

Lawson also praised Pinson for his offensive prowess and superior all-around ability, stating, "I always felt Vada had more talent in his little finger than most guys have in their whole body. Vada could run, and he had surprising power. I don't recall anybody getting to 1,500 hits faster than Vada did."

Commenting on the totality of Pinson's game, Tim McCarver said, "Vada was a five-tool guy. Real quiet. He didn't get a lot of attention, but the guys on the field knew how good he was. Ask any player in the years that he played, and they'll tell you he was one of the best. . . . Vada could beat you in a lot of ways. He could beat you with his arm or his legs or his power or his average. Vada Pinson was one of the more underrated players in my day. He was similar to Curt Flood, but Vada had more power and a stronger arm and was perhaps a little bit faster."

Choosing to focus on Pinson's hitting ability, Maury Wills stated, "When I came into the majors, and for a long time after that, Vada may have been the best hitter in the National League. He and Frank Robinson made up as good a 1–2 punch as there was."

Former Braves and Reds pitcher Tony Cloninger also had high praise for Pinson, saying, "I remember what a jump he got on the ball in center field, what a clutch hitter he was, and what a class person he was. He was a great ballplayer."

Meanwhile, Frank Robinson said of his close friend and former roommate, "The numbers don't tell the true story. Vada was underrated and underappreciated as a player. He brought a whole lot more to the game than just cold numbers. . . . He was the first guy I saw who consistently put pressure on outfielders with his speed. Not just with balls that he hit into the gaps. He'd hit ground balls to straightaway center and turn them into doubles. Same thing with a two-hopper to the first baseman. He'd beat it out. The pitcher couldn't get over there fast enough to cover."

With Robinson forming an especially strong bond with Pinson, the former remembered in his autobiography, *Extra Innings*, "Some writers were reporting that Vada Pinson and I formed a 'Negro clique . . . that is gnawing at the morale of the club.' . . . What nonsense. Certainly, Vada and I had been virtually inseparable for five years, but often duos and trios on the team palled around together, and they weren't called clique members."

Unfortunately, the pairing of Pinson and Robinson came to an end following the conclusion of the 1965 campaign when the Reds foolishly traded Robby to the Baltimore Orioles for pitcher Milt Pappas. Yet, despite losing his closest friend on the team, Pinson had two more solid seasons for the Reds before his skills began to diminish somewhat. After hitting 16 homers, driving in 76 runs, scoring 70 times, stealing 18 bases, batting .288, and compiling an OPS of .768 in 1966, Pinson hit 18 homers, knocked in 66 runs, scored 90 times, batted .288, posted an OPS of .771, led the NL with 13 triples, and ranked among the league leaders with 187 hits and 26 thefts the following year. But with the 30-year-old Pinson experiencing a precipitous decline in offensive production in 1968, finishing the season with just five homers, 48 RBIs, 60 RBIs, a .271 batting average, and an OPS of .694, the Reds dealt him to the Cardinals at the end of the year for promising young outfielder Bobby Tolan and pitcher Wayne Granger.

Pinson, who left Cincinnati with career totals of 186 homers, 814 RBIs, 978 runs scored, 1,881 hits, 342 doubles, 96 triples, and 221 stolen bases, a batting average of .297, an on-base percentage of .341, and a slugging percentage of .469, ended up spending just one injury-marred year in St. Louis, hitting 10 homers, driving in 70 runs, and batting .255 in 1969, before being traded to the Cleveland Indians prior to the start of the ensuing campaign. An American Leaguer for the rest of his career, Pinson split the next six seasons between the Indians (1970–1971), Angels

(1972–1973), and Royals (1974–1975), serving all three teams as a corner outfielder, before announcing his retirement early in 1976 after being released by the Milwaukee Brewers during spring training. Over parts of 18 big-league seasons, Pinson hit 256 homers, knocked in 1,169 runs, scored 1,365 times, collected 2,757 hits, 485 doubles, and 127 triples, stole 305 bases, batted .286, compiled a .327 on-base percentage, and posted a .442 slugging percentage.

Following his playing days, Pinson began an 18-year career in coaching that saw him serve at different times as hitting instructor for the Mariners, White Sox, Tigers, and Marlins. Retiring from baseball altogether at the end of 1994, Pinson returned to Oakland, where he died at only 57 years of age on October 21, 1995, after suffering a stroke two weeks earlier.

Upon learning of his longtime friend's passing, Curt Flood said, "I always remember Vada Pinson's smile. It was always present. If not on his face, it was in his voice."

Former Reds manager Sparky Anderson recollected, "He looked like his feet never touched the ground. He was so fast, had so many doubles, all his numbers, 2,800 hits; he was such a player. And a gentleman. If there is one word I'd use to describe him, it's that: He was a gentleman. . . . Vada never got the recognition; he never got any recognition at all. But not one time did I ever hear Vada badmouth anybody about it. He never said a bad word about it."

Although fans of Pinson have long contended that he deserves serious consideration for the Baseball Hall of Fame, he curiously has never come close to gaining induction. Expressing his surprise over the lack of support Pinson has received, former Reds outfielder Jerry Lynch stated, "What bothers me is: how could a guy have over 2,700 hits and not be in the Hall of Fame?"

In attempting to explain his former teammate's exclusion from Cooperstown, Tommy Harper speculated, "Vada was just a steady ballplayer, and sometimes the steady ballplayers who are not in a big media market get overlooked, even though their numbers are there. Vada played for a long time, but if you would ask anybody about the Cincinnati Reds, they immediately go to the Big Red Machine, and they're always gonna go 'Pete Rose, Frank Robinson.' Or 'Frank Robinson, Pete Rose.'"

Harper continued, "Vada was just a person I always considered to be Hall of Fame caliber, because the way I look at it, he has longevity, being steady, and putting up good numbers for a number of years. He came up short of 3,000 hits. As far as a center fielder, in his day, he was considered one of the best."

REDS CAREER HIGHLIGHTS

Best Season

Although Pinson hit more homers, knocked in more runs, and scored more times in two or three other seasons, he made his greatest overall impact in the pennant-winning campaign of 1961, when he earned a third-place finish in the NL MVP voting by hitting 16 homers, driving in 87 runs, scoring 101 times, stealing 23 bases, and establishing career-high marks with 208 hits, a .343 batting average, a .379 on-base percentage, and an OPS of .883, while also leading all NL center fielders with 391 putouts and a career-best 19 assists.

Memorable Moments/Greatest Performances

Pinson made his first big-league homer a memorable one, knocking in all four runs the Reds scored during a 4–1 win over the Pirates on April 18, 1958, with a third-inning grand slam off Pittsburgh starter Ron Kline.

Pinson homered twice in one game for the first time in his career during an 8–5 win over the Pirates on May 29, 1959, concluding the contest with three hits, three RBIs, and three runs scored.

Pinson helped lead the Reds to a 15–13 win over the Phillies on August 14, 1959, by going 5-for-6 with two doubles, one RBI, and four runs scored.

Pinson proved to be the difference in a 4–2 win over the Phillies on May 28, 1962, knocking in all four runs the Reds scored with a pair of two-run homers.

Pinson contributed to a 14–3 victory over the Dodgers on July 9, 1961, by collecting three hits, walking twice, and scoring a career-high five runs.

Pinson went a perfect 5-for-5 at the plate during a 10–5 win over the Giants on September 1, 1962.

Pinson hit safely in 27 consecutive games from September 3 to October 3, 1965, going 42-for-113 (.372), with two homers, one triple, six doubles, six walks, 15 RBIs, and 19 runs scored.

Pinson gave the Reds a 5–4 victory over the Braves on June 2, 1967, when he drove home the winning run from third base with a two-out bases loaded single in the bottom of the 11th inning that represented his fourth hit of the game.

Notable Achievements

- Hit at least 20 home runs six times.
- Knocked in at least 100 runs twice.
- Scored more than 100 runs four times.
- Batted over .300 four times, topping the .340 mark once.
- Posted slugging percentage over .500 three times.
- Amassed more than 200 hits four times.
- Finished in double digits in triples five times.
- Topped 30 doubles seven times.
- Stole more than 20 bases seven times.
- Led NL in runs scored once, hits twice, triples twice, doubles twice, and at-bats twice.
- Finished second in NL in batting average once, hits three times, triples once, doubles twice, and stolen bases twice.
- Led NL outfielders in putouts three times and fielding percentage once.
- Led NL center fielders in assists three times.
- Ranks among Reds career leaders in RBIs (12th), runs scored (8th), hits (8th), extra-base hits (7th), triples (5th), doubles (6th), total bases (9th), stolen bases (12th), games played (9th), plate appearances (9th), and at-bats (9th).
- 1961 NL champion.
- 1961 Gold Glove Award winner.
- Finished in top 10 of NL MVP voting twice, placing third in 1961.
- Two-time NL All-Star selection (1959 and 1960).

9

EDD ROUSH

An excellent line-drive hitter who posted a lifetime batting average of .323 over 18 big-league seasons, Edd Roush spent most of his peak years in Cincinnati, where he established himself as arguably the National League's finest contact hitter. A member of the Reds for parts of 12 seasons, Roush hit well over .300 for them 10 straight times from 1917 to 1926, winning in the process two NL batting titles. An outstanding baserunner and superb defensive outfielder as well, Roush did a magnificent job of patrolling center field at Redland Field, with his superior all-around play earning him two top-10 finishes in the NL MVP voting and an eventual place in Cooperstown.

Born in Oakland City, Indiana, on May 8, 1893, Edd J. Roush grew up with his twin brother, Fred, on the family's dairy farm, where he developed a distaste for farmwork at an early age, recalling, "One of my chores was to milk the cows, which meant getting up before dawn and going out to that cold dark barn. I didn't expect to make it all the way to the big leagues; I just had to get away from them damn cows."

The son of a former semipro baseball player, Roush, who spent most of his spare time playing baseball and basketball, hoped to pursue a career on the diamond himself. Although a natural left-hander, Roush learned to throw and bat right-handed due to the scarcity of left-handed gloves in his hometown.

After getting his start in organized ball at Oakland City High School, Roush began competing semiprofessionally with the Oakland City Walk-overs in 1909 when one of the team's regular outfielders failed to show up for a game, remembering, "We waited for five minutes, and the outfielder never did show, so they gave me a uniform and put me in right field. Turned out I got a couple of hits that day and I became Oakland City's regular right fielder for the rest of the season."

After jumping to a rival team from Princeton early in 1911, Roush entered the professional ranks later that year when he joined Henderson

Edd Roush won two batting titles during his time in Cincinnati.

(Kentucky) of the Kitty League. Roush subsequently split the 1912 campaign and the first part of 1913 between Princeton of the Ohio Valley League and Evansville of the Kitty League, before having his contract purchased by the Chicago White Sox in August 1913. Appearing in nine games with Chicago the rest of the year, Roush garnered just 12 total plate appearances, before the White Sox elected to send him back to the minor leagues the following season.

However, rather than returning to the minors, Roush signed with the Indianapolis Hoosiers of the upstart Federal League, for whom he batted

.325 in 74 games in 1914. Remaining with the Hoosiers when they moved to Newark and renamed themselves the Pepper the following year, Roush batted .298 and stole 28 bases in 145 games, before heading to New York when Giants manager John McGraw purchased his contract following the demise of the Federal League at the end of the year.

Roush ended up batting just .188 in 39 games with the Giants over the first four months of the 1916 campaign, during which time he came to hate playing for the dictatorial McGraw, recalling, "If you made a bad play, he'd cuss you out, yell at you, call you all sorts of names. That didn't go with me."

Included in a five-player trade with the Reds on July 20 that also sent the aging Christy Mathewson and Bill McKechnie to Cincinnati for infielder Buck Herzog and outfielder Red Killefer, Roush improved his performance dramatically following his arrival in the Queen City. After laying claim to the starting center field job, Roush batted .287, scored 34 runs, and stole 15 bases in 69 games and 300 total plate appearances the rest of the year, before emerging as one of the senior circuit's best players in 1917, when, in addition to leading the league with a .341 batting average, he finished third in OPS (.833) and hits (178), fourth in triples (14), and fifth in runs scored (82).

Subsequently bypassed for military duty in 1918, Roush remained in the States, where he batted .333 and compiled a league-leading .455 slugging percentage and .823 OPS during the war-shortened campaign. However, Roush experienced tragedy late in the year when his lineman father died from head injuries after falling off a telephone pole.

After winning his second batting title in 1919 with a mark of .321, Roush continued to perform at an elite level when MLB began using a livelier ball in 1920, posting the following numbers over the course of the next seven seasons, with only his injury-marred 1922 campaign being excluded from the graphic:

YEAR	HR	RBI	RUNS	HITS	AVG	OBP	SLG	OPS
1920	4	90	81	196	.339	.386	.453	.839
1921	4	71	68	147	.352	.403	.502	.905
1923	6	88	88	185	.351	.406	.531	.938
1924	3	72	67	168	.348	.376	.501	.877
1925	8	83	91	183	.339	.383	.494	.878
1926	7	79	95	182	.323	.366	.462	.828

In addition to ranking among the NL leaders in batting average each year, Roush consistently placed near the top of the league rankings in OPS and triples, with his career-high 21 three-baggers in 1924 leading the league. Roush also topped the circuit with 41 doubles in 1923 and finished second in the league with 36 stolen bases in 1920.

Employing an unusual batting style in which he snapped the bat at the ball with his arms and placed line drives to all parts of the field by shifting his feet after the ball left the pitcher's hand and altering the timing of his swing, the left-handed-hitting Roush also adjusted his position in the batter's box based on the opposing pitcher. Although only 5'11" and 170 pounds, Roush possessed extraordinary strength in his arms and hands that he developed while working on his family's farm as a youth, enabling him to wield a 48-ounce bat that ranks among the heaviest ever used. Nevertheless, Roush proved to be more of a spray hitter than a slugger, never hitting more than eight homers or driving in more than 90 runs in a season.

In describing his choice of weapons and his approach at the plate, Roush said, "It was a shorter bat, with a big handle, and I tried to hit to all fields. Didn't swing my head off, just snapped at the ball. . . . Some batters, and good ones too, scoff at the whole theory of place hitting, calling it a myth. They are wrong, however. . . . Place hitting is, in a sense, glorified bunting. I only take a half swing at the ball, and the weight of the bat, rather than my swing, is what drives it."

Roush's style of hitting and keen batting eye helped make him one of the most difficult players in the game to strike out; in more than 8,000 total plate appearances over the course of his career, he fanned just 260 times. An excellent bunter as well, Roush recorded a total of 186 sacrifice hits as a member of the Reds, which represents a franchise record.

As well as Roush performed on offense, he truly separated himself from the other players who manned his position with his exceptional defensive work in center field. Often compared defensively to the great Tris Speaker, Roush received high praise in the December 1920 edition of *Baseball Magazine*, which, after calling him the greatest outfielder in the National League, claimed, "In ground covering, he has no superiors and few approximate equals."

Combining excellent speed with sound judgment and the ability to track the flight of the baseball, even after turning his back to the plate, Roush covered a tremendous amount of territory, with former Reds teammate Heinie Groh saying, "Eddie used to take care of the whole outfield, not just center field. He was far and away the best outfielder I ever saw."

A hard-nosed player who gave no quarter to the opposition, Roush had a strong dislike for pitchers who threw at him, often retaliating by spiking opposing infielders on the basepaths. Revealing his warlike mentality during a 1980s interview, Roush said, "That thing was a business with me. It wasn't no fun. I'll tell you that right quick. I played that game to win, and, when you play to win, you don't play for fun. . . . When I was a kid, yeah, it was a lot of fun playing. It was a lot of fun playing in the minor leagues. But when you got in the major leagues, the damn thing was a business. It was *then*. I don't know what the hell it is now."

Displaying his contempt for modern-day players, Roush continued, "Two-thirds of them playing today, if they had played back in my day, we'd have killed every one of them. They threw at you in those days, and they didn't throw over the top of your head, either. . . . Back when I played, if the three outfielders, the third baseman, and the first baseman didn't hit .300, they didn't last very long. Today, if one of them hits .300, they're lucky. Anybody who wants to see them play today is nuts."

Infuriated by the notion that the Reds won the 1919 World Series only because the White Sox failed to put forth their best effort, Roush insisted that Cincinnati had the better team, saying, "They threw the first ballgame. But they didn't get their money after the first ballgame, so they went out and tried to win."

Although Roush had one of his better offensive seasons in 1926, the Reds traded him back to the Giants for future Hall of Fame first baseman George "High Pockets" Kelly at the end of the year. Roush spent the next three seasons in New York, missing much of the 1928 campaign after undergoing surgery to repair torn stomach muscles, but batting over .300 the other two years. After sitting out the entire 1930 season in one of his many salary disputes, Roush returned to Cincinnati for one final season, batting .271 in 101 games in 1931, before announcing his retirement at the end of the year with career totals of 68 homers, 981 RBIs, 1,099 runs scored, 2,376 hits, 339 doubles, 182 triples, and 268 stolen bases, a batting average of .323, an on-base percentage of .369, and a slugging percentage of .446. Over parts of 12 seasons in Cincinnati, Roush hit 47 homers, knocked in 763 runs, scored 815 times, collected 1,784 hits, 260 doubles, and 152 triples, stole 199 bases, batted .331, compiled an on-base percentage of .377, and posted a slugging percentage of .462.

Following his playing days, Roush returned to the family farm in Indiana, where he spent the next several years living with his wife Essie and their daughter Mary. Later relocating to Bradenton, Florida, after Essie passed away, Roush served on the town's school board, briefly served as president of the Board of Directors of First Bank and Trust Company, and ran the Montgomery cemetery for close to 35 years.

Voted the greatest player in Reds history during a 1969 celebration of the 100th anniversary of professional baseball, Roush lived for another 19 years, dying from a heart attack at the age of 94 on March 21, 1988, while visiting the Reds spring training complex in Bradenton. Roush, who had earlier survived two mild strokes and a heart attack, was the last surviving member of the 1919 World Series champion Reds at the time of his passing.

REDS CAREER HIGHLIGHTS

Best Season

It could be argued that Roush had his finest season for the Reds in 1917, when, in one of the last years of the so-called Dead Ball Era, he led the NL with a .341 batting average and ranked among the league leaders with an OPS of .833, 67 RBIs, 82 runs scored, 178 hits, and 14 triples. Nevertheless, with a livelier ball in use by 1923, Roush posted a far-more impressive stat-line, batting .351, compiling an OPS of .938, knocking in 88 runs, scoring 88 times, amassing 185 hits, collecting 18 triples, and leading the league with a career-high 41 doubles.

Memorable Moments/Greatest Performances

Roush led the Reds to a 9–5 win over the Giants on July 14, 1918, by going 4-for-5 with a homer, double, five RBIs, and two runs scored, delivering the game's big blow in the bottom of the eighth inning, when he homered off New York starter Al Demaree with two men out and two men on.

Roush delivered the decisive blow of an 8–4 win over the Brooklyn Robins on August 19, 1918, when he homered with the bases loaded off Hall of Fame southpaw Rube Marquard in the bottom of the seventh inning.

Although Roush batted just .214 against the White Sox in the 1919 World Series, he knocked in seven runs and led both teams with six runs scored.

Roush contributed to a 13–10 victory over the Braves on August 10, 1920, by going 4-for-5 with two triples, four RBIs, and three runs scored.

Roush hit safely in 27 consecutive games from August 27 to September 21, 1920, going 46-for-114 (.404), with two homers, one triple, seven doubles, 22 RBIs, and 14 runs scored.

Roush collected five hits and knocked in five runs during a 15–8 win over the Phillies on September 26, 1922.

Roush fashioned another 27-game hitting streak from May 16 to June 25, 1924, this time going 40-for-100 (.400), with a homer, three triples, five doubles, 13 RBIs, and 14 runs scored.

Roush gave the Reds a 2–1 victory over the Phillies on July 8, 1924, when he drove home the winning run from third base with his third hit of the game in the bottom of the 16th inning.

Roush led the Reds to a 10–8 win over Brooklyn on July 17, 1924, by going 4-for-5 with two triples, five RBIs, and two runs scored.

Notable Achievements

- Batted over .320 ten times, topping the .350 mark three times.
- Compiled on-base percentage over .400 three times.
- Posted slugging percentage over .500 three times.
- Posted OPS over .900 twice.
- Finished in double digits in triples 10 times, surpassing 20 three-baggers once.
- Topped 30 doubles twice.
- Stole more than 20 bases six times.
- Led NL in batting average twice, slugging percentage once, OPS once, triples once, doubles once, and sacrifice hits once.
- Finished second in NL in batting average twice, RBIs once, triples twice, doubles once, extra-base hits once, total bases once, and stolen bases once.
- Led NL outfielders in putouts once.
- Led NL center fielders in assists twice, double plays turned three times, and fielding percentage three times.
- Holds franchise record for most sacrifice hits (186).
- Ranks among Reds career leaders in batting average (2nd), hits (9th), triples (2nd), doubles (12th), total bases (12th), OPS (12th), games played (12th), plate appearances (11th), and at-bats (11th).
- 1919 NL champion.
- 1919 world champion.
- Finished in top 10 of NL MVP voting twice.
- Elected to Baseball Hall of Fame by members of Veterans Committee in 1962.

10

ERIC DAVIS

An extraordinarily gifted player who drew comparisons to Willie Mays and Hank Aaron early in his career, Eric Davis unfortunately sustained a series of injuries that prevented him from ever fully maximizing his tremendous physical talent. Nevertheless, Davis accomplished enough during his nine seasons in Cincinnati to earn a prominent place in these rankings. The first player in major-league history to surpass 30 home runs and 50 steals in the same season, Davis hit more than 20 homers and stole more than 20 bases six times each, while also driving in more than 100 runs twice and scoring more than 100 times once. A three-time Gold Glove Award winner, Davis excelled in the field as well, with his superior all-around play earning him two All-Star selections and a pair of top-10 finishes in the NL MVP voting. A major contributor to the Reds' last world championship ballclub, Davis left behind a legacy that clearly makes him one of the greatest players in team annals. Still, we are all left to wonder what might have been had he been more fortunate.

Born in Los Angeles, California, on May 29, 1962, Eric Keith Davis grew up in South Central L.A., where danger lurked around every corner. Recounting an incident that occurred at the playground one day when someone began firing a pistol, Eric's father, Jimmy, recalled, "Here I was, there to protect Eric, but the shooting was so close, I panicked. All I could say was just, 'Eric, hit the dirt.' We all ran behind the school. That's the kind of area it is. It's a blessing he got out without getting hurt."

With drugs readily available in the area as well, Davis managed to avoid falling into the trap of addiction by competing in sports, excelling in particular in baseball and basketball at Fremont High School, where he often went up against childhood friend Darryl Strawberry, who attended high school in nearby Crenshaw. Later admitting that he preferred basketball over baseball until his senior year, when he batted .635 and stole 50 bases in only 19 games as Fremont's starting shortstop, Davis said, "I guess the first time I took baseball seriously was when the scouts started paying attention to me.

In 1987, Eric Davis became the first player in MLB history to surpass 30 homers and 50 steals in the same season.

Darryl (at Crenshaw) always had more scouts watching him. There weren't too many scouts who would come down to Fremont looking for talent."

Offered tryouts by the Dodgers and Milwaukee Brewers, Davis made an extremely favorable impression on both teams, saying of his tryout with the Brewers, "They got me at 6.36 (seconds in the 60-yard dash). They didn't believe it. They timed me again. Same thing. They didn't sign me."

Ultimately signed by the Reds for $18,000 after they selected him in the eighth round of the June 1980 MLB Amateur Draft, Davis spent most of the next five seasons in the minor leagues, moving from shortstop to center field. Promoted to the parent club in May 1984 after beginning the season at Triple-A Wichita, Davis remained in Cincinnati for the next two months, before being put on the disabled list and eventually returned to the minors after injuring his knee while sliding into second base during a July game against the Mets. Rejoining the Reds in September, Davis went on a hitting spree that enabled him to finish the season with 10 homers and 30 RBIs in only 174 official at-bats, although he also struck out 48 times and batted just .224.

Impressed with Davis's overall performance, but somewhat concerned over his high strikeout total, Reds player-manager Pete Rose said, "I told him to just be quick with the bat and the homers will come. I told him, too, that I'd be watching him like a hawk. The kid understands. He has a chance to be the best player on this club."

Davis subsequently split the 1985 campaign between the Reds and their Triple-A affiliate in Denver, hitting eight homers, driving in 18 runs, scoring 26 times, stealing 16 bases, and batting .246 in 56 games with the parent club, before arriving in Cincinnati to stay the following year. Commenting on his three-month stint in the minors, Davis said, "The only thing good about going back was that it helped me mentally. It was a test of my character, especially when I failed after all the media hype last spring."

After getting off to a slow start in 1986, Davis caught fire once Rose inserted him into the everyday starting lineup and moved him from the leadoff spot in the lineup to the middle of the batting order in mid-June. Manning either center field or left the rest of the year, Davis earned a 12th-place finish in the NL MVP voting by hitting 27 homers, driving in 71 runs, batting .277, and ranking among the league leaders with 97 runs scored, 80 stolen bases, a .523 slugging percentage, and an OPS of .901. Later crediting Reds batting coach Billy DeMars for his improved performance at the plate, the right-handed-hitting Davis claimed that DeMars got him to shorten his swing and go with the pitch, rather than trying to pull everything.

Named the Reds' full-time starter in center field in 1987, Davis performed magnificently during the season's first half, hitting 27 homers, driving in 68 runs, and compiling a batting average of .321 by the All-Star break, with his superb all-around play and unique skill set drawing him praise from some of the game's most prominent figures.

Commenting on his former team's star outfielder, Johnny Bench stated, "I was watching some early films of Hank Aaron the other day. Eric has that same strength, the ability to create things at the last second with his bat."

Aaron himself said, "Eric Davis has unlimited ability—awesome ability. I don't think he'll be Willie Mays. That would take some doing. But, on the other hand, I don't think he has a weakness, either."

Pete Rose told *Sports Illustrated*, "Eric is the one guy who can lead our league in home runs and stolen bases. Name me another cleanup hitter who can steal 100 bases. Name one. It's like having an atomic bomb sitting next to you in the dugout."

Reds teammate Dave Parker told that same publication, "As an overall package, there's no one in either league who can play with Eric Davis. . . . Eric is blessed with world-class speed, great leaping ability, the body to play until he is 42, tremendous bat speed and power, and a throwing arm you wouldn't believe."

However, Davis, who heard the comparisons being made between himself and some of the all-time greats, remained more pragmatic, saying, "I'm being compared to the impossible. I never saw Mays, Aaron, or Clemente play. What about the people I face every day? Tim Raines is the best? [Don] Mattingly is the best? Why not compare me to my peers?"

Forced to miss more than two weeks of action due to a rib injury he sustained when he crashed into the outfield wall at Wrigley Field while taking an extra-base hit away from Ryne Sandberg, Davis slumped somewhat during the second half of the 1987 campaign. Nevertheless, he finished the season with 37 homers, 100 RBIs, 120 runs scored, 50 stolen bases, a .293 batting average, and an OPS of .991, becoming in the process the first player to record at least 30 home runs and 50 steals in the same season.

Blessed with a rare combination of power and speed, Davis had the ability to drive the ball more than 450 feet from home plate despite his slender 6'2", 180-pound frame. Davis also did an exceptional job of creating havoc on the basepaths and patrolling center field at Riverfront Stadium, covering a tremendous amount of ground, while often using his outstanding leaping ability to turn apparent home runs into long outs. Meanwhile, Davis's strong throwing arm enabled him to amass at least 10 outfield assists on two separate occasions.

Despite missing several games in each of the next three seasons due to a series of injuries that included a torn hamstring, swollen elbow, bruised knee, strained wrist, and lacerated kidney, Davis continued to perform at an extremely high level, averaging 28 homers, 93 RBIs, 80 runs scored, and 26 stolen bases from 1988 to 1990. Particularly outstanding in 1989, Davis earned All-Star honors and a ninth-place finish in the NL MVP voting by batting .281, swiping 21 bags, and ranking among the league leaders with 34 homers, 101 RBIs, a .541 slugging percentage, and an OPS of .908.

Yet, even though Davis's all-out style of play proved to be the cause of his numerous stints on the disabled list, he often found his heart and dedication to his team being questioned, once saying, "I've heard both sides. I heard I don't play hurt, and now I hear I shouldn't play hurt. I know some of my teammates and the manager have said things, but not to me. They say it to the media."

After helping the Reds capture the NL pennant in 1990 by hitting 24 homers, driving in 86 runs, scoring 84 times, stealing 21 bases, batting .260, and posting an OPS of .833 during the regular season, Davis spent 40 days in the hospital with a lacerated kidney he sustained when he dove after a flyball hit by Oakland's Willie McGee in the final game of the World Series. Although subsequently advised by doctors to sit out the entire 1991 campaign, Davis displayed his mettle by returning to action on Opening Day. Clearly not himself, Davis batted just .235, hit only 11 homers, and knocked in just 33 runs, in 89 games and 340 total plate appearances, before being dealt to the Dodgers for pitchers Tim Belcher and John Wetteland at the end of the year.

Commenting on the trade following his arrival in Los Angeles, Davis said, "The reality is they [the Reds] felt I couldn't perform any more. The No. 1 thing about how I performed last year was I had a kidney torn in three places. They held me accountable for that."

Davis subsequently spent two injury-marred years in Los Angeles, and another in Detroit, before announcing his retirement at only 32 years of age after undergoing surgery for a herniated disc in his neck in 1994. But after spending the ensuing campaign overseeing several businesses and working out, Davis decided to mount a comeback in 1996. Rejoining the Reds after earning a spot on the big-league roster during spring training, Davis ended up winning the NL Comeback Player of the Year Award by hitting 26 homers, driving in 83 runs, scoring 81 times, stealing 23 bases, batting .287, and posting an OPS of .917, in 129 games and just under 500 total plate appearances as the team's primary starter in center field.

Nevertheless, the Reds decided not to re-sign Davis at the end of the year, prompting him to ink a free agent deal with Baltimore. Off to a fast start in 1997, Davis hit eight homers, knocked in 25 runs, and batted .304 for the Orioles through May 25, before missing the next four months after undergoing surgery for colon cancer. However, he returned to the lineup later in the year, just in time to help the Orioles clinch the AL East title, with his courageous effort resulting in him being named the winner of the Roberto Clemente Award as baseball's most inspirational player, and the Fred Hutchinson Award, which is presented annually to the player who best exemplifies character, dedication, and competitive spirit.

In discussing his ordeal afterward, Davis said, "I was able to get operated on four days after I was diagnosed. It was just a matter of getting this baseball-sized tumor out of me."

Davis ended up spending one more year in Baltimore, hitting 28 homers, driving in 89 runs, scoring 81 times, and batting .327 for the Orioles in 1998, before splitting the next three seasons between the Cardinals and Giants. After assuming a part-time role with both teams, Davis announced his retirement following the conclusion of the 2001 campaign, ending his career with 282 homers, 934 RBIs, 938 runs scored, 1,430 hits, 239 doubles, 26 triples, 349 stolen bases, a .269 batting average, a .359 on-base percentage, and a .482 slugging percentage. During his time in Cincinnati, Davis hit 203 homers, knocked in 615 runs, scored 635 times, collected 886 hits, 139 doubles, and 18 triples, stole 270 bases, batted .271, compiled an on-base percentage of .367, and posted a slugging percentage of .510.

Following his playing days, Davis spent several years dabbling in real estate and serving as a special assistant and adviser to Reds GM Walt Jocketty, before eventually settling into the position of minor-league outfield and baserunning coordinator.

REDS CAREER HIGHLIGHTS

Best Season

Davis had his finest season for the Reds in 1987, when, despite appearing in only 129 games and garnering just 474 official at-bats, he earned a ninth-place finish in the NL MVP voting and a spot on the *Sporting News* NL All-Star Team by batting .293, knocking in 100 runs, and ranking among the league leaders with 37 homers, 120 runs scored, 50 steals, 84 bases on balls, a .399 on-base percentage, a .593 slugging percentage, and an OPS of .991, establishing in the process career-high marks in eight different offensive categories. Displaying the totality of his game, Davis also earned Gold Glove honors for the first of three straight times by leading all NL center fielders in putouts (378) and assists (10).

Memorable Moments/Greatest Performances

Davis led the Reds to a 5–4 win over the Pirates on August 25, 1986, by going 3-for-4 with two homers, a stolen base, and four RBIs.

Two days later, Davis delivered the decisive blow of a 9–5 win over the Pirates when he homered with the bases loaded off Don Robinson in the top of the ninth inning.

Davis helped lead the Reds to a 14–2 rout of the Giants on September 10, 1986, by hitting three home runs, driving in four runs, and scoring five times, with two of his homers coming off Vida Blue.

Davis again homered three times during a 9–6 win over the Phillies on May 3, 1987, finishing the game with four hits, six RBIs, and four runs scored.

Davis gave the Reds a 5–4 win over the Giants on August 2, 1987, when he led off the bottom of the 11th inning with a home run off Jeff Robinson.

Davis hit for the cycle during a 9–4 win over the Padres on June 2, 1989, going 4-for-4 with six RBIs.

Davis provided most of the offensive firepower during a 4–3 victory over the Pirates on August 24, 1990, going 4-for-4 with a homer, double, and four runs scored.

Davis helped spark the Reds to a 7–0 victory over Oakland in Game 1 of the 1990 World Series by hitting a two-run homer off Dave Stewart in the bottom of the first inning.

Davis led the Reds to an 11–9 win over the Rockies on May 24, 1996, by going 4-for-5 with two homers, a double, and five RBIs.

Notable Achievements

- Hit more than 20 home runs six times, topping 30 homers twice.
- Knocked in more than 100 runs twice.
- Scored more than 100 runs once.
- Posted slugging percentage over .500 five times.
- Posted OPS over .900 four times.
- Stole more than 20 bases six times, topping 30 thefts three times and 50 thefts twice.
- Hit three home runs in one game twice (vs. Giants on September 10, 1986, and vs. Phillies on May 3, 1987).
- Hit for the cycle vs. San Diego on June 2, 1989.

- Finished second in NL in slugging percentage once and stolen bases once.
- Finished third in NL in home runs once, runs scored twice, slugging percentage once, and OPS twice.
- Led NL outfielders in putouts once.
- Led NL center fielders in assists once.
- Ranks among Reds career leaders in home runs (10th), stolen bases (9th), slugging percentage (7th), and OPS (6th).
- 1990 division champion.
- 1990 NL champion.
- 1990 world champion.
- Five-time NL Player of the Week.
- Four-time NL Player of the Month.
- Two-time Silver Slugger Award winner (1987 and 1989).
- Three-time Gold Glove Award winner (1987, 1988, and 1989).
- Two-time Reds team MVP (1987 and 1989).
- Finished in top 10 of NL MVP voting twice.
- Two-time NL All-Star selection (1987 and 1989).
- Two-time Sporting News NL All-Star selection (1987 and 1989).

11

TED KLUSZEWSKI

Once asked to name the five strongest players in baseball, Hall of Fame manager Leo Durocher surprisingly failed to include Ted Kluszewski on his list. Pointed out to him that he neglected to mention the powerful Reds first baseman, Durocher countered, "Kluszewski? I'm talking about human beings!"

Perhaps the most intimidating hitter of his era, Kluszewski, his huge biceps exposed by the sleeveless uniform he wore to allow his bulging muscles to move, instilled fear in opposing pitchers every time he stepped to the plate. Blessed with incredible physical strength, "Big Klu," as he came to be known, proved to be one of the game's top home-run hitters and run producers before a bad back brought his period of dominance to an end, hitting at least 40 homers three times and knocking in more than 100 runs five times. More than just a slugger, Kluszewski, who spent parts of 11 seasons in Cincinnati, also batted over .300 on seven separate occasions for the Reds, while striking out fewer than 300 times in just over 5,400 total plate appearances. A solid defender as well, Kluszewski led all NL first basemen in putouts twice, double plays turned three times, and fielding percentage five times, with his excellent all-around play earning him four All-Star selections and three top-10 finishes in the NL MVP voting.

Born in Summit Argo, Illinois, on September 10, 1924, Theodore Bernard Kluszewski grew up with his five siblings some 10 miles southwest of Chicago, not far from Comiskey Park, the longtime home of the White Sox. The son of Polish immigrants, Kluszewski, who weighed 14 pounds at birth, developed into a star in multiple sports during his teenage years, excelling in both football and baseball at Argo Community High School.

Ineligible for military duty during World War II due to a childhood pelvic procedure, Kluszewski accepted an athletic scholarship to Indiana University, where he continued to compete in both sports. An outstanding tight end and defensive lineman on the gridiron, Kluszewski, said Mark Deal, the school's assistant athletic director for alumni relations, "was a big

Ted Kluszewski hit at least 40 home runs for the Reds three straight times.

man, and a terrific football player." Meanwhile, Kluszewski excelled as a center fielder on the diamond, setting a school record in 1945 that stood for 50 years by compiling a batting average of .443.

Discovered by the Reds by chance, Kluszewski benefited from the wartime travel restrictions that forced the team to train at Indiana University from 1943 to 1945. After Reds groundskeeper Matty Schwab observed

Kluszewski hitting balls over an embankment near the baseball diamond that no other Reds player even approached, Cincinnati scouts offered the 20-year-old Hoosier a contract. While Kluszewski chose not to sign immediately since he did not wish to endanger his collegiate football eligibility, he ultimately inked a deal with the club following his graduation in 1946.

Kluszewski subsequently spent two years advancing through Cincinnati's farm system, batting .325 and .377, with his excellent hitting earning him a brief trial with the parent club in 1947. Joining the Reds for good the following year, Kluszewski hit 12 homers, knocked in 57 runs, batted .274, and posted an OPS of .758, in 113 games and just under 400 official at-bats. Named the Reds' everyday first baseman prior to the start of the 1949 campaign, Kluszewski acquitted himself well in his first year as a full-time starter, batting .309 and posting an OPS of .743, although his eight homers and 68 RBIs proved to be something of a disappointment. Far more productive in 1950, Kluszewski hit 25 homers, knocked in 111 runs, batted .307, and compiled an OPS of .863, while also striking out fewer times (28) than he walked (33) for the first of seven straight seasons. But even though Kluszewski remained a solid player the next two years, performing especially well in 1952, when he finished third in the league with a .320 batting average, a .509 slugging percentage, an OPS of .892, and a career-high 11 triples, he failed to develop into the consistent power threat the team envisioned when it originally signed him, totaling only 29 home runs and 163 RBIs.

It was also during his first few years in Cincinnati that the left-handed-hitting Kluszewski, who stood 6'2" and weighed close to 240 pounds, cut off the sleeves of his uniform because they constricted his large biceps and shoulders, thereby interfering with his swing. Revealing years later that his bold fashion statement agitated the Reds front office, Kluszewski recalled, "They got pretty upset, but it was either that or change my swing—and I wasn't about to change my swing."

Kluszewski further exposed his massive arms by electing not to wear a T-shirt underneath his uniform, prompting former White Sox teammate Billy Pierce to say nearly a half-century later, "I remember the first time that I saw Ted in those cut-off sleeves. They were good-sized. He was a big man. A big man."

Free of all constrictions, Kluszewski finally found his power stroke in 1953, when he began an exceptional four-year run during which he posted the following numbers:

YEAR	HR	RBI	RUNS	HITS	AVG	OBP	SLG	OPS
1953	40	108	97	180	.316	.380	.570	.950
1954	**49**	**141**	104	187	.326	.407	.642	1.049
1955	47	113	116	**192**	.314	.382	.585	.967
1956	35	102	91	156	.302	.362	.536	.898

Averaging 43 homers and 116 RBIs during that four-year stretch, Kluszewski reached the seats more times (171) than any other player in the game. In addition to ranking among the NL leaders in homers and RBIs all four years, Kluszewski annually placed near the top of the league rankings in batting average, slugging percentage, OPS, hits, and total bases, earning in the process four straight All-Star selections and three top-10 finishes in the NL MVP voting. And with Kluszewski never striking out more than 40 times in any of those campaigns, he twice came within a homer or two of becoming just the second player in MLB history to fan fewer than 50 times in a season in which he also hit 50 home runs (Johnny Mize accomplished the feat for the Giants in 1947).

Even though Kluszewski employed a short, compact swing that enabled him to make consistent contact against both right-handed and left-handed pitching, he possessed enough natural strength to hit the ball out of any part of the ballpark. Meanwhile, Kluszewski's keen batting eye and tremendous discipline at the plate allowed him to consistently hit for a high batting average and walk more often than he struck out.

While Kluszewski often drew praise for his exceptional hitting, he seldom received the credit he deserved for being one of the league's better fielding first basemen. Although Kluszewski possessed limited range, rarely moving more than one step to either side, he proved to be an extremely capable defender who combined sure hands and nimble footwork around the bag to lead all players at his position in fielding percentage five straight times, setting in the process a major-league record.

In discussing his fellow first sacker, former Yankees star Bill Skowron said, "Everybody knows Ted could hit a baseball. What some people don't know is that he was a hell of a first baseman and a hell of a nice guy, too."

With Kluszewski apparently headed for his fourth straight season of at least 40 home runs in 1956, he suffered a back injury during a clubhouse scuffle early in September that limited him to just two homers the rest of the year. Relegated to pinch-hitting duty for most of the ensuing campaign after aggravating the injury early in the year, Kluszewski hit just six homers and knocked in only 21 runs in 133 total trips to the plate.

Recalling the difficulties he experienced at the time, Kluszewski said, "On Opening Day, I made a sudden, quick movement to field a ball, and the pain was unbearable. Finally, it was decided that I had a slipped disc. Some doctors recommended an operation, and some didn't. But none would assure me that I would still have as much mobility, and I decided against going under the knife."

Dealt to the Pirates for first baseman Dee Fondy the following offseason, Kluszewski never regained his earlier form, forcing him to assume the role of a platoon player over the course of his four remaining big-league seasons, which he split between the Pirates, Chicago White Sox, and Los Angeles Angels. While in Chicago, though, Kluszewski made his only World Series appearance, hitting three homers, driving in 10 runs, and batting .391 in a losing effort against the Dodgers in the 1959 Fall Classic.

Choosing to announce his retirement after hitting 15 home runs in only 263 at-bats with the expansion Angels in 1961, Kluszewski ended his playing career with 279 homers, 1,028 RBIs, 848 runs scored, 1,766 hits, 290 doubles, 29 triples, a .298 batting average, a .353 on-base percentage, and a .498 slugging percentage. During his time in Cincinnati, Kluszewski hit 251 homers, knocked in 886 runs, scored 745 times, collected 1,499 hits, 244 doubles, and 23 triples, batted .302, compiled an on-base percentage of .357, and posted a slugging percentage of .512.

Following his playing days, Kluszewski remained away from the game for nearly a decade, spending most of his time overseeing the operation of Ted Kluszewski's Steak House, which he first established in the Walnut Hills neighborhood of Cincinnati in 1958. However, Kluszewski decided to return to baseball in 1970, when he assumed the role of Reds hitting coach. He subsequently spent the next nine years serving the team in that capacity, tutoring the likes of Big Red Machine members Johnny Bench, Tony Pérez, Joe Morgan, Pete Rose, Ken Griffey, and George Foster, whose power stroke he helped develop. Opting to become the organization's minor-league batting instructor after Sparky Anderson left the team following the conclusion of the 1978 campaign, Kluszewski spent the next eight years in that post, before retiring from coaching after suffering a massive heart attack in 1986 that forced him to undergo emergency bypass surgery. Plagued by health problems the rest of his life, Kluszewski lived until May 29, 1988, when he died at the age of 63 following another heart attack. Less than three weeks later, the Reds retired his #18 jersey before a game against the San Diego Padres at Cinergy Field.

In remembering his former coach, Pete Rose said, "There are a lot of coaches who have received more notoriety than Klu, but I don't think anyone's had more success. He was just a prince. I never heard a bad word said about him. He was a nice man, a gentle man."

REDS CAREER HIGHLIGHTS

Best Season

Kluszewski played his best ball for the Reds from 1953 to 1955, hitting at least 40 homers, driving in more than 100 runs, batting well over .300, and posting an OPS well over .900 all three years, while also scoring more than 100 runs twice. Particularly dominant in 1954, Kluszewski earned a runner-up finish to Willie Mays in the NL MVP voting and the first of his three consecutive *Sporting News* All-Star nominations by establishing career-high marks with 49 homers, 141 RBIs, 368 total bases, a .326 batting average, a .407 on-base percentage, a .642 slugging percentage, and an OPS of 1.049.

Memorable Moments/Greatest Performances

Kluszewski helped lead the Reds to a 7–6 win over the Braves on September 18, 1949, by going 4-for-5 with a homer, two doubles, four RBIs, and two runs scored, with his first-inning grand slam giving them an early 4–0 lead.

Kluszewski's three hits, two homers, and three RBIs provided the impetus for a 4–1 win over the Cubs on May 30, 1950.

Kluszewski led the Reds to an 11–7 win over the Dodgers on August 6, 1950, by going 4-for-4 with a homer, double, walk, five RBIs, and three runs scored.

Kluszewski contributed to a lopsided 12–2 victory over the Pirates on April 20, 1952, by driving in seven runs with a homer and a pair of triples.

Kluszewski proved to be a thorn in the side of the Pirates again on September 12, 1954, going 3-for-5 with two homers and six RBIs during an 11–5 Reds win.

Kluszewski's second solo homer of the game with two men out in the bottom of the 10th inning gave the Reds a 6–5 win over the Dodgers on June 16, 1955.

Kluszewski began a torrid stretch that saw him hit eight home runs in eight games by hitting three homers, driving in five runs, and scoring four times during a 19–15 victory over St. Louis in the first game of a doubleheader sweep of the Cardinals on July 1, 1956.

Notable Achievements

- Hit at least 40 home runs three times, topping 20 homers on two other occasions.
- Knocked in more than 100 runs five times.
- Scored more than 100 runs twice.
- Batted over .300 seven times.
- Compiled on-base percentage over .400 once.
- Posted slugging percentage over .500 six times, finishing with mark over .600 once.
- Posted OPS over 1.000 once, finishing with mark above .900 two other times.
- Finished in double digits in triples once.
- Topped 30 doubles twice.
- Hit three home runs in one game vs. Cardinals on July 1, 1956.
- Led NL in home runs once, RBIs once, and hits once.
- Finished second in NL in home runs once, doubles once, and total bases once.
- Finished third in NL in RBIs once, runs scored once, batting average once, slugging percentage twice, OPS twice, triples once, and total bases once.
- Led NL first basemen in putouts twice, double plays turned three times, and fielding percentage five times.
- Ranks among Reds career leaders in home runs (6th), RBIs (9th), slugging percentage (5th), OPS (9th), hits (12th), extra-base hits (11th), and total bases (11th).
- Finished in top 10 of NL MVP voting three times, placing as high as second in 1954.
- Four-time NL All-Star selection (1953, 1954, 1955, and 1956).
- Three-time *Sporting News* MLB All-Star selection (1954, 1955, and 1956).
- #18 retired by Reds.

12

GEORGE FOSTER

A powerful right-handed batter who set single-season franchise records for most home runs, RBIs, and total bases that still stand, George Foster spent parts of 11 seasons in Cincinnati, serving as a regular member of the Reds' starting outfield in eight of those. The team's primary starter in left field from 1975 to 1981, Foster established himself as one of the NL's premier sluggers during that time, leading the league in homers twice and RBIs three times, while also batting over .300 on four separate occasions. The only major-league player to hit as many as 50 home runs in a season between 1966 and 1989, Foster accomplished the feat in 1977, when he earned NL MVP honors after finishing second in the balloting the previous year. A major contributor to Reds teams that won back-to-back world championships, Foster also gained All-Star recognition five times, before being traded to the Mets following the conclusion of the 1981 campaign.

Born in Tuscaloosa, Alabama, on December 1, 1948, George Arthur Foster moved with his mother and two older siblings to Hawthorne, California, when his parents separated shortly after he turned eight years of age. After getting his start in organized baseball in the local Little League, Foster competed in multiple sports at Leuzinger High School in nearby Lawndale, before breaking his leg while playing basketball in his senior year. Unable to compete on the diamond that spring, the slightly built Foster adopted a workout regimen that enabled him to gain weight and increase his strength.

Returning to the ballfield following his graduation, Foster played in a fall league, where Giants scout Jack French first spotted him. Selected by the Giants in the third round of the January 1968 MLB Draft after further honing his skills at El Camino Junior College in Torrance, California, Foster signed with the team of his boyhood hero, Willie Mays.

Foster subsequently spent the next three years advancing through San Francisco's farm system, appearing in a handful of games with the parent club in both 1969 and 1970, before making the Giants' roster as a reserve

George Foster's 52 homers and 149 RBIs in 1977 both represent single-season franchise records.

outfielder in 1971. But after spending the season's first two months backing up Willie Mays, Ken Henderson, and Bobby Bonds, who became his close friend and mentor, Foster headed to Cincinnati when the Giants traded him to the Reds on May 29 for infielder Frank Duffy and pitcher Vern Geishert.

With regular starting center fielder Bobby Tolan sidelined for the entire year with an injury, Foster spent the final four months of the 1971 campaign manning center for the Reds, hitting 10 homers, driving in 50 runs, and batting .234, in 104 games and just over 400 total plate appearances. But following Tolan's return to action in 1972, Foster once again assumed the role of a fourth outfielder, limiting him to just two homers, 12 RBIs, and a batting average of .200, in 59 games and 145 official at-bats.

Sent down to the minors the following year, Foster spent most of the season at Triple-A Indianapolis, where he roomed with future Reds teammate Ken Griffey, who later said of their early days together, "At first, we had a hard time communicating because he was so upset about being sent down, but after a while we'd just have such a good time on the field, just laughing, that he forgot his situation and started to play ball."

While at Indianapolis, Foster also embraced Christianity and adopted a healthier lifestyle that included eating better and shunning alcohol and tobacco. Returning to Cincinnati during the latter stages of the 1973 campaign with a new attitude and a more chiseled physique, Foster batted .282, posted an OPS of 1.016, hit four homers, and knocked in nine runs, in only 17 games and 39 official at-bats. Impressed with the way Foster contacted the ball at the plate, Reds manager Sparky Anderson suggested, "When George gets into a pitch, no one hits a ball harder than he does—not Willie Stargell, Willie McCovey, or Lee May."

Although Foster failed to establish himself as a full-time starter in 1974, he received far more playing time. Appearing in 106 games and garnering 314 total plate appearances, Foster hit seven homers, knocked in 41 runs, batted .264, and posted an OPS of .749, while splitting his time between center and right. Named the team's regular left fielder in 1975 after Pete Rose agreed to move to third base, Foster responded by hitting 23 homers, driving in 78 runs, scoring 71 times, batting an even .300, and compiling an OPS of .875. Having worked extensively with Reds hitting instructor Ted Kluszewski on his batting stance and pitch recognition, Foster subsequently emerged as a tremendous force on offense, posting the following numbers over the course of the next three seasons:

YEAR	HR	RBI	RUNS	HITS	AVG	OBP	SLG	OPS
1976	29	**121**	86	172	.306	.364	.530	.894
1977	**52**	**149**	**124**	197	.320	.382	**.631**	**1.013**
1978	**40**	**120**	97	170	.281	.360	.546	.906

In addition to leading the NL in home runs twice and RBIs three straight times, Foster ranked among the league leaders in slugging percentage, OPS, runs scored, and total bases each season, topping the circuit in all six categories in 1977, when he earned NL MVP honors. Named to the NL All-Star team each year, Foster also earned three consecutive *Sporting News* All-Star nominations. A solid postseason performer as well, Foster, who batted .364 against Pittsburgh in the 1975 NLCS, helped lead the Reds to a four-game sweep of the Yankees in the 1976 World Series by driving in four runs, batting .429, and posting an OPS of 1.000.

Tall and lean at 6'1" and 195 pounds, Foster, with his 30-inch waist, lacked the girth of some of the game's other top sluggers. But his exceptional strength and superior bat speed enabled him to hit the ball as hard and as far as virtually any other player in either league. Blessed with tremendous power to all fields, Foster, who swung a big, black, 35-ounce, 35-inch bat, had the ability to hit the ball out of any part of the ballpark. And even though he consistently ranked among the league leaders in strikeouts, Foster batted over .300 in four of the seven seasons in which he served as a regular member of the Reds' starting outfield.

Somewhat less proficient with the glove, Foster never developed into anything more than an average defender. But although he lacked superior instincts and a strong throwing arm, Foster possessed decent speed and caught most everything within his reach, leading all NL left fielders in fielding percentage on four separate occasions during his time in Cincinnati.

An extremely private person, Foster, who once saw a hypnotist to help him deal with the pressures of playing in the major leagues, differed from most of his Reds teammates in that he shunned the spotlight and never seemed comfortable talking to the media. Shy and reserved, the soft-spoken Foster typically spent nights on the road reading a book in his hotel room, and often could be seen in the Reds' clubhouse with his nose buried in the Bible.

Commenting on the clean-living lifestyle of Foster, who neither smoked, drank, nor cursed, Sparky Anderson stated, "I've got to believe that Foster is the cleanest living athlete in sports. The way he takes care of his body, there's no telling how long he'll be able to play this game."

Plagued by injuries in 1979, Foster appeared in only 121 games and garnered just 505 total plate appearances. Nevertheless, he managed to hit 30 homers, drive in 98 runs, bat .302, and compile an OPS of .948. Limited by injury to 144 games the following year, Foster hit 25 homers, knocked in 93 runs, and batted just .273. But Foster returned to top form during the strike-interrupted 1981 campaign, when, over the course of a 108-game schedule, he batted .295 and ranked among the league leaders with 22 homers, 90 RBIs, a .519 slugging percentage, and an OPS of .892, earning in the process the last of his five All-Star selections.

Despite Foster's strong showing in 1981, the Reds decided to part ways with him at the end of the year. With Foster approaching free agency and seeking a long-term contract, the Reds completed a trade with the Mets on February 10, 1982, that sent the 33-year-old outfielder to New York for catcher Alex Treviño and pitchers Jim Kern and Greg Harris.

Foster, who, over parts of 11 seasons in Cincinnati, hit 244 homers, knocked in 861 runs, scored 680 times, collected 1,276 hits, 207 doubles, and 37 triples, stole 46 bases, batted .286, compiled a .356 on-base percentage, and posted a .514 slugging percentage, ended up spending most of the next five seasons with the Mets after inking a five-year, $10 million deal with them. However, despite knocking in 90 runs in 1983 and another 86 the following year, Foster never came close to attaining the same level of success he reached in Cincinnati, causing him to eventually become a target of the boo-birds at his home ballpark. Released by the Mets during the latter stages of the 1986 campaign, Foster signed with the White Sox, with whom he spent three weeks before being released again. Unable to garner interest from any other team, Foster announced his retirement, ending his big-league career with 348 homers, 1,239 RBIs, 986 runs scored, 1,925 hits, 307 doubles, 47 triples, 51 stolen bases, a .274 batting average, a .338 on-base percentage, and a .480 slugging percentage.

Following his playing days, Foster remained away from the game for several years, until he returned to the Reds organization in the late 1990s, first as a minor-league hitting instructor, and later as a special instructor with the team. Foster, who has also coached in high school and college, later opened the George Foster Baseball Clinic. Inducted into the Reds Hall of Fame in 2003, Foster received high praise from former Reds beat writer Hal McCoy, who called him "the greatest person in baseball," adding, "I mean as a person, not just as a player. He never raises his voice, no matter how harassed he may be by fans. I asked him once if he'd let me use his name for Building Bridges, an organization for underprivileged kids. He said, 'No, you'll have more than my name. I'll be there too.'"

Meanwhile, in selecting his own personal Reds All-Time Team in 2006, former Reds pitcher and longtime announcer Joe Nuxhall made Foster his first choice for the outfield, saying, "Good gracious, Foster might have hit 55 or 60 [home runs] at Great American Ball Park. He would bang them off the scoreboard, I guarantee. I'd bet my life that he would."

REDS CAREER HIGHLIGHTS

Best Season

Was there ever any doubt? Foster had one of the greatest single seasons in franchise history in 1977, when he earned NL MVP honors and one of his four *Sporting News* NL All-Star nominations by leading the league with 52 homers, 149 RBIs, 124 runs scored, 388 total bases, a .631 slugging percentage, and an OPS of 1.013, while also ranking among the circuit leaders with a .320 batting average and 197 hits.

Memorable Moments/Greatest Performances

Foster contributed to a 9–3 victory over the Cubs on August 11, 1975, by going 5-for-5 with a double, two RBIs, and one run scored.

Foster provided most of the offensive firepower during a 6–1 win over the Pirates on August 14, 1975, homering twice and knocking in five runs off Pittsburgh left-hander Jerry Reuss.

Foster highlighted a 4-for-4, five-RBI performance with a grand slam homer that led to a lopsided 11–0 victory over the Padres on May 23, 1976.

Foster helped lead the Reds to a 23–9 rout of the Braves on April 25, 1977, by going 4-for-4 with two homers, a double, a walk, seven RBIs, and five runs scored.

Foster had a huge game against the Braves on July 14, 1977, homering three times and driving in five runs during a 7–1 Reds win.

Foster led the Reds to an 8–6 win over the Montreal Expos on July 17, 1978, by going 3-for-4 with two homers, a double, five RBIs, and three runs scored.

Foster's third hit and second homer of the game gave the Reds a 14-inning, 10–8 walkoff win over the Braves on October 1, 1978.

Foster homered, doubled, and went a perfect 5-for-5 at the plate during a 6–5 win over the Astros on April 21, 1980.

Foster helped lead the Reds to an 8–7 win over the Pirates on August 29, 1980, by homering, doubling, and knocking in six runs.

Notable Achievements

- Hit 52 home runs in 1977.
- Surpassed 20 homers six other times.
- Knocked in more than 100 runs three times.

- Scored more than 100 runs once.
- Batted over .300 four times.
- Posted slugging percentage over .500 seven times, finishing with mark over .600 twice.
- Posted OPS over 1.000 twice, finishing with mark above .900 two other times.
- Topped 30 doubles once.
- Hit three home runs in one game vs. Braves on July 14, 1977.
- Led NL in home runs twice, RBIs three times, runs scored once, total bases once, slugging percentage once, and OPS once.
- Finished second in NL in RBIs once, total bases once, and slugging percentage once.
- Led NL outfielders with .994 fielding percentage in 1976.
- Led NL left fielders in fielding percentage four times.
- Holds Reds single-season records for most home runs (52), RBIs (149), and total bases (388).
- Ranks among Reds career leaders in home runs (7th), RBIs (10th), slugging percentage (tied for 3rd), and OPS (8th).
- Five-time division champion (1972, 1973, 1975, 1976, and 1979).
- Three-time NL champion (1972, 1975, and 1976).
- Two-time world champion (1975 and 1976).
- Three-time NL Player of the Week.
- Six-time NL Player of the Month.
- 1981 Silver Slugger Award winner.
- 1977 Reds team MVP.
- 1977 NL MVP.
- Finished in top 10 of NL MVP voting three other times, placing second once and third once.
- Five-time NL All-Star selection (1976, 1977, 1978, 1979, and 1981).
- Four-time *Sporting News* NL All-Star selection (1976, 1977, 1978, and 1981).

13

BUCKY WALTERS

A mediocre pitcher for the Philadelphia Phillies early in his career, Bucky Walters blossomed into one of the finest hurlers in the game following his arrival in Cincinnati in 1938. A member of the Reds for parts of 11 seasons, Walters won more than 20 games three times, en route to posting more victories than any other pitcher in either league from 1939 to 1946. Also first among all big-league hurlers in complete games and innings pitched during that same timeframe, Walters completed more than 20 of his starts six times and threw more than 300 innings on three separate occasions, earning in the process five All-Star nominations, one NL MVP award, and two other top-five finishes in the balloting. Along the way, Walters led the Reds to two pennants and one world championship, with his brilliant pitching in the 1940 World Series proving to be the difference in a seven-game victory over the Detroit Tigers. Amazingly, Walters accomplished all he did after beginning his professional career as a third baseman.

Born in Philadelphia, Pennsylvania, on April 19, 1909, William Henry Walters Jr. grew up with his six younger siblings in the Mount Airy section of Germantown—the same region in which his ancestors settled shortly after William Penn founded the Pennsylvania colony. The son of a Bell Telephone Company employee who also played for the company baseball team, Walters began swinging a bat at the age of six, before developing his skills on the local sandlots.

After excelling on the diamond for two years at Germantown High School, Walters left school early to become an electrician. However, Walters chose to pursue a career in baseball instead after he made an extremely favorable impression on a scout while competing in a sandlot game one afternoon, recalling, "A fellow who had a contract with a club in Montgomery, Alabama, saw me playing shortstop, and after the game he asked me if I'd like to play pro ball. I guess he heard the quickest 'Yes, sir' anybody ever heard."

Bucky Walters earned NL MVP honors in 1939, when he won the pitcher's version of the Triple Crown.

Although Walters did not end up signing with Montgomery, he began his pro career shortly thereafter with High Point (North Carolina) in the Piedmont League, for whom he batted .300 and compiled a record of 5–6 and an ERA of 5.29 in 1929 as a combination infielder/pitcher. Subsequently purchased by the Boston Braves, Walters spent three seasons advancing through their farm system as a third baseman, also making brief appearances with the parent club in both 1931 and 1932, before being sold to the Red Sox after batting .376 in 91 games with the San Francisco

Missions of the Pacific Coast League in 1933. Following his purchase by the Red Sox, Walters spent two months playing third base for them, hitting four homers, driving in 28 runs, and batting .256, before suffering a broken thumb that essentially brought his days as an everyday player to an end.

Looking back on how Walters's injury impacted his career, Joe Brown, former chairman of the Hall of Fame Veterans Committee, said, "Had he not been injured after joining Boston, he would have been a very successful third baseman. He had, as they say, all the tools."

With Walters struggling at the plate upon his return to action in 1934, the Red Sox sold him to the Phillies. But after Walters failed to regain his batting stroke in Philadelphia, Phillies manager Jimmy Wilson moved him to the mound prior to the start of the 1935 campaign, explaining years later, "Walters had the strongest arm on the club. . . . The way he fired the ball from third to first, you could see he couldn't miss as a pitcher. But selling him [on the idea] was something else."

Wilson added, "It was Bucky's spirit, not necessarily his ability to throw a fastball. . . . I figured that all anybody needed to be a pitcher was guts like Walters had. So, I made him a pitcher. That's one place in baseball where you have guts—or you don't."

However, Walters initially resisted his manager's idea, with Wilson recalling, "He hit four or five out of the park, and every time that happened, he was more determined than ever he wanted no part of pitching. . . . I had to get him a little plastered to convince him he could be a great pitcher."

Remembering how Wilson persuaded him to change positions, Walters joked, "I became a pitcher in a chicken shack somewhere between Orlando and Winter Haven."

After compiling a record of 9–9 and an ERA of 4.17 in his first year as a full-time starter, Walters posted an overall mark of just 25–36 for losing Phillies teams over the course of the next two seasons. But after winning just four of his first 12 decisions and compiling an ERA of 5.23 during the first two months of the 1938 campaign, Walters became a member of the Reds when they acquired him from the Phillies for catcher Spud Davis, pitcher Al Hollingsworth, and $50,000 on June 13.

Although Walters had reservations about leaving his hometown, later saying, "Actually . . . I didn't want to go. I'd have rather stayed in the East, with my family," he adapted quickly to his new environment, going 11–6 with a 3.69 ERA the rest of the year, before establishing himself as arguably the finest pitcher in the game the next three seasons by posting the following numbers:

YEAR	W-L	ERA	SO	SHO	CG	IP	WHIP
1939	**27-11**	**2.29**	**137**	2	**31**	**319.0**	**1.125**
1940	**22-10**	**2.48**	115	3	**29**	**305.0**	**1.092**
1941	19-15	2.83	129	5	**27**	**302.0**	1.258

The NL leader in complete games and innings pitched all three seasons, Walters also led the league in wins, ERA, and WHIP twice each, capturing the pitcher's version of the Triple Crown in 1939 by topping the senior circuit in strikeouts as well. In addition to gaining All-Star recognition three straight times, Walters earned NL MVP honors in 1939, before placing third in the balloting the following year. Meanwhile, the Reds won the pennant in both 1939 and 1940 and captured their second world championship in the second of those campaigns by defeating the Tigers in the World Series. A huge contributor to the team's victory in the Fall Classic, Walters won both his starts, tossing two complete games, during which he allowed just eight hits and three runs.

Relying primarily on a sinking fastball, curveball, and an early version of the slider, which he learned from Hall of Fame pitcher Chief Bender during his time in Philadelphia, the right-handed-throwing Walters, who stood 6'1" and weighed close to 185 pounds, did an excellent job of keeping hitters off-balance by changing speeds. Although Walters had good velocity on his fastball, he depended more on pitch location and movement to navigate his way through opposing lineups.

Known for his fierce competitive spirit and ability to excel in big games, Walters drew praise from former Reds infielder Bill Werber, who said of his onetime teammate, "Big, important games never fazed him, and he seemed to get better as the game went on. We could count on him. He had a good fastball, a decent curve, and a sinker that bore in on right-handed batters. As a former infielder, he could field his position as well as anyone in the game. Best of all, he had good control and an excellent knowledge of the batters' weaknesses. . . . Bucky was a quiet fellow, not given to much conversation, but he was a fierce competitor."

One of the best-hitting pitchers in the game as well, Walters hit 23 homers, knocked in 234 runs, and compiled a batting average of .243 over the course of his career, reaching the seats eight times, driving in 105 runs, and batting .235, in just under 1,000 total plate appearances as a member of the Reds.

The victim of poor run support in 1942, Walters compiled a record of just 15–14. Nevertheless, he earned his fourth consecutive All-Star nomination by ranking among the league leaders with a 2.66 ERA, a WHIP of 1.167, 109 strikeouts, 21 complete games, and 253⅔ innings pitched.

Despite being classified 1-A by his draft board, Walters never received the call to duty during World War II. However, he did his part for the war effort by giving motivational speeches to troops on USO tours.

Meanwhile, back in the States, a somewhat compromised Walters, who sustained a leg injury during spring training and suffered from a troubled appendix that required offseason surgery to repair, compiled a record of just 15–15 and an ERA of 3.54 in 1943. But he rebounded in 1944 to lead all NL hurlers with 23 victories (against eight losses) and rank among the leaders with a 2.40 ERA, a WHIP of 1.123, 27 complete games, and 285 innings pitched, earning in the process his final All-Star selection and a fifth-place finish in the league MVP voting.

Unfortunately, Walters's days as a dominant pitcher ended on July 31, 1945, when he injured his arm during a 2–0 shutout of the Cardinals. Able to appear in only two more games the rest of the year, Walters finished the season with a record of 10–10 and an ERA of 2.68. He subsequently started just 22 games in 1946, going 10–7 with a 2.56 ERA, before compiling a record of 8–8 and an inordinately high ERA of 5.75 the following year. Named manager of the Reds during the latter stages of the 1948 campaign after making just seven mound appearances, Walters remained in that position for a little over one year, before being replaced with just three games remaining in the 1949 season after leading the team to an overall record of 81–123.

After being fired by the Reds, Walters attempted a brief comeback with the Braves, appearing in only one game with them in 1950, before being released and subsequently announcing his retirement. Over parts of 16 big-league seasons, Walters compiled an overall record of 198–160, an ERA of 3.30, and a WHIP of 1.324, threw 242 complete games and 42 shutouts, and struck out 1,107 batters in 3,104⅔ innings pitched. During his time in Cincinnati, Walters posted a mark of 160–107, an ERA of 2.93, and a WHIP of 1.251, tossed 195 complete games and 32 shutouts, and recorded 879 strikeouts in 2,355⅔ innings of work. From 1935 to 1949, Walters won more games, threw more complete games, and tossed more shutouts than any other pitcher in the major leagues.

Following his playing days, Walters spent eight years serving as pitching coach of the Braves (1950–1955) and Giants (1956–1957), before returning to his hometown of Philadelphia, where he scouted for the Phillies for much of the 1960s. Walters also worked in sales and public relations for the Ferco Machine Screw Company until 1977, when he lost a leg due to arteriosclerosis. Failing to recover fully from the disease, Walters developed kidney problems that forced him to undergo dialysis for many years. Walters lived until April 20, 1991, when he died in the Philadelphia suburb of Abington, Pennsylvania, just one day after turning 82 years of age.

REDS CAREER HIGHLIGHTS

Best Season

Although Walters also performed magnificently in 1940 and 1944, he had the finest season of his career in 1939, when he captured NL MVP honors by leading the league with 27 wins, a 2.29 ERA, a WHIP of 1.125, 137 strikeouts, 31 complete games, 319 innings pitched, and 36 starts.

Memorable Moments/Greatest Performances

Walters yielded just three hits and three walks during a 3–0 shutout of the Pirates on April 27, 1940.

In addition to surrendering just five hits and two walks during a 3–2 complete-game victory over the Phillies on August 26, 1940, Walters helped his own cause by going 2-for-2 at the plate with a homer and two RBIs.

Walters helped lead the Reds to a seven-game victory over Detroit in the 1940 World Series by defeating the Tigers twice. Winning both his starts, Walters threw two complete games and compiled an ERA of 1.50, allowing just three runs and eight hits in 18 total innings of work. Particularly outstanding in Game 6, a 4–0 victory that evened the Fall Classic at three games apiece, Walters surrendered just five hits, homered, and knocked in two runs.

Walters dominated the St. Louis lineup on May 10, 1942, allowing just four hits, issuing two walks, and recording a career-high 10 strikeouts during a 3–0 shutout of the Cardinals.

Walters flirted with perfection on May 14, 1944, issuing no walks and yielding only a single to Boston second baseman Connie Ryan with two men out in the top of the eighth inning of a 4–0 shutout of the Braves.

Walters surrendered just two hits and four walks during a 3–0 whitewashing of the Pirates on June 20, 1944.

Walters worked all 13 innings of a 1–0 win over the Cardinals on April 26, 1944, allowing seven hits, issuing two bases on balls, and recording three strikeouts.

Walters displayed his mettle again during a 12-inning, 2–1 win over the Phillies on August 20, 1944. Going the distance, Walters allowed seven hits and just one run, while also going 4-for-5 at the plate and knocking in the game's winning run with an RBI single in the bottom of the 12th.

Although Walters surrendered 15 hits and four earned runs over the first 7⅓ innings of a 10–8 win over the Braves on May 20, 1945, he excelled at the plate, driving in three runs with a pair of homers.

Walters turned in the last dominant performance of his career on July 26, 1947, when he allowed just two hits and one walk during a 1–0 shutout of the Phillies.

Notable Achievements

- Won more than 20 games three times, posting 19 victories another time.
- Posted winning percentage above .700 twice.
- Compiled ERA under 3.00 seven times, finishing with mark under 2.50 three times.
- Threw more than 20 complete games six times, completing more than 30 of his starts once.
- Threw more than 300 innings three times, tossing more than 250 frames two other times.
- Led NL pitchers in wins three times, ERA twice, WHIP twice, strikeouts once, complete games three times, innings pitched three times, and starts once.
- Finished second in NL in ERA once, shutouts once, and complete games once.
- Won NL Pitching Triple Crown in 1939.
- Holds franchise record for most shutouts (32).
- Ranks among Reds career leaders in wins (4th), complete games (4th), innings pitched (5th), and games started (5th).
- Two-time NL champion (1939 and 1940).
- 1940 world champion.
- 1939 NL MVP.
- Finished in top five of NL MVP voting two other times.
- Five-time NL All-Star selection (1939, 1940, 1941, 1942, and 1944).
- Two-time *Sporting News* MLB All-Star selection (1939 and 1940).

14
EPPA RIXEY

The National League's career leader in victories by a left-hander until Warren Spahn surpassed his total in 1959, Eppa Rixey won 266 games over the course of 21 big-league seasons, 13 of which he spent in Cincinnati. After performing erratically for the Phillies his first eight years in the league, Rixey proved to be a model of consistency during his time in the Queen City, winning at least 19 games five times between 1921 and 1928, while also compiling an ERA under 3.00 on four separate occasions. A control pitcher who became known for his durability and refusal to give in to opposing batters, Rixey also threw more than 20 complete games four times and worked more than 300 innings three times, en route to setting franchise records for most wins, innings pitched, and games started that still stand. Rixey ranks extremely high in team annals in shutouts, complete games, and pitching appearances as well, with his total body of work eventually gaining him induction into the Baseball Hall of Fame.

Born in Culpeper, Virginia, on May 3, 1891, Eppa Rixey attended school there until the age of 10, when he moved with his family some 45 miles southwest, to Charlottesville, Virginia. Establishing himself as a standout athlete during his teenage years, Rixey starred in baseball and basketball at Charlottesville High School, before enrolling at the University of Virginia, where he continued to excel in both sports. Especially proficient on the diamond, Rixey pitched so well for the Cavaliers that NL umpire Cy Rigler, who moonlighted on the university's basketball and baseball staffs, recommended him to the Philadelphia Phillies.

Signed by the Phillies as soon as he graduated, Rixey bypassed the minor leagues completely, arriving in the City of Brotherly Love in June 1912, a little over one month after celebrating his 21st birthday. Performing well over the final three-and-a-half months of the season, Rixey compiled a record of 10–10 and an ERA of 2.50, completed 10 of his 20 starts, and tossed three shutouts. Rixey followed that up with another decent

Eppa Rixey won more games and threw more innings than anyone else in team annals.

showing in 1913, going 9–5 with a 3.12 ERA, before slumping to a mark of 2–11 and an ERA of 4.37 in the ensuing campaign.

Although Rixey compiled an overall record of just 49–43 over the course of the next three seasons, he pitched well for the Phillies, proving to be especially effective in 1916, when he went 22–10 with a 1.85 ERA, 20 complete games, and 287 innings pitched. Rixey subsequently missed the entire 1918 campaign while serving in the military during World War I. Assigned to the Chemical Warfare Division in Europe, along with fellow baseball stars Ty Cobb and Christy Mathewson, Rixey saw action on the front lines for a division that was charged with carrying out mustard gas attacks.

Failing to regain his earlier form when he returned to the States in 1919, Rixey posted marks of just 6–12 and 11–22 for last-place teams the next two seasons, prompting the Phillies to trade him to the Reds for pitcher Jimmy Ring and outfielder Greasy Neale following the conclusion of the 1920 campaign. Experiencing a rebirth upon his arrival in Cincinnati, Rixey began an excellent eight-year stretch during which he ranked among the NL's top hurlers. Particularly outstanding from 1921 to 1925, Rixey posted the following numbers those five seasons:

YEAR	W-L	ERA	SO	SHO	CG	IP	WHIP
1921	19-18	2.78	76	2	21	301.0	1.296
1922	**25**-13	3.53	80	2	26	**313.1**	1.219
1923	20-15	2.80	97	3	23	309.0	1.291
1924	15-14	2.76	57	**4**	15	238.1	1.116
1925	21-11	2.88	69	2	22	287.1	1.215

Consistently placing among the NL leaders in every category but strikeouts, Rixey topped the circuit in wins, shutouts, and innings pitched once each, while also finishing second in the league in wins once, ERA twice, complete games once, and WHIP once. Rixey, who posted a total of 100 victories during that five-year period, set a record in the first of those campaigns that is not likely to be equaled by allowing just one home run in 301 innings of work. Meanwhile, the Reds placed second in the NL in both 1922 and 1923, seriously contending for the pennant in 1923, when they finished just 4½ games off the pace.

The gangly Rixey, who stood 6'5" and weighed 210 pounds, possessed outstanding control, even though it took him a few years to develop a delivery that allowed him to get his body parts to work in sync. A finesse pitcher despite his size, Rixey lacked an overpowering fastball but kept hitters off-balance by mixing in his breaking pitches with his heater. Typically working deep into the count, Rixey never gave in to opposing batters, whose intelligence he questioned, saying in 1927, "How dumb can the hitters in this league get? I've been doing this for 15 years. When they're batting with the count two balls and no strikes, or three and one, they're always looking for the fastball, and they never get it."

Extremely durable, Rixey threw more than 280 innings eight times over the course of his career, doing so five times as a member of the Reds. An excellent fielder as well, Rixey drew praise for the totality of his game from former Cincinnati catcher, Bubbles Hargrave, who stated, "Eppa was just great. He was great as a pitcher, fielder, and competitor. I look on him as the most outstanding player I came in contact with during my entire career."

One of the most intelligent players of his era, Rixey, who earned a master's degree in chemistry and another in Latin by returning to Charlottesville during the offseason, spent the winter months teaching Latin at Episcopal High School in Washington, DC, Rixey also wrote poetry in his spare time, specializing in sonnets and triolets. While most ballplayers of the day resented college men, Rixey won over his teammates with his affable personality, dry wit, and Southern drawl, which earned him the absurd nickname "Jephtha." Yet, despite his friendly demeanor and gentlemanly ways, Rixey possessed a fierce competitive spirit that displayed itself from time to time when he desecrated a locker room or disappeared for a day or two following a difficult loss.

Rixey had his last big year for the Reds in 1928, when, at the age of 37, he compiled a record of 19–18 and an ERA of 3.43, led all NL hurlers with 37 starts, and ranked among the league leaders with 17 complete games and 291⅓ innings pitched. Rixey remained in Cincinnati for five more years, assuming a less prominent role each season, before announcing his retirement following the conclusion of the 1933 campaign with a career record of 266–251, an ERA of 3.15, a WHIP of 1.272, 290 complete games, 37 shutouts, 14 saves, and 1,350 strikeouts in just under 4,500 total innings of work. In his 13 years with the Reds, Rixey compiled an overall record of 179–148, pitched to an ERA of 3.33, posted a WHIP of 1.286, threw 180 complete games and 23 shutouts, collected eight saves, and struck out 660 batters in 2,890⅔ innings pitched.

Following his playing days, Rixey remained in Cincinnati, where he spent many years working in his father-in-law's successful insurance company, eventually assuming the role of president. Rixey lived until February 28, 1963, when he died of a heart attack at the age of 71, one month after the members of the Veterans Committee elected him to the Baseball Hall of Fame. Visiting Cooperstown shortly after he learned of his election, Rixey sent family and friends a postcard with a message that read: "I finally made it! I guess they are really scraping the bottom of the barrel, aren't they?"

REDS CAREER HIGHLIGHTS

Best Season

Although Rixey established career-highs in wins (25), complete games (26), and innings pitched (313⅓) in 1922, he pitched slightly better three years later. While Rixey won fewer games (21), completed fewer of his starts (22), and threw fewer innings (287⅓) in 1925, he finished second in the league with a 2.88 ERA, which represented a significantly lower mark than the 3.53 ERA he posted three years earlier.

Memorable Moments/Greatest Performances

Rixey worked all 13 innings of a 2–1 win over the Pirates on September 5, 1921, allowing eight hits and recording three strikeouts.

Rixey yielded just three hits and two walks during a 3–0 shutout of the Cardinals on April 26, 1922.

Rixey turned in an outstanding all-around effort on June 28, 1924, allowing eight hits and one walk during a complete-game 5–2 victory over the Cardinals, while also going 4-for-4 at the plate with a homer, double, two RBIs, and two runs scored.

Rixey threw 33⅔ consecutive scoreless innings from July 8 to July 21, 1924, beginning his streak during a 16-inning, 2–1 win over the Phillies in which he went the distance. Rixey's finest performance during that period came on July 18, when he allowed just three harmless singles during a 4–0 shutout of the Brooklyn Robins (Dodgers).

In addition to working all 11 innings of a 3–2 victory over Brooklyn on September 24, 1925, Rixey drove in the winning run from second base with his third hit of the game in the bottom of the 11th.

Rixey continued to torment the Robins on August 27, 1926, yielding just three hits and three walks during a 4–0 Reds win.

Rixey turned in a similarly impressive performance on April 17, 1928, allowing just three hits and one walk during a complete-game 2–1 victory over the Boston Braves.

Notable Achievements

- Won at least 20 games three times, posting 19 victories two other times.
- Compiled ERA under 3.00 five times.
- Threw more than 20 complete games four times.

- Threw more than 300 innings three times, tossing more than 250 frames two other times.
- Led NL pitchers in wins once, shutouts once, innings pitched once, assists once, and starts twice.
- Finished second in NL in wins once, winning percentage once, ERA twice, WHIP once, and complete games once.
- Holds franchise records for most wins, innings pitched, and games started.
- Ranks among Reds career leaders in shutouts (tied for 8th), complete games (9th), and pitching appearances (7th).
- Elected to Baseball Hall of Fame by members of Veterans Committee in 1963.

15

ERNIE LOMBARDI

Although he is remembered primarily for his legendary lack of foot speed, prominent proboscis that earned him the nickname "Schnozz," and infamous "Snooze" at home plate during the 1939 World Series, Ernie Lombardi proved to be one of the NL's finest hitters for most of his career, much of which he spent in Cincinnati. One of only two catchers in MLB history to win multiple batting titles, Lombardi accomplished the feat for the first time as a member of the Reds, for whom he starred from 1932 to 1941. En route to compiling one of the highest lifetime marks in team annals, Lombardi batted over .330 on four separate occasions during his time in the Queen City, while also hitting 20 homers once and posting an OPS over .900 twice. A major contributor to Reds teams that won two pennants and one World Series, Lombardi earned five All-Star selections and one league MVP trophy, before moving on to Boston and New York, where his strong play over the course of the next six seasons garnered him three more All-Star nominations and an eventual place in Cooperstown.

Born in Oakland, California, on April 6, 1908, Ernesto Natali Lombardi maintained a strong connection to his Italian roots during his youth. The son of Italian immigrants who owned a grocery store that he helped them run as a teenager, Lombardi spent his early days playing bocce ball, a sport that developed into its present form in Italy, before getting his start in baseball at the age of 12 as a member of the Ravioli Meat Market team.

Later developing into a standout on the diamond at McClymonds High School, Lombardi received an offer to play for the Oakland Oaks of the Pacific Coast League following his graduation. He subsequently spent three years starting behind the plate for the Oaks, posting batting averages of .377, .366, and .370, before having his contract purchased by the Dodgers.

Joining the Dodgers at the start of the 1931 campaign, Lombardi acquitted himself well in his first big-league season, batting .297, hitting four homers, and driving in 23 runs, in 73 games and 196 total plate appearances. But with the Dodgers rich in receivers, they completed a trade with

Ernie Lombardi is one of only two catchers in MLB history to win multiple batting titles.

the Reds at the end of the year that sent Lombardi, outfielder Babe Herman, and third baseman Wally Gilbert to Cincinnati for second baseman Tony Cuccinello, third baseman Joe Stripp, and catcher Clyde Sukeforth.

Laying claim to the starting catcher's job immediately upon his arrival in Cincinnati, the 24-year-old Lombardi had a solid first season in the Queen City, batting .303, posting an OPS of .851, hitting 11 homers, and driving in 68 runs, in 118 games and just over 400 official at-bats. Plagued by injuries for much of 1933, Lombardi appeared in only 107 games, limiting him to just four homers and 47 RBIs, although he managed to bat a very respectable .283. Healthy for most of the ensuing campaign, Lombardi hit nine homers, knocked in 62 runs, batted .305, and posted an OPS of .769, before establishing himself as a force on offense in 1935, when, in addition to hitting 12 homers and driving in 64 runs, he ranked among the league leaders with a batting average of .343 and an OPS of .918.

Lombardi subsequently gained All-Star recognition in each of the next two seasons by compiling batting averages of .333 and .334, before displacing Cubs catcher Gabby Hartnett as the finest receiver in the league in 1938, when he earned NL MVP honors and the third of his five straight All-Star nominations by topping the circuit with a .342 batting average and ranking among the leaders with 19 homers, 95 RBIs, 167 hits, and an OPS of .915.

A powerful right-handed batter who stood 6'3" and weighed 230 pounds before ballooning up to almost 300 pounds during the latter stages of his career, Lombardi swung an enormous 42-ounce bat that his huge hands and massive wrists and forearms enabled him to handle with ease. Gripping his weapon with interlocking fingers, very much like a golf club, Lombardi stated, "Sometimes when I am in a slump, I use a regular grip in batting practice, but always I feel sort of funny, and I go back to the golf grip. No one ever told me to take a regular grip on a bat."

Blessed with tremendous strength and bat speed, Lombardi drove fierce line drives to all parts of the ballpark, although he pulled most of his homers to left, once hitting a ball so far over the left field wall in Cincinnati that it landed on top of a laundry building across the street. Nevertheless, Lombardi proved to be more of a contact hitter than a pure slugger, hitting as many as 20 home runs in a season just once in his entire career, while never striking out more than 25 times in any single campaign.

Lombardi's ability to hit the ball with authority, combined with his slowness afoot (baseball historian Bill James called him "the slowest man to ever play major league baseball well"), caused opposing infielders to play him extraordinarily deep. Typically positioning themselves on the outfield grass when Lombardi stepped into the batter's box, infielders cut off many would-be hits, prompting noted sportswriter Arthur Daley to suggest, "You almost come to the conclusion that he [Lombardi] was the greatest hitter of all time. Every hit he made . . . was an honest one."

Meanwhile, Harry Craft said of his former Reds teammate, "He was the best right-handed hitter I ever saw. And he was an exceptional player in every way, except running. If he hadn't been so slow, he would have had an even better batting average."

While Lombardi drew praise for his hitting prowess, he received mixed reviews for his defense. Slow and plodding, Lombardi had a difficult time fielding bunts or moving from side to side, causing him to lead all NL receivers in passed balls nine times over the course of his career. He also finished first among players at his position in errors on four separate occasions. On the other hand, Lombardi had a very strong throwing arm that he liked to show off, with Johnny Vander Meer saying of his former batterymate, "Lom would pick off six or seven guys a year throwing side-arm behind left-handed hitters." Lombardi also reputedly handled the pitching staff well and called a good game.

Known as a gentle giant, Lombardi became a beloved figure in Cincinnati due to his offensive productivity and easygoing and affable personality that allowed him to willingly accept jokes about his large nose, which the Hall of Fame website referenced as "a massive protuberance." Oddly enough, Lombardi proved to be especially popular with the ladies, who often waited for him outside Crosley Field to shower him with affection.

Lombardi followed up his MVP campaign with another outstanding season in 1939, helping to lead the Reds to the NL pennant by hitting 20 homers, driving in 85 runs, batting .287, and compiling an OPS of .829. However, the Reds subsequently suffered a four-game sweep at the hands of the Yankees in the World Series, with Lombardi experiencing an embarrassing moment in Game 4 that continued to haunt him for the rest of his life.

With the score tied at 4–4 in the top of the 10th inning, one man out, and Yankee runners on first and third, Joe DiMaggio singled to right field, driving in Frank Crosetti from third base with the go-ahead run. But when Reds outfielder Ival Goodman misplayed the ball in right, Charlie Keller scored all the way from first, allegedly hitting Lombardi in the groin by accident as he crossed home plate. Dazed by the blow, Lombardi, who had failed to wear a protective cup, remained unaware that the ball sat just a few feet away from him as DiMaggio circled the bases and slid home with a third run, just avoiding a late tag by the disheveled catcher.

Subsequently lambasted by the press, which referred to the play as "Lombardi's Big Snooze," Lombardi became what Bill James called in his *Historical Baseball Abstract*, "the Bill Buckner of the 1930s, even more innocent than Buckner, and Buckner has plenty of people who should be holding up their hands to share his disgrace."

But while the above account has since become part of baseball lore, Keller later denied ever touching Lombardi, with Johnny Vander Meer supporting that contention when he said, "Ival Goodman's throw from right field short-hopped Lom and caught him in the groin and paralyzed him. Anybody but Lombardi, they would have had to carry him off the field."

Redeeming himself somewhat the following year, Lombardi batted .319, posted an OPS of .871, and knocked in 74 runs for the world champion Reds, earning in the process a ninth-place finish in the NL MVP voting. But after Lombardi batted just .264 and drove home only 60 runs in 1941, the Reds sold him to the Braves at the end of the year.

Lombardi, who, during his time in Cincinnati, hit 120 homers, knocked in 682 runs, scored 420 times, collected 1,238 hits, 220 doubles, and 24 triples, batted .311, compiled an on-base percentage of .359, and posted a slugging percentage of .469, ended up spending just one season in Boston, hitting 11 homers, driving in 46 runs, and batting a league-leading .330 for the Braves in 1942, before joining the Giants, with whom he ended his career five years later. Deciding to hang up his cleats following the conclusion of the 1947 campaign, Lombardi retired with career totals of 190 home runs, 990 RBIs, 601 runs scored, 1,792 hits, 277 doubles, and 27 triples, a lifetime batting average of .306, an on-base percentage of .358, and a slugging percentage of .460.

Following his playing days, Lombardi ran a liquor store in San Leandro, California, for some time, before taking a job as an attendant in the Candlestick Park press office. Lombardi also later worked as a gas station attendant in his hometown of Oakland. Troubled by references to the "Big Snooze" and his failure to gain induction into the Baseball Hall of Fame, Lombardi lapsed into depression later in life and once even tried to commit suicide, slitting his throat from ear to ear with a razor, before being saved by medics. Eventually admitted to a sanitarium, Lombardi lived until September 26, 1977, when he died at the age of 69 following a long illness. Posthumously inducted into the Baseball Hall of Fame by the members of the Veterans Committee in 1985, Lombardi received the additional honors of being included in Lawrence Ritter's and Donald Honig's 1981 book *The 100 Greatest Baseball Players of All Time*, having a bronze statue of him erected at the entrance of Great American Ball Park, and having the award presented annually to the Reds' team MVP by the Cincinnati Chapter of the BBWAA named after him.

REDS CAREER HIGHLIGHTS

Best Season

Lombardi's MVP campaign of 1938 proved to be the finest of his career. In addition to leading the NL with a .342 batting average, Lombardi ranked in the league's top 10 in seven other offensive categories, including homers (19), RBIs (95), on-base percentage (.391), and slugging percentage (.524).

Memorable Moments/Greatest Performances

After hitting safely in four of his six previous plate appearances, Lombardi capped off a four-run rally in the bottom of the 12th inning with a two-run triple that gave the Reds a 9–8 win over the Braves on May 7, 1932.

Lombardi led the Reds to a 16–15 victory over the Cardinals on July 6, 1934, by going 5-for-5 with a homer, triple, six RBIs, and four runs scored.

Lombardi contributed to a 15–4 win over the Phillies on May 8, 1935, by going 5-for-6 with four doubles, one RBI, and one run scored.

Lombardi went a perfect 6-for-6 at the plate during a 21–10 win over the Phillies on May 9, 1937, finishing the game with five RBIs and three runs scored.

Lombardi helped lead the Reds to an 8–4 victory over the Dodgers on September 14, 1938, by homering twice and knocking in five runs.

Notable Achievements

- Hit 20 home runs once.
- Batted over .300 seven times, topping the .330 mark on four occasions.
- Posted slugging percentage over .500 twice.
- Posted OPS over .900 twice.
- Topped 30 doubles once.
- Had six hits in one game vs. Phillies on May 9, 1937.
- Led NL with .342 batting average in 1938.
- Finished second in NL with .319 batting average in 1940.
- Ranks among Reds career leaders in batting average (tied for 7th) and intentional bases on balls (6th).
- Two-time NL champion (1939 and 1940).
- 1940 world champion.

- 1938 NL MVP.
- Finished ninth in 1940 NL MVP voting.
- Five-time NL All-Star selection (1936, 1937, 1938, 1939, and 1940).
- Elected to Baseball Hall of Fame by members of Veterans Committee in 1986.

16

FRANK MCCORMICK

One of the finest all-around first basemen of his era, Frank McCormick spent parts of 10 seasons in Cincinnati, excelling both at the bat and in the field for the Reds. A .300 hitter on seven separate occasions, McCormick also knocked in more than 100 runs four times, hit 20 homers once, and led the NL in hits three times, earning in the process eight All-Star nominations, one NL MVP award, and two other top-five finishes in the balloting. Outstanding with the glove as well, McCormick led all NL first sackers in putouts six times, assists twice, double plays turned four times, and fielding percentage on three separate occasions, with his excellent all-around play making him a key contributor to Reds teams that won two pennants and one World Series.

Born in New York City on June 9, 1911, Frank Andrew McCormick knew at an early age that he wanted to pursue a career in baseball. After spending his formative years competing on the local sandlots, McCormick further honed his skills in a church league and high school. Originally an outfielder, McCormick tried out unsuccessfully for the Philadelphia Athletics, Washington Senators, and New York Giants, before finally getting his start in pro ball as a first baseman in the farm system of the Reds, who signed him following a tryout in 1934.

Assigned to the Beckley Black Knights of the Class C Middle Atlantic League, McCormick made an extremely favorable impression in his first year as a pro, earning a late-season callup to Cincinnati by batting .347 in 120 games at Beckley. Although McCormick performed well in his brief stint with the parent club, batting .313 and knocking in five runs in just 16 plate appearances, the Reds returned him to the minors at the end of the year. McCormick subsequently spent most of the next three seasons in the minor leagues, struggling somewhat at the plate at first, before improving his performance dramatically after modifying his batting grip at the suggestion of Durham manager Johnny Gooch. Developing into a top prospect at Durham, McCormick hit 15 homers, collected 211 hits, and

Frank McCormick led the NL in hits three straight times.

led the Piedmont League with a .381 batting average in 1936, before batting .322 for the Syracuse Chiefs the following year. Promoted to the Reds for good during the latter stages of the 1937 campaign, the 26-year-old McCormick batted .325 and knocked in nine runs in 24 games and 87 total plate appearances.

Named the Reds starting first baseman prior to the start of the 1938 season, McCormick began an extremely successful three-year run during which he posted the following numbers:

YEAR	HR	RBI	RUNS	HITS	AVG	OBP	SLG	OPS
1938	5	106	89	**209**	.327	.348	.425	.773
1939	18	**128**	99	**209**	.332	.374	.495	.869
1940	19	127	93	**191**	.309	.367	.482	.850

In addition to leading the NL in hits all three years, McCormick placed at, or near, the top of the league rankings in RBIs, runs scored, batting average, doubles, and total bases each season, leading the league with a career-high 44 two-baggers in 1940. After finishing fifth in the NL MVP voting, being accorded a spot on the NL All-Star team for the first of nine straight times, and being named the unofficial "Rookie of the Year" by the Associated Press in 1938, McCormick finished fourth in the MVP balloting the following year, before winning the award in 1940. Meanwhile, the Reds captured back-to-back pennants in 1939 and 1940 and defeated the Detroit Tigers in the 1940 World Series.

Although the right-handed-hitting McCormick stood 6'4" and weighed 205 pounds, he proved to be more of a line-drive hitter than a pure slugger, reaching the 20-homer plateau just once his entire career. Nevertheless, McCormick, who usually assumed either the third or fourth spot in the batting order, served as the Reds' foremost run producer, leading the team in RBIs seven times, while also finishing first on the club in batting average six times, slugging percentage five times, and home runs on four separate occasions.

A notorious first-ball hitter, McCormick rarely walked, drawing as many as 50 bases on balls in a season just three times over the course of his career. But he struck out even less frequently, never fanning more than 26 times in any single campaign. In fact, McCormick recorded more home runs than strikeouts in three different seasons, striking out just 189 times in more than 6,200 total plate appearances during his career.

An outstanding fielder as well, McCormick compiled a lifetime fielding percentage of .995, once going 131 consecutive games without committing an error. Chosen as the "retrospective Gold Glove" first baseman of the decade of the 1940s by STATS, Inc., the right-handed-throwing McCormick drew high praise from noted baseball historian Bill James, who called him, "one of the best defensive first basemen ever to play the game." Also extremely durable, McCormick started every game the Reds played from 1938 to 1941, appearing in 652 consecutive contests, before seeing his streak come to an end early in 1942.

Although McCormick spent much of the 1941 campaign wearing a back brace after injuring himself while diving into a hotel swimming pool, he had another solid season, hitting 17 homers, driving in 97 runs, scoring 77 times, batting .269, and compiling an OPS of .740. Forced to wear the back brace again in 1942, McCormick earned the fifth of his nine consecutive All-Star nominations by hitting 13 homers, knocking in 89 runs, and batting .277.

Deferred from military service during World War II because of the injury to his back, McCormick remained an effective player during the war years of 1943–1945, although he never again reached the heights he attained earlier in his career. Having his last big year for the Reds in 1944, McCormick earned a 13th-place finish in the NL MVP voting by batting .305, posting an OPS of .853, scoring 85 runs, and ranking among the league leaders with 20 homers, 102 RBIs, 177 hits, and 37 doubles. But after McCormick's numbers slipped to 10 homers, 81 RBIs, and a .276 batting average in 1945, the rebuilding Reds sold him to the Philadelphia Phillies for $30,000 during the following offseason.

McCormick, who left Cincinnati with career totals of 110 homers, 803 RBIs, 631 runs scored, 1,439 hits, 285 doubles, 20 triples, and 23 stolen bases, a .301 batting average, a .350 on-base percentage, and a .437 slugging percentage, ended up spending a little over one season in Philadelphia, hitting 11 homers, driving in 66 runs, and batting .284 for the Phillies in 1946, before spending most of 1947 and all of 1948 serving the Boston Braves as a part-time player. Choosing to announce his retirement following the conclusion of the 1948 campaign, McCormick ended his career with 128 home runs, 954 RBIs, 722 runs scored, 1,711 hits, 334 doubles, 26 triples, a .299 batting average, an on-base percentage of .348, and a slugging percentage of .434.

Following his playing days, McCormick managed in the minor leagues for three seasons, before returning to Cincinnati, where he spent more than a decade serving the Reds in various capacities, including coach, scout, and broadcaster. Eventually moving back to his hometown of New York, McCormick became the director of ticket sales for the Yankees, a position he held until November 21, 1982, when he died of cancer at the age of 71.

REDS CAREER HIGHLIGHTS

Best Season

McCormick earned *Sporting News* All-Star and NL MVP honors in 1940, when he helped lead the Reds to their second straight pennant by hitting 19 homers, finishing second in the league with 127 RBIs, scoring 93 times, batting .309, posting an OPS of .850, and topping the senior circuit with 191 hits and 44 doubles. But McCormick posted slightly better overall numbers the previous season, when he earned a fourth-place finish in the MVP balloting by hitting 18 homers, finishing second in the league with a .332 batting average and 312 total bases, and establishing career-high marks with 99 runs scored, an OPS of .869, and a league-leading 128 RBIs and 209 hits.

Memorable Moments/Greatest Performances

McCormick contributed to an 11–4 victory over the Cardinals on August 22, 1938, by going 5-for-6 with a double, one RBI, and four runs scored.

McCormick went a perfect 5-for-5 at the plate during a 9–1 win over the Cubs on September 10, 1938.

McCormick led the Reds to a 6–0 win over the Pirates on June 27, 1939, by going 4-for-4 with a homer and four RBIs.

McCormick contributed to a 23–2 rout of the Dodgers on June 8, 1940, by going 4-for-5 with a walk, an RBI, and a career-high five runs scored.

McCormick helped lead the Reds to a 12–9 win over Boston on August 4, 1940, by driving in six runs with two doubles and a pair of singles.

McCormick capped a six-run rally in the bottom of the ninth inning with a three-run homer that gave the Reds a 9–6 win over the Braves on May 20, 1941.

McCormick delivered the only run scored during a 1–0 win over the Cardinals on April 26, 1944, when he homered with two men out in the bottom of the 13th inning.

McCormick helped pace the Reds to a 9–3 win over the Giants on July 30, 1944, by driving in five runs with a double and a pair of homers.

Notable Achievements

- Hit 20 home runs once.
- Knocked in more than 100 runs four times.
- Batted over .300 seven times, topping the .320 mark on three occasions.
- Surpassed 200 hits twice.
- Topped 30 doubles six times, surpassing 40 two-baggers on three occasions.
- Led NL in RBIs once, hits three times, doubles once, and at-bats twice.
- Finished second in NL in RBIs once, batting average once, doubles once, and total bases twice.
- Led NL first basemen in putouts six times, assists twice, double plays turned four times, and fielding percentage three times.
- Two-time NL champion (1939 and 1940).
- 1940 world champion.
- 1940 NL MVP.
- Finished in top 10 of NL MVP voting three other times, placing in top five twice.
- Eight-time NL All-Star selection (1938, 1939, 1940, 1941, 1942, 1943, 1944, and 1945).
- 1940 *Sporting News* MLB All-Star selection.

17

DAVE CONCEPCIÓN

Identified by Joe Morgan as "the greatest shortstop I've ever played with, or I've ever seen," Dave Concepción combined with his Hall of Fame double-play partner to give the Reds the NL's premier middle-infield tandem for much of the 1970s. The finest all-around shortstop in the game for nearly a decade, Concepción excelled at the bat, on the basepaths, and in the field, batting over .300 three times, stealing more than 20 bases seven times, and leading all players at his position in assists twice and putouts, double plays turned, and fielding percentage once each. A key member of Reds teams that won six division titles, four pennants, and two World Series, Concepción earned nine All-Star nominations and two top-10 finishes in the NL MVP voting, before being further honored following the conclusion of his playing career by having his #13 retired by the club.

Born in Ocumare de la Costa, Aragua State, Venezuela, on June 17, 1948, David Ismael Concepción grew up idolizing fellow countrymen Chico Carrasquel and Luis Aparicio, who he hoped to emulate by playing shortstop in the major leagues. After excelling on the diamond at Agustin Codazzi High School, Concepción worked briefly as a bank teller and played for a local amateur baseball team, whose coach, Wilfredo Calvino, a scout for the Reds, signed him to a professional contract in September 1967.

Advancing rapidly through Cincinnati's farm system, Concepción spent just two seasons in the minors, before joining the parent club prior to the start of the 1970 campaign after batting a combined .310 for Double-A Asheville and Triple-A Indianapolis the previous year. Displaying a high aptitude on the basepaths during his relatively brief stint in Indianapolis, Concepción drew praise from Indians manager Vern Rapp, who said, "Concepción has the best baserunning instincts I've ever seen in a youngster. He stole 11 bases in 12 attempts, and he was only with us about a month."

Following his arrival in Cincinnati, the slightly built Concepción, who stood 6'2" and weighed only 155 pounds at the time, received his initiation to the Reds from Pete Rose, who joked that he would not be in danger of

Dave Concepción earned All-Star honors nine times.

pulling a muscle in his legs, but, rather, a bone. But Rose also acknowledged, "They tell me that the kid can play shortstop with a pair of pliers."

Concepción ended up spending his first big-league season sharing playing time at short with veteran infielder Woody Woodward, doing a respectable job offensively, but proving to be something of a disappointment with the glove. While Concepción batted .260, homered once, knocked in 19 runs, scored 38 times, and stole 10 bases in fewer than 300 plate appearances, he committed 22 errors in just 93 games in the field. Although Concepción tightened up his defense the next two seasons, he struggled at the plate, posting batting averages of just .205 and .209 that prevented him from becoming a regular member of the everyday starting lineup.

Having added some much-needed weight onto his slender frame by 1973, a more physically mature Concepción finally laid claim to the starting shortstop job. Acquitting himself extremely well in his first year as a full-time starter, Concepción earned All-Star honors by hitting eight homers, driving in 46 runs, stealing 22 bases, batting .287, and posting an OPS of .760 through the first four months of the campaign. However, Concepción's season ended abruptly on July 22 when he broke the fibula in his left leg while sliding into third base during a 6–0 win over the Montreal Expos. Although the Reds went on to win the division title, they ended up losing to the Mets in the NLCS, with Pete Rose later saying that Concepción's absence "probably cost us the league championship."

Fully recovered by the start of the 1974 season, Concepción established himself as the league's finest player at his position by hitting 14 homers, knocking in 82 runs, scoring 70 times, stealing 41 bases, batting .281, and posting an OPS of .732, while also earning Gold Glove honors for the first of four straight times by leading all NL shortstops with 536 assists. Although Concepción compiled slightly less impressive offensive numbers the next two seasons, totaling 14 homers, 118 RBIs, 136 runs scored, and 54 stolen bases from 1975 to 1976, while posting batting averages of .274 and .281, his strong all-around play made him a huge contributor to Reds teams that won back-to-back pennants and world championships.

In discussing Concepción's varied skill set, former Dodgers shortstop Pee Wee Reese stated, "Mark Belanger may be a little smoother than Concepción. Larry Bowa is very quick. Rick Burleson is a leader type. Bill Russell has an accurate arm. But no one does everything as well as Concepción. It's possible that no one ever has."

Agreeing with Reese's assessment, Reds third base coach Alex Grammas said, "There are some mighty good shortstops in the league today. But Concepción is a notch ahead of them all in all-around ability because his bat is stronger and his range in the field is greater."

Although the right-handed-swinging Concepción never truly established himself as an elite hitter, he fared much better at the plate than most other shortstops of his time, consistently batting over .280, posting an OPS over .700, and driving in somewhere between 60 and 80 runs. A solid line-drive hitter with occasional power, Concepción finished in double digits in homers twice and amassed at least 25 doubles on nine separate occasions. An excellent baserunner as well, Concepción twice stole more than 30 bases, swiping more than 20 bags five other times.

In addition to the many contributions he made on offense, Concepción proved to be one of the finest defensive shortstops in the game. Blessed with outstanding range and soft hands, Concepción annually ranked among the top players at his position in putouts and assists. And after developing a sore throwing arm, Concepción learned how to use Riverfront Stadium's artificial surface to his advantage, perfecting the art of throwing the ball on a hop to first base when fielding grounders deep in the shortstop hole. In discussing his often-used maneuver, Concepción said, "I didn't invent that throw. I saw another fellow do it. I saw Brooks Robinson do it to Lee May here in 1970. Then, when my arm hurt, I decided, 'Why not try it?'"

After gaining All-Star recognition in both 1975 and 1976, Concepción earned that distinction in each of the next six seasons as well. Performing especially well in 1978 and 1979, Concepción hit six homers, knocked in 67 runs, scored 75 times, batted .301, and posted an OPS of .763 in the first of those campaigns, before hitting 16 homers, driving in 84 runs, scoring 91 times, batting .281, and compiling an OPS of .764 in the second.

Gradually assuming a more prominent role on the team as his career progressed and stars such as Tony Pérez, Joe Morgan, and Pete Rose went elsewhere, Concepción eventually became more of a leader and one of the club's senior statesmen, with Johnny Bench saying of his longtime teammate, "The other people move away, and all of a sudden you notice the antique work of art in the corner."

Meanwhile, after hitting toward the bottom of the Reds' star-studded lineup his first several years in Cincinnati, Concepción spent the second half of his career batting anywhere from second to sixth.

Concepción remained the Reds' starting shortstop through the 1985 season, experiencing a considerable decline in offensive production after undergoing shoulder surgery at the end of 1982. Replaced by Barry Larkin at short in 1986, Concepción assumed the role of a utility infielder his last three seasons in Cincinnati, before announcing his retirement after being released by the Reds following the conclusion of the 1988 campaign. Prior to leaving the game, though, Concepción showed that he still had something left in 1987, when, appearing in 104 games and garnering 311 plate appearances, he compiled a career-high batting average of .319.

In his 19 years with the Reds, Concepción hit 101 homers, knocked in 950 runs, scored 993 times, collected 2,326 hits, 389 doubles, and 48 triples, stole 321 bases, batted .267, compiled a .322 on-base percentage, and posted a .357 slugging percentage. The winner of two Silver Sluggers and five Gold Gloves, Concepción recorded the 13th-most assists (7,024) of any player in MLB history and the 11th-most (6,594) of any shortstop.

Following his playing days, Concepción returned to his native Venezuela, where, after briefly managing his hometown Aragua Tigers, he became an executive in a trucking business and the owner of a farm.

Inducted into the Reds Hall of Fame in 2000, Concepción received plaudits for the integral role he played on the dominant team of his era from fellow shortstop Ozzie Smith, who said, "In my estimation, he was one of the most important pieces on that team. When a team is successful, you look no farther than the middle of the diamond—shortstop, center field, and catching. And when I think of The Big Red Machine, Davey Concepción was the guy who stabilized them in the middle. . . . He was the guy who gave the pitcher the confidence that, if he got a ground ball, he was going to get an out. That's what it is all about—giving pitchers the confidence to know that if I got a ground ball in a crucial situation or needed a double play, I was going to get it."

CAREER HIGHLIGHTS

Best Season

Had the 1981 season not been interrupted by a players' strike, Concepción likely would have posted the best offensive numbers of his career, with his solid hitting and deft fielding earning him a fourth-place finish in the NL MVP balloting. However, with Concepción appearing in only 106 games and garnering just 421 official at-bats during the strike-shortened campaign, the 1979 season would have to be considered his finest. In addition to winning the last of his five Gold Gloves, batting .281, compiling an OPS of .764, and stealing 19 bases, Concepción established career-high marks with 16 homers, 84 RBIs, 91 runs scored, 64 bases on balls, and 245 total bases, earning in the process a ninth-place finish in the league MVP voting.

Memorable Moments/Greatest Performances

Concepción helped lead the Reds to a 4–3 victory over the Giants on July 5, 1973, by going 5-for-5 with a triple, double, two RBIs, and one run scored, with his two-out single in the bottom of the ninth inning plating the game's winning run.

Concepción starred during the Reds' three-game sweep of Pittsburgh in the 1975 NLCS, batting .455 (5-for-11) with a homer, two runs scored, two stolen bases, and an OPS of 1.227.

Concepción contributed to an 11–2 win over the Cardinals on June 4, 1976, by going 5-for-6 with two RBIs and one run scored.

Concepción led the Reds to a 7–3 win over the Mets on August 13, 1976, by going 4-for-4 with two homers, a double, and three RBIs.

After knocking in two runs earlier in the contest, Concepción delivered a two-run bases loaded single in the bottom of the ninth inning that gave the Reds an 8–7 win over the Phillies on August 28, 1976.

Concepción continued his assault on Mets pitching on July 16, 1978, going 4-for-5 with a homer, two doubles, four RBIs, and two runs scored during a 9–2 Reds win.

Concepción led the Reds to an 8–5 victory over the Padres on April 29, 1981, by going 4-for-4 with two homers, a walk, and a career-high six RBIs.

Concepción homered, singled, and knocked in five runs during a 9–5 win over the Cubs on May 20, 1983, breaking the game open with an eighth-inning grand slam.

Concepción helped lead the Reds to a 5–3 win over the Braves on April 16, 1986, by homering twice and knocking in three runs.

Notable Achievements

- Batted over .300 three times.
- Topped 30 doubles twice.
- Stole more than 20 bases seven times, topping 30 thefts twice.
- Finished third in NL in hits once and doubles once.
- Led NL shortstops in putouts once, assists twice, double plays turned once, and fielding percentage once.
- Holds share of franchise record for most seasons played (19).
- Ranks among Reds career leaders in RBIs (8th), runs scored (7th), hits (3rd), extra-base hits (9th), doubles (4th), total bases (6th), bases on balls (8th), stolen bases (6th), sacrifice flies (2nd), games played (2nd), plate appearances (2nd), and at-bats (2nd).
- Six-time division champion (1970, 1972, 1973, 1975, 1976, and 1979).
- Four-time NL champion (1970, 1972, 1975, and 1976).
- Two-time world champion (1975 and 1976).
- Two-time NL Player of the Week.
- April 1981 NL Player of the Month.
- Two-time Silver Slugger Award winner (1981 and 1982).
- Five-time Gold Glove Award winner (1974, 1975, 1976, 1977, and 1979).

- 1981 Reds team MVP.
- Finished in top 10 of NL MVP voting twice, placing in top five once.
- Nine-time NL All-Star selection (1973, 1975, 1976, 1977, 1978, 1979, 1980, 1981, and 1982).
- Three-time *Sporting News* NL All-Star selection (1974, 1976, and 1981).
- #13 retired by Reds.

18

BRANDON PHILLIPS

An outstanding all-around second baseman who performed well both at the bat and in the field, Brandon Phillips spent 11 seasons in Cincinnati serving as the emotional leader of teams that won two division titles. A solid offensive player, Phillips surpassed 20 homers three times, scored more than 100 runs twice, knocked in more than 100 runs and batted over .300 once each, and stole more than 20 bases five times. Even stronger in the field, Phillips won four Gold Gloves by leading all players at his position in putouts, assists, and fielding percentage on multiple occasions. Yet Phillips, who earned three All-Star nominations during his time in the Queen City, became best known for the passion and sheer sense of joy he exhibited on the playing field.

Born in Raleigh, North Carolina, on June 28, 1981, Brandon Emil Phillips moved with his family at an early age to Stone Mountain, Georgia, where he spent his youth rooting for the Cincinnati Reds and his favorite player, Barry Larkin. Acquiring his love of baseball from his father, who runs the Phillips Baseball Center in Pine Lake, Georgia, Phillips starred at shortstop for the Redan High School Raiders for three years, while also performing so well in football that he received scholarship offers from the University of Georgia for both sports.

After initially signing a letter of intent to attend Georgia on a dual scholarship, Phillips decided to put his education on hold when the Montreal Expos selected him in the second round of the June 1999 MLB Amateur Draft. Phillips subsequently spent the next few years slowly advancing through the Montreal farm system, before heading to Cleveland when the Indians acquired him as part of a six-player trade they completed with the Expos on June 27, 2002.

Shuttling back and forth between the Indians and their top minor-league affiliate in Buffalo the next four seasons, Phillips appeared in a total of 135 games with the parent club, hitting six homers, driving in 38 runs, and batting just .206, before beginning his major-league career in earnest when

Brandon Phillips won four Gold Gloves as a member of the Reds.
Courtesy of Mike Morbeck

the Reds acquired him from Cleveland for a player to be named later on April 7, 2006.

Less than three months shy of his 25th birthday by the time he arrived in Cincinnati, Phillips acquitted himself extremely well in his first full big-league season after laying claim to the starting second base job, hitting 17 homers, knocking in 75 runs, scoring 65 times, batting .276, stealing 25 bases, and finishing third among all players at his position with 331 putouts. Improving upon those numbers in 2007, Phillips hit 30 homers, knocked in 94 runs, scored 107 times, swiped 32 bags, batted .288, and led all NL second sackers with 341 putouts, 433 assists, and a .990 fielding percentage. Though somewhat less productive at the plate in 2008, Phillips had another solid season, concluding the campaign with 21 homers, 78 RBIs, 80 runs scored, 23 steals, and a .261 batting average, while also earning Gold Glove honors for the first time by once again posting the best fielding percentage of any NL second baseman.

Continuing his strong play in 2009, Phillips hit 20 homers, knocked in 98 runs, scored 78 times, stole 25 bases, batted .276, and posted an OPS of .776, before helping the Reds capture the division title the following year by hitting 18 homers, driving in 59 runs, scoring 100 times, batting .275, and compiling an OPS of .762. An All-Star in 2010, Phillips also earned Gold Glove honors by leading all NL second sackers in assists and committing just three errors in the field all year.

A solid hitter, the right-handed-swinging Phillips, who stood 6-foot and weighed 210 pounds, spent most of his time in Cincinnati batting either second, third, or fourth. Blessed with good power to all fields, Phillips hit at least 17 homers eight straight times, surpassed 30 doubles four times, and knocked in more than 90 runs on three separate occasions, giving the Reds outstanding production for a player who manned his position. An excellent baserunner as well, Phillips displayed good speed and superior instincts on the basepaths, with his only weakness on offense being his lack of patience at the plate (he never walked more than 46 times in a season).

Known even more for his wizardry with the glove, Phillips proved to be one of the finest defensive second basemen in the game, exhibiting excellent range, soft hands, and a strong throwing arm. A flashy fielder, Phillips employed colorful maneuvers such as the "between-the-legs flip," the "between-the-legs double play flip," and the "behind-the-back double play flip."

Always one to speak his mind, Phillips never attempted to hide his feelings from anyone, be it fans, opponents, or members of the media. Extremely competitive as well, Phillips played the game with an edge, creating a major controversy in mid-August 2008, when he made some unflattering remarks about the Cardinals just prior to the start of a three-game series between the Reds and their NL Central Division rivals.

Quoted by the *Dayton Daily News* as saying, "I hate the Cardinals. All they do is bitch and moan about everything, all of them, they're little bitches, all of them. . . . I hate the Cardinals," Phillips had hell to pay the next evening when he became involved in a bench-clearing brawl between the two teams at home plate. Coming to bat in the bottom of the first inning, Phillips, as he always did, tapped his bat against the shin pads of St.

Louis catcher Yadier Molina and the home plate umpire. Having read Phillips's comments, Molina responded by kicking his bat, setting off a melee during which Reds pitcher Johnny Cueto kicked Jason LaRue in his face, resulting in a concussion that helped bring the latter's career to an early end.

Yet even though Phillips perhaps spoke out of turn at times, he became a favorite of the hometown fans, who grew increasingly fond of his ever-present smile and engaging personality.

After winning his third Gold Glove and earning his second straight All-Star nomination and lone Silver Slugger in 2011 by hitting 18 homers, driving in 82 runs, scoring 94 times, batting .300, and posting an OPS of .810, Phillips helped lead the Reds to their second division title in three seasons the following year by hitting another 18 homers, knocking in 77 runs, scoring 86 times, batting .281, and compiling an OPS of .750, garnering in the process a 13th-place finish in the NL MVP voting. Although Phillips's batting average and OPS slipped to .261 and .706, respectively, in 2013, he gained All-Star recognition again by hitting 18 homers, driving in 103 runs, and scoring 80 others, while also capturing Gold Glove honors for the fourth and final time in his career.

Plagued by a torn ligament in his thumb that forced him to miss more than a month of action in 2014, Phillips finished the year with just eight homers, 51 RBIs, 44 runs scored, and a .266 batting average. Although Phillips rebounded somewhat the next two seasons, totaling 23 homers while posting batting averages of .294 and .291, he never quite regained his earlier form, prompting the Reds to trade him to the Braves for a pair of minor-league pitchers on February 12, 2017.

Phillips, who, during his time in Cincinnati, hit 191 homers, knocked in 851 runs, scored 877 times, collected 1,774 hits, 311 doubles, and 32 triples, stole 194 bases, batted .279, compiled a .325 on-base percentage, and posted a .429 slugging percentage, ended up spending most of the 2017 campaign in Atlanta, hitting 11 homers, driving in 52 runs, and batting .291 in 120 games with the Braves, before finishing out the season with the Los Angeles Angels. A free agent at the end of the year, Phillips signed with the Red Sox, with whom he appeared in only nine games, before being granted his release. Following unsuccessful comeback attempts with the Vallejo Admirals of the independent Pacific Association, the Diablos Rojos del México of the Mexican League, and the Baseball Brilliance of the Yinzer Baseball Confederacy the next two seasons, Phillips officially announced his retirement, ending his major-league career with 211 homers, 951 RBIs, 1,005 runs scored, 2,029 hits, 368 doubles, 35 triples, 209 stolen bases, a .275 batting average, a .320 on-base percentage, and a .420 slugging percentage.

Although some outsiders considered Phillips to be more style than substance, Joey Votto suggested otherwise when he said of his longtime teammate, "He and I played side-by-side together for a long time and Brandon had a little bit of a public persona that people looked at him as perhaps a flash. . . . He was very fundamentally sound. That's why he could get away with a lot of the more extreme things that he did—the behind-the-back, the between-the-legs, that sort of thing. . . . He played every day, and I watched him play through a lot of different injuries that may have caused other players to hit the pause button. He worked every single day. He was routine-oriented and steadfast in his work. He took a great deal of pride in wearing the Cincinnati Reds uniform, and he had a genuine love and fondness for this city and uniform, and for being part of the team. Getting to play next to him, I learned a great deal, and I felt a great deal of respect for him. . . . To me, when I think of a Cincinnati Red, I really do think of Brandon Phillips."

Following his playing days, Phillips spent two seasons serving as a co-owner of the Lexington Legends of the Atlantic League of Professional Baseball, before leaving the franchise when a new ownership group purchased the team. Phillips, who is married to fitness model and professional wrestler Jade Cargill, subsequently purchased with his wife the Texas Smoke, a softball team that competes in the Women's Professional Fastpitch League.

REDS CAREER HIGHLIGHTS

Best Season

It could be argued that Phillips played his best ball for the Reds in 2011, when, in addition to earning Gold Glove honors and his lone *Sporting News* NL All-Star selection, he won his only Silver Slugger Award by hitting 18 homers, driving in 82 runs, scoring 94 times, batting an even .300, posting an OPS of .810, and ranking among the league leaders with 183 hits and 38 doubles. But Phillips posted slightly better overall numbers in 2007, when he batted .288, knocked in 94 runs, and established career-high marks in seven different offensive categories, including home runs (30), runs scored (107), hits (187), stolen bases (32), and OPS (.816). Furthermore, Phillips led all NL second basemen in putouts, assists, and fielding percentage, making the 2007 campaign the finest all-around season of his career.

Memorable Moments/Greatest Performances

Phillips helped lead the Reds to a 12–8 win over the Brewers on April 20, 2006, by driving in six runs with a single and a pair of homers, with his sixth-inning grand slam breaking the game open.

Phillips hit safely in 22 consecutive games from April 26 to May 20, 2007, going 34-for-97 (.351), with four homers, two triples, seven doubles, 15 RBIs, and 13 runs scored.

Phillips led the Reds to an 8–4 win over the Mets on July 13, 2007, by going 3-for-5 with a homer, double, six RBIs, and two runs scored, delivering the game's big blow in the top of the first inning when he homered off John Maine with the bases loaded.

Phillips provided much of the offensive firepower during a 7–0 win over the Marlins on May 5, 2009, driving in six runs with a homer and a pair of singles.

Phillips knocked in all six runs the Reds scored during a 6–2 win over the Cubs on June 10, 2013, plating four of those with a third-inning grand slam.

Phillips contributed to a 15–5 rout of the Pirates on July 30, 2015, by going 4-for-5 with two homers, seven RBIs, and two stolen bases, becoming in the process the first player in major-league history to hit two three-run homers, drive in seven runs, and steal two bases in the same game.

Notable Achievements

- Surpassed 20 home runs three times, topping 30 homers once.
- Knocked in more than 100 runs once.
- Scored more than 100 runs twice.
- Batted over .300 once.
- Topped 30 doubles five times.
- Stole more than 20 bases five times, topping 30 thefts once.
- Led NL second basemen in putouts twice, assists three times, and fielding percentage three times.
- Ranks among Reds career leaders in home runs (12th), RBIs (11th), runs scored (tied for 10th), doubles (9th), hits (10th), extra-base hits (10th), total bases (10th), sacrifice flies (5th), games played (8th), at-bats (8th), and plate appearances (8th).
- Two-time division champion (2010 and 2012).
- April 23, 2006, NL Player of the Week.
- 2011 Silver Slugger Award winner.

- Four-time Gold Glove Award winner (2008, 2010, 2011, and 2013).
- Three-time Reds team MVP (2007, 2009, and 2012).
- Three-time NL All-Star selection (2010, 2011, and 2013).
- 2011 Sporting News NL All-Star selection.

19

GUS BELL

The patriarch of a rare three-generation baseball family that also includes son, Buddy, and grandsons, David and Mike, Gus Bell established himself as one of the NL's better all-around outfielders during the 1950s. Spending most of his peak seasons with the Reds after beginning his career with the Pittsburgh Pirates, Bell batted over .300 twice, hit more than 25 homers three times, and knocked in more than 100 runs on four separate occasions, earning in the process four All-Star selections. The Reds' starting center fielder most of his time in Cincinnati, Bell proved to be a solid defender as well, leading all NL outfielders in fielding percentage twice, before splitting his final three big-league seasons between the New York Mets and Milwaukee Braves.

Born in Louisville, Kentucky, on November 15, 1928, David Russell Bell acquired the nickname "Gus" during his formative years because he spent much of his youth rooting for longtime New York Giants catcher Gus Mancuso. Hoping to follow in his hero's footsteps, Bell starred behind the plate at Bishop Benedict Joseph Flaget High School, performing so well that the Pittsburgh Pirates signed him as soon as he graduated.

Bell subsequently spent three years advancing through Pittsburgh's farm system, batting .319 for the C-level Keokuk Pirates in 1948 and .325 for the Albany Senators in the A-level Eastern League the following year, before earning a promotion to the parent club early in 1950 by getting off to a torrid start at Triple-A Indianapolis. Acquitting himself extremely well over the final five months of the 1950 campaign, Bell hit eight homers, knocked in 53 runs, scored 62 times, and batted .282 in 111 games as the Bucs' starting right fielder.

Inserted into the cleanup spot in the batting order the following year, right behind Hall of Fame slugger Ralph Kiner, Bell responded by finishing second on the team with 16 homers, 89 RBIs, and 80 runs scored, batting .278, and leading the league with 12 triples. Somewhat less productive in 1952, Bell again hit 16 homers but knocked in just 59 runs, scored only

Gus Bell knocked in more than 100 runs four times for the Reds.

53 times, and batted just .250, prompting the Pirates to trade him to the Reds at the end of the year for outfielder Cal Abrams and a pair of minor leaguers.

While his subpar performance undoubtedly contributed to his departure from Pittsburgh, Bell, who angered Pirates GM Branch Rickey during spring training by insisting that his family travel with him, later claimed that his differences with Rickey ultimately led to his exile, saying, "Rickey took a dislike to me because I refused to be one of his hungry ballplayers."

Shifted to center field upon his arrival in Cincinnati, Bell emerged as one of the NL's finest players at that position, beginning an excellent four-year run during which he posted the following numbers:

YEAR	HR	RBI	RUNS	HITS	AVG	OBP	SLG	OPS
1953	30	105	102	183	.300	.354	.525	.879
1954	17	101	104	185	.299	.349	.465	.814
1955	27	104	88	188	.308	.361	.510	.871
1956	29	84	82	176	.292	.347	.501	.848

In addition to ranking in the league's top 10 in home runs and RBIs in three of those four seasons, Bell placed near the top of the league rankings in hits, doubles, and total bases all four years, earning in the process three All-Star nominations. Meanwhile, Bell's strong performance in 1956 helped the Reds finish just two games behind the pennant-winning Dodgers, with their 221 home runs as a team tying the then-single-season MLB record previously set by the 1947 New York Giants.

A strong left-handed batter, the 6'1", 195-pound Bell possessed good power at the plate and drove the ball well to all fields. Although more of a line-drive hitter than a pure slugger, Bell proved to be one of the NL's top power threats during the mid-1950s, combining with Ted Kluszewski to give the Reds a formidable pair of lefty bats in the middle of their lineup. Though not particularly fleet afoot, Bell also ran the bases well and did an excellent job in center field, annually ranking among the league leaders in outfield putouts and assists.

Impressed with the totality of Bell's game, Reds manager Birdie Tebbetts stated at one point during the 1954 campaign, "I'm tired of hearing about Mays and Snider. Bell is my boy for the position. He's really a great player."

And years later, former Reds teammate Hersh Freeman said, "Gus Bell was one of the all-time great center fielders; a good hitter, a good team man, a good all-around ballplayer."

Despite being limited by injuries to 121 games, 13 home runs, 61 RBIs, and 65 runs scored in 1957, Bell batted .292, helping him gain All-Star recognition as part of a ballot-stuffing campaign waged by Reds fans. But after being voted onto the starting team, along with teammates Frank Robinson, Wally Post, Ed Bailey, Johnny Temple, Roy McMillan, and Don Hoak, Bell had to settle for a reserve role when NL president Warren Giles replaced him and Post with Hank Aaron and Willie Mays, removing an injured Post from the squad altogether.

Bell subsequently experienced a major decline in offensive production in 1958, hitting just 10 homers, driving in only 46 runs, and batting just .252, in 112 games and fewer than 400 official at-bats. But he rebounded nicely after being moved back to his original position of right field in 1959, hitting 19 homers, ranking among the league leaders with a career-high 115 RBIs, batting .293, and posting an OPS of .770. However, after Bell slumped to 12 homers, 62 RBIs, and a .262 batting average in 1960, he assumed a part-time role the following year. Subsequently left unprotected in the October 1961 expansion draft, Bell became a member of the New York Mets when they selected him with the eighth overall pick.

Bell, who left the Reds having hit 160 homers, driven in 711 runs, scored 634 times, collected 1,343 hits, 228 doubles and 35 triples, stolen 24 bases, batted .288, compiled a .335 on-base percentage, and posted a .454 slugging percentage as a member of the team, ended up spending less than two months in New York, batting just .149 for the Mets, before being sold to the Milwaukee Braves on May 21, 1962. After hitting five homers, knocking in 24 runs, and batting .285 for the Braves in a part-time role the rest of the year, Bell appeared in only a handful of games with them in 1963, before being released during the early stages of the 1964 campaign. Bell announced his retirement shortly thereafter, ending his career with 206 home runs, 942 RBIs, 865 runs scored, 1,823 hits, 311 doubles, 66 triples, 30 stolen bases, a .281 batting average, a .330 on-base percentage, and a .445 slugging percentage.

Following his playing days, Bell worked for an auto dealership, ran an employment agency, and scouted for the Cleveland Indians and Texas Rangers. Inducted into the Reds Hall of Fame in 1964, Bell lived until May 7, 1995, when he died from a heart attack at the age of 66.

REDS CAREER HIGHLIGHTS

Best Season

Bell's first year in Cincinnati proved to be the finest of his career. En route to earning the first of his four All-Star nominations in 1953, Bell batted .300, compiled an OPS of .879, knocked in 105 runs, scored 102 times, and ranked among the league leaders with 30 homers, 183 hits, 37 doubles, and 320 total bases.

Memorable Moments/Greatest Performances

Bell led the Reds to a 9–5 win over the Giants on May 4, 1953, by going 4-for-5 with a homer, five RBIs, and two runs scored, delivering the game's big blow in the top of the seventh inning, when he homered with the bases loaded.

Bell homered, scored two runs, and hit safely in five of his six trips to the plate during an 11-inning, 6–5 win over the Dodgers on September 10, 1953.

Bell helped lead the Reds to a 9–4 win over the Phillies on July 16, 1954, by going 3-for-5 with two homers, a double, and six RBIs.

Bell proved to be the lone bright spot in a 5–3 loss to the Phillies on July 21, 1955, driving in all the runs the Reds scored with three solo homers.

Bell led the Reds to a 14–5 win over the Braves on September 21, 1955, by going 4-for-4 with a homer, double, walk, and career-high eight RBIs, four of which came on a first-inning grand slam.

Bell had a huge game against the Cubs on May 29, 1956, going 5-for-5 with three homers and seven RBIs during a 10–4 Reds win.

Bell led the Reds to a 6–4 win over the Pirates on September 15, 1956, by going 4-for-5 with two homers and four RBIs.

Bell contributed to an 11–5 victory over the Cardinals on July 15, 1959, by going 5-for-6 with two doubles, two RBIs, and one run scored.

Notable Achievements

- Hit more than 25 home runs three times, surpassing 30 homers once.
- Knocked in more than 100 runs four times.
- Scored more than 100 runs twice.
- Batted over .300 twice.
- Posted slugging percentage over .500 three times.
- Topped 30 doubles four times.
- Hit three home runs in one game twice (vs. Phillies on July 21, 1955, and vs. Cubs on May 29, 1956).
- Finished third in NL with 188 hits in 1955.
- Led NL outfielders in fielding percentage twice.
- Led NL right fielders in putouts once and double plays turned once.
- 1961 NL champion.
- Four-time NL All-Star selection (1953, 1954, 1956, and 1957).

20

KEN GRIFFEY SR.

The senior member of one of the finest father-son duos in baseball history, Ken Griffey performed well both at the bat and in the field for four different teams during a lengthy major-league career that spanned 19 years. Playing most of his best ball for the Reds, with whom he served two tours of duty over parts of 12 seasons, Griffey batted over .300 six times, scored more than 100 runs twice, and stole more than 20 bases three times, while also doing an excellent job of patrolling right field at Riverfront Stadium. Perhaps the most unheralded member of Reds teams that won four division titles, two pennants, and two World Series, Griffey spent most of his time in Cincinnati being overshadowed by superstar teammates Johnny Bench, Pete Rose, Joe Morgan, and Tony Pérez. Nevertheless, Griffey managed to earn three NL All-Star selections and one top-10 finish in the league MVP voting, before departing for New York, where he began the second half of his distinguished career.

Born in Donora, Pennsylvania, on April 10, 1950, George Kenneth Griffey grew up with his four siblings in Washington County, some 20 miles south of Pittsburgh. The son of a former high school teammate of Stan Musial who left the family in 1952 after his company closed its plant in Pittsburgh and transferred him to Cleveland, Griffey hardly knew his father, revealing during a 2016 interview with ESPN that he did not see him again for another 14 years.

Forced to live in poverty, Griffey found solace in sports, starring in baseball, football, basketball, and track at Donora High School. A hard-hitting, fine-fielding center fielder on the diamond, Griffey also excelled on the hardwood, once scoring 40 points and amassing 27 rebounds during a game against Charleroi Area High School. A standout in track as well, Griffey competed in the 220-yard dash, the low hurdles, and the high jump, setting a Washington County record in May 1969 by leaping 6 feet ¾ inches. But Griffey experienced his greatest success on the gridiron, where he specialized in making long runs as a combination receiver/halfback.

Ken Griffey Sr. batted over .300 six times as a member of the Reds.

Offered athletic scholarships to several universities as graduation neared, Griffey initially hoped to play football in college. But with his girlfriend expecting and wedding plans in his immediate future, Griffey chose instead to sign with the Reds when they offered him a contract worth $500 a month after they selected him in the 29th round of the 1969 MLB Amateur Draft.

Griffey spent most of the next five years advancing through Cincinnati's farm system, gradually emerging as one of the organization's top prospects. Performing especially well in his final three seasons, Griffey batted .342 and stole 25 bases in just 88 games with the Tampa Tarpons of the

Florida State League in 1971, before batting .318, hitting 14 homers, and swiping 31 bags as a member of the Trois-Rivieres of the Double-A Eastern League the following year. Griffey then earned a late-season callup to Cincinnati in 1973 by batting .327 for Indianapolis of the Triple-A American Association. Faring extremely well in his first trial with the Reds, Griffey batted .384, hit three homers, knocked in 14 runs, and scored 19 times in 25 games and close to 100 total plate appearances, while playing right field almost exclusively.

Griffey subsequently split the 1974 campaign between the Reds and their Triple-A affiliate, batting .251, homering twice, driving in 19 runs, and scoring 24 times in 88 games with the parent club, before arriving in Cincinnati to stay the following year. Named the team's starting right fielder prior to the start of the regular season, Griffey contributed to the first of the Reds back-to-back world championship ballclubs by batting .305, compiling an on-base percentage of .391 and an OPS of .793, stealing 16 bases, and ranking among the league leaders with 95 runs scored and nine triples. Continuing his solid play in the postseason, Griffey batted .333 and knocked in four runs during Cincinnati's three-game sweep of Pittsburgh in the NLCS, before batting .269, driving in four runs, scoring four times, and stealing two bases against Boston in the World Series. Increasing his offensive output in 1976, Griffey earned All-Star honors and an eighth-place finish in the NL MVP balloting by hitting six homers, driving in 74 runs, and placing near the top of the league rankings with 111 runs scored, 189 hits, 34 stolen bases, a .336 batting average, a .401 on-base percentage, and an OPS of .851.

One of the league's most consistent performers, the 5'11," 195-pound Griffey, who batted left-handed and generally hit out of the number two spot in the Reds lineup, proved to be an outstanding line-drive hitter who rarely struck out, knew how to work the opposing pitcher, and possessed occasional home-run power. Blessed with exceptional running speed, Griffey also ran the bases extremely well and did an excellent job in right field, with his strong all-around play making him arguably the most overlooked member of Cincinnati's Big Red Machine.

Appreciated by his teammates, though, Griffey received high praise from Joe Morgan, who said, "He was the best fastball hitter I had seen. It did not matter where you pitched him—in, out, up, or down—he was always able to handle the heat. He had speed, he could throw, he was smart in the outfield and never missed a cutoff man."

Yet, as Griffey recalled, Morgan's exalted status in the Reds' hierarchy of players prevented him from taking full advantage of his exceptional athletic ability. After Griffey spent the first several weeks of the 1975 campaign batting either sixth or seventh in the Cincinnati lineup, manager Sparky Anderson told him in mid-May, "Kenny, I'm moving you up to the number two spot in the lineup. That's because I think you're a great hitter. But there's one thing you need to know. From now on, I don't want you stealing any bases. You got Joe Morgan hitting after you, and he's the best damn player in the game of baseball, and he doesn't like when people steal bases when he's batting. It distracts him. So, you don't steal."

Always a team player, Griffey bit his lip and did not complain. But he stated years later, "I could have been a whole hell of a lot different player. I could have been a very selfish player. I could have been like Joe Morgan. . . . Joe knew he couldn't run with me. I could have stolen just as many bases as he did. I could have stolen more bases. Back in 1973, I was the best there was at stealing bases. . . . Sparky told me I couldn't steal bases because it bothered Joe's hitting. . . . I sacrificed for the team. I always sacrificed for the team."

Although the Reds failed to repeat as NL champions in 1977, Griffey earned his second All-Star nomination by hitting 12 homers, driving in 57 runs, collecting 35 doubles, stealing 17 bases, posting an OPS of .855, and ranking among the league leaders with a .318 batting average, 117 runs scored, and 186 hits. Griffey followed that up with another solid season, batting .288, scoring 90 runs, and stealing 23 bases in 1978, before compiling a batting average of .316 and an OPS of .845 in the ensuing campaign despite being limited by injuries to only 95 games. Healthy for most of 1980, Griffey gained All-Star recognition for the third and final time by hitting 13 homers, driving in a career-high 85 runs, swiping 23 bags, scoring 89 times, batting .284, and posting an OPS of .818. Griffey subsequently batted .311 and scored 65 runs during the strike-interrupted 1981 campaign, before being dealt to the Yankees for two marginal prospects at the end of the year.

Griffey ended up spending four-and-a-half productive years in New York, batting over .300 twice, while splitting his time between first base and all three outfield positions. But with Riverfront Stadium's hard artificial surface having taken its toll on him, Griffey experienced constant discomfort in his knees, preventing him from ever again displaying the same speed on the basepaths he exhibited earlier in his career. Traded to the Braves midway through the 1986 campaign, Griffey remained in Atlanta for two years, before signing with the Reds as a free agent following his release in August 1988. Griffey spent most of the next two seasons with the organization that gave him his start, batting .263, hitting eight homers, and driving in 30 runs for the Reds in a part-time role in 1989, before ending his career with the Seattle Mariners early in 1991. While in Seattle, though, Griffey made history when he became the first father to play on the same team as his son, experiencing a truly surreal moment on September 14, 1990, when he and Ken Jr. homered consecutively in the first inning of a 7–5 loss to California.

Recalling his brief stint in Seattle, Griffey Sr., who, unlike his own father, has always taken great interest in the fortunes of his sons, said, "A lot of times, I'd look over to center field, and this is no lie, I still saw the hat too big for his head, a baggy uniform, and he's got number 30 across his chest and back. That's a father-son game I was remembering when he was just a little kid, and I was with the Reds."

Choosing to announce his retirement two months into the 1991 campaign, Griffey ended his career with 152 homers, 859 RBIs, 1,129 runs scored, 2,143 hits, 364 doubles, 77 triples, 200 stolen bases, a .296 batting average, a .359 on-base percentage, and a .431 slugging percentage. As a member of the Reds, Griffey hit 71 homers, knocked in 466 runs, scored 709 times, collected 1,275 hits, 212 doubles, and 63 triples, stole 156 bases, batted .303, compiled an on-base percentage of .370, and posted a slugging percentage of .434.

Following his playing days, Griffey, who currently resides with his wife, Alberta, in Winter Garden, Florida, overcame a bout with prostate cancer to begin a career in coaching and managing that has seen him serve as batting coach for the Dayton Dragons, the Reds' Class A minor-league affiliate (2010), and manager of the Bakersfield Blaze, the team's Class A California League affiliate (2011–2013). Still a member of the organization, Griffey serves as a roving instructor who tutors his pupils on the art of hitting and bunting.

REDS CAREER HIGHLIGHTS

Best Season

Although Griffey hit more homers, scored a few more runs, and posted a slightly higher OPS the following year, he had the most impactful season of his career in 1976. Playing an integral role on one of the greatest teams in MLB history, Griffey earned his lone *Sporting News* NL All-Star nomination and an eighth-place finish in the NL MVP voting by finishing second in the league with a .336 batting average, while also ranking among the leaders with a .401 on-base percentage, .851 OPS, 111 runs scored, 189 hits, nine triples, and 34 stolen bases.

Memorable Moments/Greatest Performances

Griffey drove home the decisive run of a 3–2 win over the Red Sox in Game 2 of the 1975 World Series with a two-out double in the top of the ninth inning.

Griffey came up big in the clutch on August 11, 1976, hitting a game-tying two-out, two-run homer off Cubs right-hander Joe Coleman in the top of the ninth inning. The Reds subsequently pushed across three runs in the ensuing frame, giving them a 13–10 victory over Chicago.

Griffey performed exceptionally well during the Reds' three-game sweep of the Phillies in the 1976 NLCS, going 5-for-13 (.385) with a triple, two walks, two RBIs, two runs scored, two stolen bases, and an OPS of 1.005.

Griffey proved to be huge factor in a 3–2 win over the Expos on May 18, 1978, going 4-for-4 with two RBIs and one run scored, with his two-run double in the top of the eighth inning keying a three-run rally by the Reds.

Griffey helped lead the Reds to a 5–2 win over the Padres on May 27, 1978, by going 4-for-4 with a walk, an RBI, and three runs scored.

Griffey starred in defeat on August 21, 1978, going 3-for-5 with two homers and six RBIs during a 14–9 loss to the Cardinals.

Notable Achievements

- Batted over .300 six times.
- Compiled on-base percentage over .400 twice.
- Posted slugging percentage over .500 once.
- Posted OPS over .900 once.
- Scored more than 100 runs twice.
- Finished in double digits in triples once.
- Topped 30 doubles twice.
- Stole more than 20 bases three times, topping 30 thefts once.
- Finished second in NL in batting average once and runs scored once.
- Led NL right fielders with .990 fielding percentage in 1977.
- Four-time division champion (1973, 1975, 1976, and 1979).
- Two-time NL champion (1975 and 1976).
- Two-time world champion (1975 and 1976).
- 1980 Reds team MVP.
- Finished eighth in 1976 NL MVP voting.
- Three-time NL All-Star selection (1976, 1977, and 1980).
- 1976 Sporting News NL All-Star selection.

21

DAVE PARKER

Recognized as the finest all-around player in the game during the late-1970s, Dave Parker suffered a precipitous fall from grace his last few years with the Pittsburgh Pirates that caused him to leave the Steel City a hated man. But after signing with the Reds as a free agent following the conclusion of the 1983 campaign, Parker experienced a rebirth, earning two All-Star selections and a pair of top-five finishes in the NL MVP voting over the course of the next four seasons by batting over .300 once, while also hitting more than 30 homers and knocking in more than 100 runs twice each. A three-time Reds team MVP who also gained *Sporting News* NL All-Star recognition twice during his time in the Queen City, Parker created excitement in Cincinnati with his outstanding hitting and outgoing persona, making him one of the most popular players in team annals.

Born in Grenada, Mississippi, on June 9, 1951, David Gene Parker moved with his family at the age of five to Cincinnati, Ohio, where he grew up with his five siblings just a stone's throw from Crosley Field. A fan of the Reds as a youth, Parker remembered, "Frank Robinson and Vada Pinson would come out, and there I'd be, waiting for them. And believe it or not, they were always nice to me. They'd come out and give me a glove or a ball."

After learning to play baseball on the stadium's parking lots, Parker further honed his skills at Courter Technical High School, where he also excelled in football and basketball, later saying, "Football was my first love. I loved it because it's a contact game. I liked to run over people."

Performing especially well on both the diamond and gridiron his junior year, Parker led his team in batting average, homers, and RBIs, while splitting his time between catcher, pitcher, and the outfield. Meanwhile, Parker garnered interest from more than 60 college football programs by earning First-Team All-Public High School League honors as a running back. However, Parker sustained a season-ending injury to his left knee in the first game of his senior year that ended his dream of playing college football and greatly reduced his draft stock heading into the June 1970 MLB Draft.

Dave Parker earned a runner-up finish in the 1985 NL MVP voting as a member of the Reds.

Ultimately selected by the Pirates in the 14th round, Parker spent parts of the next four seasons in the minors, before joining the parent club in July 1973, one month after celebrating his 22nd birthday. Platooned mostly against right-handed pitching the rest of the year, and for all of 1974 as well, the left-handed-swinging Parker posted batting averages of .288 and .282, before finally becoming a regular member of the everyday starting lineup in 1975.

Excelling in his first season as a full-time starter, Parker earned a third-place finish in the NL MVP voting by hitting 25 homers, driving in

101 runs, batting .308, compiling an OPS of .898, and leading the league with a slugging percentage of .541. After posting slightly less impressive numbers in 1976, Parker began an exceptional three-year run during which he established himself as arguably the NL's most complete player, averaging 25 homers, 100 RBIs, 106 runs scored, 19 stolen bases, and 18 outfield assists from 1977 to 1979, while also winning two batting titles, three Gold Gloves, and one league MVP trophy. Particularly outstanding in 1978, Parker earned NL MVP honors by hitting 30 homers, driving in 117 runs, scoring 102 times, and leading the league with a .334 batting average, .585 slugging percentage, and .979 OPS.

Blessed with good power at the plate, a cannon for an arm, and surprising speed for a man his size, the 6'5", 230-pound Parker possessed tremendous natural ability, with Willie Stargell saying of his teammate, "The talent Dave Parker has is just awesome. He can excel in every phase of the game."

Pirates manager Chuck Tanner expressed similar sentiments when he stated, "Dave Parker can beat you in every way. He can beat you with the home run or the single. He can beat you with his speed, or his throwing arm, or his defense. He is the complete player."

Tanner also praised his right fielder for the intensity he brought with him to the playing field each day, saying, "There isn't a player alive who plays the game the way Dave Parker does. Every game is the seventh game of the World Series to him. There isn't a player alive who can do the things on the field that Parker can do. None."

Parker's superior all-around play prompted the Pirates to reward him with a five-year contract prior to the start of the 1979 season that made him baseball's first million-dollar-a-year player. But while Parker enjoyed the perks of his increased income, he eventually came to realize that it changed the way the fans viewed him, saying, "I think it took away from people looking at me as Dave Parker, hustling ballplayer, and turned it into Dave Parker, million-dollar man. . . . Basically, this [Pittsburgh] is a coal-mining, steel-melting city. These people work hard for their money, and it's hard for them to imagine making this type of money playing games."

The hometown fans grew increasingly resentful of Parker in 1980, when he became involved in two separate lawsuits for failing to live up to his financial responsibilities, and his common-law wife, Stella Miller-Parker, filed for divorce, accusing him of adultery and "cruel and barbarous treatment." Parker's image received an additional blow when a series of injuries, a gradual 20- to 30-pound increase in weight, and a growing dependency on cocaine caused his on-field performance to suffer, cutting into his playing time significantly and greatly diminishing his offensive production.

After posting solid, but unspectacular, numbers in 1980, Parker appeared in a total of just 140 games over the course of the next two seasons, although he did everything he could to take the field, with Jane Gross of the *New York Times* reporting after a game with the Mets that his left knee was "so sore that he limped to the plate, looked like a lame horse on the base paths, and was forced to play deeper than usual in the field because he had trouble going back for the ball."

Meanwhile, Pittsburgh manager Chuck Tanner told Gross, "He plays a lot of times when he can hardly walk into the clubhouse. Every time I take him out of the lineup because he's hurting, he says he wants to play, and I play him every time he asks."

Much more of a factor in 1983 after discontinuing his use of cocaine and improving his health by shedding some of his excess weight, Parker hit 12 homers, knocked in 69 runs, and batted .279, prompting the Reds to offer him a two-year free agent contract at the end of the year. Upon inking his deal with the Reds, Parker said, "Pittsburgh took a lot out of me. I always sacrificed my body in Pittsburgh. I tried to come back too soon from injuries. That was my stupidity. It made my game decline. I should have done what every player does when he's hurt—sit on the bench."

Giving the Reds a solid return on their investment his first year in Cincinnati, Parker hit 16 homers, knocked in 94 runs, scored 73 times, batted .285, and posted an OPS of .738. Subsequently rewarded with a three-year contract extension, Parker earned All-Star honors and a second-place finish in the NL MVP voting in 1985 by leading the league with 125 RBIs, 42 doubles, and 350 total bases, while also placing in the top five in homers (34), hits (198), batting average (.312), slugging percentage (.551), and OPS (.916).

Unfortunately, Parker's testimony in a federal court drug trial held in Pittsburgh in September of 1985 overshadowed his tremendous on-field performance. Granted immunity in exchange for his testimony against a man charged with distributing cocaine to major-league players, Parker admitted to using the drug "with consistency" from 1979 to 1982, and to arranging cocaine transactions during his time with the Pirates, saying, "It was the sort of in-thing to do. Cocaine was becoming pretty popular in society. It was constantly available because of who I was."

Parker also claimed that he stopped using cocaine during the latter stages of the 1982 campaign because, "I felt my game was slipping. I think cocaine played a part in that. . . . I felt my game was more important than cocaine. I was getting married. I thought that was more important than cocaine. It's a matter of priority."

Avoiding a one-year suspension initially doled out by MLB commissioner Peter Ueberroth by agreeing to contribute 10 percent of his 1986 salary to programs dedicated to fighting drug abuse, submit to drug tests for the rest of his career, participate in antidrug programs established by baseball, and do 200 hours of community service, Parker garnered his second straight All-Star selection and a fifth-place finish in the NL MVP balloting in 1986 by batting .273, compiling an OPS of .807, scoring 89 runs, finishing second in the league with 31 homers and 116 RBIs, and topping the circuit with 304 total bases.

Although Parker no longer ran the bases as well or covered as much territory in the outfield as he did earlier in his career, he hit the ball just as hard, possessed the same powerful throwing arm, and remained one of the game's most intimidating batters, with Paul Molitor, who played with him in Milwaukee in 1990, saying of his former teammate, "He had a presence because of his size alone, but he hit line drives as hard as anybody I've ever played with—and that was in the latter stages of his career. He could beat you in a lot of ways."

Parker also retained his leadership ability and raucous sense of humor that helped bring out the best in his teammates. Known for his knee-slapping one-liners, Parker said of himself, "If you first meet me in the clubhouse, you'd say I'm very insulting. Loud. Maybe you'd even think in terms of a bully."

But Parker added, "I'm a motivator. I'll point out guys' faults. I'll tell a guy he's pulling out, that he couldn't hit a balloon. He thinks to himself, 'I'll show that turkey.' It makes him better."

Claiming that Parker's remarks achieved their desired goal, former Pirates teammate Phil Garner stated, "If you feel down, sorry for yourself, he gets the spark going in you. Dave's found that picking on someone makes guys rally round, laugh. Suddenly, they're ready. It's group therapy."

Jerry Reuss, Parker's teammate in Pittsburgh from 1974 to 1978, added, "It didn't matter where you were born, your ethnic heritage, religious background, marital status. Dave was an equal-opportunity offender. Nothing was sacred. Nor was it personal. But it was a daily comedy routine."

Parker remained with the Reds for one more season, hitting 26 homers, driving in 97 runs, scoring 77 times, batting .253, and posting an OPS of .744 for them in 1987, before being traded to the Athletics for pitchers José Rijo and Tim Birtsas at the end of the year. Parker, who, during his time in Cincinnati, hit 107 homers, knocked in 432 runs, scored 327 times, collected 694 hits, 129 doubles, and seven triples, stole 24 bases, batted .281, compiled a .334 on-base percentage, and posted a .469 slugging percentage, ended up spending the remainder of his career in the AL, serving the Athletics, Brewers, Angels, and Blue Jays almost exclusively as a designated hitter. Playing his best ball for the Athletics in 1989 and the Brewers in 1990, Parker hit 22 homers, knocked in 97 runs, and batted .264 in the first of those campaigns, before earning the last of his seven All-Star nominations in the second by reaching the seats 21 times, driving in 92 runs, and batting .289. Choosing to announce his retirement after spending the final two weeks of the 1991 season with the Blue Jays, Parker ended his career with 339 homers, 1,493 RBIs, 1,272 runs scored, 2,712 hits, 526 doubles, 75 triples, 154 stolen bases, a .290 batting average, a .339 on-base percentage, and a .471 slugging percentage.

Following his playing days, Parker began a brief career in coaching that included one-year stints with the Angels, Cardinals, and Pirates. He also owned several Popeyes Chicken franchises in the Cincinnati area that he sold in 2012 after being diagnosed with Parkinson's disease. Parker subsequently created the Dave Parker 39 Foundation (39 being the uniform number he wore throughout his major-league career), which strives to find a cure for Parkinson's and make life better for those who have been stricken with the disease. The now 74-year-old Parker, who has had both of his knees replaced, currently resides near Cincinnati, in Loveland, Ohio, where, in addition to raising awareness for Parkinson's through his foundation, he enjoys playing golf and spending time with his wife, Kellye, and their grandchildren.

Inducted into the Reds Hall of Fame in 2014, Parker discussed what the honor meant to him when he said, "It means an awful lot to me—something I'll cherish forever. I grew up playing stickball off the (outside) wall at Crosley Field. The Reds were always part of my life, growing up in the city. To make my mark here as an athlete, to come back home and play for my hometown team and be elected to the Reds Hall of Fame? Man, that's a great honor. I have a lot of people to thank."

REDS CAREER HIGHLIGHTS

Best Season

Parker posted impressive numbers for the Reds in 1986, finishing second in the NL with 31 homers and 116 RBIs, while topping the circuit with 304 total bases, batting .273, and compiling an OPS of .807. But he performed even better the previous season, earning *Sporting News* NL All-Star honors and a runner-up finish to Willie McGee in the NL MVP voting by leading the league with 125 RBIs, 42 doubles, 350 total bases, and 80 extra-base hits, while also ranking among the leaders with 34 homers, 198 hits, a .312 batting average, a .551 slugging percentage, and an OPS of .916.

Memorable Moments/Greatest Performances

Parker helped lead the Reds to an 8–7 win over the Padres on August 5, 1985, by going 4-for-5 with a homer, two doubles, three RBIs, and two runs scored.

Parker contributed to a lopsided 11–2 victory over the Cubs on September 5, 1986, by driving in five runs with a single and a pair of homers.

Parker led the Reds to an 11–3 win over the Astros on April 26, 1987, by knocking in five runs with a pair of homers.

After homering with one man aboard earlier in the contest, Parker gave the Reds a 7–6 win over the Giants on June 8, 1987, by delivering a two-run single in the bottom of the ninth inning.

Parker proved to be the difference in an 8–4 win over the Expos on July 23, 1987, knocking in six runs with a homer, double, and single.

Parker again hit safely three times, homered, and knocked in six runs during a 15–5 win over the Padres on July 29, 1987.

Parker contributed to a 21–6 rout of the Braves on September 15, 1987, by going 5-for-5 with two homers, a double, eight RBIs, and four runs scored.

Notable Achievements

- Hit more than 30 home runs twice, topping 20 homers another time.
- Knocked in more than 100 runs twice.
- Batted over .300 once.
- Posted slugging percentage over .500 once.
- Posted OPS over .900 once.
- Topped 30 doubles twice.
- Led NL in RBIs once, doubles once, extra-base hits once, and total bases twice.
- Finished second in NL in home runs twice, RBIs once, hits once, and slugging percentage once.
- Three-time NL Player of the Week.
- May 1985 NL Player of the Month.

- Two-time Silver Slugger Award winner (1985 and 1986).
- Three-time Reds team MVP (1984, 1985, and 1986).
- Finished in top five of NL MVP voting twice, placing as high as second in 1985.
- Two-time NL All-Star selection (1985 and 1986).
- Two-time Sporting News NL All-Star selection (1985 and 1986).

22

JAKE BECKLEY

Second all-time only to Eddie Murray in games played at first base, Jake Beckley recorded more putouts at that post than any other player in MLB history over the course of a 20-year big-league career that included stints with five different teams. A member of the Reds for parts of seven seasons, Beckley batted well over .300 for them six times, en route to compiling the third-highest batting average in team annals. An excellent line-drive hitter who possessed the ability to drive the ball deep into the outfield gaps, Beckley, who plied his trade in Cincinnati at the turn of the 20th century, also finished second in the NL in home runs once and collected at least 10 triples five times during his time in the Queen City, adding to the outstanding numbers that eventually earned him a place in Cooperstown.

Born in Hannibal, Missouri, on August 4, 1867, Jacob Peter Beckley grew up on a farm in Shelby County, just a few miles west of the Mississippi River town that Mark Twain made famous. After getting his start in organized ball playing for several semipro teams in the area, Beckley turned pro at the age of 18 when he joined the Leavenworth Oilers of the Western Association. Beckley subsequently split the next two seasons between Leavenworth and another Western League team in Lincoln, Nebraska, manning multiple positions, before settling in at first base. After being sold to the St. Louis Whites of the Western Association at the end of 1887, Beckley remained in Missouri for just two months, before the National League's Pittsburgh Alleghenies purchased him from the Whites for $4,500 midway through the 1888 campaign.

Still only 20 years old, Beckley performed well in his first big-league season, batting .343, driving in 27 runs, and scoring 35 times in just 71 games and 283 official at-bats. Beckley followed that up by batting .301, hitting nine homers, knocking in 97 runs, and scoring 91 times in 1889, establishing himself in the process as the best player on a team that finished 10 games under .500.

Jake Beckley batted over .300 for the Reds six times.

Offered more money by the Pittsburgh Burghers of the newly formed Players League at the end of 1889, Beckley chose to join several of his teammates in leaving the Alleghenies, saying at the time, "I'm only in this game for the money anyway." But after batting .323, driving in 123 runs, scoring 110 times, and belting a league-leading 22 triples in 1890, Beckley rejoined the Alleghenies (soon to be renamed the Pirates) when the Players League folded at the end of the year.

Beckley subsequently remained in Pittsburgh for the next five-and-a-half years, playing some of the best ball of his career for the Pirates. In addition to batting over .300, posting an OPS well over .800, and knocking in more than 100 runs three times each, Beckley scored more than 100 runs four times and amassed 19 triples five straight times, while also leading all players at his position in putouts three times and assists on four separate occasions. But, with Beckley struggling at the plate during the first half of the 1896 season, the Pirates traded him to the New York Giants on July 25. Released by the Giants on May 22, 1897, after failing to regain his stroke, Beckley signed with the Reds five days later, in what proved to be a coup by the Queen City's NL representative.

Experiencing a rebirth in Cincinnati, Beckley batted .345, posted an OPS of .894, knocked in 76 runs, and scored 76 others over the final four months of the 1897 campaign, before batting .294, compiling an OPS of .764, driving in 72 runs, and scoring 86 times in only 118 games the following year. Beckley then had his two most productive seasons for the Reds in 1899 and 1900, knocking in 99 runs, scoring 87 times, batting .333, and ranking among the league leaders with 16 triples in the first of those campaigns, before driving in 94 runs, scoring 98 times, batting .341, and collecting a career-high 190 hits in the second.

Despite never hitting more than 10 home runs in a season, the solidly built Beckley, who stood 5'10" and weighed 200 pounds, possessed a powerful left-handed swing that enabled him to consistently place near the top of the league rankings in doubles and triples. Nicknamed "Eagle Eye" for his batting prowess, Beckley never struck out more than 46 times in a season his entire career, fanning a total of only 157 times in almost 4,000 total plate appearances during his time in Cincinnati. An exceptional bunter, Beckley had the ability to lay down a sacrifice bunt by holding the thicker end of the bat and contacting the ball with the bat's handle (a now-illegal practice). And even though Beckley lacked superior running speed, he ran the bases well, stealing at least 20 bags in a season on eight separate occasions, including four times as a member of the Reds. An extremely capable fielder as well, the left-handed-throwing Beckley possessed good range and quick reflexes around the bag, with his only weakness being his poor throwing arm, which often allowed runners to take an extra base on him. Nevertheless, in addition to leading all NL first basemen in putouts six times, Beckley led all players at his position in assists four times and double plays turned twice.

One of the game's quirkier players, Beckley occasionally attempted to bend the rules, once running almost directly from second base to home and sliding in without a throw. However, even though the umpire failed to take notice of Beckley's devious maneuver, he called him out, yelling at him, "You big son of a bitch, you got here too fast!" Beckley also enjoyed employing the hidden-ball trick, attempting it on every new player who entered the league. Either hiding the ball in his clothing, under his armpit, or under the base sack, Beckley waited for the unsuspecting runner to wander off first base before applying the tag to him.

Despite suffering an early-season beaning that knocked him unconscious for more than five minutes, Beckley had another solid year in 1901, batting .307 with 79 RBIs, 78 runs scored, 13 triples, and 36 doubles. Beckley continued to perform well for the Reds the next two seasons, totaling 150 RBIs and 167 runs scored, while posting batting averages of .330 and .327. But, with second-year player/manager Joe Kelley wanting to move from the outfield to first base, the Reds sold Beckley to the St. Louis Cardinals following the conclusion of the 1903 campaign.

Beckley, who, during his time in Cincinnati, hit 26 homers, knocked in 570 runs, scored 592 times, collected 1,126 hits, 178 doubles, and 77 triples, stole 114 bases, batted .325, compiled an on-base percentage of .375, and posted a slugging percentage of .443, ended up spending the next four seasons in St. Louis, batting .325 for the Cardinals in 1904, before being released by them on June 15, 1907. Following his release by the Cardinals, Beckley spent three years playing in the minor leagues, before finally retiring as an active player in 1911.

Beckley, who, in addition to recording the most putouts of any player in MLB history (23,767), ended his big-league career with 87 home runs, 1,581 RBIs, 1,603 runs scored, 2,938 hits, 473 doubles, 244 triples, 315 stolen bases, a .308 batting average, a .361 on-base percentage, and a .436 slugging percentage, briefly returned to his hometown of Hannibal following his retirement, before moving to Kansas City, where he spent the next several years operating a grain business. Beckley also served as a baseball coach at William Jewell College in nearby Liberty, Missouri, and spent one season umpiring for the independent Federal League.

Suffering from a weak heart, Beckley passed away at only 50 years of age on June 25, 1918. More than 50 years later, the members of the Veterans Committee elected him to the Baseball Hall of Fame, with Beckley officially gaining induction on August 9, 1971, as part of a class that also included legendary Negro League hurler Satchel Paige.

REDS CAREER HIGHLIGHTS

Best Season

Beckley posted extremely comparable numbers in 1899 and 1900, finishing with a few more RBIs (99–94) and triples (16–10) in the first of those campaigns, while scoring more runs (98–87) and collecting more hits (190–172) in the second. But, with Beckley compiling a significantly higher OPS (.856–.822) and the Reds winning 21 more games as a team in 1899, we'll identify that as his finest season in Cincinnati.

Memorable Moments/Greatest Performances

Beckley led the Reds to a 10–4 win in the first game of their doubleheader sweep of the St. Louis Browns on September 26, 1897, by becoming the first player in franchise history to hit three homers in one game.

Beckley accomplished the rare feat of collecting three triples in one game during a 5–4 victory over the Boston Beaneaters on May 19, 1898.

Beckley helped lead the Reds to a 7–4 win over the Pirates on August 3, 1901, by going 3-for-6 with a homer, double, two RBIs, and three runs scored.

Beckley nearly hit for the cycle on August 5, 2001, when he went 3-for-4 with a homer, triple, single, four RBIs, and three runs scored during a 10–7 win over the Chicago Orphans (Cubs).

Beckley contributed to a lopsided 14–4 victory over the Cardinals on April 26, 1902, by going 4-for-5 with a homer, stolen base, two RBIs, and two runs scored.

Beckley had another big day against the Cardinals on August 30, 1902, going 4-for-5 with a double, stolen base, one RBI, and three runs scored during a 13–2 Reds win.

Notable Achievements

- Batted over .300 six times, topping the .320 mark on five occasions.
- Finished in double digits in triples five times.
- Topped 30 doubles once.
- Stole at least 20 bases four times.
- Hit three home runs in one game vs. St. Louis Browns on September 26, 1897.
- Finished second in NL in home runs once.

- Led NL first basemen in putouts twice and double plays turned twice.
- Holds MLB career record for most putouts (23,767).
- Ranks fourth in MLB history with 244 career triples.
- Ranks among Reds career leaders in batting average (3rd) and triples (10th).
- Elected to Baseball Hall of Fame by members of Veterans Committee in 1971.

23

PAUL DERRINGER

A hard-throwing right-hander who became known for his high leg-kick, pinpoint control, and volatile temperament, Paul Derringer spent parts of 10 seasons in Cincinnati, recording the second most starts and the third most victories of any pitcher in franchise history during that time. After playing for losing ballclubs his first five years in the Queen City, Derringer emerged as one of the central figures on teams that won two pennants and one World Series, earning a victory over Detroit in the decisive seventh game of the 1940 Fall Classic. A four-time 20-game winner, Derringer also compiled an ERA under 3.00 twice, completed at least 20 of his starts four times, and threw more than 300 innings twice, earning in the process six All-Star selections and two top-five finishes in the NL MVP voting, before going to Chicago, where he spent his final three big-league seasons with the Cubs.

Born in the small town of Springfield, Kentucky, on October 17, 1906, Samuel Paul Derringer grew up some 55 miles southwest of Lexington, not far from where the parents of Abraham Lincoln lived. The son of a tobacco farmer and former semipro baseball player who turned down an offer from the NL's Louisville Colonels to remain on his farm, Derringer starred in multiple sports at Springfield High School, excelling in football, basketball, and baseball. Originally a catcher on the diamond, Derringer gradually transitioned to the mound, where he performed so well that the St. Louis Cardinals signed him right out of high school.

Beginning his pro career in 1927 with the Danville Veterans of the Three-I League, Derringer compiled an overall record of 25–19 for them over the course of the next two seasons, before moving on to Rochester, where, after going 17–12 in 1929, he won 23 games the following year. Promoted to the parent club in 1931 at the expense of Dizzy Dean, who Cardinals GM Branch Rickey returned to the minors instead, Derringer had an excellent year for the eventual world champions, compiling a record of 18–8 and an ERA of 3.36, while ranking among the league leaders with

Paul Derringer recorded the third most wins of any pitcher in team annals.

134 strikeouts and four shutouts. But after losing both his starts and posting an ERA of 4.26 against the Philadelphia Athletics in the World Series, Derringer continued to struggle in 1932, going just 11–14 with a 4.05 ERA. With Derringer subsequently dropping his first two decisions in 1933, the Cardinals completed a trade with the Reds on May 7 that sent the 26-year-old right-hander, veteran infielder Sparky Adams, and relief pitcher Allyn Stout to Cincinnati for shortstop Leo Durocher and pitchers Dutch Henry and Jack Ogden.

Although Derringer pitched fairly well upon his arrival in Cincinnati, compiling an ERA of 3.23 and throwing 16 complete games over the final five months of the campaign, the failures of the last-place Reds as a team doomed him to an overall mark of 7–27 that left him just two defeats shy of the modern NL record for most losses in a season that Boston's Vic Willis set in 1905. Following a mediocre 1934 campaign in which he went 15–21 with a 3.59 ERA, Derringer established himself as one of the NL's best pitchers in 1935, earning All-Star honors for the first time by compiling a record of 22–13, an ERA of 3.51, and a WHIP of 1.243, while ranking among the league leaders with 120 strikeouts, three shutouts, 20 complete games, and 276⅔ innings pitched. Despite winning 19 games and throwing 282⅓ innings the following year, Derringer pitched somewhat less effectively, tasting defeat 19 times, while compiling an ERA of 4.02. Derringer subsequently went just 10–14 with a 4.04 ERA in 1937, before beginning an outstanding three-year run during which he posted the following numbers:

YEAR	W-L	ERA	SO	SHO	CG	IP	WHIP
1938	21-14	2.93	132	4	**26**	**307.0**	1.186
1939	25-7	2.93	128	5	28	301.0	1.183
1940	20-12	3.06	115	3	26	296.2	1.106

Rivaling teammate Bucky Walters as the NL's finest pitcher over that three-year stretch, Derringer finished either first or second in the league in complete games, innings pitched, and wins all three years, while also placing second in WHIP twice and strikeouts and shutouts once each. An NL All-Star each season, Derringer also earned one *Sporting News* MLB All-Star nomination and three top-10 finishes in the league MVP voting, placing in the top five of the balloting twice. Meanwhile, the Reds won the NL pennant in both 1939 and 1940 and defeated the Detroit Tigers in seven games in the 1940 World Series, with Derringer posting victories in Games 4 and 7. And even though Derringer failed to defeat the Yankees in the 1939 Fall Classic, he pitched well in his two starts, compiling an ERA of 2.35 and yielding just nine hits in 15⅓ innings of work, while recording nine strikeouts.

One of the NL's hardest throwers, the 6'3", 205-pound Derringer possessed a blazing fastball that he delivered to home plate with an exceptionally high leg-kick that saw him raise his front (left) leg so high that it nearly touched his glove. Despite his unorthodox delivery, Derringer had tremendous command of his pitches, which also included an excellent curve and a rarely used knuckleball. Nicknamed "The Control King," Derringer led all NL hurlers in strikeouts-to-walks ratio and fewest bases on balls allowed per nine innings pitched twice each, issuing a total of only 761 free passes in 3,645 innings of work over the course of his career.

In discussing Derringer in Rick Van Blair's 1994 book *Dugout to Foxhole: Interviews with Baseball Players Whose Careers Were Affected by World War II*, former Phillies third baseman Pinky May said, "Paul Derringer had a great curveball. He rolled that curveball right off the table and had a good fastball, too. If I had to pick the toughest pitcher I ever hit against, it would be Paul Derringer."

While Derringer had great command of his pitches, he often failed to display the same control over his emotions. Quick to anger, Derringer frequently manifested his rage in a violent manner, doing so on one occasion at the expense of Reds general manager Larry MacPhail. With MacPhail in the middle of a lengthy tirade against him for failing to slide on a close play at home plate, Derringer grew weary of the tongue-lashing, picked up an inkwell on the GM's desk, and threw it at him, barely missing his head. After a stunned MacPhail said, "You might have killed me, Derringer," the latter responded, "That's what I was meaning to do." The equally excitable MacPhail subsequently took out his checkbook and made out a $750 check to Derringer with a note that read, "Thank you for missing my head." Derringer also once engaged in an on-field brawl with former Cardinals teammate and longtime antagonist Dizzy Dean that resulted in both men being ejected from the contest.

Derringer's days as a big winner ended in 1941, when he went just 12–14 with a 3.31 ERA. Nevertheless, he pitched well enough to earn his fourth straight All-Star selection, before being similarly honored the following year, when he compiled a record of 10–11 and an ERA of 3.06. Sold to the Cubs following the conclusion of the 1942 campaign, Derringer ended up spending three years in Chicago, posting an overall mark of 33–38 during that time, before announcing his retirement with a career record of 223–212, an ERA of 3.46, a WHIP of 1.282, 251 complete games, 32 shutouts, 29 saves, and 1,507 strikeouts in 3,645 total innings of work. Over parts of 10 seasons in Cincinnati, Derringer compiled a record of 161–150, an ERA of 3.36, and a WHIP of 1.241, threw 189 complete games and 24 shutouts, collected 17 saves, and struck out 1,062 batters in 2,615⅓ innings pitched.

Following his playing days, Derringer, who spent his offseasons working in the drugstore business with his brother-in-law in West Frankfort, Illinois, became a plastics salesman and worked as a troubleshooter for the

American Automobile Association. Inducted into the Reds Hall of Fame in 1958, Derringer lived until November 17, 1987, when he died in Sarasota, Florida, one month after turning 81 years of age. Said to be destitute at the time of his passing, Derringer left behind one daughter and his third wife.

REDS CAREER HIGHLIGHTS

Best Season

Although Derringer perhaps pitched just as well the previous year, his third-place finish in the NL MVP voting and career-best 25 victories, .781 winning percentage, 2.93 ERA, and 28 complete games in 1939 made that his most impactful season.

Memorable Moments/Greatest Performances

Derringer won a 1–0 pitchers' duel with Cardinals Hall of Fame hurler Jesse Haines on August 6, 1933, yielding just three hits and one walk over 12 innings.

Derringer started and won the first night game ever played in the major leagues on May 24, 1935, earning a 2–1 complete-game victory over the Phillies at Crosley Field by allowing just six hits and one run.

Derringer shut out the Pirates on just three hits on May 10, 1936, walking no one and striking out five during a 6–0 Reds win.

Although Derringer allowed four runs on nine hits over the first eight innings of a 6–4 win over the Cubs on August 20, 1937, he knocked in five runs with a single and two doubles.

Derringer yielded just three hits and one walk during a 5–0 shutout of the Cardinals on April 25, 1938.

In addition to throwing a complete-game five-hitter on July 26, 1938, Derringer hit the first of his two career homers off Boston starter Jim Turner during a 6–2 win over the Bees.

Derringer reached the seats again during a 9–1 victory over the Cubs on August 18, 1938, this time homering off Chicago starter Charlie Root with one man aboard.

Derringer tossed a one-hit shutout on May 26, 1940, yielding just two walks and a first-inning single to St. Louis third baseman Stu Martin during a 4–0 win over the Cardinals.

Derringer threw another one-hit shutout on July 6, 1940, with only Cubs third baseman Stan Hack reaching base against him with a walk and a sixth-inning single during a 4–0 Reds win.

Derringer surrendered just two hits during a 6–1 complete-game victory over the Giants on July 21, 1940, with one of New York's safeties coming on an eighth-inning home run by first baseman Babe Young.

Derringer gave the Reds their second world championship by yielding seven hits and just one unearned run during a complete-game 2–1 victory over the Tigers in Game 7 of the 1940 World Series.

Although an unearned run scored by the Dodgers in the top of the 16th inning doomed him to defeat, Derringer displayed his mettle by working all 16 innings of a 2–1 loss to Brooklyn on June 22, 1941.

Notable Achievements

- Won at least 20 games four times.
- Posted winning percentage over .700 once.
- Compiled ERA under 3.00 twice.
- Threw at least 20 complete games four times.
- Threw more than 300 innings twice, tossing more than 250 frames four other times.
- Led NL pitchers in winning percentage once, complete games once, innings pitched once, and starts three times.
- Finished second in NL in wins three times, WHIP twice, strikeouts once, shutouts once, complete games twice, and innings pitched twice.
- Ranks among Reds career leaders in wins (3rd), innings pitched (3rd), complete games (5th), shutouts (tied for 5th), strikeouts (9th), pitching appearances (tied for 9th), and games started (2nd).
- Two-time NL champion (1939 and 1940).
- 1940 world champion.
- Finished in top 10 of NL MVP voting three times, placing in the top five twice.
- Six-time NL All-Star selection (1935, 1938, 1939, 1940, 1941, and 1942).
- 1940 *Sporting News* MLB All-Star selection.

24

SEAN CASEY

One of the most popular players ever to don a Reds uniform, Sean Casey spent eight seasons in Cincinnati endearing himself to everyone with whom he came into contact with his friendly demeanor, engaging personality, and giving nature. Nicknamed "The Mayor" because of his enthusiasm for meeting and helping others, Casey proved to be one of baseball's best ambassadors through his determination to assist his teammates and community in any way possible. An excellent on-field performer as well, Casey earned three All-Star nominations by batting over .300 five times, hitting at least 20 homers three times, scoring more than 100 runs twice, and posting an OPS over .900 on three separate occasions, before leaving the Queen City and splitting his final three seasons between the Pirates, Tigers, and Red Sox.

Born in Willingboro, New Jersey, on July 2, 1974, Sean Thomas Casey moved with his parents and older sister at an early age to Upper St. Clair Township, Pennsylvania, where he learned to play baseball on the local sandlots. A right-handed thrower but left-handed batter, Casey often practiced his swing at home by hitting a tethered ball into a net in the garage, before further developing his stroke during his teenage years at the Bethel Park Grand Slam batting cages

Eventually developing into a star on the diamond at Upper St. Clair High School, Casey helped lead the Panthers to the Western Pennsylvania Interscholastic Athletic League championship as a senior in 1992, prompting John Carroll University, a small Division III school near Cleveland, to offer him a baseball scholarship. Seeking a better offer, Casey politely declined and wrote to several larger institutions, including Penn State, Notre Dame, and Clemson. However, with only the University of Richmond responding, Casey accepted a $1,000 annual scholarship to a school with a yearly tuition of $22,000.

Excelling at first base for the Richmond Spiders the next three years, Casey earned Freshman All-America honors in 1993 by batting

Sean Casey earned three All-Star nominations during his time in Cincinnati.

.386 and posting an on-base percentage of .447, before gaining First-Team All-Colonial Athletic Association (CAA) recognition the following year by compiling a batting average of .371. Even better his junior year, Casey became the first CAA player to win the Triple Crown, earning in the process Second-Team All-America and Eastern College Athletic Conference (ECAC) Player of the Year honors. While in college, Casey also spent one season playing for the Brewster (Massachusetts) Whitecaps in the Cape Cod Baseball League, whose manager, Mike Kirby, nicknamed him "The Mayor" for his willingness to talk to and shake hands with many of the people in the stands each game.

With Casey having posted a composite batting average of .405 and driven in 158 runs in 158 games at Richmond, he decided to leave school after his junior year when the Cleveland Indians selected him in the second round of the June 1995 MLB Amateur Draft, with the 53rd overall pick. Casey subsequently spent most of the next three seasons advancing through Cleveland's farm system, performing well at each stop, before making a brief appearance with the parent club during the latter stages of the 1997 campaign. But with star first baseman Jim Thome blocking Casey's path to the big leagues, Cleveland traded him to the Reds for veteran right-handed pitcher Dave Burba just prior to the start of the 1998 regular season.

Casey's time in Cincinnati began ominously when a throw from a teammate during batting practice on April 2 struck him just below the right eye, causing him to be placed on a stretcher and taken to a local hospital, where doctors discovered that his orbital bone had been shattered. Unable to see clearly the next few weeks after undergoing surgery, Casey had to come to terms with the fact that he might never play baseball again. But, remarkably, after beginning rehabilitation and taking batting practice with his former hitting coach, Frank Porco, Casey found that the vision in his once-injured eye had improved to 20/10. Commenting on his protégé's amazing recovery, Porco said at the time, "A miracle took place. . . . I talked to a doctor. . . . You've got a better chance to win the lottery than to have your eyesight improve in that kind of surgery. One in a hundred million."

Rejoining the Reds a little over one month after sustaining his near-career-ending injury, Casey ended up hitting seven homers, driving in 52 runs, batting .272, and posting an OPS of .782, in 96 games and 351 total plate appearances his first year in Cincinnati.

Beginning the 1999 season as the Reds' starting first baseman, Casey went on to establish himself as one of the NL's better all-around hitters, earning All-Star honors by hitting 25 homers, knocking in 99 runs, scoring 103 times, compiling an OPS of .938, and ranking among the league leaders with 197 hits, 42 doubles, and a .332 batting average. Casey followed that up with two more solid seasons, hitting 20 homers, driving in 85 runs, batting .315, and posting an OPS of .902 in 2000, before gaining All-Star recognition again in 2001 by reaching the seats 13 times, knocking in 89 runs, batting .310, and compiling an OPS of .827.

Although the left-handed-hitting Casey stood 6'4" and weighed 215 pounds, he rarely swung for the fences, preferring instead to make consistent contact with the ball and drive it to all fields. Regularly ranking among the league leaders in most at-bats per strikeout, Casey fanned more than 65 times in a season just twice his entire career, once striking out only 36 times in more than 600 total plate appearances. Meanwhile, Casey placed in the league's top-10 in batting average on three separate occasions, finishing as high as fourth in 1999.

As Casey rose to prominence in the Queen City for his contributions on the ballfield, he became known for his willingness to give of himself to others. Volunteering for several charitable causes, Casey became heavily involved with the Make-A-Wish Foundation, frequently visited the Cincinnati Children's Hospital and Shriners Hospital for Children, started "Casey's Crew," which provided 24 complimentary field-level tickets to disadvantaged youngsters for every Saturday home game, and participated with his wife, Mandi, in the Big Brothers/Big Sisters program.

Expressing his admiration for Casey as a person, Reds beat writer Hal McCoy commented, "There's no debate, and there never will be a debate. Sean Casey is the nicest guy in professional baseball. Ever."

Mandi Casey also spoke highly of her husband, saying, "Sean's integrity and sincerity are unquestioned. What you see is what you get."

Following an injury-marred 2002 campaign during which he hit just six homers, knocked in only 42 runs, and batted just .261, Casey rebounded somewhat in 2003, finishing the season with 14 homers, 80 RBIs, and a .291 batting average. Reestablishing himself as one of the league's top hitters in 2004, Casey earned team MVP honors and the last of his three All-Star nominations by hitting 24 homers, driving in 99 runs, scoring 101 times, collecting a career-high 44 doubles, batting .324, compiling an on-base percentage of .381, and posting a slugging percentage of .534.

Casey remained in Cincinnati for one more year, hitting nine homers, knocking in 58 runs, scoring 75 times, batting .312, posting an OPS of .795, and leading all NL first basemen with a .998 fielding percentage in 2005, before being traded to the Pirates the following offseason for pitcher David Williams.

Upon learning of the team's decision to part ways with him, Casey said, "That stinks. I want to play for the Cincinnati Reds. I don't want to go anywhere else. I love Cincinnati and the team and the fans and the charitable work I do here. . . . A piece of my heart will always be in Cincinnati."

Commenting on his teammate's impending departure, Reds outfielder Austin Kearns stated, "He was a leader in the clubhouse and out on the field. It's always a risk when you trade a guy like that."

Meanwhile, Kathy List, the executive director of Big Brothers/Big Sisters of Greater Cincinnati, called the trade "a loss for the Reds and a loss for the community."

Casey, who left the Reds having hit 118 homers, driven in 604 runs, scored 588 times, collected 1,223 hits, 256 doubles, and 11 triples, batted .305, compiled a .371 on-base percentage, and posted a .463 slugging percentage as a member of the team, ended up splitting the 2006 campaign between the Pirates and Tigers, hitting eight homers, knocking in 59 runs, and batting .272 for both teams. After posting a mark of .296 for Detroit in 2007, Casey signed as a free agent with the Red Sox, for whom he batted .322 in a part-time role in 2008, before announcing his retirement at the end of the year. Over parts of 12 big-league seasons, Casey hit 130 homers, knocked in 735 runs, scored 690 times, amassed 1,531 hits, 322 doubles, and 12 triples, batted .302, compiled a .367 on-base percentage, and posted a .447 slugging percentage.

Following his playing days, Casey, who has two sons and two daughters, accepted an analyst position with the MLB Network, saying at the time, "This is a way to stay in the game and to shift to my number one priority—spending more time with my family."

After surviving a life-threatening blood clot that split and entered both lungs in January 2014, Casey continued to serve as a baseball analyst until July 10, 2023, when the Yankees hired him as their hitting coach. Casey remained in that post until the end of the year, when he rejoined MLB Network.

REDS CAREER HIGHLIGHTS

Best Season

Casey posted nearly identical numbers in 1999 and 2004, ranking among the league leaders in batting average, hits, and doubles both years, while also hitting nearly the same number of homers, knocking in 99 runs, and scoring just over 100 times each season. Ultimately, the Reds' close second-place finish in the NL Central Division in the first of those campaigns, which helped Casey garner his lone top-20 selection in the league MVP voting (he finished 14th), prompted me to identify 1999 as his finest season in Cincinnati.

Memorable Moments/Greatest Performances

Casey helped lead the Reds to a 24–12 win over the Rockies on May 19, 1999, by going 4-for-4 with two homers, three walks, six RBIs, and five runs scored.

Casey led the Reds to a 9–4 win over the Royals on June 5, 1999, by homering twice and driving in five runs.

Casey continued his hot-hitting the next day, going 5-for-6 with a double, two RBIs, and three runs scored during a 14–3 win over Kansas City.

Casey contributed to an 8–2 victory over the Pirates on April 9, 2001, by going 4-for-4 with a homer, double, five RBIs, and two runs scored.

Casey gave the Reds a 2–1 win over the Astros on August 18, 2002, when he hit a solo homer off reliever Ricky Stone with one man out in the bottom of the 10th inning.

Casey led the Reds to a 6–4 win over the Mets on June 23, 2004, by going 5-for-6 with two homers and four RBIs, with his two-run blast off John Franco in the top of the 12th inning providing the margin of victory.

Casey starred in defeat on May 18, 2005, going a perfect 5-for-5 with a homer, double, four RBIs, and two runs scored during a 10–6 loss to the Mets.

Notable Achievements

- Surpassed 20 home runs three times.
- Scored more than 100 runs twice.
- Batted over .300 five times, topping the .320 mark twice.
- Posted slugging percentage over .500 three times.
- Posted OPS over .900 three times.
- Topped 30 doubles five times, surpassing 40 two-baggers on three occasions.
- Led NL first basemen with .998 fielding percentage in 2005.
- 2004 Reds team MVP.
- Three-time NL All-Star selection (1999, 2001, and 2004).

25

ADAM DUNN

One of only two players in franchise history to reach the 40-homer plateau in consecutive seasons, Adam Dunn accomplished the feat four straight times from 2004 to 2007, establishing himself in the process as one of the game's top sluggers. A member of the Reds for parts of eight seasons, Dunn also knocked in more than 100 runs three times, drew more than 100 bases on balls five times, and posted an OPS over .900 on four separate occasions, before being dealt to the Arizona Diamondbacks in August 2008. Yet despite his tremendous slugging, Dunn often found himself being criticized for his high strikeout totals, below-average defense, and what some perceived to be a lackadaisical attitude, making him very much a polarizing figure during his time in Cincinnati.

Born in Houston, Texas, on November 9, 1979, Adam Troy Dunn grew up some 40 miles north, in the town of Porter, where he learned how to play baseball at an early age from his father, who taught him how to hit from the left side of the plate even though he did everything else right-handed. Eventually developing into a star in multiple sports at nearby New Caney High School, Dunn excelled in both baseball and football, performing so well at quarterback on the gridiron that several major college programs recruited him as graduation neared. Ultimately choosing the University of Texas over Tennessee, Texas A&M, and Notre Dame, Dunn committed to play quarterback for the Longhorns, causing every major-league team to bypass him in the first round of the June 1998 MLB Amateur Draft.

Recalling how his decision affected his draft stock, Dunn said, "That's what I let everyone know, that I was going to play football, but I'd like to play baseball, too. I guess that scared a lot of teams off."

Nevertheless, with Dunn considered a top prospect in baseball as well, the Reds selected him in the second round, with Johnny Almaraz, the team's assistant director of scouting at the time, remembering, "He threw 94 miles

Adam Dunn hit at least 40 home runs for the Reds four straight times.

an hour, he ran four-flat down the line, and he could hit a ball 400 feet. His power was unbelievable."

After agreeing with the Reds on a deal that allowed him to play minor-league ball during the summer and return to Austin in August to prepare for the football season, Dunn redshirted his freshman year at Texas while serving as a backup to starting QB Major Applewhite. But when the Longhorns coaching staff asked him to move to tight end following the signing of star recruit Chris Simms prior to the start of his sophomore season, Dunn chose to concentrate solely on baseball, later saying, "College football is brutal. If you're not kissing the right person's ass, you're done. I figured I might as well play baseball, make money, and have fun."

Dunn subsequently spent the next two-and-a-half years in the minor leagues, before joining the Reds in late-July 2001 after hitting 32 homers, driving in 84 runs, and posting a composite batting average of .334 for Double-A Chattanooga and Triple-A Louisville over the first four months of the campaign. Continuing his hot hitting following his arrival in Cincinnati, Dunn hit 19 homers, knocked in 43 runs, batted .262, and compiled an OPS of .948 in 66 games and 286 total plate appearances with the parent club, earning in the process a fourth-place finish in the NL Rookie of the Year voting.

Impressed with Dunn's strong performance, Reds manager Bob Boone stated at the end of the year, "Very few guys have ever come up and dominated as Adam did. In five or six years I believe he'll be in a class with Sosa, Bonds, and Helton."

Splitting the ensuing campaign between left field and first base, Dunn earned All-Star honors by hitting 26 homers, driving in 71 runs, scoring 84 times, drawing 128 bases on balls, compiling an on-base percentage of .400, and posting a slugging percentage of .454, although he also batted just .249 and finished second in the league with 170 strikeouts. Less productive in 2003, Dunn homered 27 times but knocked in only 57 runs and batted just .215, with his season coming to a premature end in mid-August when he sprained his thumb while attempting a diving catch in the outfield. Playing left field almost exclusively the next four years, Dunn established himself as a premier power hitter by posting the following numbers:

YEAR	HR	RBI	RUNS	BB	AVG	OBP	SLG	OPS
2004	46	102	105	108	.266	.388	.569	.956
2005	40	101	107	114	.247	.387	.540	.927
2006	40	92	99	112	.234	.365	.490	.855
2007	40	106	101	101	.264	.386	.554	.940

In addition to ranking among the NL leaders in homers all four years, Dunn placed near the top of the league rankings in walks each season, enabling him to compile very respectable on-base percentages despite his rather mediocre batting averages. Unfortunately, Dunn also led both leagues in strikeouts in three of those four seasons, setting a new major-league record (since broken) by fanning 195 times in 2004. Yet, despite his high strikeout totals, Dunn exhibited good plate discipline, rarely swinging at bad pitches, and averaging more pitches per time at-bat than almost anyone else in either league.

Dunn's greatest strength as a hitter, though, proved to be his ability to reach the seats. Blessed with tremendous power to all fields, the left-handed-swinging Dunn, who stood 6'6" and weighed 285 pounds, had the ability to hit the ball out of any part of the ballpark, delivering the longest home run in the history of Great American Ball Park on August 10, 2004, when he drove a pitch from Los Angeles Dodgers right-hander José Lima some 535 feet over the batter's eye in center field, onto Mehring Way, and into a section of the Ohio River that is considered part of Kentucky.

Commenting on his teammate's ability to alter the outcome of a game with one swing of the bat, Sean Casey told John McMurray of *Baseball Digest* in September 2005, "He's one of those special talents who comes around once every 20 years, you know what I mean? Adam is someone who really changes a game and can hit the ball as far as anybody in the league."

An extremely down-to-earth person who appreciated the simple things in life, Dunn very much enjoyed playing in Cincinnati his first few years in the league, telling Jeff Pearlman of *Sports Illustrated* in 2005, "Cincinnati is the perfect fit for me. It's a small city, and I've met a lot of good people who like to fish. For me, New York or Los Angeles would be more difficult. I'm a small-town guy and moving to a huge city might be an adjustment."

However, Dunn grew increasingly uncomfortable in what he came to view as his second home after he began to receive criticism for his subpar defensive play, prolonged slumps, and penchant for striking out. In addressing his tendency to perform poorly at the plate for extended periods of time, Dunn stated, "When I'm going bad, I'm the worst player in the league. There's no arguing that. When I'm in that little funk that I get in, you know, every year for 'x' amount of times, I'm the worst in the league."

When asked if his strikeouts bothered him, Dunn responded, "It depends on when, you know. If it's the first inning, two outs, nobody on, you know I'm not going to lie to you, I'm trying to get in the seats. And you know if I strike out, okay, whatever; but if there are guys, runners in scoring position, things like that, and you strike out too, that, to me, that's bad."

Unable to provide a reasonable explanation for his subpar defense, Dunn had to accept the fact that he led all NL left fielders in errors four times and, despite his above-average foot speed, lacked the quickness, agility, and instincts to ever establish himself as anything more than a marginal defensive outfielder.

Also censured by some for a perceived lack of interest in the game, Dunn drew particularly harsh criticism from longtime Reds announcer

Marty Brennaman, who said of him in 2007, "I think he was overweight last year. He walks to his position. He walks off the field. You see no energy whatsoever, and that disappoints the heck out of me."

Brennaman also criticized Dunn for his inability to hit in the clutch, saying, "He homers, but he doesn't drive in runs."

Eligible for free agency following the conclusion of the 2008 campaign, Dunn hit 32 homers, knocked in 74 runs, batted .233, and compiled an OPS of .901 over the season's first 114 games, before the Reds traded him to the Diamondbacks on August 11 for minor-league pitcher Dallas Buck and two players to be named later.

Commenting on Dunn's impending departure upon learning of the deal, Reds manager Dusty Baker said, "It's tougher to lose a good guy, you know, than the 40-home-run guy. It's going to be tough to replace his offense, but it's even tougher to replace the man."

Meanwhile, with the Reds on their way to a fifth-place finish in the NL Central, Dunn stated, "It was one of those pleasant surprises. To come off the terrible month that we had in Cincinnati, and you get a phone call today saying you're being traded to a first-place team. As a player, that's all you could ask for."

Finishing out the year in Arizona, Dunn, who left Cincinnati with career totals of 270 home runs, 646 RBIs, 678 runs scored, 920 hits, 192 doubles, eight triples, and 58 stolen bases, a .247 batting average, a .380 on-base percentage, and a .520 slugging percentage, reached the seats another eight times, giving him at least 40 home runs for the fifth straight season. Dunn also knocked in 26 more runs, enabling him to surpass the 100-RBI mark for the fourth time in his career.

Nevertheless, Dunn continued to be the target of negative comments after he hit the free agent market at the end of the year, with Toronto Blue Jays GM J. P. Ricciardi responding to a question about the possibility of his team acquiring the power-hitting outfielder by saying, "Do you know the guy doesn't really like baseball that much? Do you know the guy doesn't have a passion to play the game that much? How much do you know about the player? There's a reason why you're attracted to some players, and there's a reason why you're not attracted to some players. I don't think you'd be very happy if we brought Adam Dunn here."

However, Washington Nationals general manager Mike Rizzo felt differently, stating, "Dunn was the most misunderstood player I have heard about in recent memory. The way he was misconstrued (in Cincinnati) was almost unbelievable. He plays banged up. He'd go out there 162 games if you'd let him. He's the most consistent player in the game the last six years."

Inked to a two-year deal by the Nationals, Dunn hit 38 homers and knocked in more than 100 runs in each of the next two seasons, before signing with the White Sox when he became a free agent again at the end of 2010. Dunn subsequently spent most of the next four seasons in Chicago, earning the last of his two All-Star nominations in 2012 by hitting 41 homers and driving in 96 runs, despite batting just .204 and leading the majors with 222 strikeouts. Dealt to the Athletics during the latter stages of the 2014 campaign, Dunn finished out the season in Oakland, before announcing his retirement at the end of the year with career totals of 462 homers, 1,168 RBIs, 1,097 runs scored, 1,631 hits, 334 doubles, 10 triples, 63 stolen bases, 1,317 walks, and 2,379 strikeouts, a lifetime batting average of .237, a .364 on-base percentage, and a .490 slugging percentage, with his 2,379 Ks placing him third on MLB's all-time strikeout list.

Following his playing days, Dunn moved back to his home state of Texas, where he currently resides with his family in the city of Houston. Inducted into the Reds Hall of Fame in 2018, Dunn said at the time, "In my opinion, obviously, the Reds Hall of Fame is second to only one, and that would be Cooperstown. Some of the greatest players to not only play for the Reds, but to ever play the game have been inducted into the Reds Hall of Fame. I can't put into words how big of an honor that is."

Dunn then added, "I was a kid. I grew up in Cincinnati, essentially. The relationships that I made will be lifelong. They lasted a lot longer than the baseball did. That's something that people can't take away."

REDS CAREER HIGHLIGHTS

Best Season

Dunn played his best ball for the Reds from 2004 to 2007, hitting at least 40 homers each year, while also surpassing 100 RBIs and 100 runs scored three times each. With Dunn posting his best overall numbers in 2004 and 2007, I opted to go with the first of those campaigns since, in addition to compiling a slightly higher OPS (.956–.940), Dunn hit six more homers (46–40), collected 13 more hits (151–138), and amassed 34 more total bases (323–289).

Memorable Moments/Greatest Performances

Dunn helped lead the Reds to an 8–5 win over the Rangers on June 11, 2002, by scoring three times and knocking in four runs with a double and a pair of homers.

Dunn provided much of the offensive firepower during a 7–5 win over the Brewers on May 11, 2003, going 3-for-4 with two homers and five RBIs.

Dunn delivered the decisive blow of a 7–6 win over the Braves on May 26, 2003, when he hit a pinch-hit grand slam home run in the top of the 11th inning.

After homering with no one on base earlier in the contest, Dunn gave the Reds a 6–3 win over the Montreal Expos on June 5, 2004, when he homered with two men out and two men on in the bottom of the 10th inning.

Dunn proved to be the difference in a 7–5 win over the Phillies on May 12, 2005, knocking in five runs with a pair of homers.

Dunn gave the Reds a dramatic 9–8 win over Cleveland on June 30, 2006, when he homered off reliever Bob Wickman with two men out and the bases loaded in the bottom of the ninth inning.

Notable Achievements

- Hit more than 20 home runs seven times, surpassing 40 homers on four occasions.
- Knocked in more than 100 runs three times.
- Scored more than 100 runs three times.
- Drew more than 100 bases on balls five times.
- Compiled on-base percentage of .400 once.
- Posted slugging percentage over .500 five times.
- Posted OPS over .900 four times.
- Topped 30 doubles twice.
- Finished second in NL in home runs once and walks once.
- Ranks among Reds career leaders in home runs (5th), bases on balls (7th), on-base percentage (8th), slugging percentage (2nd), and OPS (3rd).
- Two-time NL Player of the Week.
- July 2005 NL Player of the Month.
- 2002 NL All-Star selection.

26

JIM MALONEY

Known for his blazing fastball and ability to dominate the opposition on any given day, Jim Maloney spent parts of 11 seasons in Cincinnati, striking out more batters during that time than any other pitcher in franchise history, while also throwing two no-hitters, five one-hitters, and 10 two-hitters. The winner of at least 20 games twice, Maloney also compiled an ERA under 3.00 five times and recorded more than 200 strikeouts on four separate occasions, with his 265 Ks in 1963 representing the second-highest single-season total in team annals. A member of Reds teams that won two NL pennants, Maloney earned one All-Star nomination, before having his career shortened by injuries that robbed him of the chance to pitch for The Big Red Machine.

Born in Fresno, California, on June 2, 1940, James William Maloney grew up with his sister Jeanne in a typical post–World War II middle-class American family. The son of a former semiprofessional baseball player who later opened one of the largest used-car dealerships in Fresno, Maloney developed into quite an athlete himself at Fresno High School, excelling in baseball, basketball, and football. Particularly outstanding on the diamond, Maloney led the Warriors to three straight Northern Yosemite League championships by batting .310, .340, and .500 as the team's starting shortstop.

Scouted by all 16 major-league teams his senior year, Maloney received several contract offers following his graduation. However, even though Maloney rarely pitched in high school, Reds West Coast scout Bobby Mattick believed that he had the ability to develop into a great pitcher after watching him perform at a team tryout at Crosley Field. Heeding Mattick's advice, Maloney spent two semesters honing his pitching skills at UC Berkeley and Fresno City College, before signing with the Reds.

Recalling the events that transpired at the time, Maloney said, "There were 16 major-league teams that talked to my dad the night I graduated from high school. They were offering money in the range of $40,000 to $50,000. My dad said I was worth more money, so I didn't sign. I had a

Jim Maloney struck out more batters than anyone else in franchise history.

scholarship offer to Stanford, but my grades weren't quite good enough. They wanted me to go to a junior college, but my dad liked the coach at Cal—George Wolfman. I ended up going to Berkeley. I had a hard time there. I was in a fraternity, and there was lots of stuff going on. At the end of one semester, I figured I'd better go home. So, I went to Fresno City College."

Maloney continued, "I could have signed as an infielder or pitcher. Some teams wanted me to go as an infielder. I played shortstop in high school and rarely pitched. . . . Cincinnati wanted me as a pitcher, and they pursued me as a pitcher. . . . A lot of teams were offering me a bonus and a major league contract. I had just started at Fresno City College when Bobby Mattick sneaked into town. He told my dad the Reds had the money, and he was to sign the boy, and get him out of there. . . . We went down to Hotel California in Fresno. He had a room down there, so we ended up signing. I got a bonus and a major-league contract. I never had a minor-league contract. In those days, the minimum salary was $7,000, and the Reds offered me a major league contract for three years at $10,000 a year. I was going to make more than the minimum salary for three years, and they gave me a bonus. The whole thing was worth about a hundred grand. That was good money in 1959."

Initially sent to Tampa to briefly work out with the Reds at their spring training camp, Maloney remembered being somewhat starstruck at first, recounting, "When I went into the clubhouse, there were the guys that I'd read about in the sports magazines. There was Frank Robinson, Gus Bell, Wally Post, Vada Pinson, Ed Bailey, Roy McMillan, Ted Kluszewski, and some big guys. When I came up in spring training, Gus Bell and Wally Post took me under their wing. They told me to follow what they did, and to keep my mouth shut. It was like a fraternity hazing deal. I was in awe, took directions, and shut up."

Subsequently assigned to the Topeka Hawks in the Class B Illinois-Indiana-Iowa (Three-I) League, Maloney struggled at first, recalling, "I didn't have a clue how to pitch. I was just trying to throw my fastball past the hitters. They were rocking me around. I got a sore arm."

But Maloney eventually righted himself, with then-Hawks manager Johnny Vander Meer remembering, "Jim found himself the last month of the season. He was letting go of his fastball too quick, and he had numerous faults, which was natural for a kid who had such limited experience. He finished with a 6–7 record and 84 bases on balls in 124 innings."

Promoted to Nashville in the Double-A Southern Association in 1960, Maloney spent most of the year being tutored by pitching coach Jim Turner, recalling, "Turner started working with me from the day I reported for spring training. He talked about nothing but pitching and never stopped."

Maloney, who, with the help of Turner, learned how to relax on the mound, developed a curveball, and improved his control, added, "I threw a fastball, curve, and changeup. My changeup was mediocre. I sure would like to have learned how to throw that full circle change that they throw today. I didn't know anything about it. Turner had me change off the curveball. I threw a real hard curveball that was maybe three-quarters speed that acted like a changeup. That helped me. I used that in the big leagues. They did not have a speed gun in those days, but I'd say I was pitching close to 100 miles per hour on my fastball."

After earning Southern Association All-Star honors by compiling a record of 14–5 and an ERA of 2.80, Maloney joined the parent club in late July. Struggling somewhat in his first tour of duty at the major-league level, the 20-year-old Maloney went just 2–6 with a 4.66 ERA. Although Maloney subsequently remained with the Reds throughout the entirety of the 1961 campaign, he developed arm and shoulder problems during spring training that plagued him the rest of the year. Limited to just 27 appearances and 94⅔ innings, Maloney posted a record of 6–7 and an ERA of 4.37, while splitting his time between starting and relieving. Improving his performance dramatically the following year after becoming a regular member of the starting rotation in mid-June, Maloney finished the season with a record of 9–7 and an ERA of 3.51, while also striking out 105 batters in 115⅓ innings pitched. Finally reaching his full potential in 1963, Maloney established himself as one of the finest pitchers in the senior circuit by going 23–7 with a 2.77 ERA, setting a new club record (since broken) by striking out 265 batters, and throwing six shutouts, 13 complete games, and 250⅓ innings.

In explaining his transformation, Maloney later said, "When I first came up, I wasn't ready. I just wasn't mature enough to pitch in the big leagues. . . . Toward the end of the 1962 season, I started to really believe in myself and have confidence that I belonged on the major-league level. If I made my pitches, I could get guys out regularly."

Widely recognized as one of the game's toughest pitchers to hit, the right-handed-throwing Maloney, who stood 6'2" and weighed 195 pounds, received praise from Pirates center fielder Bill Virdon, who said, "Even when you know he's going to throw hard, he can throw the ball past you. . . . He's mixing up his pitches and getting them over the plate."

Roberto Clemente said of Maloney, "That fellow could throw as hard as anybody."

Meanwhile, Reds catcher Johnny Edwards credited his batterymate's newfound success to his development into more of a complete pitcher, stating, "Jim's fastball is his big pitch, and it will be for years. But now he can get the curveball over and it's giving him more confidence in his changeup."

Despite missing a handful of starts in 1964 due to shoulder problems, Maloney pitched well, going 15–10 with a 2.71 ERA, 214 strikeouts, and 11 complete games. Healthy for most of 1965, Maloney earned All-Star honors for the only time in his career by compiling a record of 20–9, throwing 255⅓ innings and 14 complete games, and ranking among the league leaders with a 2.54 ERA, 244 strikeouts, and five shutouts. Maloney followed that up with three more solid seasons, posting an overall record of 47–29 from 1966 to 1968, while compiling an ERA under 3.00, striking out more than 200 batters, and leading the league in shutouts once each.

But Maloney's arm and shoulder woes finally began to get the better of him in 1969. Forced to get regular cortisone injections and take extra time off between starts, Maloney started only 27 contests and registered just 102 strikeouts, although he won 12 of his 17 decisions and pitched to an ERA of 2.77.

Claiming that Maloney's muscular build made it necessary for him to receive vigorous pre- and postgame arm treatments, Reds trainer Bill Cooper stated, "Instead of stretching his muscles when he pitches, he rips them. That was okay when he was younger and the muscles healed quickly. But at 29–30, they don't heal that fast anymore."

Maloney's inability to take the mound every fourth or fifth day caused some of his teammates to question his mettle and the severity of his injuries, with one anonymous player telling sportswriter Pat Jordan, "It's not the pain that bothers Jim . . . it's the mental strain that's wearing him down. You think it don't bother him knowing he's starting each game with only 50 percent of his stuff; or not knowing which pitch will be his last; or knowing the team's fighting for a pennant and he's not contributing like he used to? Hell, that kind of anxiety can ruin a guy."

Responding to those teammates who doubted him, Maloney stated, "If some of them want to think my arm isn't sore, okay. I can't help that. They'll just have to take my word."

After holding out for more money following the conclusion of the 1969 campaign, Maloney found himself being resented even more by his teammates and the hometown fans, who believed the accusations made by Reds general manager Bob Howsam in the media that questioned his durability, injuries, and commitment to baseball. Finally joining the Reds in training camp after agreeing to a slight pay cut, Maloney expressed his sense of disillusionment, saying, "You know what makes this game really tough? There's no security and no friendships. Hell, if my arm goes tomorrow, you think I'll still be with the Cincinnati Reds?"

Ironically, Maloney's days in Cincinnati came to an end shortly thereafter when he ruptured the Achilles tendon in his left ankle while running out a groundball in just his second start of the season. Able to appear in only five more games the rest of the year, Maloney finished the season with a record of 0–1 and an ERA of 11.34, before being traded to the California Angels for pitcher Greg Garrett on December 15, 1970. Maloney ended up spending just one season in California, making only 13 appearances and compiling a record of 0–3 for the Angels in 1971, before being released at the end of the year. After subsequently failing to earn a roster spot with either the Cardinals or Giants, Maloney announced his retirement in June 1972, shortly after celebrating his 32nd birthday. Over parts of 12 big-league seasons, Maloney compiled an overall record of 134–84, an ERA of 3.19, and a WHIP of 1.259, threw 74 complete games and 30 shutouts, and struck out 1,605 batters in 1,849 total innings of work, posting virtually all those numbers during his time in Cincinnati.

Following his playing days, Maloney returned to his hometown of Fresno, where he became a car salesman at his father's business. However, Maloney had a difficult time adjusting to a more sedentary lifestyle, revealing during a 2012 interview, "I had a hard time sliding into the real world. I got into alcohol and drank as a player. When I got out of baseball, I became an alcoholic. By 1985, I was out of my house and my wife was filing for divorce. I had a nice home and three children. I ended up in a treatment center in Arizona. In February of 1985, I went through that program in 42 days, came back to Fresno, and went back to school. I became a drug and alcohol counselor. I reconnected with my high school sweetheart after a 40th high school reunion, and we've been married for 11 years. I've been sober for 27 years."

More than a decade later, Maloney, who is 84 years old as of this writing, continues to reside in Fresno with his second wife, Lyn.

REDS CAREER HIGHLIGHTS

Best Season

Maloney had a big year for the Reds in 1965, earning his lone All-Star selection by compiling a record of 20–9, a career-best ERA of 2.54 that placed him fourth in the league rankings, and a WHIP of 1.171, while finishing fifth in the circuit with 244 strikeouts. But Maloney performed slightly better in 1963, when, despite being snubbed for the All-Star team, he compiled an ERA of 2.77, threw 250⅓ innings, and established career-best marks in wins (23), strikeouts (265), shutouts (6), and WHIP (1.083), ranking among the league leaders in each of the last four categories.

Memorable Moments/Greatest Performances

Maloney earned a 2–0 victory over the Milwaukee Braves on May 21, 1963, by recording 16 strikeouts and yielding just two hits and four walks over 8⅓ shutout innings, at one point fanning eight consecutive batters.

Maloney struck out 13 batters and allowed just one hit and three walks during a 1–0 shutout of the Cubs on July 23, 1963, holding Chicago hitless after center fielder Ellis Burton singled in the first inning.

Maloney recorded seven strikeouts and yielded just two hits and one walk during a 4–0 shutout of the Giants on August 13, 1963, allowing only a pair of harmless singles to Harvey Kuenn and Felipe Alou.

Maloney tossed a one-hit shutout against the Mets on September 25, 1964, allowing just two walks and a second-inning single by outfielder Joe Christopher during a 3–0 Reds win.

Maloney threw another one-hit shutout on April 19, 1965, recording eight strikeouts, walking three batters, and yielding just an eighth-inning single by Denis Menke during a 2–0 win over the Braves.

Although an 11th-inning homer by Mets outfielder Johnny Lewis made a 1–0 loser out of Maloney on June 14, 1965, he dominated New York's lineup throughout the contest, allowing just two hits and one walk, while registering a franchise-record 18 strikeouts.

Despite issuing 10 bases on balls, Maloney no-hit the Cubs on August 19, 1965, striking out 12 batters during a 1–0 Reds win in which he threw a total of 187 pitches.

Maloney surrendered just two hits and one walk during a 4–0 shutout of the Mets on May 17, 1966, yielding only a first-inning single by second baseman Ron Hunt and a second-inning single by outfielder Ron Swoboda.

Maloney tossed a one-hit shutout against the Dodgers on May 28, 1968, recording 10 strikeouts and allowing just a fifth-inning single by shortstop Zoilo Versalles during a 7–0 Reds win.

Maloney threw 27 consecutive scoreless innings from September 21 to September 29, 1968, with the highlight of his streak coming on September 25, when he struck out 11 batters and yielded just two hits and one walk during a 3–0 shutout of the Pirates at Forbes Field.

Although he issued five bases on balls, Maloney threw the second no-hitter of his career on April 30, 1969, when he also recorded 13 strike-outs during a 10–0 win over the Astros.

Maloney dominated Houston's lineup again on September 26, 1969, striking out nine batters and allowing just two walks and a third-inning single by Joe Morgan during a 3–0, one-hit shutout of the Astros.

Notable Achievements

- Won at least 20 games twice.
- Posted winning percentage over .700 twice.
- Compiled ERA under 3.00 five times.
- Struck out more than 200 batters four times.
- Threw more than 250 innings twice, tossing more than 200 frames three other times.
- Threw two no-hitters (vs. Cubs on August 19, 1965, and vs. Astros on April 30, 1969).
- Led NL pitchers with five shutouts in 1966.
- Finished second in NL with 265 strikeouts in 1963.
- Finished third in NL in wins once, winning percentage twice, and shutouts once.
- Holds franchise record for most career strikeouts (1,592).
- Ranks among Reds career leaders in wins (7th), winning percentage (tied for 5th), shutouts (2nd), and games started (10th).
- Two-time NL champion (1961 and 1970).
- 1963 Reds team MVP.
- 1965 NL All-Star selection.

27

DON GULLETT

In discussing Don Gullett, Pete Rose said of his teammate, "Gullett's the only guy who can throw a baseball through a car wash and not get the ball wet."

Often described as a harder-throwing version of Hall of Fame southpaw Whitey Ford, Don Gullett served as the ace of the Reds' pitching staff most of his time in Cincinnati despite being plagued by arm and shoulder problems that ended up shortening his career. A member of the Reds for seven seasons, Gullett helped lead them to five division titles, four pennants, and two world championships by winning at least 15 games four times, while also compiling an ERA under 3.00 and throwing more than 200 innings three times each. The holder of the franchise record for highest career winning percentage, Gullett earned one top-five finish in the Cy Young voting and one *Sporting News* NL All-Star nomination, before signing with the Yankees as a free agent following the conclusion of the 1976 campaign.

Born in Lynn, Kentucky, on January 6, 1951, Donald Edward Gullett grew up with his seven siblings in the northeastern part of the state, some two-and-a-half hours outside of Cincinnati. Developing into an outstanding all-around athlete during his teenage years, Gullett starred in baseball, football, and basketball at McKell High School, performing so well on the diamond (he won 30 games his senior year) that pro scouts came from miles around to watch him pitch. Excelling on the gridiron and hardwood as well, Gullett once tallied 72 points in a football game (on 11 touchdowns and six extra points) and 47 points in a basketball game, prompting several major colleges to recruit him for all three sports. But with baseball remaining his first love, Gullett chose to sign with the Reds when they selected him in the first round of the June 1969 MLB Draft, with the 14th overall pick.

Advancing rapidly through Cincinnati's farm system, Gullett spent just one year in the minors, compiling a record of 7–2 and an ERA of 1.96 with the Sioux Falls Packers of the Northern League in 1969, before being promoted to the parent club prior to the start of the ensuing campaign. Still

Don Gullett posted the highest career winning percentage of any pitcher in team annals.

only 19 years old, Gullett spent his first big-league season working almost exclusively out of the bullpen, going 5–2 with a 2.43 ERA, six saves, and 76 strikeouts in 77⅔ innings pitched for a Reds team that captured the NL pennant.

Making an extremely favorable impression on Johnny Bench during the early stages of his rookie season, Gullett drew praise from the Reds star receiver, who stated, "He throws smoke, and I mean real good heat."

Joining the starting rotation in 1971, Gullett proved to be easily the best pitcher on a team that finished the year four games under .500, compiling a record of 16–6, ranking among the league leaders with a 2.65 ERA, tossing three shutouts, and striking out 107 batters in 217⅔ innings pitched. Stricken with hepatitis early in 1972, Gullett took a step backward, posting a mark of just 9–10 and an ERA of 3.94, while splitting his time between starting and relieving. Returning to top form the following year, Gullett helped lead the Reds to their third division title in four seasons by going 18–8 with a 3.51 ERA, completing seven of his starts, throwing four shutouts, and registering 153 strikeouts in 228⅓ innings pitched.

Gushing over the performance of his ace left-hander, Reds manager Sparky Anderson stated at one point during the campaign, "Barring an injury, he is almost sure of making the Hall of Fame. With Gullett's body and the way he stays in shape, I know he's going to pitch until he's at least 35. So, doing that, you know he's going to win at least 250 games with the start he has."

An extremely hard thrower early in his career, the 6-foot, 190-pound Gullett depended primarily on his high-octane fastball, deceptive changeup, and excellent control to navigate his way through opposing lineups his first few years in the league. But by 1974 he had added to his repertoire of pitches a forkball, which dropped sharply as it neared home plate, making him that much tougher. Armed with his new weapon, Gullett had one of his finest seasons, compiling a record of 17–11 and an ERA of 3.04, while also establishing career-high marks with 183 strikeouts, 243 innings pitched, and 10 complete games.

Claiming that his new offering made him a more complete pitcher, Gullett said, "The forkball has made the difference, even though 75 to 80 percent of my pitches are still hard stuff. It used to be, though, that when I got behind, I was throwing what they were looking for—the fastball."

Gullett subsequently began the 1975 season in fine fashion, compiling an 8–3 record and a 2.09 ERA over the first two months of the campaign. However, a line drive off the bat of Braves shortstop Larvell Blanks during a game on June 11 struck Gullett on his left hand, fracturing his thumb, and putting him on the disabled list for the next two months. Nevertheless, Gullett picked up right where he left off when he returned to action on August 18, hurling five scoreless innings during a 3–2 win over the Cardinals. Commenting on Gullett's extraordinary effort after such a long layoff, Reds pitching coach Larry Shepard stated, "I feel like a music teacher watching a great pianist at work. He gives me goose bumps."

Gullett won five of his next six decisions as well, thereby finishing the season with a record of 15–4 and an ERA of 2.42 that earned him a fifth-place finish in the NL Cy Young balloting. Continuing his strong pitching in the postseason, Gullett won his lone start against Pittsburgh in the NLCS, going the distance during an 8–3 victory in Game 1, before winning one of his two decisions against Boston in the World Series.

Following the Reds' seven-game victory over the Red Sox in the Fall Classic, the quiet and unassuming Gullett returned to his 75-acre farm in Greenup County, Kentucky, where he spent the offseason raising Black Angus cattle. Deeply religious and extremely down-to-earth, Gullett eschewed drinking, carousing, and chasing women, preferring instead to spend his free time hunting, fishing, and listening to country music.

Although Gullett continued to pitch well for the second of Cincinnati's back-to-back championship teams in 1976, posting an ERA of 3.00 and a winning percentage of .786, neck and shoulder problems sidelined him for much of the year, limiting him to just 20 starts and 11 victories.

With the Reds subsequently refusing to offer him a long-term contract when he became a free agent at the end of the year, Gullett signed with the Yankees for six years and $2 million, making him one of the highest-paid players in the game. Expressing his joy upon inking Gullett to the deal, Yankees president Gabe Paul told UPI, "Don Gullett is the modern Whitey Ford. His won-lost record is just phenomenal."

Unfortunately, Gullett, who, during his time in Cincinnati, compiled an overall record of 91–44, an ERA of 3.03, and a WHIP of 1.208, threw 35 complete games and 13 shutouts, collected 11 saves, and struck out 777 batters in 1,187 total innings of work, continued to experience injury problems in New York. Although Gullett somehow managed to go 14–4 for a Yankees team that ended up winning the World Series in 1977, he spent much of the season pitching in pain, forcing him to go on the disabled list multiple times. After making just eight starts the following year, Gullett underwent surgery for a double tear of his rotator cuff that essentially ended his pitching career. Released by the Yankees on October 30, 1980, after sitting out the previous two seasons, Gullett announced his retirement shortly thereafter, still shy of his 30th birthday.

Returning to his home in Kentucky, Gullett went back to farming, although he had to take a brief hiatus after suffering a heart attack in 1986 that nearly claimed his life. Gullett subsequently quit smoking and remained healthy until 1989, when he suffered another heart attack that forced him to undergo triple-bypass surgery. Eventually making a full recovery, Gullett began a career in coaching, spending two seasons serving as a pitching coach in the minor leagues, before assuming the same role in Cincinnati from 1993 to 2005. Gullett lived until February 14, 2024, when he passed away in Columbus, Ohio, at the age of 73.

Inducted into the Reds Hall of Fame two decades earlier, Gullett looked back on his career somewhat wistfully at the time, saying, "I always felt when I took the mound that I would win every game. I'll always wonder what I might have done with seven or eight more years. It's the goal of every player to get into the Hall of Fame in Cooperstown. I'm not saying I would have or could have made it. But we'll never know."

Some years earlier, Gullett told *Baseball Digest*, "You want to try and trade arms. Sometimes you dream of some miraculous recovery. Sometimes, I dream that I came back as a right-handed pitcher—and then I would be Don Gullett, the right-handed pitcher. By some stretch of the imagination, I dream that when I wake up my left arm will be like it was. But, when I really do wake up, my left arm is always like it is."

REDS CAREER HIGHLIGHTS

Best Season

Although Gullett won more games in each of the two previous seasons, he pitched his best ball for the Reds in 1975, when, despite being limited by injury to just 22 starts and 159⅔ innings, he earned a fifth-place finish in the NL Cy Young voting by compiling a record of 15–4 and a career-best ERA of 2.42 and WHIP of 1.146.

Memorable Moments/Greatest Performances

Gullett earned a victory in the second game of a doubleheader split with the Mets on August 23, 1970, by working four perfect innings of relief during a 7–5 Reds win, recording eight strikeouts, six of which came in succession.

Gullett tossed a complete-game three hitter against the Phillies on August 25, 1972, striking out 10 batters during a 6–1 win, while also going 2-for-4 at the plate with a pair of RBIs.

Gullett surrendered just two singles and two walks during a 1–0 shutout of the Cubs on August 7, 1973.

Gullett outdueled Houston southpaw Jerry Reuss on September 18, 1973, allowing just four hits, issuing no walks, and recording 11 strikeouts during a 1–0 shutout of the Astros.

Gullett hurled another gem against Houston on July 31, 1974, striking out eight and yielding just two walks and a pair of harmless singles to shortstop Roger Metzger during a 4–0 Reds win.

Gullett tossed another two-hit shutout on April 13, 1975, with only Dave Winfield and catcher Randy Hundley hitting safely against him during a 10–0 win over the Padres.

In addition to earning a complete-game 8–3 win over the Pirates in Game 1 of the 1975 NLCS, Gullett knocked in three runs with the only home run of his career.

Gullett also came up big for the Reds in Game 1 of the 1976 NLCS, yielding just two hits and one run over the first eight innings of a 6–3 win over the Phillies, while also going 2-for-4 at the plate with a double and three RBIs.

Notable Achievements

- Won at least 15 games four times, topping 17 victories twice.
- Posted winning percentage over .700 four times.
- Compiled ERA under 3.00 three times, finishing with mark under 2.50 twice.
- Threw more than 200 innings three times.
- Led NL pitchers with .727 winning percentage in 1971.
- Finished second in NL in winning percentage twice.
- Holds franchise record for highest career winning percentage (.674).
- Five-time division champion (1970, 1972, 1973, 1975, and 1976).
- Four-time NL champion (1970, 1972, 1975, and 1976).
- Two-time world champion (1975 and 1976).
- April 13, 1975, NL Player of the Week.
- July 1974 NL Player of the Month.
- Finished fifth in 1975 NL Cy Young voting.
- 1974 *Sporting News* NL All-Star selection.

28

JOSÉ RIJO

Remembered most for his superb pitching in the 1990 World Series that earned him Series MVP honors, José Rijo helped lead the Reds to their last world championship by recording two victories over the Oakland Athletics in their four-game sweep of the heavily favored AL champions. Yet Rijo accomplished a great deal more during his time in Cincinnati, winning at least 14 games four times and compiling an ERA under 3.00 on seven separate occasions despite being plagued by injuries that forced him to miss five full seasons. A onetime NL All-Star who also earned one *Sporting News* All-Star nomination and two top-five finishes in the NL Cy Young voting, Rijo established himself as one of the Reds career leaders in winning percentage and strikeouts, before finally succumbing to the arm woes that prevented him from ever fully reaching his enormous potential.

Born some 20 miles east of Santo Domingo, in the municipality of San Cristóbal, in San Cristóbal Province, Dominican Republic, on May 13, 1965, José Antonio Rijo Abreu grew up barely knowing his father, who left the family shortly after he celebrated his fourth birthday. Spending most of his youth living in an aluminum-roofed four-bedroom house with his mother, grandparents, aunts, uncles, and 12 siblings, Rijo learned to do without, recalling years later, "We were so poor I had to play ball in a friend's shoes, which were too small. The shoes were so tight and worn out I had blisters on each of my toes."

Finding solace in sports, Rijo frequently ignored his studies and played baseball and basketball instead, remembering, "That's all I thought about—playing ball. I'd even miss meals—tell my mother I wasn't hungry—so I could go to the stadium."

Eventually developing into an excellent pitcher, Rijo quit school in the ninth grade to pursue a career in baseball, signing with the Yankees as an amateur free agent on August 1, 1980, at only 15 years of age. In explaining his decision, Rijo said, "I signed because I hated school, and my family

José Rijo earned 1990 World Series MVP honors by defeating Oakland twice.

needed the money. I knew leaving school was a big gamble. If I didn't succeed in baseball, I didn't know what I would do."

Rijo subsequently spent nearly four years advancing through New York's farm system, before joining the Yankees in 1984 after compiling an overall record of 18–7 and an ERA of 1.88 at the Class A and Double-A levels the previous season.

Still only 19 years old, Rijo struggled in his first big-league season, going just 2–8 with a 4.76 ERA and two saves while working primarily out of the bullpen. Included in a multiplayer trade with Oakland at the end of the year that brought star outfielder Rickey Henderson to New York, Rijo split the next three seasons between the A's and their Triple-A affiliate in Tacoma, posting a composite record of 17–22 with the parent club, before being dealt to the Reds, along with pitcher Tim Birtsas, for aging slugger Dave Parker on December 8, 1987.

Although the right-handed-throwing Rijo never found consistency during his time in Oakland, he later credited Hall of Fame pitcher Juan Marichal—his father-in-law and the organization's Latin American scouting director at the time—for much of the success he eventually experienced, saying, "I owe a lot to Juan. He taught me how to have patience, how to concentrate, how to prepare yourself before a game. . . . He told me to concentrate better and take the game more seriously. There's a big difference in José Rijo today. When I was there (in Oakland), I had good velocity and a good slider, but my head and my mind weren't in the baseball. When I started my relationship with Juan Marichal, my father-in-law, there was a big change in my career."

Taking with him to Cincinnati the lessons he learned from Marichal, Rijo soon developed into one of the NL's foremost pitchers. After spending the first half of the 1988 campaign assuming the role of a middle-inning reliever, Rijo joined the starting rotation in mid-June, doing so against his wishes. Although Rijo expressed a desire to return to the bullpen after allowing just one run on two hits in six innings of work in his first start, Reds manager Pete Rose had other ideas, telling reporters, "He wants to go back to the bullpen? Tell him he can go back to the bullpen—until Tuesday night against Houston, his next start. . . . I have him penciled in for 21 more starts between now and the end of the season. He's a real horse, and he's going to win a lot of games—as a starter."

Living up to Rose's expectations, Rijo ended up finishing the season with a 13–8 record, an ERA of 2.39, a WHIP of 1.130, and 160 strikeouts in 162 innings pitched, despite experiencing tendinitis in his right elbow that sidelined him for three weeks. Continuing to perform well through the first half of the 1989 campaign, Rijo posted a mark of 7–6 and an ERA of 2.84 through mid-July. However, a stress fracture in his lower back forced him to miss the final two and a half months of the season.

Despite missing almost a month of action in 1990 as well after straining a muscle in his right shoulder, Rijo emerged as the ace of the Reds' pitching staff, compiling a record of 14–8, an ERA of 2.70, and a WHIP of 1.162, while also striking out 152 batters in 197 innings of work. Rijo then punctuated his outstanding season by defeating his former team, the Athletics, twice in the World Series, with his magnificent pitching leading the Reds to their first world championship in 14 years.

His confidence buoyed by the success he experienced the previous season, Rijo told reporters during 1991 spring training, "I'm capable of doing a lot of things if I can stay healthy for a full season. That's what I'm praying for, to be healthy for one full year and see what I can do. I've got one goal in mind, being in the All-Star Game and being the Cy Young winner."

Unfortunately, Rijo found himself being bitten by the injury bug again in 1991, breaking his ankle while trying to steal second base during a game against the Montreal Expos on June 20. Yet even though he spent the next six weeks on the disabled list, Rijo had arguably his finest season to date, earning a fourth-place finish in the Cy Young voting by posting a record of 15–6 that gave him a league-best .714 winning percentage, leading all NL hurlers with a WHIP of 1.077, and ranking among the circuit leaders with an ERA of 2.51 and 172 strikeouts.

Praising Rijo for his exceptional mound work, Reds manager Lou Piniella stated during the latter stages of the campaign, "José is developing into the best pitcher in the National League, pure and simple. He's really got it all together out there."

Primarily a fastball/slider pitcher, the 6'1", 200-pound Rijo relied heavily on the second offering to navigate his way through opposing lineups, although he typically refrained from throwing it between starts and in early exhibition games due to the stress that it placed on his elbow. Blessed with excellent velocity on his fastball, Rijo employed both a regular heater and a split-finger version, making him that much tougher on opposing hitters.

Posting 15 victories again in 1992, Rijo finished the season with a record of 15–10, an ERA of 2.56, and 171 strikeouts in 211 innings pitched, despite being plagued for much of the year by an inflamed right elbow that forced him to spend two weeks on the disabled list. Displaying his ability to pitch in pain, Rijo chose not to have surgery, saying in late July, "All I know is it's not getting any better. I'm trying to take it like a man. But I'm not having any fun even though we're winning. . . . I'm trying. I'm doing my best. It's bad, but I've been able to swallow my pain and go out and pitch . . . but it's getting harder and harder."

Finally healthy for a full season in 1993, Rijo earned a fifth-place finish in the NL Cy Young voting by compiling a record of 14–9, ranking among the league leaders with 257⅓ innings pitched, a 2.48 ERA, and a WHIP of 1.088, and topping the circuit with 227 strikeouts and 36 starts. Turning in another strong performance during the strike-shortened 1994 campaign, Rijo gained All-Star recognition for the only time in his career by going 9–6 with a 3.08 ERA and 171 strikeouts in 172⅓ innings pitched.

However, Rijo's days as an elite pitcher ended the following year when, after compiling a record of 5–4 and an ERA of 4.17 through 14 starts, he suffered a partial tear of the UCL tendon in his right elbow that forced him to undergo Tommy John surgery. Unfortunately, the procedure that Rijo had done on August 22, 1995, resulted in complications that forced him to eventually go under the knife three more times. Spending the 1996–2000 campaigns recuperating from his many operations, Rijo ended up missing five full seasons, before he gradually began to work his way up again through the Reds farm system.

Rejoining the parent club in 2001, Rijo performed relatively well in his 13 relief appearances, even though he lacked some of the bite on his once sharp-breaking slider. Less successful in 2002, Rijo posted a mark of 5–4 and an ERA of 5.14 in nine starts and 22 relief outings, before his comeback bid ended the following spring when the development of painful bone spurs in his oft-injured elbow forced him to announce his retirement.

Rijo, who did 10 stints on the disabled list during his time in Cincinnati, ended his playing career with a record of 116–91, an ERA of 3.24, a WHIP of 1.262, 22 complete games, four shutouts, and 1,606 strikeouts in 1,880 total innings of work. As a member of the Reds, Rijo went 97–61 with a 2.83 ERA, a WHIP of 1.187, 17 complete games, four shutouts, and 1,251 strikeouts in 1,478 innings pitched.

After retiring as an active player, Rijo spent the next few years working at his baseball academy in the Dominican Republic and serving as an assistant to the general manager of the Washington Nationals, before losing both his job and his academy in 2009 following a disclosure that one of the players he scouted and brought into the organization had provided a fake name and an inaccurate date of birth at the time of his signing. Rijo ran into trouble again in 2012, when he was investigated for his association with a person accused of drug trafficking and money laundering. However, the law did not find Rijo guilty of any wrongdoing. Since that time, Rijo has again become a hero in his native land by helping young Dominicans develop their baseball skills and pursue their dreams of playing the game professionally.

REDS CAREER HIGHLIGHTS

Best Season

Rijo performed exceptionally well for the Reds in 1991, earning *Sporting News* NL All-Star honors and a fourth-place finish in the Cy Young voting by compiling a record of 15–6, leading the league with a 1.077 WHIP, and ranking among the leaders with a 2.51 ERA and 172 strikeouts. But Rijo proved to be a bit more dominant in 1993, when en route to posting a record of 14–9, he finished second in the league with a 2.48 ERA, placed third in the circuit with a WHIP of 1.088, and established career-high marks with 257⅓ innings pitched and a league-leading 227 strikeouts.

Memorable Moments/Greatest Performances

In addition to allowing just one run on seven hits over the first five innings of an 11–2 win over the Mets on July 19, 1988, Rijo hit the first of his two career homers.

Rijo tossed a five-hit shutout against the Dodgers on June 9, 1989, walking one batter and striking out five during a 4–0 Reds win.

Rijo surrendered just two hits and recorded 12 strikeouts during a 4–0 shutout of the Giants on September 17, 1990, yielding only a single and double to San Francisco right fielder Kevin Bass.

Rijo earned 1990 World Series MVP honors by going 2–0 with a 0.59 ERA and 14 strikeouts in 15⅓ total innings of work during Cincinnati's four-game sweep of Oakland. After throwing seven shutout innings during a 7–0 win in Game 1, Rijo clinched the Series for the Reds by recording nine strikeouts and allowing just two hits, three walks, and one run over the first 8⅓ innings of a 2–1 victory in Game 4.

Rijo shut out the Mets on just two hits on August 24, 1991, striking out nine batters, issuing one walk, and yielding just a fifth-inning single to second baseman Gregg Jefferies and a ninth-inning single to shortstop Kevin Elster during a 7–0 Reds win.

Rijo allowed just one hit and issued no walks during a 6–0 shutout of the Rockies on September 25, 1993, yielding only a second-inning single to Colorado third baseman Charlie Hayes.

Notable Achievements

- Won 15 games twice.
- Posted winning percentage over .700 once.
- Compiled ERA under 3.00 seven times, finishing with mark under 2.50 on three occasions.
- Struck out more than 200 batters once.
- Threw more than 250 innings once, tossing more than 200 innings two other times.
- Led NL pitchers in winning percentage once, WHIP once, strikeouts once, and starts twice.
- Finished second in NL in ERA twice, strikeouts once, and innings pitched once.
- Ranks among Reds career leaders in winning percentage (9th), WHIP (11th), and strikeouts (tied for 4th).
- Two-time division champion (1990 and 1995).
- 1990 NL champion.
- 1990 world champion.
- Two-time NL Player of the Week.
- September 1992 NL Pitcher of the Month.
- 1990 World Series MVP.
- Finished in top five of NL Cy Young voting twice.
- 1991 *Sporting News* NL All-Star selection.
- 1994 NL All-Star selection.

29

KEN GRIFFEY JR.

Once considered the man most likely to displace Hank Aaron as MLB's all-time home-run king, Ken Griffey Jr. established himself as arguably the finest all-around player in the game during the first half of his career, which he spent in Seattle. While patrolling center field for the Mariners from 1989 to 1999, Griffey won 10 Gold Gloves and earned 10 All-Star selections, seven Silver Sluggers, one AL MVP award, and four other top-five finishes in the voting by hitting at least 40 homers six times, surpassing 100 RBIs seven times, and batting .300 or better on seven separate occasions. Unfortunately, a string of debilitating injuries prevented Griffey from maintaining his extraordinarily high level of play after he joined his hometown Cincinnati Reds in 2000. Nevertheless, Junior, as he came to be known, performed well enough over the course of the next nine seasons to earn three more All-Star nominations, one *Sporting News* All-Star selection, and one team MVP award, with his total body of work gaining him almost unanimous admission to the Baseball Hall of Fame the first time his name appeared on the ballot in 2016.

Born in Donora, Pennsylvania, on November 21, 1969, George Kenneth Griffey Jr. grew up around baseball, creating many of his fondest childhood memories while playing in the clubhouse of the Reds, with whom his father won back-to-back world championships in 1975 and 1976. Eventually developing into an outstanding all-around athlete himself after moving with his family to Cincinnati, Ohio, at the age of three, Griffey Jr. starred in both baseball and football at Archbishop Moeller High School, excelling on the diamond as a center fielder and the gridiron as a wide receiver.

Although Griffey received several scholarship offers to play football in college, he decided to pursue a career in baseball when the Seattle Mariners selected him with the first overall pick of the June 1987 MLB Amateur Draft. Recalling the rare combination of power, speed, and tremendous defensive ability that Griffey possessed at the time, legendary Atlanta Braves

Ken Griffey Jr. earned three of his 13 All-Star selections as a member of the Reds.
Courtesy of Dirk Hansen

manager Bobby Cox, then the team's general manager, stated, "I saw Ken Griffey Jr. in high school at Moeller High in Cincinnati, and he was the best prospect I've ever seen in my life. There was nobody even close to him; he was outstanding."

Not yet 18 years of age, Griffey seemed to have everything a young man could ask for. However, just a few months after being drafted by Seattle, Griffey attempted to take his life by swallowing 277 aspirin. Citing repeated arguments with his father, depression, and anger as the reasons for his attempted suicide, Griffey later revealed, "It seemed like everyone was yelling at me in baseball, then I came home, and everyone was yelling at me there. . . . I got depressed. I got angry. I didn't want to live."

Fortunately, the mother of Griffey's girlfriend saved his life by driving him to the hospital as soon as she discovered his condition. But after being resuscitated in the intensive care unit, Junior found himself being admonished by his father, causing him to rip the IV from his arm. Ultimately, though, the incident helped create a greater understanding between the two men, whose relationship improved dramatically as a result.

Feeling less burdened emotionally, Griffey spent the next two years honing his skills in the minor leagues, before joining the Mariners prior to the start of the 1989 campaign. Acquitting himself extremely well in his first big-league season, Griffey earned a third-place finish in the AL Rookie of the Year voting by hitting 16 homers, driving in 61 runs, stealing 16 bases, and batting .264, despite missing six weeks with a broken bone in his left hand. Developing into one of the finest all-around players in the junior circuit over the course of the next three seasons, Griffey gained All-Star recognition each year by averaging 24 homers and 94 RBIs, posting batting averages of .300, .327, and .308, and winning the first three of his 10 straight Gold Gloves.

Though still evolving as a player his first few years in Seattle, Griffey displayed his vast array of skills for all to see. A true five-tool player, the left-handed-swinging Griffey drove the ball with power to all fields, hit for a high batting average, ran the bases well, and did a superb job in the outfield, making several spectacular catches, while also throwing out opposing baserunners who dared to challenge his arm.

Griffey's extraordinary ability made him one of baseball's most popular and recognizable figures. Adding to the amount of notoriety he received was the enthusiasm he brought with him to the ballpark each day. Wearing a smile on his face and his cap turned backward during pregame practice, Junior didn't seem to have a care in the world, revealing his carefree attitude on one occasion when he said, "As long as I have fun playing, the stats will take care of themselves."

After hitting 27 homers, knocking in 103 runs, and batting .308 the previous year, a more physically mature Griffey, who, after beginning his major-league career as a slender 6'3", 195-pounder, gradually added some 25 or 30 pounds onto his frame, took the next step in his development in 1993, when he earned a fifth-place finish in the AL MVP voting by batting .309, ranking among the league leaders with 45 home runs, 109 RBIs,

113 runs scored, and an OPS of 1.025, and topping the circuit with 359 total bases. Griffey followed that up with another outstanding year, earning a runner-up finish in the 1994 AL MVP balloting by hitting a league-leading 40 homers, knocking in 90 runs, batting .323, and posting an OPS of 1.076 during the strike-shortened campaign, before missing more than half of the 1995 season with a broken wrist.

Griffey subsequently began an extraordinary four-year run during which he averaged 52 homers, 142 RBIs, and 123 runs scored, while also batting over .300 and posting an OPS over 1.000 twice each. Particularly outstanding in 1997, Griffey earned AL MVP and *Sporting News* MLB Player of the Year honors by leading the league with 56 homers, 147 RBIs, 125 runs scored, 393 total bases, and a .656 slugging percentage, while also batting .304 and finishing second in the circuit with an OPS of 1.028.

But after receiving the Players Choice Award as Major League Baseball's Player of the Decade following the conclusion of the 1999 campaign, Griffey rejected an eight-year, $135 million offer from the Mariners and requested a trade to another team, eventually narrowing his choice of ballclubs down to the Reds. With Griffey set to become a free agent at the end of the year, the Mariners granted his request, dealing him to the Reds on February 10, 2000, for a package of four players that included outfielder Mike Cameron.

Happy to be returning to Cincinnati, Griffey stated upon his arrival, "Well, I'm finally home. This is my hometown. I grew up here. It doesn't matter how much money you make; it's where you feel happy. Cincinnati is the place where I thought I would be happy."

Attempting to put into perspective the acquisition of Griffey, Reds GM Jim Bowden said, "February 10, 2000, will go down in Reds history and in baseball history as the night when one of the biggest trades in the history of our sport took place, when the Michael Jordan of baseball came home to Cincinnati. . . . This is a general manager's dream. In baseball history, Babe Ruth was traded. Rogers Hornsby traded, and now Ken Griffey Jr."

Meanwhile, Seattle Mariners president Chuck Armstrong stated simply, "We gave up Babe Ruth."

Despite being plagued by a sore hamstring throughout the 2000 campaign that forced him to miss almost three weeks of action, Griffey posted excellent numbers his first year with the Reds, earning All-Star honors by hitting 40 homers, knocking in 118 runs, scoring 100 times, batting .271, and compiling an OPS of .942. But Griffey subsequently sustained a litany of injuries over the course of the next four seasons that decreased his bat speed and significantly reduced both his playing time and offensive production. Limited to a total of just 317 games from 2001 to 2004 by maladies that included tears to both hamstrings, a torn patella in his right knee, a ruptured ankle tendon, and a dislocated shoulder, Griffey hit only 63 homers, essentially ending his pursuit of the all-time home-run record.

Yet, even in his somewhat diminished state, Griffey made an extremely favorable impression on his Reds teammates whenever he found himself able to take the field, with Barry Larkin recalling, "Ken Griffey Jr. had the prettiest swing I have ever seen. Not only was the swing pretty, but it was effective. He hit for average, for power, and he hit in situations. He played the game the right way offensively, he impacted the game defensively. Junior had great range, tremendous athleticism, and a cannon of an arm. And he played with a smile on his face. It was an honor to play alongside one of the greatest players in the history of the game."

Adam Dunn, a teammate of Griffey for eight seasons, stated, "Ken made things that were not supposed to be easy look easy. There were very few players who had more fun playing the game. He loved playing, and we loved watching him play. Ken is one of my favorite people, both as a professional and on a personal level. He not only is a hall of famer on the field, but he also is one off it."

Former Reds pitcher Danny Graves added, "Junior was one of my favorite teammates. He had a great clubhouse presence and made the game look so easy. Watching his routes and the jumps on balls hit to him, it was like he knew where the batters were going to hit it before it was hit. He had the most accurate arm of any center fielder I've ever seen, always on the money. And, of course, he had the sweetest swing ever."

Healthy for much of 2005 after undergoing an experimental procedure the previous year that involved reattaching his ruptured right hamstring with three titanium screws, Griffey earned NL Comeback Player of the Year honors by hitting 35 homers, driving in 92 runs, scoring 85 times, batting .301, and ranking among the league leaders with a slugging percentage of .576 and an OPS of .946. Despite being bitten by the injury bug again in 2006, Griffey managed to hit 27 homers and knock in 72 runs in only 109 games, although his batting average slipped to .252. Shifted to right field the following year, Griffey appeared in 144 games and garnered more than 600 total plate appearances, before suffering a season-ending groin strain in mid-September. Nevertheless, prior to sustaining his injury, Griffey hit 30 homers, knocked in 93 runs, scored 78 times, batted .277, and posted an OPS of .869, earning in the process the last of his 13 All-Star nominations. Failing to perform at the same level the first four months of the 2008 campaign, the 38-year-old Griffey hit 15 homers, knocked in

53 runs, and batted just .245, before being traded to the Chicago White Sox on July 21 for relief pitcher Nick Masset and utility infielder Danny Richar.

Griffey, who left Cincinnati having hit 210 homers, driven in 602 runs, scored 533 times, collected 904 hits, 173 doubles, and eight triples, stolen 17 bases, and compiled a batting average of .270, an on-base percentage of .362, and a slugging percentage of .514 as a member of the Reds, finished out the season in Chicago, before re-signing with the Mariners when he became a free agent at the end of the year. Griffey subsequently spent all of 2009 and the first two months of the ensuing campaign serving the Mariners primarily as a designated hitter, before announcing his retirement at the end of May with career totals of 630 home runs, 1,836 RBIs, 1,662 runs scored, 2,781 hits, 524 doubles, 38 triples, and 184 stolen bases, a lifetime batting average of .284, a .370 on-base percentage, and a .538 slugging percentage. In addition to ranking seventh all-time in career homers, Griffey recorded the eighth-most extra-base hits (1,192) of any player in MLB history and the ninth-most putouts (5,606) of any outfielder.

After retiring as an active player, Griffey joined the Mariners' front office as a special consultant, a position he held until 2021, when he became a member of the team's ownership group. Griffey, who currently resides with his family in Winter Garden, Florida, also serves as a member of the Baseball Hall of Fame's Board of Directors and a senior adviser to MLB commissioner Rob Manfred.

Looking back on his years with the Reds, Griffey said, "You had your ups and your downs. I spent a little more time on the DL than I care to talk about. . . . Being able to wear the same uniform and, at the same time, the same number my father wore, is something that you only dream of."

Meanwhile, longtime Reds beat writer Hal McCoy summed up Griffey's time in the Queen City thusly: "Due to injuries, we in Cincinnati did not get to see the real Junior, but we saw enough. He was still one of the best players of all time. We were privileged to see home run numbers 400, 500, and 600 in a Reds uniform. More importantly to me, Junior was a good friend and a Hall of Fame person."

REDS CAREER HIGHLIGHTS

Best Season

Griffey's first year with the Reds proved to be his finest in Cincinnati. Appearing in more than 130 games for one of only two times as a member of the team, Griffey earned his 11th consecutive All-Star nomination by hitting 40 homers, driving in 118 runs, scoring 100 times, batting .271, and posting an OPS of .942.

Memorable Moments/Greatest Performances

Griffey led the Reds to an 8–7 win over the Astros on May 13, 2000, by going 3-for-4 with two homers, a double, four RBIs, and three runs scored, with his two-run homer off Billy Wagner in the top of the ninth inning providing the margin of victory.

Griffey helped lead the Reds to a 14–5 win over Cleveland on July 8, 2000, by going 4-for-6 with two homers, a double, and eight RBIs.

Griffey contributed to a 15–6 victory over Colorado on July 13, 2000, by homering twice, knocking in four runs, and scoring four times.

After tying the score at 3–3 with a solo home run in the top of the ninth inning, Griffey delivered the decisive blow of a 4–3 win over the Marlins on May 30, 2003, by homering with two men out and no one on base two frames later.

Griffey led the Reds to a 9–6 win over Milwaukee on May 6, 2004, by going 3-for-5 with a homer, five RBIs, and two runs scored.

Griffey became the 20th player to amass 500 career home runs on June 20, 2004, when, with his father watching from the stands, he reached the seats off Matt Morris with no one aboard in the top of the sixth inning of a 6–0 win over the Cardinals.

Griffey gave the Reds a 5–4 walkoff win over the Washington Nationals on May 11, 2006, when he homered with one man out and two men on base in the bottom of the 11th inning.

Griffey homered twice, doubled, and knocked in four runs during an 8–7 win over the Cardinals on June 5, 2006, with his three-run homer off Jason Isringhausen in the top of the ninth inning proving to be the game's decisive blow.

Griffey hit the 600th home run of his career off Mark Hendrickson in the first inning of a 9–4 win over the Marlins on June 9, 2008.

Notable Achievements

- Surpassed 20 home runs six times, topping 30 homers on three occasions.
- Knocked in more than 100 runs once.
- Scored 100 runs once.
- Batted over .300 once.
- Posted slugging percentage over .500 three times.
- Posted OPS over .900 three times.
- Topped 30 doubles once.
- Ranks among Reds career leaders in home runs (9th), slugging percentage (tied for 3rd), and OPS (7th).
- Ranks seventh in MLB history with 630 home runs.
- May 13, 2007, NL Player of the Week.
- 2005 Reds team MVP.
- 2005 NL Comeback Player of the Year.
- Three-time NL All-Star selection (2000, 2004, and 2007).
- 2005 *Sporting News* NL All-Star selection.
- Number 93 on the *Sporting News*' 1999 list of Baseball's 100 Greatest Players.
- Elected to Baseball Hall of Fame by members of BBWAA in 2016.

30
JOHN FRANCO

Although he is remembered more for his years in New York, John Franco previously spent six seasons in Cincinnati excelling for the Reds out of the bullpen. Assuming the role of closer his last four years in the Queen City, Franco established himself as one of the NL's premier relievers, leading the league in saves once and ranking among the leaders the other three years. The 1988 *Sporting News* NL Fireman of the Year, Franco, who ranks third in franchise history in career saves, also earned three All-Star nominations, before departing for New York, where he spent the next 14 years anchoring the Mets' bullpen.

Born in Brooklyn, New York, on September 17, 1960, John Anthony Franco grew up with his older brother James Jr. in the Gravesend section of South Brooklyn, in a 28-building project called the Marlboro Houses. The son of a city sanitation worker who switched his allegiance from the Dodgers to the Mets when the former relocated to California in 1958, John spent his youth rooting for the Mets as well, while learning to play the game on the sandlots of Marine Park, Bay Eighth Street, Erasmus Field, and the Parade Grounds, saying years later, "One field was worse than the next."

Developing into a standout on the diamond at nearby Lafayette High School, Franco performed especially well in his senior year, when he compiled a record of 14–1 and averaged 17 strikeouts a game. But with Franco standing only 5-feet-7 and weighing just 140 pounds at the time, no team selected him in the annual MLB Draft, prompting him to enroll at St. John's University in Queens, where he combined with future AL Cy Young Award winner Frank Viola for three years to give the Red Storm a formidable pitching tandem.

Looking back on his college days, Franco, who tossed multiple no-hitters despite missing part of his sophomore year with an arm injury, said, "I had a great experience at St. John's. We ruled the East back then. One of my big regrets was that I hurt my arm and didn't get a chance to

John Franco ranks third in franchise history in career saves.

pitch in the College World Series. I think if I was healthy, we'd have had a really good chance to win that year."

Choosing to forgo his final year of college, Franco entered the June 1981 MLB Amateur Draft, where the Dodgers selected him in the fifth round. Franco subsequently spent two years advancing through the Los Angeles farm system, during which time he learned his signature pitch—the changeup—from fellow southpaw Sandy Koufax, a roving minor-league instructor for the organization at the time.

Dealt to the Reds for utility infielder Rafael Landestoy on May 9, 1983, Franco, who had previously worked exclusively as a starter, joined the team's Triple-A affiliate in Indianapolis, where he struggled terribly the rest of the year while splitting his time between starting and relieving. Nevertheless, Franco benefited from the input of minor-league pitching instructor Fred Norman, a left-handed hurler for the Reds during their glory days of the 1970s, who, in Franco's words, "tinkered with me a little bit and my changeup."

Promoted to the parent club during the early stages of the 1984 campaign after beginning the year at Wichita in the American Association, Franco performed well in his first big-league season, compiling a record of 6–2 and an ERA of 2.61, striking out 55 batters, and collecting four saves in 54 relief appearances and 79.1 total innings of work. Assuming a similar role in 1985, Franco earned the trust of manager Pete Rose by going 12–3 with a 2.18 ERA, striking out 61 batters in 99 innings pitched, and saving 12 games while serving as a left-handed complement to righty reliever Ted Power. Replacing Power as the Reds' primary closer in 1986, Franco gained All-Star recognition for the first time by compiling a record of 6–6 and an ERA of 2.94, registering 84 strikeouts in 101 innings of work, and finishing fifth in the league with 29 saves. An All-Star again in 1987, Franco won eight of his 13 decisions, posted an ERA of 2.52, and ranked among the league leaders with 32 saves, before earning MVP consideration the following year by establishing career-best marks with a 1.57 ERA and a league-leading 39 saves, with his fabulous pitching also earning him NL Rolaids Reliever of the Year honors.

Though small in stature, the 5'10", 170-pound Franco possessed a good fastball that typically registered somewhere in the low 90s on the radar gun. However, Franco considered his "out pitch" to be his changeup, which many likened to a screwball since it tended to break away from right-handed batters.

In discussing his former college teammate, Frank Viola stated, "Here's this little guy, but he was a power pitcher—90-plus fastball, real good breaking ball, incredible poise on the mound. But his style had to change after he blew his arm out in college and hurt it again in the pros. So, he went from a power pitcher to a control pitcher—a guy with great location and a devastating changeup. And that's all he really needs. Two pitches."

Adding that Franco's streetwise personality and use of psychology made him valuable in the clubhouse and more effective on the mound, Viola said, "We both have good heads. . . . What we do best is think ahead of the hitters, set them up, and make them crazy."

New York Mets manager Davey Johnson also expressed his admiration for Franco, calling him in 1989 "the most consistent reliever we've got in our league."

Meanwhile, Padres Hall of Fame outfielder Tony Gwynn said of Franco, "He's good, real good. He can throw anything for a strike."

Franco spent one more year in Cincinnati, earning his third All-Star nomination in 1989 by compiling an ERA of 3.12 and finishing third in the league with 32 saves, before heading for New York when the Reds included him in a four-player trade they completed with the Mets on December 6 that sent hard-throwing reliever Randy Myers to the Queen City.

While Reds GM Bob Quinn cited at the time Franco's impending free agency as part of his reason for making the deal, local newspapers instead pointed to the fact that the 29-year-old left-hander's name had surfaced in connection with the gambling scandal surrounding Pete Rose—an allegation that Franco denied.

Franco, who left Cincinnati with an overall record of 42–30, an ERA of 2.49, a WHIP of 1.269, 148 saves, and 367 strikeouts in 528 total innings of work, ended up spending 14 years in his hometown of New York, where he remained one of the NL's top closers for the next decade. Amassing at least 30 saves for the Mets five times, Franco led the league in that category twice, while also compiling an ERA under 2.00 on two separate occasions. Meanwhile, Franco, who served as team captain much of his time in New York, maintained a strong presence in and around the city, particularly following the terrorist attack on the World Trade Center on September 11, 2001. Deeply affected by the events that transpired, Franco later said, "I lost friends who were firemen, policemen, people who worked for Cantor Fitzgerald (the investment bank). That stuff stays with you forever."

Named that year's recipient of the Lou Gehrig Memorial Award, which is presented annually to the player who "best demonstrates his character and integrity both on and off the field," Franco later received high praise from former New York City fire commissioner Sal Cassano, who said, "He helped us get through a very difficult time. It hit home because his uncle was a firefighter, and his dad worked for the city. He did so much, bringing players to meet with kids who'd lost their parents."

Choosing to leave the city he loved at the end of 2004 after losing his closer's job a few years earlier, Franco signed as a free agent with the Houston Astros, with whom he appeared in 31 games, before announcing his retirement midway through the 2005 campaign. Over parts of 21 big-league seasons, Franco compiled a record of 90–87, an ERA of 2.89, and a WHIP of 1.333, collected 424 saves, and struck out 975 batters in 1,245⅔ innings pitched. Currently fifth on MLB's all-time saves list, Franco saved more games than any other left-hander in the history of the game.

Since retiring as an active player, Franco has remained heavily involved with youth baseball in New York City and has also served as an ambassador and guest instructor for the Mets at various times.

Looking back on his playing career, Franco said, "You can't judge a person by his size, but you could judge 'em by the heart he has. And I have always had a big heart. Every time I went out there, I gave 150 percent. It wasn't pretty at times, but I was under control, and I knew what I was doing. And I enjoyed every minute of it, through the good times and the bad times."

REDS CAREER HIGHLIGHTS

Best Season

Franco had an outstanding season for the Reds in 1985, compiling a record of 12–3 and an ERA of 2.18, while saving 12 games after assuming the role of closer. But he performed even better in 1988, when he earned a 12th-place finish in the NL MVP voting by winning six of his 12 decisions and posting career-best marks in ERA (1.57), WHIP (1.012), and saves (39), with the last figure leading all NL relievers.

Memorable Moments/Greatest Performances

Franco did yeoman's work on May 30, 1984, working four scoreless innings during a 6–4 victory over the Pirates that the Reds eventually won in 14 innings.

Franco helped the Reds earn a 13-inning, 2–1 win over the Astros on September 22, 1984, by working three hitless innings during which he issued two walks and recorded three strikeouts.

Franco earned a 3–2 victory over the Cubs on August 23, 1985, by allowing just one hit and one walk over the final three innings.

Franco contributed to a 7–6 win over the Cardinals on August 28, 1985, by yielding just one hit and recording three strikeouts over three scoreless innings.

Franco earned a 10–6 win over the Phillies on July 20, 1987, by allowing just one walk and registering four strikeouts over the final two innings.

Franco threw 28⅔ consecutive scoreless innings from July 15 to September 11, 1988.

Notable Achievements

- Saved more than 30 games three times.
- Won 12 games in 1985.
- Compiled ERA under 3.00 five times, finishing with mark under 2.00 once.
- Threw more than 100 innings once.
- Led NL with 39 saves in 1988.
- Ranks among Reds career leaders in saves (3rd) and pitching appearances (tied for 9th).
- Two-time NL Player of the Week.
- July 1988 NL Pitcher of the Month.
- 1988 *Sporting News* NL Fireman of the Year.
- 1988 NL Rolaids Reliever of the Year.
- Three-time NL All-Star selection (1986, 1987, and 1989).

31

TOM SEAVER

Identified by legendary broadcaster Vin Scully as "the best right-handed pitcher I ever saw," Tom Seaver gained general recognition as the finest hurler of his generation over the course of a 20-year Hall of Fame career that included stints with four different teams. Most closely associated with the Mets, Seaver became known simply as "The Franchise" during his time in New York for the level of respectability he brought to an organization that previously experienced very little success. A nine-time All-Star as a member of the Mets, Seaver also won three Cy Young Awards, before being traded to the Reds in what the New York newspapers referred to as "The Midnight Massacre." Continuing to perform at an elite level the next six years in Cincinnati, Seaver earned three more All-Star selections and another three top-five finishes in the Cy Young voting by winning 16 games twice, compiling an ERA under 3.00 three times, and striking out more than 200 batters once, before returning to New York for a second tour of duty with the club that gave him his start.

Born in Fresno, California, on November 17, 1944, George Thomas Seaver developed a love for the game of baseball at an early age, recalling that when he tried unsuccessfully to sign up for Little League ball one year before he became eligible, "I went home and cried."

Developing into an outstanding all-around athlete during his teenage years, Seaver starred in baseball and basketball at Fresno High School, earning All-City honors in both sports. Following his graduation in 1962, Seaver enrolled at Fresno City College, where he performed well enough on the diamond the next two seasons to draw interest from Southern Cal head baseball coach Rod Dedeaux, who recruited him for the Trojans. After proving himself worthy of a scholarship by excelling on the mound for the semiprofessional Alaska Goldpanners in the summer of 1964, Seaver posted a record of 10–2 as a sophomore at USC, prompting the Dodgers to select him in the 10th round of the June 1965 MLB Amateur Draft. But with the

Tom Seaver earned three top-five finishes in the NL Cy Young voting during his time in Cincinnati.

Dodgers offering him just $2,000 to sign with them, Seaver chose instead to return to school.

Although the Braves subsequently selected Seaver in the first round of the January 1966 MLB Draft, with the 20th overall pick, they did not sign him until after USC began its season, violating in the process MLB rules. His contract voided by MLB commissioner William Eckert, Seaver became the prize in a lottery held among teams willing to match Atlanta's signing bonus of $51,000. Beating out two other teams for his services, the Mets inked Seaver to a deal, after which he spent just one season in the minors before joining the parent club.

Performing exceptionally well in his first big-league season, the 22-year-old Seaver earned NL Rookie of the Year honors and the first of his seven consecutive All-Star nominations by compiling a record of 16–13 and an ERA of 2.76 for a team that won only 61 games. After posting another 16 victories and ranking among the NL leaders with a 2.20 ERA, a WHIP of 0.978, 205 strikeouts, five shutouts, and 278 innings pitched the following year, "Tom Terrific" took his game up a notch in 1969, leading the Mets to their first world championship by compiling a record of 25–7 and an ERA of 2.21, registering 208 strikeouts, completing 18 of his starts, and throwing 273 innings, with his fabulous performance earning him NL Cy Young honors and a runner-up finish in the league MVP voting.

Continuing to excel on the mound the next four seasons, Seaver posted an overall record of 78–44 for the light-hitting Mets, while also leading the NL in ERA three times, WHIP twice, strikeouts three times, and complete games once. Particularly outstanding in 1971 and 1973, Seaver earned a second-place finish in the Cy Young voting in the first of those campaigns by going 20–10 with a career-high 21 complete games and league-leading 1.76 ERA, 0.946 WHIP, and 289 strikeouts, before winning the award two years later by compiling a record of 19–10 and leading all NL hurlers with a 2.08 ERA, 251 strikeouts, 18 complete games, and a WHIP of 0.976.

The 6'1", 200-pound Seaver, whose repertoire of pitches included a mid-90s fastball, an excellent curve, and an outstanding slider, employed near-perfect pitching mechanics on the mound that thousands of Little Leaguers during the 1960s and 1970s tried to imitate. A classic power pitcher, Seaver used a drop-and-drive delivery that caused his back (right) knee to scrape the dirt on the mound as he released the ball.

In addition to his natural ability and superior mechanics, Seaver possessed a tremendous intellect that helped set him apart from other hurlers. A student of pitching, Seaver received high praise for his knowledge of his craft from Johnny Bench, who said, "I never knew a pitcher with such knowledge of pitching. He had such a great mind, he could out-think the hitters."

With Seaver also familiarizing himself with the tendencies of opposing batters, Bench added, "Some pitchers I could put on autopilot. Tom Seaver knew what he wanted to do and how he wanted to do it. When he pitched, I called the pitches he wanted to throw, not the ones I wanted him to throw."

After a sore hip limited him to just 11 victories in 1974, Seaver returned to top form the following year, when he earned Cy Young honors for the third time by going 22–9 with a 2.38 ERA and league-leading 243 strikeouts. Although Seaver subsequently set a major-league record by striking out more than 200 batters (235) for the ninth straight time and ranked among the league leaders with a 2.59 ERA, five shutouts, and 271 innings pitched, the Mets' feeble offense relegated him to a record of just 14–11 in 1976, which proved to be his last full season in New York for quite some time. With contract squabbles and philosophical differences with Mets GM M. Donald Grant creating an adversarial relationship between the two parties, the Mets completed a trade with the Reds on June 15, 1977, that sent Seaver to Cincinnati for pitcher Pat Zachry, second baseman Doug Flynn, and young outfielders Steve Henderson and Dan Norman.

While news of the deal broke the hearts of Mets fans, Reds manager Sparky Anderson exulted, "This gives us the premier pitcher in baseball. Seaver just keeps climbing, and he may be the all-time all-timer before he is through."

Meanwhile, Dodger second baseman Davey Lopes expressed concern over the addition of Seaver to his team's chief rival, saying, "This makes the Reds definitely a stronger club. This has to be one of the biggest steals since the Babe Ruth trade. A trade is supposed to help both teams. But I don't think the Mets are as good a club as they were before. I can't see how they improved their team one iota."

Proving Lopes to be prophetic, the demoralized Mets entered an extended period of futility that lasted nearly a decade. Meanwhile, Seaver helped the Reds remain a consistent contender in the NL West for the next few years. After winning seven of his 10 decisions in New York over the first two months of the 1977 campaign, Seaver posted a record of 14–3 for the Reds the rest of the year that gave him an overall mark of 21–6. The 32-year-old right-hander also finished the season with a 2.58 ERA, 196 strikeouts, 19 complete games, 261⅓ innings pitched, and a league-leading seven shutouts and 1.014 WHIP, earning in the process his 10th All-Star nomination and a third-place finish in the Cy Young voting.

Commenting on the performance of his new teammate at one point during the campaign, Joe Morgan stated, "It is something to watch him pitch. I always marveled at him when I was on the other team. But now, seeing him all the time, I say to myself, 'How did you ever get a hit off him?'"

A true professional who fans, teammates, opponents, and journalists alike admired, Seaver also drew praise from Sparky Anderson for the way he blended in with the rest of the team, with the Reds manager saying, "Seaver was a joy to have around. He is such a bright young guy that his weird sense of humor almost seems out of character. His personality fit right in with the veterans. They accepted him, and he accepted them. Moreover, Tom was of tremendous help to our young pitchers who frequently sought his advice."

Seaver subsequently gained All-Star recognition in 1978 by going 16–14 with a 2.88 ERA, 226 strikeouts, eight complete games, and 259⅔ innings pitched, before helping the Reds capture the division title the following year by compiling a record of 16–6 and an ERA of 3.14, while also registering 131 strikeouts, completing nine of his starts, and tossing a league-high five shutouts. Plagued by arm problems in 1980, Seaver went just 10–8 with a 3.64 ERA. But he rebounded nicely during the strike-interrupted 1981 campaign, earning the last of his 12 All-Star nominations and a runner-up finish to Fernando Valenzuela in the NL Cy Young balloting by going 14–2 with a 2.54 ERA.

Hampered by injuries again in 1982, Seaver compiled a record of just 5–13 and an ERA of 5.50, prompting the Reds to trade him back to the Mets at the end of the year for three undistinguished players. Seaver, who, over parts of six seasons in Cincinnati, posted an overall record of 75–46, an ERA of 3.18, and a WHIP of 1.177, threw 42 complete games and 12 shutouts, and struck out 731 batters in 1,085⅔ innings pitched, ended up spending just one year back in New York, going 9–14 with a 3.55 ERA for a poor Mets team in 1983, before being left unprotected in the free agent compensation pool at season's end. Subsequently claimed by the Chicago White Sox, Seaver split the next three seasons between the White Sox and Boston Red Sox, posting a total of 31 victories during his time in Chicago, before announcing his retirement following the conclusion of the 1986 campaign.

Over 20 big-league seasons, Seaver compiled a record of 311–205, an ERA of 2.86, and a WHIP of 1.121, threw 231 complete games and 61 shutouts, and struck out 3,640 batters in 4,783 total innings of work. The winner of at least 20 games five times, Seaver also compiled an ERA under 2.50 five times, threw at least 18 complete games six times, tossed more than 250 innings 11 times, and struck out more than 200 batters on ten separate occasions. A decent hitter as well, Seaver homered 12 times, knocked in 86 runs, and batted .154 in a total of 1,552 plate appearances over the course of his career.

Elected to the Baseball Hall of Fame the first time his name appeared on the ballot, Seaver, who Hank Aaron identified as the toughest pitcher he ever faced, and Bob Gibson, Juan Marichal, Jim Palmer, Nolan Ryan,

Steve Carlton, Bert Blyleven, and Don Sutton all named as the best pitcher of their generation in an ESPN poll, entered Cooperstown having received the highest percentage of votes ever accorded any player up until that time (98.84 percent).

Following his playing days, Seaver spent five seasons serving as a broadcaster on Yankees telecasts and another seven announcing Mets games, while also working as a public relations representative for the Chase Manhattan Bank. Eventually leaving his home in Connecticut and returning to his native California with his wife, Nancy, Seaver established a winery in the city of Calistoga, which he continued to operate until the dementia he developed some six years earlier forced him to retire from public life in 2019. The man once known as "The Franchise" and "Tom Terrific" lived until August 31, 2020, when he died in his sleep at the age of 75 from complications of Lewy body disease and COVID-19.

Upon learning of his passing, Reds chief executive officer Bob Castellini released a statement that read: "Tom Seaver was one of the best and most inspirational pitchers to play the game. We are grateful that Tom's Hall of Fame career included time with the Reds. We are proud to count his name among the greats in the Reds Hall of Fame. He will be missed."

Ed Kranepool said of his longtime Mets teammate, "He turned the organization around from a laughingstock ballclub into a complete team instantly. You knew every time out you were going to be a competitive team. . . . It's a sad day in Metsville. We lost our star and our leader."

Ron Swoboda, another former Mets teammate, stated, "You put a bunch of guys together of varying abilities and you know who the great ones are. When you played behind Tom Seaver, you were playing behind greatness. And you saw it almost every game."

Meanwhile, Johnny Bench said of his former Reds batterymate, "He was probably the best man's man you'd ever want to be around. He played on many different teams, and on each one he had the respect and admiration and the love of all the players around him. I mean, he was Tom Seaver after all."

REDS CAREER HIGHLIGHTS

Best Season

It could be argued that Seaver pitched his best ball as a member of the Reds after he first joined them in 1977, compiling a record of 14–3, an ERA of

2.34, and a WHIP of 0.956 over the final two-and-a-half months of the season. But, with Seaver spending the entire strike-shortened 1981 campaign in Cincinnati, we'll opt for that instead. En route to earning a runner-up finish in the Cy Young voting and a 10th-place finish in the MVP balloting, Seaver led all NL hurlers with 14 wins and an .875 winning percentage, posted an ERA of 2.54 and a WHIP of 1.118, and placed near the top of the league rankings with 166⅓ innings pitched.

Memorable Moments/Greatest Performances

In addition to allowing just two hits, walking four batters, and yielding just one unearned run during a 7–1 win over the Braves on July 14, 1977, Seaver helped his own cause by hitting a solo home run.

Seaver threw 27⅔ consecutive scoreless innings from September 15 to September 30, 1977, with the highlight of his streak coming on September 20, when he allowed just two hits and one walk during a 4–0 shutout of the Padres.

Seaver threw the only no-hitter of his career on June 16, 1978, when he issued three walks and recorded three strikeouts during a 4–0 win over the Cardinals.

Seaver tossed a two-hit shutout on April 19, 1979, yielding just three walks, a third-inning double by shortstop Pepe Frias, and an eighth-inning single by third baseman Jerry Royster during a 2–0 win over the Braves.

Seaver punctuated a 4–0, six-hit shutout of the Astros on May 8, 1981, by knocking in two runs with a seventh-inning homer.

Notable Achievements

- Won 16 games twice.
- Posted winning percentage over .700 three times.
- Compiled ERA under 3.00 three times.
- Posted WHIP under 1.000 once.
- Struck out more than 200 batters once.
- Threw more than 250 innings once, tossing more than 200 innings one other time.
- Threw no-hitter vs. St. Louis Cardinals on June 16, 1978.
- Led NL pitchers in wins once, winning percentage once, and shutouts twice.
- Finished second in NL in wins once, winning percentage twice, ERA once, and complete games once.

- Holds Reds single-season record for highest winning percentage (.875 in 1981).
- Ranks among Reds career leaders in winning percentage (8th) and WHIP (7th).
- 1979 division champion.
- Two-time NL Player of the Week.
- Two-time NL Pitcher of the Month.
- Finished in top five of NL Cy Young voting three times, placing as high as second in 1981.
- Three-time NL All-Star selection (1977, 1978, and 1981).
- 1981 *Sporting News* NL All-Star selection.
- Number 32 on the *Sporting News*' 1999 list of Baseball's 100 Greatest Players.
- Elected to Baseball Hall of Fame by members of BBWAA in 1992.

32

AROLDIS CHAPMAN

One of the hardest throwers the game has ever seen, Aroldis Chapman spent six seasons in Cincinnati overpowering opposing batters with his blazing fastball that frequently registered more than 100 mph on the radar gun. The Reds' closer his last four years in the Queen City, Chapman established himself as arguably the NL's most dominant reliever, amassing more than 30 saves and recording more than 100 strikeouts each season, while also compiling an ERA under 2.00 twice. A four-time NL All-Star, Chapman, who ranks fourth in franchise history in saves, helped lead the Reds to two division titles, before his involvement in an ugly domestic violence dispute hastened his departure from Cincinnati.

Born in Holguín, Cuba, on February 28, 1988, Albertin Aroldis Chapman grew up with his two sisters some 450 miles southeast of the nation's capital and largest city, Havana. Raised by his mother and father in a three-bedroom house, Chapman, whose grandparents had emigrated from Jamaica to Cuba to receive a better education, began playing organized baseball with a local team at the age of 15.

After spending his earliest days on the diamond at first base, Chapman moved to the mound at the suggestion of his school's coach, who took note of his strong throwing arm. Displaying a natural affinity for his new position, Chapman found himself pitching for the Sabuesos de Holguín Hounds of the Cuban National League before long, compiling an overall record of 24–19 and striking out a total of 365 batters in 327 innings of work from 2005 to 2009. Used primarily as a starter, Chapman proved to be particularly effective in 2009, posting a mark of 11–4 and registering 130 strikeouts in 118⅓ innings pitched, although he struggled with his control, issuing 62 bases on balls.

Eventually landing a spot on the Cuban national team after trying unsuccessfully to defect from his homeland in the spring of 2008, Chapman made a name for himself at the 2009 World Baseball Classic, where he displayed his ability to throw the ball by opposing hitters. However, while

Aroldis Chapman recorded more than 30 saves for the Reds four straight times.
Courtesy of Keith Allison

in Rotterdam, Netherlands, Chapman walked out the front door of the team hotel one day, entered an automobile driven by an acquaintance, and never returned. After defecting to Andorra, Chapman established residency in that small European country, from where he petitioned MLB to grant him free agent status.

Unfamiliar with the United States and its big-league ballclubs, Chapman had no idea where to go once he became a free agent, with his agent, Randy Hendricks, recalling, "We took him through a Google map that showed every major-league club, and we could zoom in on a state and describe the teams."

Eventually settling on a team whose players donned a cap with a distinctive "C" that reminded him of his former ballclub, Chapman chose to sign with the Reds, who, following an extensive workout, inked him to a six-year contract worth $30.25 million on January 10, 2010.

Although the left-handed-throwing Chapman, who stood 6'4" and weighed 235 pounds, possessed tremendous natural ability, he lacked polish when he first joined the Reds organization, with Cincinnati GM Walt Jocketty saying at the time, "What we think he needs now is some refinement in his delivery, because everything else is there. This is a talent that doesn't come along very often."

In addition to spending most of the 2010 season fine-tuning his delivery at Triple-A Louisville, Chapman worked on developing an offspeed pitch to supplement his overpowering fastball. Meanwhile, after starting 13 games for the Reds' top minor-league affiliate, Chapman gradually transitioned to the bullpen, posting an overall record of 9–6, compiling an ERA of 3.57, registering eight saves, and striking out 125 batters in 95⅔ innings pitched, before being summoned to the big leagues at the end of August. Acquitting himself extremely well over the final month of the campaign, Chapman helped the Reds capture the NL Central Division title by going 2–2 with a 2.03 ERA and registering 19 strikeouts in just 13⅓ innings of work. Plagued by control problems while serving as a setup man the following year, Chapman issued 41 bases on balls in just 50 innings pitched and posted a rather mediocre ERA of 3.60. Nevertheless, he managed to compile a record of 4–1 and strike out 71 of the 207 batters he faced.

After toying with the idea of moving Chapman into the starting rotation prior to the start of the 2012 regular season, Reds manager Dusty Baker decided to leave him in the bullpen when newly acquired reliever Ryan Madson tore a ligament in his elbow during spring training. Subsequently inserted into the role of closer, Chapman responded well to the challenge, earning All-Star honors for the first of four straight times by compiling an ERA of 1.51 and a WHIP of 0.809, while also finishing third in the league with 38 saves and striking out 122 batters in 71⅔ innings of work. Continuing his outstanding pitching in 2013, Chapman posted an ERA of 2.54, once again finished third in the NL with 38 saves, and recorded 112 strikeouts in 63⅔ innings pitched. Despite missing the first month of the 2014 regular season after undergoing surgery to repair a skull fracture that he sustained when a line drive struck him just above the left eye during a spring training game, Chapman had another excellent year, compiling an ERA of 2.00, posting a WHIP of 0.833, collecting 36 saves, and striking out 106 batters in 54 innings of work.

Employing a three-quarters delivery, Chapman relied heavily on his four-seam fastball that typically approached home plate at a speed of somewhere between 97 and 101 mph. Chapman, whose heater earned him the nickname "The Cuban Missile," also occasionally mixed in a slider that averaged 87–88 miles per hour on the radar gun, a splitter, and a changeup. Made even more imposing by his long frame and powerful physique, Chapman further intimidated opposing batters with the wildness he exhibited on the mound from time to time.

Although the Reds finished well out of contention in 2015, Chapman performed brilliantly, winning four of his eight decisions, compiling an ERA of 1.63, saving 33 games, and recording 116 strikeouts in 66⅓ innings pitched. But Chapman, who had been sued three years earlier for allegedly serving as "an informant for Cuban state authorities after a failed defection attempt and helping turn in another man in order to get back on the country's national baseball team," found himself embroiled in controversy again in December 2015, when news broke that he had been involved in an alleged domestic violence incident with his girlfriend at his home in Davie, Florida, five weeks earlier.

According to a police report obtained by ESPN, Chapman's girlfriend accused him of pushing her against a wall and choking her during a verbal altercation that began after she "found something on his phone that she did not like." Chapman was also said to have fired eight shots with a handgun while alone in his garage, seven of which hit a concrete wall, with the other going through a window into an open field. While Chapman admitted knocking the woman to the floor by poking her on the shoulder, he denied choking her. And the report submitted by police indicated that they found no injuries or redness around her neck.

Due to conflicting stories, a lack of cooperating witnesses, and no physical injuries to his girlfriend, Chapman escaped being charged with domestic violence. But the incident caused a trade that the Reds had in place with the Dodgers for Chapman to fall through. Instead, they dealt him to the Yankees three weeks later for four minor leaguers.

Chapman, who left Cincinnati with an overall record of 19–20, 146 saves, an ERA of 2.17, a WHIP of 1.016, and 546 strikeouts in 319 innings pitched, ended up being suspended by MLB for the first

30 games of the 2016 season for violating the league's domestic violence policy. Upon his return to action in early May, Chapman performed extremely well for the Yankees the next three months, compiling an ERA of 2.01 and saving 20 games for them, before being dealt to the Cubs for top infield prospect Gleyber Torres just prior to the trade deadline. After helping the Cubs win their first World Series in more than a century, Chapman re-signed with the Yankees when he became a free agent at the end of the year. Chapman subsequently spent the next six seasons in New York, earning three more All-Star selections, before leaving the Yankees at the end of 2022 after losing his closer's role during the early stages of the campaign. Following his departure from New York, Chapman split the 2023 season between Kansas City and Texas, serving both teams as a setup man and winning his second world championship as a member of the Rangers. A free agent again at the end of the year, Chapman signed with the Pittsburgh Pirates, with whom he assumed the role of a setup man. The now 37-year-old Chapman will enter the 2025 campaign with a career record of 55–45, an ERA of 2.63, 335 saves, and 1,246 strikeouts in 760 total innings of work.

REDS CAREER HIGHLIGHTS

Best Season

Chapman turned in his most dominant performance as a member of the Reds in 2012, when he earned an eighth-place finish in the Cy Young voting and a 12th-place finish in the MVP balloting by winning five of his 10 decisions, ranking third in the NL with 38 saves, posting career-best marks in ERA (1.51) and WHIP (0.809), recording 122 strikeouts in 71⅔ innings pitched, and holding opposing hitters to a batting average of just .141. Particularly outstanding from June 26 to August 17, Chapman did not allow a run in 23 straight mound appearances and converted a team-record 27 consecutive save opportunities.

Memorable Moments/Greatest Performances

Chapman made history on September 24, 2010, when, during a 4–3 loss to the San Diego Padres, he threw a pitch to Tony Gwynn Jr. that registered an unprecedented 105.1 miles per hour on the radar gun.

Chapman worked two perfect innings during a 4–3 victory over the Giants on July 29, 2011, that the Reds ultimately won in 13 innings, striking out four of the six batters he faced.

Chapman earned a win over the Cardinals on April 11, 2012, by striking out five of the seven batters he faced over the final two innings of a 4–3 Reds victory.

During a 6–5 win over the Pirates on July 11, 2014, Chapman broke a major-league record previously held by Bruce Sutter for the most consecutive relief appearances with a strikeout, fanning at least one batter in his 40th straight outing. Chapman's streak, which began on August 21, 2013, ultimately reached 49 consecutive games, lasting until August 13, 2014.

Notable Achievements

- Saved more than 30 games four times.
- Compiled ERA under 3.00 five times, finishing with mark under 2.00 twice.
- Posted WHIP under 1.000 twice.
- Struck out more than 100 batters four times.
- Finished third in NL in saves twice.
- Ranks fourth in franchise history with 146 career saves.
- Two-time division champion (2010 and 2012).
- Four-time NL All-Star selection (2012, 2013, 2014, and 2015).

33

HEINIE GROH

Although he is remembered primarily for his unusually shaped bat that resembled a milk bottle with a slender, elongated handle, Heinie Groh proved to be one of the finest all-around third basemen of his generation. A solid hitter and excellent fielder for both the Reds and Giants, Groh had most of his finest seasons in Cincinnati, batting over .300, finishing in double digits in triples, and stealing more than 20 bases four times each from 1913 to 1921, while also leading all NL third sackers in putouts three times, fielding percentage twice, and double plays turned on six separate occasions. The captain of the Reds' 1919 world championship ballclub, Groh spent parts of nine seasons in Cincinnati, before returning to New York, where he began his 16-year major-league career in 1912.

Born to German immigrant parents in Rochester, New York, on September 18, 1889, Henry Knight Groh developed a serious interest in baseball at an early age, with both he and his older brother, Lew, spending countless hours competing on the local sandlots. After further honing his skills in high school, Groh received an offer to play shortstop for the Oshkosh Indians of the Wisconsin/Illinois League. However, Groh experienced very little success in his first foray into professional baseball, compiling a batting average of just .161 for the Indians in 1908.

Determined to improve his performance at the plate, Groh worked extremely hard the following offseason, later telling baseball historian Lawrence Ritter, "I kept practicing and practicing at it, and the next year I hit about .285, and the year after that I made it to .300."

After three years at Oshkosh, Groh spent the first few months of the 1911 season with Decatur in the Three-I League, before being assigned to Buffalo of the Eastern League when the New York Giants purchased his contract in July. Promoted to the parent club the following year after batting .333 at Buffalo, Groh appeared in only 27 games, before being returned to the minors for more seasoning.

Heinie Groh served as captain of Cincinnati's 1919 world championship ballclub.

Although the diminutive Groh, who, depending on the source, stood somewhere between 5'6" and 5'8" and weighed close to 160 pounds, compiled a respectable .271 batting average during his brief stint in New York, he struggled to make consistent contact at the plate. Discussing Groh's plight in his book *The Cincinnati Reds*, baseball historian Lee Allen wrote, "Groh decided he needed a bat with plenty of hitting space. But the big bats that he would have liked to use were unsuited to him because he could hardly swing them. So, he started cutting down the size of the handle until the bat was light enough for him to swing. . . . The handle was only about 6" long, but the bat weighed 41 ounces."

Armed with his new "bottle bat," Groh returned to the Giants in 1913. However, after appearing in only four games with them, he headed to Cincinnati when the Reds completed a trade with the Giants on May 22 that sent pitcher Art Fromme and infielder Eddie Grant to New York for Groh, outfielder Josh Devore, and pitcher Red Ames.

Named the starting second baseman upon his arrival in Cincinnati, Groh performed well over the final four months of the 1913 campaign, batting .282, posting an OPS of .729, driving in 48 runs, and scoring 51 times in 117 games and 460 total plate appearances. Although Groh had another solid season at the plate in 1914, batting .288 and compiling an OPS of .749, he struggled somewhat in the field, committing a league-high 44 errors at second, prompting the Reds to move him to third base the following year.

Adapting well to his new position, Groh led all NL third sackers in double plays turned for the first of six straight times, while also finishing second in putouts and fielding percentage. Meanwhile, after being inserted into the leadoff spot in the batting order, Groh batted .290, posted an OPS of .745, led the Reds with 32 doubles, and finished second on the team with 170 hits and 72 runs scored. Although Groh subsequently batted just .269 in 1916, his league-leading 84 bases on balls allowed him to rank among the circuit leaders with a .370 on-base percentage and 85 runs scored. Groh followed that up with two of his most productive offensive seasons, batting .304, compiling an OPS of .796, scoring 91 runs, and leading the league with a .385 on-base percentage, 182 hits, and 39 doubles in 1917, before batting .320, posting an OPS of .791, and topping the circuit with a .395 on-base percentage, 28 doubles, and 86 runs scored in 1918.

Although the right-handed-swinging Groh possessed very little power at the plate, he proved to be a solid line-drive hitter who knew how to take full advantage of his diminutive stature to consistently rank among the league leaders in bases on balls. Employing a unique batting stance in which he crouched down low at the extreme front of the batter's box with both feet facing the pitcher, Groh choked up on the bat and slapped at the ball. Extremely difficult to strike out, Groh never fanned more than 37 times in a season. An adept bunter, Groh also excelled at executing the hit-and-run.

Gradually establishing himself as arguably the finest defensive third baseman in the game as well, Groh, who compiled a lifetime fielding percentage of .967 at the hot corner that ranks as the best among players who manned that position prior to 1920, employed a relatively simple technique, saying, "I'd get in front of the ball one way or the other and, if I couldn't catch it, I'd let it hit me, and then I'd grab in on the bounce and throw to first."

Moved down to the number three spot in the lineup in 1919, Groh spent most of the championship campaign batting between Jake Daubert and Edd Roush, enabling him to post some of the best numbers of his career. Ranking among the NL leaders in most offensive categories, Groh topped the circuit with an OPS of .823 and placed in the league's top five in batting average (.310), on-base percentage (.392), slugging percentage (.431), RBIs (63), runs scored (79), and walks (56). Although Groh subsequently batted just .172 against Chicago in the World Series, he drew six bases on balls and scored six runs, in helping the Reds defeat the White Sox in eight games. And, while it later surfaced that several Chicago players had conspired to throw the Series, Groh remained convinced that the Reds had the better team, saying many years later, "I think we'd have beaten them either way. That's what I thought then, and I still think so today."

Groh remained in Cincinnati for two more years, batting .298, posting an OPS of .768, and scoring 86 runs in 1920, before batting a career-high .331 and compiling an OPS of .815 the following season despite being limited by injuries to just 97 games and 357 official at-bats. But, with Groh having been involved in a contentious holdout following the conclusion of the 1920 campaign, the Reds traded him back to the Giants for veteran outfielder George Burns and catcher/first baseman Mike González on December 6, 1921.

Groh, who left Cincinnati having hit 17 homers, driven in 408 runs, scored 663 times, collected 1,323 hits, 224 doubles, and 75 triples, stolen 158 bases, batted .298, compiled a .378 on-base percentage, and posted a .394 slugging percentage his nine years there, ended up spending five seasons in New York, helping to lead the Giants to three pennants and one world championship, before sustaining a serious knee injury during the latter stages of the 1924 campaign that brought his days as a full-time player to an end. Released by the Giants in 1926, Groh later signed with the Pittsburgh Pirates, for whom he appeared in just 14 games in 1927, before announcing his retirement at the end of the year. Over parts of 16 big-league seasons, Groh hit 26 homers, knocked in 566 runs, scored 918 times, collected 1,774 hits, 308 doubles, and 87 triples, stole 180 bases, batted .292, compiled an on-base percentage of .373, and posted a slugging percentage of .384.

Following his major-league career, Groh remained in the game, first as a manager and part-time player in the minors, and, later, as a scout.

Eventually returning to Cincinnati, Groh worked as a cashier at River Downs Racetrack until he retired to private life. Inducted into the Reds Hall of Fame in 1963, Groh lived until August 22, 1968, when he died of a respiratory ailment at the age of 78.

REDS CAREER HIGHLIGHTS

Best Season

Although Groh posted a slightly higher batting average, on-base percentage, and OPS in each of the next two seasons, he had his best all-around year for the Reds in 1917, when he led the NL with 182 hits, 39 doubles, and a .385 on-base percentage, ranked among the circuit leaders with a .304 batting average, a .411 slugging percentage, an OPS of .796, 91 runs scored, 71 bases on balls, and 246 total bases, and led all players at his position in putouts, double plays turned, and fielding percentage.

Memorable Moments/Greatest Performances

Groh led the Reds to a 12–7 victory over the Cubs in the second game of their doubleheader sweep of the Chicagoans on July 5, 1915, by hitting for the cycle, going a perfect 5-for-5 with four runs scored.

Although the Reds lost to the Cubs in 14 innings by a score of 5–4 the very next day, Groh remained hot at the plate, going 4-for-6 with a walk.

Groh knocked in the only run scored during a 1–0 win over the Phillies on June 17, 1916, when he led off the game with a home run.

Groh hit safely in 23 straight games from July 14 to August 8, 1917, going 34-for-88 (.386), with eight doubles, 11 bases on balls, four RBIs, and 12 runs scored.

Groh helped lead the Reds to a 9–7 win over the Cardinals on June 22, 1918, by going 4-for-5 with a homer, stolen base, and three runs scored.

Groh proved to be a thorn in the side of the Cardinals again on May 7, 1920, going 4-for-6 with a double, two RBIs, and three runs scored during a 15–11 Reds win.

Notable Achievements

- Batted over .300 four times, topping the .320 mark twice.
- Finished in double digits in triples four times.

- Surpassed 30 doubles twice.
- Stole more than 20 bases four times.
- Hit for the cycle vs. Chicago Cubs on July 5, 1915.
- Led NL in on-base percentage twice, OPS once, runs scored once, hits once, doubles twice, bases on balls once, and plate appearances once.
- Finished second in NL in on-base percentage once, OPS once, runs scored twice, hits once, total bases once, and bases on balls once.
- Led NL third basemen in putouts three times, double plays turned six times, and fielding percentage twice.
- 1919 NL champion.
- 1919 world champion.

34

JOHNNY TEMPLE

A hard-nosed player who approached the game with an old-school mentality, Johnny Temple spent parts of nine seasons in Cincinnati giving no quarter to the opposition. Fighting with everyone from opponents to umpires and media members, Temple, in the words of one local sportswriter, proved to be "a throw-back to the old-time, hell-bent-for-leather tobacco-chewing players of the Ty Cobb Era." A pretty fair second baseman as well, Temple, despite his physical limitations, willed himself into becoming arguably the National League's finest all-around player at his position for much of the 1950s. A solid hitter and excellent baserunner, Temple batted over .300 three times and compiled an on-base percentage over .400, scored more than 100 runs, and stole more than 20 bases once each. Outstanding with the glove as well, Temple led all NL second basemen in putouts three times, assists once, and double plays turned once, with his strong play earning him three All-Star selections.

Born in Lexington, North Carolina, on August 8, 1927, John Ellis Temple grew up with his three brothers on a small farm located some 50 miles southwest, in Reeds Crossroads Township, North Carolina. Recalling his uninspiring surroundings, Temple said, "A big Saturday night (in Reeds Crossroads) was sitting in a car at the highway intersection watching the caution light flicker on and off."

After breaking and severely burning his left leg below the kneecap at the age of 16 while helping family members escape a house fire, Temple developed into a star in multiple sports at Reeds High School, donning a protective device on his injured leg to help him overcome his handicaps. Particularly outstanding in basketball, Temple performed well enough to earn a scholarship to Duke University. However, he chose to leave Duke after just two weeks, remembering, "I found out that was no place for a poor farm boy to be, even on a scholarship. I didn't have the kind of clothes those college kids wear. So, I went home to Catawba College (in Salisbury, North Carolina)."

Johnny Temple combined with Roy McMillan during the 1950s to give the Reds one of the finest double-play tandems in baseball.

But Temple's stay at Catawba did not last much longer. After lettering in football and basketball, Temple left the school prior to the start of the baseball season, explaining years later, "I had a limited scholarship, but I didn't have enough money to buy clothes and the other things, so I quit and went into the Navy."

Temple subsequently spent the tail end of World War II serving on the aircraft carrier USS *Randolph*, where, while performing for Navy teams, he discovered that he enjoyed playing baseball enough to pursue a career in the major leagues.

But Temple had an uphill climb, with his smallish frame causing local pro teams to snub him and big-league scouts to turn their attention elsewhere. Finally signed by the Reds in 1948 for $150 a month following a tryout in Mooresville, North Carolina, during which he lied about his age (he told them he was only 18), Temple spent most of the next five seasons in the minor leagues, during which time he moved from shortstop to second base.

While Temple made a successful transition to his new post and hit well at every stop, he also frequently put his combative nature on display for all to see, engaging in fisticuffs with two different opposing pitchers while playing for the Double-A Texas League Tulsa Oilers in 1951. Recalling the difficulties he encountered, Temple said, "Every player in the Texas League wanted to fight me. At least that's the way it seemed to me. I know that most of my trouble was of my own making. I felt like everyone in the league was picking on me. It was absolutely the worst year of my life."

Finally promoted to the parent club in 1952, Temple appeared in a total of 30 games, batting just .196, hitting his first big-league homer, and driving in five runs, in just under 100 official at-bats. Prior to that, though, Temple incurred the wrath of home plate umpire Larry Goetz during a preseason game by arguing a called third strike, with Goetz telling him before ejecting him from the contest, "From (Stan) Musial I'd take that. But not from a runt."

After assuming a backup role again in 1953, Temple laid claim to the starting second base job the following season, beginning in the process a six-year run during which he combined with slick-fielding shortstop Roy McMillan to give the Reds one of the finest double-play tandems in baseball. The better offensive player of the two, Temple batted .307, scored 60 runs, compiled an on-base percentage of .384, posted an OPS of .751, and finished second in the league with 21 stolen bases, while also leading all NL second sackers in putouts. Inserted into the leadoff spot in the batting order in 1955, Temple did an excellent job of setting the table for middle-of-the-lineup sluggers Ted Kluszewski, Gus Bell, and Wally Post, scoring 94 runs, batting .281, compiling an on-base percentage of .365, and ranking among the league leaders with 19 steals and 80 bases on balls. Meanwhile, Temple led all NL second basemen in double plays turned and finished second among players at his position in both putouts and assists.

Continuing to perform well the next four seasons, Temple earned three All-Star nominations by batting over .300 twice, compiling an on-base percentage of at least .380 three times, scoring more than 100 runs once, and posting an OPS over .800 and drawing more than 90 bases on balls twice each. Having perhaps his finest season in 1959, Temple hit eight homers, knocked in 67 runs, posted an OPS of .809, and ranked among the league leaders with a .311 batting average, 102 runs scored, 186 hits, and 35 doubles.

Although Temple, who stood 5'10" and, despite being officially listed at 175 pounds, weighed closer to 160, possessed very little power at the plate, hitting only 22 home runs over the course of his career, he proved to be an exceptional contact hitter who never struck out more than 41 times in a season. Blessed with a keen batting eye and well-above-average speed, Temple consistently placed near the top of the league rankings in walks and stolen bases, making him one of the NL's better leadoff hitters. Meanwhile, Temple's quickness, range, and soft hands allowed him to annually rank among the top players at his position in putouts, assists, double plays turned, and fielding percentage.

Often compared during his heyday to Nellie Fox, the AL's top second baseman, Temple objected when sportswriters introduced Pittsburgh's Bill Mazeroski into the conversation during the late-1950s, telling them, "Mazeroski can't carry my glove."

However, even as Temple established a reputation as one of the better middle infielders in the game, he became known as someone who had little control over his temper, either on or off the playing field. In addition to once punching out a Cincinnati official scorer who charged him with an error on a tough play, Temple engaged in a four-year feud with Milwaukee's equally hotheaded shortstop Johnny Logan, scuffling with him on numerous occasions, before finally burying the hatchet in 1958.

Temple displayed his disdain for the opposition on another occasion, when, informed by concerned teammates that Braves catcher Del Crandall had not yet risen to his feet after being bowled over at home plate by the much smaller Reds second baseman, he barked, "He's not supposed to. That's the way you play this game."

In attempting to shed light on Temple's persona, longtime Cincinnati sportswriter Earl Lawson stated, "Because Temple and I had once exchanged swings during a clubhouse scuffle, most people figured we had little use for one another. Actually, we were good friends. Temple was a high-strung individual . . . with an inferiority complex, which he attempted to conceal beneath a cover of braggadocio."

Despite Temple's outstanding play in 1959, the Reds' desperate need for pitching prompted them to trade him to the Cleveland Indians the following offseason for 19-game winner Cal McLish, first baseman Gordy Coleman, and infielder Billy Martin. Following his arrival in Cleveland, Temple told Indians fans what to expect from him when he said, "I can't stand a guy who loafs. I play ball for all I'm worth, and I think every professional ball player should do the same. I'll do all in my power to get along with my teammates and the people of Cleveland. There's only one thing I'll never do. I'll never stop hustling."

Temple, who, during his time in Cincinnati, hit 15 homers, knocked in 300 runs, scored 533 times, collected 1,058 hits, 149 doubles, and 30 triples, stole 105 bases, batted .291, compiled an on-base percentage of .372, and posted a slugging percentage of .361, ended up spending two years in Cleveland, earning All-Star honors in 1961 by batting .276 and scoring 73 runs, before splitting the next two seasons between the Baltimore Orioles and Houston Astros. Released by the Astros following the conclusion of the 1963 campaign, Temple returned to Cincinnati, where he spent most of 1964 serving the Reds as a player-coach, appearing in only six games, before leaving the organization in August after coming to blows with fellow coach Reggie Otero.

Subsequently announcing his retirement from baseball, Temple, who ended his playing career with 22 homers, 395 RBIs, 720 runs scored, 1,484 hits, 208 doubles, 36 triples, 140 stolen bases, a .284 batting average, a .363 on-base percentage, and a .351 slugging percentage, briefly worked as a roofer, before moving to Houston, where he became the sports director at a local radio station. Ultimately choosing to enter the business world, Temple made the mistake of trusting the wrong people, causing him to lose everything he had, including his home. Arrested and accused of stealing farm equipment in western North Carolina in 1977, Temple faced a charge of grand larceny, prompting his wife, Becky, to write a heartfelt letter to Earl Lawson that read:

> After Johnny's fight with Otero, he tried to get other jobs in baseball, and most people would not show him the courtesy of returning his call. . . . People began to come to Johnny with business deals. And he decided to go into the recreational vehicle venture—campers, boats, motor homes, etc. His partner was the business manager and Johnny was the public relations man. We thought everything was fine. We had a lovely home; we were living well and had no problems. Our only child, Mike, was attending Texas A&M. Then, all of a sudden, things were not fine at all. We were in trouble with the government (taxes) and all the banks on

> our floor plans (loans for vehicle inventory). Johnny and I never had any business sense and Johnny somehow always picks the wrong person to trust.

Ultimately accorded legal assistance, Temple avoided jail time by giving testimony to the South Carolina assembly against his criminal partners. But he developed an addiction to alcohol, which contributed to the pancreatic cancer that claimed his life on January 9, 1994, when he died at the age of 66 at the home of his son in White Rock, South Carolina.

REDS CAREER HIGHLIGHTS

Best Season

Temple displayed tremendous consistency for the Reds from 1954 to 1959, never batting any lower than .281 or compiling an on-base percentage under .344, while scoring fewer than 80 runs just once. Particularly outstanding in 1959, Temple earned his third All-Star selection and a 16th-place finish in the NL MVP voting by establishing career-high marks with eight homers, 67 RBIs, 102 runs scored, 186 hits, 35 doubles, a batting average of .311, and an OPS of .809.

Memorable Moments/Greatest Performances

Temple delivered the big blow of an 8–7 win over the Giants on September 12, 1952, when he homered with the bases loaded in the second inning.

Temple contributed to a lopsided 9–1 victory over the Cardinals on June 28, 1955, by going 4-for-5 with a triple, stolen base, and five RBIs.

Temple helped lead the Reds to a 19–1 dismantling of the Pirates on July 14, 1955, by going 5-for-7 with a triple, stolen base, three RBIs, and two runs scored.

Temple continued to be a thorn in the side of Pittsburgh pitchers on July 31, 1955, going a combined 7-for-10 with two RBIs and four runs scored during a doubleheader sweep of the Pirates.

Temple played a key role in a 13-inning, 12–11 win over the Phillies on June 1, 1958, knocking in five runs with a homer and single, with four of his RBIs coming on a sixth-inning grand slam.

Notable Achievements

- Batted over .300 three times.
- Compiled on-base percentage over .400 once.
- Scored more than 100 runs once.
- Surpassed 30 doubles twice.
- Stole more than 20 bases once.
- Led NL in bases on balls once, sacrifice hits twice, sacrifice flies once, and at-bats once.
- Finished second in NL in bases on balls once and stolen bases once.
- Led NL second basemen in putouts three times, assists once, and double plays turned once.
- 1958 Reds team MVP.
- Three-time NL All-Star selection (1956, 1957, and 1959).

35
NOODLES HAHN

Hailed by the *Sporting News* in 1904 as "one of the game's greatest left-handed pitchers," Noodles Hahn ranked among the finest hurlers in the game during the first few years of the 20th century. A crafty southpaw who possessed excellent control and an outstanding curveball, Hahn won more than 20 games for the Reds four times despite pitching for mostly mediocre or losing teams. A true workhorse, Hahn threw more than 300 innings four times and completed more than 30 of his starts on five separate occasions, with his 209 complete games ranking as the second-highest total in franchise history. However, Hahn ended up paying a steep price for his heavy workload, developing arm problems that brought his pitching career to a premature end.

Born in Nashville, Tennessee, on April 29, 1879, Frank George Hahn acquired his distinctive nickname at an early age, although he claimed he didn't know why, once saying, "All I know is they always called me 'Noodles.'" However, a friend of Hahn's offered an explanation, recalling, "When Hahn was a boy in Nashville, he always had to carry his father's lunch to him. His father worked in a piano factory, and the lunch was always noodle soup, so the nickname was a natural."

While other variations of the story continued to be passed down through the years, the moniker stuck, even after Hahn began his career in organized baseball at the age of 16 with the Chattanooga team of the Southern Association in 1895. Remaining in the organization after it relocated to Mobile the following year, Hahn pitched well enough to garner interest from both the Detroit and St. Louis clubs of the Western League. Choosing to sign with Detroit, Hahn spent the next two seasons compiling an overall record of 29–35 for the Wolverines, before being sold to the Reds prior to the start of the 1899 campaign.

Still almost two months shy of his 20th birthday when he arrived at his first big-league training camp, Hahn pitched better than expected, with the *Sporting News* reporting that he had "terrific speed, good curves, and the

Noodles Hahn won more than 20 games for the Reds four times.

best control ever displayed by a green southpaw" and that he showed little of the "lack of condition" that had plagued him in the Western League.

After winning a spot in the starting rotation, Hahn continued to perform well once the regular season began, surprising everyone by posting a record of 23–8, throwing 309 innings and 32 complete games, leading all NL hurlers with 145 strikeouts, and ranking among the league leaders with a 2.68 ERA, a WHIP of 1.126, and four shutouts.

Crediting much of the success he experienced as a rookie to clean living, Hahn told the *Cincinnati Enquirer*: "This year shows me what I can do when I am not drinking. I'll never again indulge in any kind of strong drink."

A hard-luck pitcher in his second season, Hahn went just 16–20 for a Reds team that finished 15 games under .500, despite compiling a very respectable 3.27 ERA, ranking among the league leaders with 311⅓ innings pitched and 29 complete games, and topping the circuit with 132 strikeouts and four shutouts. The victim of more misfortune in 1901, Hahn won 22 games but tasted defeat 19 times, even though he pitched some of the best ball of his career. In addition to leading the league with 239 strikeouts, 375 1/3 innings pitched, and 41 complete games, Hahn ranked among the leaders with a 2.71 ERA and a WHIP of 1.170. Meanwhile, by winning 22 games for a Reds club that finished last in the NL with a record of just 52–87, Hahn posted 42 percent of his team's victories, which represents the second-highest percentage in modern NL history. (Steve Carlton collected 46 percent of the Phillies' wins in 1972.)

Though not armed with an overpowering fastball, Hahn, who stood 5'9" and weighed 160 pounds, used his outstanding control and sharp-breaking curveball to establish himself as one of the game's top strikeout artists. Describing Hahn's pitching style long after his playing career ended, sportswriter Grantland Rice wrote: "Hahn was a left-hander who belonged to the Herb Pennock, Eddie Plank school. He lacked the blazing speed of a [Lefty] Grove or a Rube Waddell, but he could tie up batters into more knots than 10 sailors could untie in a week. And you could see the seams on the ball as it came floating up."

Asked to throw an extraordinary number of innings despite his smallish frame, Hahn expressed concerns over his heavy workload following the conclusion of the 1901 campaign, telling the *Sporting News*, "I am wise enough to know that I cannot last forever and that I am greatly shortening my career by pitching as I did last season. . . . I pitched 40 games during the past season, yet I did more work than if I had pitched 80 games with a winning team behind me."

Deciding to prepare himself for the future in case his playing career ended earlier than he expected, Hahn enrolled in the Cincinnati Veterinary College during the offseason, reasoning that, while doctors, lawyers, and dentists abounded, "hoss doctors; why, they're lined up along the boulevards waiting to give those boys money."

Choosing to remain in Cincinnati after being approached by the Boston Americans of the rival American League in the winter of 1901, Hahn performed magnificently for an improved Reds team that finished .500 in 1902, compiling a record of 23–12, an ERA of 1.77, and a WHIP of

1.059, registering 142 strikeouts and six shutouts, and throwing 35 complete games and 321 innings. Hahn followed that up with another strong season, going 22–12 with a 2.52 ERA, a WHIP of 1.162, 127 strikeouts, five shutouts, 34 complete games, and 296 innings pitched in 1903, with his 2.52 ERA ranking well below the league average of 3.26.

With Hahn having won his 100th game in July 1903, just two months after celebrating his 24th birthday, he became the youngest player to reach that milestone since the rules governing the game moved the pitching mound back to its current distance of 60'6" in 1893. Taking note of Hahn's accomplishment, the *Sporting News* wrote during the early stages of the 1904 season, "He has given good service for a longer period than most southpaws, but there is no reason to believe 'Noodles' will not retain his effectiveness for several seasons."

Although Hahn finished the 1904 season with a record of just 16–18, he continued to perform at an extremely high level, ranking among the league leaders with an ERA of 2.06 and a WHIP of 0.984, while also throwing 33 complete games and 297⅔ innings. But after winning five of his eight decisions and compiling an ERA of 2.81 during the early stages of the 1905 campaign, Hahn developed a dead arm that essentially ended his playing career. Released by the Reds on August 1, Hahn received the following critique from the *Cincinnati Commercial Gazette*: "Hahn has failed to reach his old standard. Without his speed, he was robbed of much of his effectiveness."

Hahn, who, during his time in Cincinnati, compiled an overall record of 127–92, an ERA of 2.52, and a WHIP of 1.134, threw 24 shutouts and 209 complete games, and struck out 900 batters in 1,987⅓ total innings of work, spent the rest of the season pitching for some semipro teams, before signing with the AL's New York Highlanders prior to the start of the ensuing campaign. But after making just six starts and throwing only 42 innings through the first week of July, Hahn asked for and received his release from manager Clark Griffith.

Following his retirement, Hahn remained in Cincinnati, where he became a veterinary inspector for the US government. He also continued to pitch semiprofessionally for several more years and remained close to the Reds by often pitching batting practice at Crosley Field until he reached his late 60s. After moving with his wife to a town called Candler in western North Carolina in the early 1950s, Hahn lived until February 6, 1960, when he passed away at the age of 80.

REDS CAREER HIGHLIGHTS

Best Season

Hahn had a huge year for the Reds in 1901, when, despite pitching for a team that finished 35 games under .500, he won 22 games and led all NL hurlers with 239 strikeouts, 41 complete games, and 375⅓ innings pitched. Hahn also performed exceptionally well in 1899, when he led the league with 145 strikeouts and ranked among the leaders with 23 wins, a 2.68 ERA, a WHIP of 1.126, and four shutouts. But Hahn posted the best overall numbers of his career in 1902, when he compiled a record of 23–12, finished second in the league with a 1.77 ERA, posted a WHIP of 1.059, and threw six shutouts, 35 complete games, and 321 innings.

Memorable Moments/Greatest Performances

Hahn threw the 20th century's first no-hitter on July 12, 1900, when he allowed just one walk during a 4–0 win over the Phillies.

Although Hahn surrendered 11 hits during a 4–3 win over Boston on May 22, 1901, he held the Beaneaters to just two earned runs and recorded a career-high 16 strikeouts.

Hahn yielded just three singles and one walk during a 7–0 shutout of the Brooklyn Superbas on July 14, 1901.

Hahn worked all 14 innings of a 5–4 win over the Chicago Orphans (Cubs) on July 31, 1901, allowing 10 hits and two earned runs, while striking out 11.

Hahn surrendered just four hits and one walk during a 5–0 shutout of Brooklyn on May 25, 1902.

Hahn threw 32 consecutive scoreless innings from June 18 to July 6, 1903, highlighting his streak with a 5–0, four-hit shutout of the Giants on June 25.

Hahn again shut out the Giants on four hits on September 15, 1903, issuing no walks and recording six strikeouts during an 8–0 Reds win.

Hahn nearly tossed his second no-hitter in the final game of the 1903 regular season, when he yielded just one walk and a single by third baseman Dave Brain during a 1–0 shutout of the Cardinals.

Notable Achievements

- Won more than 20 games four times.
- Posted winning percentage over .700 once.
- Compiled ERA under 2.50 twice, finishing with mark under 2.00 once.
- Posted WHIP under 1.000 once.
- Struck out more than 200 batters once.
- Threw more than 30 complete games five times, completing 29 of his starts another time.
- Threw more than 300 innings four times, tossing more than 290 frames two other times.
- Threw no-hitter vs. Philadelphia Phillies on July 12, 1900.
- Led NL pitchers in strikeouts three times, shutouts once, complete games once, and innings pitched once.
- Finished second in NL in ERA once, WHIP once, and shutouts twice.
- Ranks among Reds career leaders in wins (tied for 10th), ERA (8th), WHIP (3rd), shutouts (tied for 5th), complete games (2nd), and innings pitched (11th).

36

CY SEYMOUR

The first Reds player to win a batting title, Cy Seymour accomplished the feat in 1905, when he put together one of the finest offensive seasons in team annals. More than just a one-year wonder, though, Seymour consistently ranked among the NL leaders in batting average, home runs, RBIs, hits, and total bases during his time in Cincinnati, which proved to be all too brief. The Reds' primary starter in center field from 1902 to 1906, Seymour spent less than five full seasons in the Queen City. Nevertheless, he distinguished himself by compiling the highest lifetime batting average of any player in franchise history, doing so after beginning his career as a pitcher with the New York Giants.

Born in Albany, New York, on December 9, 1872, James Bentley Seymour began his career in baseball some 160 miles north, in the city of Plattsburgh, where he competed semiprofessionally until 1896, when the minor-league Springfield Ponies of the Class A Eastern League offered him a contract. Originally a pitcher, the left-handed-throwing Seymour acquired the nickname "The Cyclone" or "Cy" while at Springfield for his blazing fastball.

After brief tours of duty with the Ponies and the New York Metropolitans of the Class A Atlantic League, Seymour joined the New York Giants, for whom he compiled a record of 2–4 and an ERA of 6.40 in 11 games and eight starts in 1896. Inserted into the starting rotation the following year, Seymour posted 18 victories and pitched to a 3.27 ERA, before winning 25 games, compiling a 3.18 ERA, and leading the league with 239 strikeouts in 1898. But, while Seymour fanned more batters than anyone else in the circuit, he also led all NL hurlers with 213 bases on balls, prompting Boston Beaneaters first baseman Fred Tenney to tell the *Wilmington Sun*, "If Cy Seymour possessed control, he would be the greatest pitcher in the country. He has the most baffling curves. It is impossible to gauge them."

Meanwhile, veteran Baltimore Orioles catcher Wilbert Robinson stated that he had never seen anyone pitch like Seymour, claiming that his

Cy Seymour holds franchise records for highest career and single-season batting average.
Courtesy of RMYAuctions.com

tendency to first throw high around the batter's head and then drop the next pitch around his feet caused him "to not know whether his head or feet were in most danger."

Seymour continued to struggle with his control in 1899, leading the league in walks for the third straight time, before his arm went dead the following year, thereby ending his pitching career. Reinventing himself as an outfielder, the 28-year-old Seymour jumped to the upstart American League, where he batted .303 and knocked in 77 runs for the Baltimore

Orioles in 1901. Released by Baltimore midway through the ensuing campaign, Seymour signed with the Reds, for whom he batted .340, posted an OPS of .792, and knocked in 37 runs during the season's second half.

Manning center field full-time for the Reds in 1903, Seymour emerged as one of the NL's best hitters, placing near the top of the league rankings in eight different offensive categories, including home runs (7), RBIs (72), batting average (.342), OPS (.861), and hits (191). After posting slightly less impressive numbers the following year (.313 AVG, .790 OPS, and 58 RBIs), Seymour reached the apex of his career in 1905, when he led the NL in almost every major offensive category. In addition to scoring 95 runs and finishing second in the league with eight homers and a .429 on-base percentage, Seymour topped the circuit with 121 RBIs, 219 hits, 40 doubles, 21 triples, 325 total bases, a .377 batting average, a .559 slugging percentage, and an OPS of .988. The only player other than Honus Wagner to win the NL batting title from 1903 to 1909, Seymour also came within one home run of capturing the Triple Crown.

Employing a smooth, left-handed swing, the 6-foot, 200-pound Seymour stood deep in the batter's box, claiming that doing so allowed him to "get that much more time to be sure which infielder is going to cover second base. A large portion of my base hits were made in this way."

Although Seymour possessed occasional power, he proved to be more of a line-drive hitter who drove the ball through the infield and into the outfield gaps. Taking a scientific approach to his craft, Seymour, unlike most other players of his time, adjusted his bat usage to the opposing pitcher, using a lighter bat when facing a hurler who depended primarily on movement and location and a heavier one when going up against a hard thrower.

In discussing Seymour's unorthodox approach to hitting, Brooklyn manager Ned Hanlon stated, "I look upon Seymour as the greatest straight ball player of the age; by that I mean he is absolutely all right if you let him play the game in his own way. But if you try to mix up any science on him, you are likely to injure his effectiveness."

Somewhat less proficient on defense, Seymour, who played an extremely shallow center field, twice led all players at his position in errors, committing as many as 36 miscues in 1903. Nevertheless, his strong throwing arm enabled him to lead all NL outfielders in assists once and double plays twice. And despite his reputation as a below-average outfielder, Seymour received praise for his defensive work in 1904 from *Sporting Life*, which suggested that he "is as speedy and graceful as ever in center field and covers a world of ground out there, more than any other center fielder in the National League."

Meanwhile, Chicago manager Frank Selee spoke highly of Seymour's range and ability to back-pedal, calling him "a marvel and a pleasure to watch."

Despite the prolific numbers that Seymour posted in 1905, the Reds chose to sell him to the Giants for the then-enormous sum of $10,000 when he experienced a decline in offensive production the following year. Dealt to the Giants on July 12, 1906, after compiling a batting average of just .257 over the first three months of the season, Seymour left Cincinnati having hit 26 homers, driven in 326 runs, scored 313 times, collected 738 hits, 106 doubles, and 53 triples, stolen 74 bases, batted .332, compiled an on-base percentage of .378, and posted a slugging percentage of .463 as a member of the Reds.

After batting .320 for the Giants the rest of the year, Seymour continued to start in center for two more seasons, hitting .294 in 1907, before batting .267 and ranking among the league leaders with 92 RBIs the following year. But after the aging Seymour assumed a part-time role for them in 1909 and for much of 1910, the Giants sold him to the Baltimore Orioles of the Class A Eastern League on August 24, 1910. Seymour subsequently spent most of the next three seasons in the minors, before briefly returning to the major leagues with the Boston Braves in 1913. Released by the Braves after compiling a batting average of just .178 for them in 84 plate appearances, Seymour announced his retirement, ending his big-league career with 52 homers, 799 RBIs, 737 runs scored, 1,724 hits, 229 doubles, 96 triples, 222 stolen bases, a .303 batting average, a .347 on-base percentage, and a .405 slugging percentage. In his five years as a pitcher, Seymour compiled a record of 61–56 and an ERA of 3.73, posted a WHIP of 1.554, completed 105 of his 141 starts, and struck out 591 batters in 1,038 innings of work, while issuing 659 bases on balls.

Following his playing days, Seymour, having been declared unfit for military duty, worked in the shipyards of New York during World War I. With his time on the docks making him susceptible to pulmonary tuberculosis, Seymour contracted the disease and died at only 46 years of age, on September 20, 1919. Rumored to be penniless at the time of his death, Seymour, who Christy Mathewson once called "a mighty batsman . . . one of the best ever," was laid to rest in the Seymour family plot in an unmarked grave next to his wife, Agnes. Though many attended his funeral, no one from organized baseball came.

REDS CAREER HIGHLIGHTS

Best Season

Seymour had easily the finest season of his career in 1905, when he led the NL in nine different offensive categories, including batting average (.377), slugging percentage (.559), OPS (.988), RBIs (121), hits (219), doubles (40), triples (21), and total bases (325), with his .377 average setting a single-season franchise record that still stands.

Memorable Moments/Greatest Performances

Seymour contributed to a 15–1 rout of the Brooklyn Superbas on August 20, 1902, by going 3-for-5 with a homer, five RBIs, and three runs scored.

Seymour helped lead the Reds to an 8–4 win over the Boston Beaneaters on May 22, 1903, by collecting three hits, driving in five runs, and scoring once.

Seymour led the Reds to a 10–5 victory over the Pirates on July 28, 1903, by going 4-for-5 with a homer, double, stolen base, and three RBIs.

Seymour fashioned a 24-game hitting streak from August 22 to September 19, 1903, going 39-for-97 (.402), with three triples, four doubles, and 20 runs scored.

Seymour helped lead the Reds to an 11–2 win over the Giants on July 14, 1904, by going 4-for-5, with a homer, three RBIs, and two runs scored.

Seymour contributed to a lopsided 15–1 victory over Boston on July 23, 1904, by going 5-for-5 with a triple, two doubles, and five runs scored.

After hitting safely in three of his four previous trips to the plate, Seymour gave the Reds an 8–7 win over Brooklyn on August 2, 1905, when he homered with no one aboard in the bottom of the 13th inning.

Seymour homered twice in one game for the only time as a member of the Reds during an 8–3 win over Brooklyn on September 24, 1905.

Notable Achievements

- Batted over .300 four times, topping the .340 mark twice.
- Compiled on-base percentage over .400 once.
- Posted slugging percentage over .500 once.
- Posted OPS over .900 once.
- Knocked in more than 100 runs once.
- Collected more than 200 hits once.

- Finished in double digits in triples three times, amassing more than 20 three-baggers once.
- Surpassed 40 doubles once.
- Stole more than 20 bases twice.
- Led NL in batting average, slugging percentage, OPS, RBIs, hits, triples, doubles, and total bases in 1905.
- Finished second in NL in home runs twice, on-base percentage once, hits once, and total bases once.
- Led NL outfielders in putouts once and double plays turned once.
- Holds Reds single-season record for highest batting average (.377 in 1905).
- Holds Reds career record for highest batting average (.332).
- Ranks among Reds career leaders in on-base percentage (tied for 11th) and OPS (11th).

37

LEE MAY

A feared slugger who surpassed 30 homers and 100 RBIs three times each over the course of an 18-year major-league career that included stints with four different teams, Lee May proved to be one of the most productive hitters of his generation. Nicknamed the "Big Bopper" for his size and ability to deliver the long ball, May homered at least 20 times in 11 straight seasons, while also driving in at least 94 runs in eight of those. A regular member of the Reds starting lineup from 1967 to 1971, May surpassed 30 home runs three times and 100 RBIs once during his time in Cincinnati, while also batting over .300 once. A capable defender as well, May led all NL first basemen in double plays turned twice, with his strong all-around play earning him two All-Star nominations. Nevertheless, May will always be remembered as much as anything for being the key piece in a trade with the Houston Astros that helped turn the Reds into baseball's dominant team.

Born in Birmingham, Alabama, on March 23, 1943, Lee Andrew May grew up in the segregated South, where he held several jobs as a youngster, including delivering newspapers and cleaning offices. The son of a semipro ballplayer, May suffered through the divorce of his parents at a relatively early age, forcing him, his younger brother, and his mom to move in with his grandmother.

Developing into an excellent all-around athlete during his teenage years, May starred in football, basketball, and baseball at A.H. Parker High School, excelling as a fullback on the gridiron and a forward on the hardwood. But May, who first drew the attention of Cincinnati Reds scout Jimmy Bragan while competing on the Alabama sandlots at the age of 13, held baseball closest to his heart, recalling years later, "They called me the 'Big Bopper.' That was fine with me. I always wanted to be a home run hitter when I was growing up. My favorite player was Harmon Killebrew. . . . I wanted to be just like Killebrew and hit a lot of homers."

Recruited by several colleges for both baseball and football as graduation neared, May received an offer to play football for the University of Nebraska.

Lee May hit more than 30 home runs three times as a member of the Reds.

However, he instead chose to sign with the Reds for $12,000, later explaining, "Well, the Reds offered me money, and I felt I had a better chance in baseball. Plus, I felt I'd have a longer career in baseball . . . and it was safer."

May subsequently spent the next six years in the minor leagues, while also briefly attending Miles College in Fairfield, Alabama, and further honing his skills during the winter months in Venezuela and Puerto Rico, remembering, "I actually planned on going to college (in the offseason), but I was always busy playing winter ball, and it just got squeezed out. They paid you better in Puerto Rico and Venezuela than your own club paid you. . . . I made $350 a month in my first year in the minors and $1,500 a month in Venezuela that same winter."

Making a successful transition from the outfield to first base while in the minors, May explained his switch in positions by saying, "I threw side-arm too much for an outfielder, and my throw would move too much from the target."

While advancing through Cincinnati's farm system, May also received a piece of advice from one of his managers, John "Red" Davis, that enabled him to better harness his power at the plate. Recalling the correction that Davis made to his batting stance, May said, "I was uppercutting the ball, and Red had me go into a semicrouch. The result was 18 home runs at Rocky Mount in 1963, 25 at Macon in 1964, and 34 at Triple-A San Diego in 1965."

Despite his outstanding production in the minors, May made only a pair of brief appearances with the parent club in 1965 and 1966 due to the presence in Cincinnati of a talented crop of first basemen that included Gordy Coleman, Deron Johnson, and Tony Pérez. But after the Reds parted ways with Coleman and moved Pérez to third base to create an opening for him, May joined the team for good in 1967. Making the most of his opportunity, May, who shared playing time at first with Johnson and saw some action at both corner outfield positions as well, ended up earning *Sporting News* NL Rookie of the Year honors by hitting 12 homers, driving in 57 runs, and batting .265 in 127 games and 438 official at-bats.

Named the full-time starter at first base after the Reds traded Johnson to Atlanta prior to the start of the ensuing campaign, May responded by hitting a team-high 22 homers, driving in 80 runs, batting .290, and posting an OPS of .805, before establishing himself as one of the NL's top sluggers in 1969, when he earned All-Star honors for the first time by batting .278, compiling an OPS of .860, and ranking among the league leaders with 38 homers, 110 RBIs, and 321 total bases. May followed that up with another extremely productive season, helping the Reds capture the NL pennant in 1970 by hitting 34 homers and knocking in 94 runs, although he batted just .253, posted an on-base percentage of only .297, and placed near the top of the league rankings in strikeouts for the third of six straight times.

Recalling the contributions that May made to the Reds during their successful run to the league championship, Johnny Bench stated, "A lot of people never realized how important he was to us when we won the pennant in '70. . . . We were stumbling around late in the year because we were all tired, but Lee was hitting home runs almost every day. And when we died in the [World] Series, he was a one-man gang."

Although the Reds dropped the Series to Baltimore in five games, May, who hit fifth in the lineup, behind Pete Rose, Bobby Tolan, Tony Pérez, and Bench, proved to be their lone bright spot, batting .389, posting an OPS of 1.283, driving in eight runs, and hitting two homers, including a game-winning three-run blast in Game 4 that gave them their only victory.

An imposing figure at the plate, the right-handed-hitting May, who stood 6'3" and weighed close to 220 pounds, wagged his bat back and forth as he awaited the pitcher's offering, all the while glaring out toward him as he stood on the mound. Very much a free swinger who readily admitted, "I deliberately try to hit a home run every time up," May never walked more than 52 times in a season. Meanwhile, he struck out at least 100 times on 10 separate occasions. However, May made up for his shortcomings in that area by hitting a lot of homers and driving in a lot of runs. Extremely strong, May possessed tremendous power to all fields, although he pulled most of his homers to left. Commenting on May's ability to reach the seats, Reds batting coach Ted Kluszewski stated, "He may be fooled on a certain pitch but the next time up he'll hit the same pitch out of the park."

Despite his size, May also proved to be surprisingly nimble in the field, consistently ranking among the NL's top first basemen in putouts, assists, double plays turned, and fielding percentage. An outstanding team leader as well, May earned the respect of his teammates wherever he went, often using his pragmatic personality and comical sense of timing to put out clubhouse fires.

Although the Reds failed to repeat as NL champions in 1971, finishing the year four games under .500, May had arguably his finest season in Cincinnati, earning his second All-Star nomination by ranking among the league leaders with 39 homers, 98 RBIs, and a .532 slugging percentage, scoring 85 times, batting .278, and posting an OPS of .864. Nevertheless, the Reds' poor showing during the regular season convinced team management that it needed to make a major move the following offseason. To that end, the Reds traded May, second baseman Tommy Helms, and veteran utility man Jimmy Stewart to the Astros for second baseman Joe Morgan, infielder Denis Menke, center fielder César Gerónimo, outfielder Ed Armbrister, and pitcher Jack Billingham. Although May and Helms subsequently played well for Houston, the deal turned out to be an excellent one for the Reds, with whom Morgan developed into one of the finest all-around players in the game. The trade also enabled Cincinnati to move Tony Pérez back to his more natural position of first base and replace him at third with the more mobile Menke.

Later admitting to being very much surprised by the deal, May claimed that it caught him totally off guard "because I had such a good year in '71 and had been named the MVP of the Reds."

May also revealed that he felt great sadness over having to leave Cincinnati, remembering, "That might have been the worst point of my life in baseball. I had never played with anybody but the Reds. We had gelled together and, all of a sudden, I got traded, kicked out of the house. It took a while to get over it."

May added, "It's like you're born into a family—you get up there in age, you leave home, but you're always part of the family. So, I guess I'll always be a Red at heart."

Despite spending the next three years playing in the Astrodome, a noted pitchers' park, May compiled outstanding numbers during his time in Houston, averaging 27 homers and 96 RBIs for the Astros, before being traded to the Baltimore Orioles following the conclusion of the 1974 campaign. May ended up spending the next six seasons in Baltimore, proving to be a perfect fit for the offensive philosophy employed by manager Earl Weaver, who believed in "waiting for the three-run homer." In discussing May on one occasion, Weaver said, "He's a guy who likes to hit the ball as hard as he can every time he goes up there . . . and when he's doing it, he can be destructive."

After averaging 24 homers and 97 RBIs his first four years in Baltimore, May experienced a precipitous decline in offensive production the next two seasons as age began to take its toll on him. A free agent at the end of 1980, May signed with the Kansas City Royals, with whom he assumed a backup role the next two seasons, before announcing his retirement. Over parts of 18 big-league seasons, May hit 354 homers, knocked in 1,244 runs, scored 959 times, amassed 2,031 hits, 340 doubles, and 31 triples, batted .267, compiled a .313 on-base percentage, and posted a .459 slugging percentage.

Following his playing days, May spent several years coaching at the major-league level, first serving as hitting coach in Kansas City, and later coaching first base for the Reds, Royals, Orioles, and Tampa Bay Devil Rays. Ending his career in baseball with the organization that first signed him, May said in 2011, "I now do PR with the Reds and have eight grandchildren who keep me and my wife pretty busy." May lived until July 29, 2017, when he died of pneumonia in a Cincinnati hospital at the age of 74.

Upon learning of his passing, former Reds announcer Al Michaels, who carpooled to Riverfront Stadium with May during their time together in Cincinnati, said of his old friend, "He was a big presence with zero bombast. Just a rock-solid guy with a great, understated sense of humor."

REDS CAREER HIGHLIGHTS

Best Season

May posted extremely comparable numbers in 1969 and 1971, and either of those seasons would make a good choice here. We'll go with 1971 since, with several of his teammates experiencing subpar campaigns, May stepped to the forefront, establishing himself as the Reds' top power threat by hitting 39 homers and driving in 98 runs, while also batting .278 and posting an OPS of .864, with his strong play earning him *Sporting News* NL All-Star honors and a 12th-place finish in the league MVP voting.

Memorable Moments/Greatest Performances

May contributed to an 11–5 victory over the Braves on October 1, 1966, by going 4-for-5 with a homer, double, four RBIs, and three runs scored.

May led the Reds to a 6–5 victory over the Mets on June 24, 1968, by knocking in four runs with a homer and triple, with his opposite field three-bagger in the bottom of the 11th inning driving in Johnny Bench with the winning run from first base.

May went on a home-run-hitting binge from May 24 to May 28, 1969, homering twice in three straight games. After reaching the seats twice and knocking in four runs during an 11–2 win over Montreal on May 24, May hit another two homers and drove home four more runs during a 7–2 victory over the Expos the very next day. May followed that up on the 28th of the month by hitting two homers and knocking in three runs during a 7–6 win over the Pirates, ending his three-game spree with six homers and 11 RBIs.

May had a huge day at the plate on July 15, 1969, homering four times and knocking in 10 runs during a doubleheader split with the Braves, ending each game with two homers and five RBIs.

May knocked in the only runs scored during a 4–0 win over the Cardinals on July 20, 1970, when he homered with the bases loaded in the top of the 10th inning.

May proved to be the difference in a 5–4 victory over the Phillies on August 15, 1970. After tying the score at 4–4 with a solo home run in the bottom of the ninth inning, May drove home the game's winning run with an RBI single five frames later, concluding the contest with four hits, two homers, and five RBIs.

May gave the Reds their only win of the 1970 World Series when he homered with two men aboard in the top of the eighth inning of Game 4, turning a 5–3 deficit into a 6–5 lead.

May provided most of the offensive firepower during a 6–3 win over the Expos on August 8, 1971, homering twice and driving in five runs, with his three-run blast in the bottom of the ninth inning providing the margin of victory.

May helped lead the Reds to a 9–4 win over the Cubs on August 25, 1971, by going 4-for-5 at the plate with two homers and five RBIs.

Notable Achievements

- Hit more than 30 home runs three times.
- Knocked in more than 100 runs once.
- Batted over .300 once.
- Posted slugging percentage over .500 three times.
- Topped 30 doubles three times.
- Finished third in NL in home runs twice.
- Led NL first basemen in double plays turned twice.
- 1970 division champion.
- 1970 NL champion.
- 1967 *Sporting News* NL Rookie of the Year.
- 1971 Reds team MVP.
- Two-time NL All-Star selection (1969 and 1971).
- 1971 Sporting News NL All-Star selection.

38

PETE DONOHUE

A member of arguably the best starting staff in franchise history, Pete Donohue spent parts of 10 seasons in Cincinnati, combining with Eppa Rixey and Dolf Luque most of that time to give the Reds a formidable threesome at the top of their rotation. The winner of at least 20 games three times, Donohue posted a total of 96 victories from 1922 to 1926, establishing himself in the process as one of the NL's top starters. Depending primarily on his outstanding changeup to navigate his way through opposing lineups, Donohue also threw at least 19 complete games and 250 innings three times each, before injuries and illness brought his days as an elite pitcher to a premature end.

Born in Athens, Texas, on November 5, 1900, Peter Joseph Donohue grew up with his six siblings on a ranch in central Henderson County, before moving with his family some 100 miles northwest, to the city of Fort Worth, where he starred as a pitcher at North Side High School. After winning 24 out of 31 games at North Side High and posting another 54 victories in two seasons with Libby of the semipro City League, Donohue enrolled at Texas Christian University in the fall of 1919. Continuing his exceptional mound work at TCU, Donahue threw four no-hitters and posted an overall record of 29–4 for the Horned Frogs over the course of the next season-and-a-half, before being lured out of college by the Reds with a $5,000 signing bonus.

Choosing the Reds over five other teams, Donohue later explained that he decided to sign with them because "they took a real interest in me. The other club representatives seemed to be only interested in my alleged pitching powers. It seemed to me that they only wanted me as a chattel to win games for them. They only wanted me as a bolt or a rod or a can to go into the old machinery. But the Cincinnati folks showed an interest in Pete Donohue. They talked to me about my health, my folks, and my studies."

Bypassing the minor leagues completely, Donohue arrived in Cincinnati midway through the 1921 campaign, still four months shy of his 21st

Pete Donohue won at least 20 games for the Reds three times during the 1920s.

birthday. Appearing in a total of 21 games during the season's second half, Donohue went 7–6 with a 3.35 ERA, threw 118⅓ innings, and completed seven of his 11 starts. Inserted into the starting rotation full-time the following season, Donohue began an outstanding five-year run during which he posted the following numbers:

YEAR	W-L	ERA	SO	SHO	CG	IP	WHIP
1922	18-9	3.12	66	2	19	242.0	1.240
1923	21-15	3.38	84	2	19	274.1	1.356
1924	16-9	3.60	72	3	16	222.1	1.277
1925	21-14	3.08	78	3	**27**	**301.0**	1.193
1926	**20**-14	3.37	73	**5**	17	**285.2**	1.180

In addition to leading all NL hurlers in innings pitched twice and wins, shutouts, and complete games once each, Donohue finished third in the league in ERA twice and WHIP once. Donohue, who consistently ranked among the league leaders in wins, shutouts, and complete games throughout the period, also started more games than any other NL pitcher twice. Meanwhile, although the Reds failed to capture the NL pennant in any of those five seasons, they seriously contended for the flag three times, finishing a close second in 1922, 1923, and 1926.

Long and lean at 6'2" and 185 pounds, the right-handed-throwing Donohue possessed only average speed on his fastball, never striking out more than 84 batters in a season. But he compensated for his lack of velocity by making extensive use of his changeup, which he developed in college.

In discussing the degree to which Donohue relied on his favorite offering, former big-league catcher, manager, and coach Bobby Bragan told the *Fort Worth Star-Telegram* years later, "He's credited with developing the changeup. Today, of course, it's a very familiar pitch, but prior to Donohue's time, pitchers threw it only occasionally, if at all. He was the first one who used it regularly, as a primary pitch."

Unfortunately, Donohue's period of excellence ended in 1927, when he compiled a record of 6–16 and an ERA of 4.11, completed just 12 of his starts, and threw only 190⅔ innings. While some attributed Donohue's fall from grace to the heavy workload he assumed the previous two seasons, the team ascribed his poor performance to an unspecified "illness."

Supporting the contention that his troubles stemmed from overuse, Donohue said during a 1954 interview with Lee Allen, "I was overworked. When Jakie May got spiked by Cliff Heathcote at first base that year (1926), Eppa Rixey, Dolf Luque, and I had to pitch out of turn the rest of the season. Rixey and Luque were stronger than I and could take it, but it was the ruination of me. One series I pitched in three consecutive games, starting and relieving."

However, following Donohue's passing many years later, his nephew, Jim Pemberton, said, "He told me he'd been spiked and nearly died of blood poisoning. They'd actually given him up, but he came back. But after that, he favored the injured leg and ruined his pitching motion."

Never again the same pitcher, Donohue spent the rest of his career relying almost exclusively on grit and determination to retire opposing batters. Remaining in Cincinnati for parts of the next three seasons, Donohue posted a composite record of 18–27 and an ERA that exceeded 5.00, prompting the Reds to trade him and outfielder Ethan Allen to the New York Giants for infielder Pat Crawford on May 27, 1930. During his time in Cincinnati, Donohue compiled an overall record of 127–110, an ERA of 3.73, and a WHIP of 1.328, threw 134 complete games and 16 shutouts, collected 13 saves, and struck out 536 batters in just under 2,000 total innings pitched.

After leaving the Queen City, Donohue split the next three seasons between the Giants, Cleveland Indians, Boston Red Sox, and several minor-league teams, before announcing his retirement in 1933 with a career record of 134–118, a 3.87 ERA, a WHIP of 1.354, 16 shutouts, 138 complete games, and 571 strikeouts in 2,112⅓ total innings of work. An excellent hitting pitcher, Donohue also hit six homers, knocked in 87 runs, and posted a lifetime batting average of .246.

Following his playing days, Donohue returned to Fort Worth, where he and his former battery mate from TCU, Rube Berry, opened Berry Bros. & Donohue Inc., a dry-cleaning business that remained in operation for 30 years. Donohue, who nearly lost his life in an automobile accident on Christmas Eve 1938, lived until February 23, 1988, when he died at the age of 87.

REDS CAREER HIGHLIGHTS

Best Season

Donohue pitched his best ball for the Reds from 1922 to 1926, performing especially well in 1925, when, in addition to compiling a record of 21–14 for a team that finished just a few games over .500, he established career-best marks in ERA (3.08), complete games (27), and innings pitched (301), earning in the process a 15th-place finish in the NL MVP voting.

Memorable Moments/Greatest Performances

Donohue yielded just three hits and two walks during a 1–0 shutout of the Phillies on May 17, 1922.

Although Donohue allowed seven hits and three earned runs during a 6–5 win over the Phillies on September 19, 1923, he helped his own cause by going 3-for-4 at the plate with a double, triple, and four RBIs.

Donohue shut out the Braves on just four hits on August 26, 1924, issuing no walks and recording four strikeouts during a 7–0 Reds win.

Donohue allowed just three hits and two walks during a 3–1 win over the Cardinals on April 25, 1925.

In addition to surrendering just one earned run during an 11–2 victory over the Phillies on May 22, 1925, Donohue went 5-for-5 at the plate with a homer and three RBIs.

Donohue yielded just four hits and walked no one during an 8–0 shutout of the Pirates on July 3, 1925.

Donohue tossed consecutive shutouts in September of 1926, surrendering just three hits and no walks during a 5–0 win over Brooklyn on the 12th of the month, before allowing just four hits and issuing no walks during a 3–0 victory over the Giants four days later.

Notable Achievements

- Won at least 20 games three times, posting 18 victories on another occasion.
- Threw more than 20 complete games once, completing 19 of his starts two other times.
- Threw more than 300 innings once, tossing more than 250 frames two other times.
- Led NL pitchers in wins once, winning percentage once, shutouts once, complete games once, innings pitched twice, and starts twice.
- Finished second in NL in wins once.
- Finished third in NL in ERA twice and WHIP once.
- Ranks among Reds career leaders in wins (tied for 10th), innings pitched (9th), complete games (12th), and games started (11th).

39

BOBBY TOLAN

An integral part of the earliest incarnation of The Big Red Machine, Bobby Tolan spent four seasons in Cincinnati, helping to lead the Reds to three division titles and two NL pennants. A speedy outfielder who excelled both at the bat and on the basepaths, Tolan hit more than 20 homers once, scored more than 100 runs and batted over .300 twice each, and stole more than 20 bases three times, topping the senior circuit one year with 57 thefts. A solid defender as well, Tolan led all NL outfielders in putouts twice, with his strong all-around play earning him one *Sporting News* All-Star nomination, before a string of injuries brought his days as an impact player to an end.

Born in Los Angeles, California, on November 19, 1945, Robert Tolan first began to make a name for himself at Fremont High School, where his outstanding play on the diamond prompted the Pittsburgh Pirates to sign him as an amateur free agent before he turned 18 years of age. The cousin of Eddie Tolan, who won gold for the United States in the 100-meter and 200-meter sprints at the 1932 Summer Olympics, the younger Tolan remained in the Pirates organization for just one year, before being selected by the Cardinals in the December 1963 minor-league draft.

Tolan subsequently spent most of the next three seasons advancing through the St. Louis farm system, during which time he moved from first base to the outfield. Making a seamless transition, Tolan excelled at every stop, performing especially well at Triple-A Jacksonville in 1965, where he batted .290 and stole 45 bases.

Impressed with Tolan's exceptional play, Jacksonville manager Grover Resinger filed a report to the parent club that read: "He's improving all the time. . . . He's going to be one of the better hitters in the game. He's a line-drive hitter, with good power to all fields. Bobby is a Billy Williams type of hitter. He's going to get stronger, and I think he has a good chance to become a 25- to 30-homer hitter. . . . His base-stealing ability is

Bobby Tolan led the NL with 57 stolen bases in 1970.

unlimited. I think he'll eventually steal 50 bases in the big leagues. He's not as fast as [Lou] Brock, but he is above average."

Meanwhile, after facing Tolan in an exhibition game that year, Dodgers shortstop Maury Wills stated, "He could challenge my base-stealing record."

Dodgers catcher John Roseboro added, "The kid looks too good to be true."

After making brief appearances with the Cardinals in each of the previous two seasons, Tolan arrived in the majors to stay in 1967, when he spent the year serving as a fourth outfielder on a team that went on to win the World Series. After assuming a similar role the following year, Tolan became a member of the Reds when they acquired him and reliever Wayne Granger from St. Louis for veteran outfielder Vada Pinson the day after the Cardinals lost the final game of the World Series to the Detroit Tigers.

Named a starter immediately upon his arrival in Cincinnati, Tolan spent the 1969 campaign batting right behind leadoff hitter Pete Rose in the Reds lineup. Acquitting himself extremely well in his first year as a full-time starter, Tolan hit 21 homers, knocked in 93 runs, batted .305, posted an OPS of .821, and ranked among the league leaders with 104 runs scored, 194 hits, 10 triples, and 26 stolen bases. Doing a solid job in the outfield as well while splitting his time between center and right, Tolan led all NL outfielders with 362 putouts. Moved to center full-time the following year, Tolan helped lead the Reds to the pennant by hitting 16 homers, driving in 80 runs, scoring 112 times, batting .316, compiling an OPS of .860, and topping the senior circuit with 57 steals, ending in the process Lou Brock's four-year stranglehold on the stolen base title.

Combining with Pete Rose his first two seasons in Cincinnati to give the Reds an excellent pair of table-setters at the top of their lineup, the lefty-swinging Tolan, who stood 5'11" and weighed close to 175 pounds, drove the ball well to all fields, occasionally exhibiting the ability to reach the seats. Employing a rather unusual batting stance, Tolan held the bat high over his head as if trying to knock a cobweb off the ceiling with a broomstick, before lowering and cocking his weapon as the pitch headed toward home plate. Tolan's offensive arsenal also included an exceptional drag bunt that he often used to leg out infield hits. And once he reached base, Tolan drove opposing pitchers to the point of distraction, frequently causing them to serve up savory offerings to middle-of-the-order sluggers Tony Pérez, Johnny Bench, and Lee May.

Following his outstanding performance in 1970, Tolan missed the ensuing campaign after sustaining a pair of serious injuries during the off-season. While competing in a charity basketball game on January 7, 1971, thereby violating a specific clause in his contract that barred him from that activity, Tolan ruptured his Achilles tendon. After undergoing surgery, Tolan tore his Achilles again in May while running in the outfield as part of his rehab.

Making a triumphant return in 1972, Tolan earned *Sporting News* NL Comeback Player of the Year honors by hitting eight homers, driving in

82 runs, scoring 88 times, stealing 42 bases, batting .283, and posting an OPS of .720 for a Reds team that captured its second NL pennant in three seasons. Although Tolan subsequently performed relatively well at the plate and on the basepaths against Oakland in the World Series, batting .269, driving in six runs, and stealing five bases, he committed a pair of defensive miscues in Game 7 that contributed to a 3–2 Reds loss.

Coming off his bounce-back year, Tolan appeared a step slower in 1973, leading to a dismal performance that resulted in a batting average of .206 and an OPS of .555. Tolan, who also concluded the campaign with just nine homers, 51 RBIs, 42 runs scored, and 15 stolen bases, suffered the additional indignity of having the green light that permitted him to steal on his own taken away from him by manager Sparky Anderson. Growing increasingly dissatisfied as the season progressed, Tolan broke team rules by growing a beard, went AWOL for two days in August, and had several squabbles with management, which remained unhappy over his 1971 basketball injury. Ultimately suspended for engaging in an altercation with one team official, Tolan developed a reputation as a malcontent who shirked his responsibilities.

Dealt to the San Diego Padres for pitcher Clay Kirby on November 9, 1973, Tolan downplayed his troubles with Reds management upon learning of the trade, saying, "I was having a bad year and I got into a little hassle with them. I think the situation got blown out of proportion. Some people said I was a troublemaker. . . . I'll tell you I'm not a troublemaker. I'm real pleased to be traded, and I'm looking forward to playing with the Padres."

Tolan, who, during his time in Cincinnati, hit 54 homers, knocked in 306 runs, scored 346 times, collected 645 hits, 101 doubles, and 23 triples, stole 140 bases, batted .282, compiled an on-base percentage of .335, and posted a slugging percentage of .417, ended up spending two seasons in San Diego, but failed to regain his earlier form. Released by the Padres following the conclusion of the 1975 campaign after posting batting averages of .266 and .255, and totaling 13 homers, 83 RBIs, and 103 runs scored for them, Tolan split the remainder of his career between the Phillies, Pirates, and Padres, assuming a backup role for all three teams, before announcing his retirement shortly after San Diego released him for a second time at the end of 1979. Over parts of 13 big-league seasons, Tolan hit 86 homers, knocked in 497 runs, scored 572 times, amassed 1,121 hits, 173 doubles, and 34 triples, stole 193 bases, batted .265, compiled an on-base percentage of .314, and posted a slugging percentage of .382.

Following his playing days, Tolan spent four years serving as a member of the Padres coaching staff, before beginning a lengthy career as a minor-league manager that included stints with the Beaumont Golden Gators of the Texas League (1984–1985), Erie Orioles of the New York–Penn League (1988–1989), and Great Falls White Sox of the Pioneer League (2006). Tolan also spent two seasons assuming the dual role of player-manager for the St. Petersburg Pelicans of the Senior Professional Baseball Association. In retirement, Tolan, who is 79 years old as of this writing, has disassociated himself from the Reds organization, choosing not to attend any team functions or reunions.

REDS CAREER HIGHLIGHTS

Best Season

Tolan performed extremely well for the Reds in 1969, when, in addition to batting .305, posting an OPS of .821, scoring 104 runs, and stealing 26 bases, he established career-high marks with 21 homers, 93 RBIs, 194 hits, 10 triples, and 302 total bases. But Tolan made a slightly greater overall impact the following season, when he helped the Reds capture the NL pennant by hitting 16 homers, driving in 80 runs, scoring 112 times, collecting 186 hits and 34 doubles, batting .316, posting an OPS of .860, and leading the league with 57 stolen bases, with his strong play earning him a top-20 finish in the NL MVP voting and a spot on the *Sporting News* NL All-Star Team.

Memorable Moments/Greatest Performances

Tolan helped lead the Reds to an 11-inning, 10–9 win over the Astros on July 19, 1969, by knocking in five runs with a homer and single.

Tolan contributed to an 8–5 victory over the Mets on August 5, 1969, by going 3-for-3 with a homer, two doubles, a walk, a stolen base, three RBIs, and a career-high four runs scored.

Tolan delivered the big blow of a 6–1 win over the Padres on April 14, 1970, when he homered with the bases loaded in the bottom of the seventh inning.

Tolan led the Reds to a 3–1 victory over the Pirates in Game 2 of the 1970 NLCS by going 3-for-4 with a solo homer, a stolen base, and three runs scored.

Tolan contributed to an 8–0 win over the Phillies on April 29, 1973, by knocking in five runs with a single and a pair of doubles.

Notable Achievements

- Hit more than 20 home runs once.
- Scored more than 100 runs twice.
- Batted over .300 twice.
- Finished in double digits in triples once.
- Topped 30 doubles once.
- Stole more than 20 bases three times.
- Led NL with 57 stolen bases in 1970.
- Led NL outfielders in putouts twice.
- Three-time division champion (1970, 1972, and 1973).
- Two-time NL champion (1970 and 1972).
- 1970 *Sporting News* NL All-Star selection.
- 1972 *Sporting News* NL Comeback Player of the Year.

40

JOHNNY CUETO

A hard-throwing right-hander who overcame early doubts about his ability to succeed at the major-league level due to his diminutive stature, Johnny Cueto spent parts of eight seasons in Cincinnati, serving as the ace of the Reds' pitching staff much of that time. A key contributor to teams that won two division titles, Cueto won at least 19 games twice, compiled an ERA under 3.00 five times, and struck out more than 200 batters once, earning in the process one All-Star nomination and two top-five finishes in the NL Cy Young voting. Battling through injuries that forced him to spend a considerable amount of time on the disabled list in both 2011 and 2013, Cueto also threw more than 200 innings twice, before the Reds' failures as a team prompted them to trade him to the Kansas City Royals for three pitching prospects in July 2015.

Born in San Pedro de Macorís, Dominican Republic, on February 15, 1986, Johnny Cueto grew up with his four siblings in modest circumstances, helping his family make ends meet by picking fruits and vegetables for neighbors. Raised in that small city that has produced so many major-league players, Cueto spent much of his youth being told that he lacked the size to pursue a career in baseball. Nevertheless, Cueto remained undeterred, drawing inspiration from his childhood idol, Pedro Martínez.

In explaining his dedication to the Hall of Fame pitcher, Cueto told Cincinnati.com in 2014: "I was short and skinny—the scouts from other organizations had rejected me. . . . Some told me I was too short, others thought I was in fact older than the age that appeared in my papers. . . . But Pedro wasn't big. And Pedro was my idol. He was the only player I liked, the only player I followed. I never watched much TV. But I knew about Pedro. Everything for me growing up was Pedro, Pedro, Pedro. He was my inspiration, the person for whom I decided to stop playing outfield to become a pitcher."

Ultimately signed by Reds scout Johnny Almaraz as an undrafted amateur free agent in 2004, Cueto spent the next three years advancing through

Johnny Cueto earned a runner-up finish in the NL Cy Young voting in 2014.

Cincinnati's farm system, before joining the parent club in 2008 after being named the organization's Minor League Pitcher of the Year for the second straight time the previous season.

Inserted into the starting rotation immediately upon his arrival in Cincinnati, the 22-year-old Cueto experienced the usual growing pains of a rookie, going just 9–14 with a 4.81 ERA and 68 bases on balls in 174 innings of work, although he also struck out 158 batters. Faring slightly better in 2009, Cueto compiled a record of 11–11 and an ERA of 4.41, issued 61 bases on balls, and registered 132 strikeouts in 171⅓ innings pitched.

Far more consistent in 2010, Cueto helped the Reds capture the NL Central Division title by going 12–7 with a 3.64 ERA and 138 strikeouts in 185⅔ innings pitched. However, the highly emotional Cueto displayed his inability to retain total control of himself for the first time during an August 10 meeting with the Cardinals, when, after being pinned to the backstop during a bench-clearing brawl between the two teams, he began to kick wildly at several St. Louis players, injuring in the process Chris Carpenter and Jason LaRue, with the latter suffering a severe concussion that forced him to retire at the end of the year. As a result, MLB issued a seven-game suspension to Cueto for what it described as his "violent and aggressive actions."

Although limited to just 24 starts in 2011 by soreness in his right triceps that forced him to spend six weeks on the disabled list, Cueto pitched effectively whenever he found himself able to take the mound, compiling a record of 9–5 and an ERA of 2.31. Fully healthy by the start of the ensuing campaign, Cueto emerged as one of the finest pitchers in the senior circuit, earning a fourth-place finish in the NL Cy Young voting by posting a record of 19–9, registering 170 strikeouts, and ranking among the league leaders with a 2.78 ERA and 217 innings pitched.

Growing increasingly effective as the season progressed after altering his pitching motion, Cueto gradually incorporated more and more of a turn into his windup, which eventually came to resemble the one employed by Luis Tiant decades earlier. Pivoting toward second base and pausing for a moment, Cueto turned his back on the batter before delivering the ball to home plate. The stocky Cueto, who, although officially listed at 5'11" and 229 pounds, actually stood closer to 5'9", presented further challenges to opposing hitters with his wide assortment of pitches, which included a four-seam fastball that typically registered somewhere between 91 and 97 miles per hour on the radar gun, an 89–94 mph two-seam fastball, an 81–88 mph slider, an 87–92 mph cut-fastball, a 78–83 mph curveball, and an 82–86 mph changeup that he only threw to left-handed batters. Known to use multiple windups over the course of a game, Cueto also possessed the ability to make adjustments on the fly, changing his approach to individual batters after noticing the flaws in their swings.

Plagued by a strained lateral muscle, tightness in his lower back, and a sore shoulder in 2013, Cueto made just 11 mound appearances, finishing the season with a record of 5–2 and an ERA of 2.82. Nevertheless, Cueto's history of success prompted manager Dusty Baker to name him the starter versus Pittsburgh in the NL Wild Card Game. But with the contest being played before a raucous Steel City crowd that constantly chanted his name, Cueto once again allowed his emotions to get the best of him. After surrendering a leadoff home run to Pirates outfielder Marlon Byrd in the bottom of the second inning, Cueto became so disturbed by the continuous chanting of the fans that he dropped the ball off the mound. Returning to the slab, Cueto yielded a home run to Pittsburgh catcher Russell Martin on the very next pitch, with the two homers providing much of the impetus for a 6–2 Pirates win during which the Reds' right-hander allowed eight hits and four earned runs in just 3⅓ innings of work.

Seeking to redeem himself the following year, Cueto put together the finest season of his career, earning his first All-Star selection, a 12th-place finish in the NL MVP voting, and a runner-up finish in the Cy Young balloting by placing second in the league with 20 victories (against nine losses), a 2.25 ERA, and a WHIP of 0.960, while also topping the circuit with 242 strikeouts, 243⅔ innings pitched, and 34 starts. Following the conclusion of the campaign, Cueto, who led all NL hurlers with 39 assists, also received the Wilson Defensive Player of the Year Award for his defensive excellence.

Cueto continued to perform well on the mound for the Reds in 2015, compiling an ERA of 2.62, posting a WHIP of 0.934, and winning seven of his 13 decisions through late July, despite receiving very little run support from his teammates. But with the Reds well out of contention on July 26, they completed a trade with the eventual world champion Kansas City Royals that sent Cueto to KC for minor-league pitchers Brandon Finnegan, John Lamb, and Cody Reed.

In explaining his decision to part ways with his team's best pitcher, Reds general manager Walt Jocketty said at the time, "Obviously, this is a tough trade. Johnny has been part of the organization for a long time. We have great affection for him as a pitcher and a person. So, it was difficult. . . . But we're in a situation where this is the best thing for our franchise now. We got three left-handed pitchers—three quality left-handed pitchers—who we think very highly of. It was tough for Kansas City to give up all three. But we were finally able to do that. There was a lot of interest in Johnny. And we felt this was the value we could get."

Meanwhile, in discussing his impending departure from Cincinnati, Cueto stated, "I know it's a good trade, but I'm very sad. I'm very thankful to my teammates, my fans, and my coaching staff. It's a very emotional time for me. But I understand it's part of the game. I'm just excited about my next step."

Cueto, who, during his time in Cincinnati, compiled an overall record of 92–63, an ERA of 3.21, and a WHIP of 1.165, threw 11 complete games and five shutouts, and struck out 1,115 batters in 1,339 total innings of work, struggled somewhat over the final two months of the regular season, going just 4–7 with a 4.76 ERA for his new team. But he subsequently helped lead the Royals to their second world championship by allowing just one run and two hits during a complete-game 7–1 victory over the Mets in Game 2 of the World Series.

A free agent at season's end, Cueto signed with the San Francisco Giants, with whom he earned his second All-Star nomination in 2016 by compiling a record of 18–5 and an ERA of 2.79, registering 198 strikeouts, and throwing a league-leading five complete games. But after experiencing arm problems the following year that limited him to just 25 starts, Cueto missed most of the next three seasons after undergoing Tommy John surgery during the early stages of the 2018 campaign. Failing to regain his earlier form after he returned to action full-time in 2021, Cueto compiled an overall record of just 16–21 over the course of the next three seasons, which he split equally between the Giants, Chicago White Sox, and Miami Marlins. Inked to a minor-league deal by the Texas Rangers on April 23, 2024, Cueto spent two months toiling in their farm system before exercising the opt-out clause in his contract and becoming a free agent again. Cueto subsequently signed with the Los Angeles Angels, with whom he made two starts, before being designated for assignment. If the now 39-year-old Cueto never throws another pitch in the majors, he will end his big-league career with a record of 144–113, an ERA of 3.52, a WHIP of 1.210, 18 complete games, 8 shutouts, and 1,857 strikeouts in 2,256⅓ innings pitched.

REDS CAREER HIGHLIGHTS

Best Season

Although Cueto had an excellent year for the Reds in 2012, earning a fourth-place finish in the NL Cy Young voting by ranking among the league leaders with 19 wins, a 2.78 ERA, and 217 innings pitched, he performed even better in 2014, when his 20 victories, 2.25 ERA, 0.960 WHIP, and league-leading 242 strikeouts and 243⅔ innings pitched earned him a runner-up finish to Clayton Kershaw in the Cy Young balloting. Particularly outstanding during the early stages of the campaign, Cueto started the season with nine straight starts in which he worked at least seven innings and allowed two runs or less.

Memorable Moments/Greatest Performances

Cueto performed brilliantly in his major-league debut, earning a victory over the Arizona Diamondbacks by recording 10 strikeouts, issuing no walks, and allowing just one run and one hit over the first seven innings of a 3–2 Reds win.

Cueto tossed a one-hit shutout on May 11, 2010, recording eight strikeouts, issuing no walks, and yielding only a third-inning infield single by Pittsburgh shortstop Ronny Cedeño during a 9–0 win over the Pirates.

Cueto surrendered just three hits, walked one batter, and struck out eight during a 9–0 shutout of the Giants on July 31, 2011.

Cueto threw another three-hit shutout on April 16, 2014, walking no one and recording 12 strikeouts during a 4–0 win over the Pirates.

Although Cueto did not figure in the decision, he allowed just three hits and struck out 11 batters over the first eight innings of a 1–0, 10-inning loss to the Braves on April 27, 2014.

Cueto yielded just three hits, walked two batters, and recorded eight strikeouts during a 5–0 shutout of the Padres on May 15, 2014.

Cueto issued one walk, struck out 11, and allowed only a first-inning single to Bryce Harper and a fifth-inning triple to shortstop Ian Desmond during a 5–0 shutout of the Washington Nationals on July 7, 2015.

Notable Achievements

- Won 20 games once, posting 19 victories another time.
- Posted winning percentage over .700 once.
- Compiled ERA under 3.00 five times, finishing with mark under 2.50 twice.
- Posted WHIP under 1.000 twice.
- Struck out more than 200 batters once.
- Threw more than 200 innings twice.
- Led NL pitchers in strikeouts once, innings pitched once, starts twice, and assists once.
- Finished second in NL in wins once, ERA once, and WHIP once.
- Ranks among Reds career leaders in WHIP (6th) and strikeouts (8th).
- Two-time division champion (2010 and 2012).
- August 10, 2014, NL Player of the Week.
- 2014 Reds team MVP.
- Finished in top five of NL Cy Young voting twice, placing as high as second in 2014.
- 2014 NL All-Star selection.

41

JOHNNY VANDER MEER

The only pitcher in major-league history to throw consecutive no-hitters, Johnny Vander Meer is known to most baseball fans for that singular achievement. Yet even though Vander Meer's remarkable feat remains his primary claim to fame, the hard-throwing left-hander accomplished considerably more during his 13-year big-league career, most of which he spent in Cincinnati. A member of the Reds for parts of 11 seasons, Vander Meer won at least 15 games five times, compiled an ERA under 3.00 three times, and led all NL hurlers in strikeouts on three separate occasions, en route to earning four All-Star selections and one *Sporting News* MLB Player of the Year nomination. Meanwhile, despite being plagued by control problems throughout his career, Vander Meer continues to rank among the franchise's all-time leaders in strikeouts, shutouts, and innings pitched more than three-quarters of a century after he threw his last pitch for the Reds.

Born in Prospect Park, New Jersey, on November 2, 1914, John Samuel Vander Meer moved with his family at the age of four to nearby Midland Park, where he got his start in organized baseball in a church league while still in elementary school. Nicknamed "The Dutch Master" because his parents emigrated to the United States from Holland, Vander Meer began pitching semiprofessionally during his early teenage years, performing so well that the Brooklyn Dodgers signed him as an amateur free agent as soon as he graduated from Midland Park High School in 1933.

After beginning his pro career with Brooklyn's minor-league affiliate in Dayton, Ohio, Vander Meer spent the next two seasons pitching for the Scranton Miners of the New York–Penn League, a Class A farm team of the Boston Bees. Dealt to the Reds for minor-league pitcher Tiny Chaplin following the conclusion of the 1935 campaign after experiencing very little success at Scranton, Vander Meer finally began to realize his potential with the Durham Bulls of the Class B Piedmont League, gaining recognition from the *Sporting News* as Minor League Player of the Year in 1936 by going 19–6 with a 2.65 ERA and 295 strikeouts in 214 innings of work.

Johnny Vander Meer's consecutive no-hitters in 1938 remains one of the greatest feats in the history of the game.

Promoted to the big leagues in 1937, Vander Meer struggled in his first stint with the Reds, earning a return trip to the minors early in the year by winning just three of his eight decisions, posting an ERA of 3.84, and walking 69 batters in 84⅓ innings pitched. But after working on a new delivery aimed at improving his control the following spring, Vander Meer became a regular member of the Reds' starting rotation. Establishing himself as one of the NL's better pitchers in 1938, Vander Meer earned All-Star honors by compiling a record of 15–10 and an ERA of 3.12, throwing 225⅓ innings,

16 complete games, and three shutouts, and finishing third in the league with 125 strikeouts, although he also walked 103 batters. Particularly outstanding during the month of June, Vander Meer went a perfect 7–0 with an ERA of 1.46, at one point throwing 33 consecutive scoreless innings and two straight no-hitters.

The first of Vander Meer's no-nos came on June 11, when he allowed just three walks during a 3–0 shutout of the Boston Braves. Returning to the mound four days later, Vander Meer issued eight bases on balls but surrendered no hits during a 6–0 win over the Dodgers, with his extraordinary feat prompting the *Sporting News* to name him its MLB Player of the Year at season's end.

Vander Meer followed up his breakout season with a disappointing 1939 campaign, going just 5–9 with a 4.67 ERA after falling ill during spring training and sustaining an injury when he slipped on a wet pitching mound in Pittsburgh. Vander Meer subsequently struggled terribly with his control early in 1940, walking 41 batters in only 48 innings of work, prompting the Reds to return him to the minors in June, before recalling him later in the year. Although Vander Meer finished the season just 3–1 with a 3.75 ERA, he contributed to Cincinnati's World Series triumph over Detroit by working three scoreless innings in his lone appearance in the Fall Classic.

Regaining his regular spot in the starting rotation in 1941, Vander Meer began an outstanding three-year stretch during which he ranked among the finest pitchers in the senior circuit. After compiling a record of 16–13, leading the league with 202 strikeouts, and placing among the leaders with a 2.82 ERA, 18 complete games, and six shutouts in 1941, Vander Meer earned All-Star honors the following year by going 18–12 with a 2.43 ERA, 21 complete games, four shutouts, 244 innings pitched, and a league-high 186 strikeouts. Although Vander Meer subsequently posted a mark of just 15–16 in 1943, he compiled an ERA of 2.87, completed 21 of his starts, finished second among NL hurlers with 289 innings pitched, and again led the league in strikeouts, this time with 174.

Despite performing well for the Reds much of his time in Cincinnati, the 6'1", 190-pound Vander Meer never truly established himself as an elite pitcher due to his inability to consistently locate his fastball. Blessed with one of the NL's best heaters, Vander Meer possessed the ability to throw the ball past opposing hitters. But he also walked far too many batters, issuing more than 100 bases on balls five times, en route to amassing a career total of 1,132 walks in just over 2,100 innings pitched.

Enlisting in the US Navy on March 3, 1944, Vander Meer spent the next two years serving his country during World War II. Initially assigned to the Welfare Recreation Department at the Sampson Naval Training Center in New York, Vander Meer spent most of 1944 pitching for the unit's baseball team, before touring the Pacific with the Fifth Fleet ballclub the following year, while being stationed mostly at Guam.

Discharged from the military on December 20, 1945, Vander Meer returned to the Reds the following spring. But despite compiling a record of 17–14 and an ERA of 3.41 in 1948, Vander Meer never regained his earlier form. Sold to the Cubs prior to the start of the 1950 campaign, Vander Meer spent one year in Chicago and another in Cleveland, going a combined 3–5 over the course of those two seasons, before announcing his retirement after being released by the Indians on June 30, 1951.

Vander Meer, who, during his time in Cincinnati, compiled a record of 116–116, an ERA of 3.41, and a WHIP of 1.382, threw 131 complete games and 29 shutouts, and struck out 1,251 batters in 2,028 innings of work, continued to pitch in the minor leagues for another five years, throwing a no-hitter for the Tulsa Oilers at the age of 37 in 1952, before retiring as a player completely. Following his playing days, Vander Meer returned to Cincinnati, where he spent 10 years serving as a manager in the Reds farm system. After leaving baseball, Vander Meer worked for the Schlitz Brewery company as a military sales manager for 20 years, before retiring to private life. Vander Meer lived until October 6, 1997, when he died of an abdominal aneurysm at his home in Tampa, Florida, at the age of 82. He was subsequently buried with a baseball in his left hand.

REDS CAREER HIGHLIGHTS

Best Season

Vander Meer's consecutive no-hitters in 1938 gained him recognition from the *Sporting News* as its MLB Player of the Year. However, Vander Meer compiled better overall numbers in both 1941 and 1942, performing especially well in the second of those campaigns. In addition to leading all NL hurlers with 186 strikeouts, Vander Meer ranked among the league leaders with 18 wins, a 2.43 ERA, a WHIP of 1.189, 21 complete games, 244 innings pitched, and four shutouts, establishing in the process career-best marks in each of the first four categories.

Memorable Moments/Greatest Performances

Vander Meer kept the opposition off the scoreboard for 33 straight innings from June 5 to June 19, 1938, highlighting his streak with consecutive no-hitters. After allowing just three walks during a 3–0 no-hitter of the Boston Braves on June 11, Vander Meer tossed another no-no four days later, issuing eight bases on balls and recording seven strikeouts during a 6–0 win over the Dodgers in the first night game ever held at Brooklyn's Ebbets Field.

Vander Meer tossed a one-hit shutout on June 6, 1941, issuing one walk, recording 12 strikeouts, and yielding only a second-inning infield single by Phillies left fielder Danny Litwhiler during a 7–0 Reds win.

Vander Meer turned in another dominant performance on September 6, 1941, allowing just two hits, issuing three walks, and recording a career-high 14 strikeouts during a 2–0 shutout of the Cardinals.

Less than two weeks later, on September 17, 1941, Vander Meer yielded just three hits and struck out 11 batters during a 1–0 shutout of the Phillies.

Vander Meer continued his dominance of the Phillies on July 12, 1942, allowing only three hits, issuing four walks, and striking out 13 during a 2–0 Reds win.

Vander Meer outdueled St. Louis pitching ace Mort Cooper on April 21, 1943, yielding just two hits, and walking five batters during a 1–0 shutout of the Cardinals.

Vander Meer performed magnificently against the Dodgers on September 11, 1946, allowing just seven hits, and recording 14 strikeouts over the first 15 innings of a game that ended in a 0–0 tie after 19 innings.

Vander Meer hit the only home run of his career during a 3–2 win over the Boston Braves on June 12, 1948, in which he allowed seven hits and two runs over the first 7⅓ innings, before turning the game over to the bullpen.

Vander Meer ended the 1948 campaign in style, yielding just two hits and four walks during a 1–0 shutout of the Pirates in the regular-season finale.

Notable Achievements

- Won at least 15 games five times, topping 17 victories twice.
- Compiled ERA under 3.00 three times.
- Struck out more than 200 batters once.

- Threw more than 20 complete games twice.
- Threw more than 250 innings once.
- Threw consecutive no-hitters (vs. Braves on June 11, 1938, and vs. Dodgers on June 15, 1938).
- Led NL pitchers in strikeouts three times and starts once.
- Finished second in NL in shutouts once and innings pitched once.
- Ranks among Reds career leaders in strikeouts (tied for 4th), shutouts (3rd), innings pitched (7th), and games started (tied for 7th).
- Two-time NL champion (1939 and 1940).
- 1940 world champion.
- 1938 *Sporting News* MLB Player of the Year.
- Four-time NL All-Star selection (1938, 1939, 1942, and 1943).
- 1938 *Sporting News* MLB All-Star selection.

42

WALLY POST

A powerful right-handed batter who became known for his tape-measure home runs, Wally Post spent parts of 12 seasons in Cincinnati, serving as a regular member of the Reds' starting outfield much of that time. Playing his best ball for the Reds from 1954 to 1957, Post hit more than 30 homers twice, knocked in more than 100 runs once, and batted over .300 once, while also doing an excellent job of patrolling right field at Crosley Field. Dealt to the Phillies prior to the start of the 1958 campaign, Post remained away from the Queen City for the next two and a half years, before returning to the Reds for a second tour of duty and making significant contributions to their 1961 pennant-winning ballclub.

Born in St. Wendelin, Ohio, on July 9, 1929, Walter Charles Post grew up with his eight siblings in the nearby village of St. Henry, just off the Ohio-Indiana state line. After receiving his early education in a one-room school in St. Wendelin, Post enrolled at St. Henry High School, where, after playing softball exclusively during his formative years, he got his start in organized baseball.

Developing into a star before long, Post excelled for the Skins at both pitcher and first base, making a particularly strong impression on head coach Charles Karcher with his hitting ability. Recalling the first home run that Post hit his freshman year, Karcher said, "We were playing in Houston, Ohio, about 25 miles from St. Henry. There was an embankment in left field that led to the highway. Nobody ever hit a ball out there. Wally did. . . . He got all of it. It went about 400 feet."

Karcher added, "Wally was a shy boy; pleasant, quick smile. Unassuming, the kind of kid you want to know and be around. He was a little chubby when he first came out for the team—about 5'9" and 165 pounds—but by the time he was a junior, he was 5'11" and 190 pounds. He was so good the Reds signed him after his junior year; he couldn't play as a senior."

Inked to a deal by the Reds at the tender age of 16, Post made a brief appearance with the team's minor-league affiliate in Middletown, Ohio,

Wally Post homered 40 times for the Reds in 1955.

in 1946, before spending the 1947 campaign with Class D Muncie of the Ohio State League, for whom he compiled a record of 17–7 and an ERA of 3.33. Promoted to the Columbia Reds of the Class A South Atlantic League the following year, Post did not fare nearly as well on the mound, winning just eight of his 19 decisions, with his lack of success prompting the organization to convert him into an outfielder. Post subsequently spent most of the next five seasons developing his outfield and batting skills at five different levels of the Reds farm system, appearing briefly with the parent club in four of those campaigns, before arriving in Cincinnati to stay in 1954 after hitting 33 homers, driving in 120 runs, and batting .289 at Triple-A Indianapolis the previous year.

Performing relatively well his first full season in the Queen City, Post hit 18 homers, knocked in 83 runs, batted .255, and compiled an OPS of .731 for a Reds team that finished six games under .500. Reaching the apex of his career the following year, Post hit 40 homers, knocked in 109 runs, scored 116 times, batted .309, and compiled an OPS of .946, ranking among the league leaders in each of those categories.

Although Post failed to gain All-Star recognition in 1955, he began to develop a reputation as one of the most powerful hitters in the senior circuit. Capable of hitting the ball as far as anyone in the league, Post, who stood 6'1" and weighed close to 200 pounds, won many a free suit by hitting the "Hit Sign, Win Suit" billboard that stood atop the laundromat across the street from Crosley Field's left field wall. Delivering one of his most notable home runs on the road, Post drove a ball off the scoreboard clock at Busch Stadium in St. Louis that closest estimates revealed would have traveled 569 feet had its flight not been interrupted. On another occasion, Post sent a ball through the supposedly indestructible new scoreboard at Crosley Field during batting practice.

While Post received far more attention for his prodigious slugging, he proved to be an excellent defensive outfielder as well, leading all NL right fielders in putouts once and finishing second two other times. Blessed with one of the league's strongest throwing arms, Post also finished among the top three players at his position in assists six straight times, twice throwing out as many as 15 runners on the basepaths.

Post followed up his banner year with another solid season, hitting 36 homers, driving in 83 runs, scoring 94 times, and posting an OPS of .807 in 1956, although he batted just .249 and led the league with 124 strikeouts. Once again unable to reach the level of excellence he attained two years earlier, Post hit 20 homers, knocked in 74 runs, scored only 68 times, and batted just .244 in 1957, prompting the Reds to trade him to the Phillies at the end of the year for veteran pitcher Harvey Haddix.

Post ended up spending the next two-plus seasons in Philadelphia, batting a composite .269 and totaling 36 homers and 168 RBIs for the Phillies, before returning to Cincinnati on June 15, 1960, when the Reds reacquired him for outfielders Tony González and Lee Walls. After batting .281, compiling an OPS of .892, hitting 17 homers, and driving in 38 runs in 77 games and 280 total plate appearances with the Reds the rest of the year, Post helped them capture the NL pennant the following season by hitting 20 homers, knocking in 57 runs, scoring 44 times, batting

.294, and compiling an OPS of .932 in 99 games, while splitting his time between both corner outfield positions. Assuming a part-time role for the Reds in 1962, Post hit 17 homers, knocked in 62 runs, and batted .263 in 109 games and 321 total plate appearances, before being sold to the Minnesota Twins during the early stages of the ensuing campaign.

Post, who left the Reds having hit 172 homers, driven in 525 runs, scored 463 times, collected 805 hits, 150 doubles, and 17 triples, stolen 19 bases, batted .266, and compiled an on-base percentage of .323 and a slugging percentage of .498 as a member of the team, spent the rest of the 1963 season serving the Twins primarily as a pinch-hitter, appearing in only 21 games with them, before being released at the end of the year. Subsequently signed by the Cleveland Indians, Post made just 11 total plate appearances, before being released again on May 9, 1964. Announcing his retirement shortly thereafter, Post ended his playing career with 210 home runs, 699 RBIs, 594 runs scored, 1,064 hits, 194 doubles, 28 triples, a .266 batting average, a .323 on-base percentage, and a .485 slugging percentage.

After retiring from baseball, Post returned to St. Henry, where he accepted a position as an officer in his father-in-law's business, the Minister Canning Company of Minister, Ohio. Post also remained in touch with his closest friend from his baseball days, Joe Nuxhall, who recalled, "There'd be winter baseball banquets in Cincinnati, and Wally would drive all the way down from St. Henry, and he and his wife would stay at our house. We'd pick up Gus Bell and his wife, and Klu [Ted Kluszewski] and his wife would be there. And I'd drive up to St. Henry and go to dances and play charity basketball games at the school gym on Sunday afternoons."

Post lived until January 6, 1982, when, after undergoing treatments for cancer the previous few weeks, he died at his son's home in St. Henry at the age of 52.

REDS CAREER HIGHLIGHTS

Best Season

Post had his finest season for the Reds in 1955, when he earned a 12th-place finish in the NL MVP voting by establishing career-high marks in virtually every offensive category, including homers (40), RBIs (109), runs scored (116), hits (186), doubles (33), total bases (345), batting average (.309), on-base percentage (.372), and slugging percentage (.574).

Memorable Moments/Greatest Performances

Post gave the Reds a dramatic 6–5 victory over the Cubs on April 24, 1954, when he hit a two-out, three-run homer in the bottom of the ninth inning.

Post contributed to a 19–1 mauling of the Pirates on July 14, 1955, by going 4-for-6 with two homers, a walk, four RBIs, and five runs scored.

Post helped lead the Reds to a 6–4 win over the Giants on July 24, 1955, by going 4-for-5 with a homer and three RBIs.

Post proved to be the difference in a 4–3 win over the Phillies on August 29, 1955, hitting a pair of solo home runs off Hall of Fame right-hander Robin Roberts, with his second blast in the top of the ninth inning providing the margin of victory.

Post had the most productive day of his career on April 29, 1956, when he collected six hits, homered four times, and knocked in eight runs during a doubleheader sweep of the Cubs. After leading the Reds to a 5–4 win in Game 1 by going 3-for-4 with two homers and four RBIs, Post put up identical numbers during their 8–4 victory in Game 2.

Notable Achievements

- Hit at least 20 home runs four times, topping 30 homers twice and 40 homers once.
- Knocked in more than 100 runs once.
- Scored more than 100 runs once.
- Batted over .300 once.
- Posted slugging percentage over .500 three times.
- Posted OPS over .900 twice.
- Topped 30 doubles once.
- Finished third in NL with 116 runs scored in 1955.
- Led NL right fielders in putouts once, assists once, and double plays turned once.
- Ranks ninth in franchise history with .498 slugging percentage.
- 1961 NL champion.
- 1955 Reds team MVP.

43

DOLF LUQUE

One of baseball's most overlooked, underappreciated, and misunderstood figures, Dolf Luque proved to be a pioneer in many ways. The first Latin American to fashion an enduring and outstanding major-league career, the Cuban-born Luque spent parts of 20 seasons pitching in the big leagues, winning close to 200 games despite being constantly subjected to the racial and cultural stereotypes that persisted during his playing days. A member of the Reds from 1918 to 1929, Luque, who also played for the Braves, Dodgers, and Giants, won a total of 154 games during his time in Cincinnati, compiling in the process the fifth-highest win total in franchise history. The author of one of the greatest single-season pitching performances in team annals, Luque also posted an ERA under 3.00 four times, threw more than 20 complete games three times, and tossed more than 300 innings twice, doing so while continuing his string of 34 straight seasons in which he played and managed in the Cuban winter leagues.

Born in La Habana, Cuba, on August 4, 1890, Adolfo Domingo de Guzmán Luque grew up in the low-rent district of Havana, where he joined the newly formed republican army during the last few years of the first decade of the 20th century. While serving as an artilleryman in the military, Luque also made a name for himself as a slugging third baseman on the infantry baseball club, prompting the amateur league Vedado Tennis Club team to recruit him when he left the service. After being converted into a pitcher, Luque signed with the Cuban League Fe ballclub in 1912, beginning in the process a professional playing career that lasted more than three decades.

Although Luque failed to win a game in his first two years as a pro, he made a favorable impression on Dr. Hernández Henríquez, a Cuban entrepreneur residing in New Jersey and operating the Long Branch franchise of the New Jersey–New York State League, who recruited him for his team. Luque subsequently split the next two seasons between Long Branch and Jersey City of the International League, compiling an overall record of

Dolf Luque led all NL pitchers with 27 wins and a 1.93 ERA in 1923.

24–15, before having his contract purchased by the Boston Braves during the latter stages of the 1914 campaign. Luque ended up appearing in just a handful of games with the Braves, spending most of the next four seasons in the minors, before beginning his major-league career in earnest with the Reds in 1918 at the rather advanced age of 27.

Starting 10 games for the Reds after joining them in late July, Luque won six of his nine decisions, pitched to an ERA of 3.80, and threw nine complete games and one shutout. Working as both a starter and a reliever in 1919, Luque performed well in his dual role, compiling a record of

10–3 and an ERA of 2.63, posting a WHIP of 1.179, completing six of his nine starts, tossing a pair of shutouts, and saving three games for Cincinnati's world championship ballclub. Used primarily as a starter in 1920, Luque established himself as one of the NL's better pitchers by going 13–9, ranking among the league leaders with a 2.51 ERA and a WHIP of 1.098, and throwing 10 complete games and 207⅔ innings.

Despite going a combined 30–42 over the course of the next two seasons, Luque pitched relatively well, compiling an ERA of 3.38, leading the NL with three shutouts, and ranking among the leaders with 102 strikeouts, 25 complete games, and 304 innings pitched in 1921, before placing in the league's top 10 with a 3.31 ERA, 18 complete games, and 261 innings pitched the following year. But Luque took his game to another level in 1923, when he helped the Reds finish second in the NL, just 4½ games behind the pennant-winning Giants, by going 27–8 with 28 complete games, 322 innings pitched, 151 strikeouts, and a league-best 1.93 ERA and six shutouts.

Although the right-handed-throwing Luque, who stood just 5'7" and weighed only 160 pounds, lacked an overpowering fastball, he possessed one of the best curves in the game, which typically broke down in the strike zone or below the batter's knees, thereby inducing an inordinately high number of groundball outs. Also blessed with excellent control and outstanding movement on his pitches, Luque worked the corners of the plate, moving the ball inside and out, and up and down, rarely giving the batter something down the middle.

An intense competitor, Luque, who slipped through the cracks of baseball's unwritten rules on segregation because of his light skin color and blue eyes, often rubbed his opponents the wrong way with his combative personality, with writer Roberto González Echevarria describing his countryman as a "snarling, vulgar, cursing, aggressive pug, who, although small at five-seven, was always ready to fight."

Known for his bad temper, Luque put that side of his persona on display for all to see one afternoon in Cincinnati in the summer of 1923, when, having grown weary of the insults and racial slurs being hurled at him from the Giants bench throughout the contest, he placed his glove and ball on the mound, charged into the New York dugout, and slugged Casey Stengel, who happened to be next to the primary instigator, outfielder Bill Cunningham.

Unfortunately, such behavior helped foster the prevailing thinking of the day that stereotyped all Latins as "combative hotheads." And with Luque also developing a reputation as someone who enjoyed drinking, gambling, and chasing women, he received less latitude than his fellow players from big-league fans and ballpark scribes for his many vices.

Although Luque never again reached the heights he attained in 1923, he remained an effective pitcher for the Reds for five more years, performing especially well in 1925, when, despite compiling a record of just 16–18, he earned a 13th-place finish in the NL MVP voting by leading the league with a 2.63 ERA, a WHIP of 1.172, and four shutouts, while also ranking among the leaders with 140 strikeouts, 22 complete games, and 291 innings pitched. But after the 39-year-old Luque posted a mark of just 5–16 and compiled an ERA of 4.50 in 1929, the Reds traded him to Brooklyn the following offseason for veteran pitcher Doug McWeeny.

Luque, who, during his time in Cincinnati, compiled an overall record of 154–152 and an ERA of 3.09, posted a WHIP of 1.265, struck out 970 batters, tossed 24 shutouts, collected 11 saves, and threw 2,668⅔ innings, ended up spending two years in Brooklyn, experiencing a moderate amount of success, before serving the Giants primarily as a reliever for parts of the next four seasons. Retiring from American baseball early in 1935, Luque ended his big-league career with a record of 194–179, an ERA of 3.24, a WHIP of 1.288, 206 complete games, 26 shutouts, 29 saves, and 1,130 strikeouts in 3,220⅓ total innings of work.

Remaining with the Giants following his retirement as an active player, Luque, who won a World Series as a member of the team in 1933, spent seven seasons serving as pitching coach under managers Bill Terry and Mel Ott, helping New York capture back-to-back pennants in 1936 and 1937. After ending his association with major-league baseball, Luque continued to manage in the Cuban winter league and the Mexican League for several more years, guiding his teams to a total of 12 pennants.

Luque lived until July 3, 1957, when he died of a heart attack in Havana at 66 years of age. Upon learning of Luque's passing, legendary sportswriter Frank Graham paid tribute to the major leagues' first true Hispanic star when he wrote: "It's hard to believe. Adolfo Luque was much too strong, too tough, too determined to die at this age of sixty-six. . . . He died of a heart attack. Did he? It sounds absurd. Luque's heart failed him in the clutch? It never did before. How many close ballgames did he pitch? How many did he win . . . or lose? When he won, it was sometimes on his heart. When he lost, it was never because his heart missed a beat. Some enemy hitter got lucky or some idiot playing behind Luque fumbled a groundball or dropped a sinking liner or was out of position so that he did not make the catch that should have been so easy for him."

REDS CAREER HIGHLIGHTS

Best Season

Luque had easily the finest season of his career in 1923, when he led all NL hurlers with 27 wins, a .771 winning percentage, a 1.93 ERA, and six shutouts, while also finishing second in the circuit with 151 strikeouts, 28 complete games, and a WHIP of 1.140.

Memorable Moments/Greatest Performances

Luque allowed just three hits and two walks during a 7–0 shutout of the Phillies on August 5, 1920.

Luque turned in a similarly impressive performance on July 27, 1921, yielding just four hits and issuing no walks during a 2–0 shutout of the Boston Braves.

Luque tossed 30⅓ consecutive scoreless innings from June 10 to June 24, 1923.

Luque outdueled Hall of Fame right-hander Burleigh Grimes on June 19, 1923, allowing just five hits and recording eight strikeouts during an 11-inning, 1–0 win over the Brooklyn Robins.

Luque won both ends of a doubleheader against the Braves on July 17, 1923, yielding five hits and two runs over the first six innings of a 4–3 victory in Game 1, before allowing 10 hits and two earned runs during a complete-game 9–5 win in Game 2.

Luque surrendered just three hits and one unearned run during a complete-game 4–1 win over the Braves on August 28, 1923.

Luque continued to dominate the Braves lineup on June 5, 1925, yielding just three hits, walking no one, and recording 10 strikeouts during a 10-inning, 1–0 Reds win.

Luque displayed his mettle on September 22, 1927, allowing just five hits and three walks over 12 innings, in earning a 2–1 win over the Brooklyn Robins.

In addition to yielding just six hits and two walks during a 7–0 shutout of the Giants on May 13, 1929, Luque went 2-for-4 at the plate with a homer and two RBIs.

Notable Achievements

- Won 27 games in 1923.
- Posted winning percentage over .700 twice.
- Compiled ERA under 3.00 four times, finishing with mark under 2.00 once.
- Threw more than 20 complete games three times.
- Threw more than 300 innings twice, tossing more than 250 frames two other times.
- Led NL pitchers in wins once, winning percentage once, ERA twice, WHIP once, and shutouts three times.
- Finished second in NL in WHIP once, strikeouts twice, complete games once, innings pitched three times, and saves once.
- Ranks among Reds career leaders in wins (5th), shutouts (tied for 5th), innings pitched (2nd), complete games (8th), pitching appearances (8th), and games started (3rd).
- 1919 NL champion.
- 1919 world champion.

44

BOB BESCHER

One of the premier base-stealers of the Dead Ball Era, Bob Bescher spent six seasons in Cincinnati, swiping the seventh-most bags of any player in team annals during that time. The NL leader in steals four straight times, Bescher stole 81 bases one year, setting in the process a post-19th-century single-season franchise record that still stands. A solid all-around player, the switch-hitting Bescher also finished in double digits in triples four times, scored more than 100 runs twice, drew more than 100 bases on balls once, and did an excellent job of patrolling left field for the Reds, with his strong play earning him one top-five finish in the NL MVP voting.

Born in London, Ohio, on February 25, 1884, Robert Henry Bescher grew up some 25 miles southwest of Columbus as an only child after his brother and sister died young. Leaving home at only 15 years of age to attend Notre Dame, which until World War I enrolled students from the first grade through graduate school, Bescher remained at South Bend for four years, participating in no varsity sports, before heading to Nebraska, where he spent a year punching cows on a cattle ranch.

Returning to Ohio in 1904, Bescher enrolled at Wittenberg College in Springfield, where he spent two seasons starring on the gridiron, using his speed and sturdy 6'1", 200-pound frame to earn All-State honors at half-back. Excelling in baseball as well, Bescher performed so well on the diamond that Lima (Ohio) of the Class C Interstate Association offered him a minor-league contract in 1906. After batting .539 in 39 games at Lima, Bescher joined the Class B Central League team in Dayton, for whom, after suffering a broken leg in his first full season, he batted 305 and stole 62 bases in 1908.

Impressed with Bescher's outstanding performance at Dayton, the Reds purchased his contract in September 1908. Acquitting himself extremely well during the season's final month, Bescher batted .272, posted an OPS of .740, knocked in 17 runs, scored 16 times, and stole 10 bases in only 32 games. Somewhat less successful at the plate in 1909, Bescher batted

Bob Bescher's total of 81 stolen bases in 1911 represents a post-19th-century single-season franchise record.

just .240, compiled an OPS of just .647, and knocked in only 34 runs. Nevertheless, he finished second on the team with 73 runs scored and led the NL with 54 stolen bases.

Despite having to undergo emergency surgery at one point during the ensuing campaign after mangling his hand on the sharp edges of the box seats while attempting to catch a foul ball, Bescher improved his overall offensive performance dramatically, batting .250, compiling an OPS of .682, hitting four homers, driving in 48 runs, scoring 95 times, drawing 81 bases on balls, and leading the league with 70 steals. Fully healthy in

1911, Bescher emerged as arguably the Reds' best player, batting .275, posting an OPS of .753, ranking among the league leaders with 106 runs scored, 165 hits, 32 doubles, and 102 bases on balls, and topping the circuit with 81 stolen bases, which established a modern NL record that stood until 1962, when Maury Wills swiped 104 bags for the Dodgers.

Hailed as the "King of Base-Stealers" by F. C. Lane of *Baseball Magazine*, Bescher, who spent most of his time in Cincinnati batting leadoff, drew praise not only for the number of steals he amassed, but also for the frequency with which he ran once he reached base. Displaying total disdain for opposing pitchers, Bescher studied their tendencies carefully to make certain that he got a good jump. And as he approached second (or third), he always slid feetfirst, eluding the infielder's tag by employing a hook slide. Gauging the height of the catcher's throw by the placement of the infielder's hands, Bescher slid to the inside part of the bag on high throws and to the outside on low tosses. Extremely aggressive on the basepaths, Bescher also frequently turned singles into doubles and doubles into triples.

Although Bescher never established himself as one of the league's best hitters, failing to bat any higher than .281 during his time in Cincinnati, he did an excellent job of setting the table for his teammates by supplementing his hit total with a significant number of walks. And once Bescher got on, he drove opposing defenses to the point of distraction with his thievery on the basepaths. Meanwhile, Bescher made good use of his great speed and strong throwing arm in left field, consistently ranking among the top players at his position in putouts and assists.

Generally reserved and good-natured off the field, Bescher nevertheless had the ability to react violently when provoked, such as the time he beat up a fellow player for throwing a bat at a friend's dog that ran onto the field during practice. On another occasion, a well-publicized disagreement between Bescher and Roger Bresnahan of the Cardinals resulted in Bescher delivering a blow to the jaw of the St. Louis player-manager that sent him to the dentist's chair.

Bescher followed up his outstanding 1911 season with an equally impressive performance in 1912, earning a fifth-place finish in the voting for the Chalmers Award, presented at that time to the player deemed to be the league's Most Valuable Player, by batting .281, posting an OPS of .777, drawing 83 bases on balls, and leading the league with 120 runs scored and 67 stolen bases. But even though Bescher subsequently posted decent numbers in 1913, concluding the campaign with a batting average of .258, an OPS of .727, 86 runs scored, 38 steals, and a league-leading 94 bases on balls, he slumped badly during the season's second half, prompting the

Reds to trade him to the Giants at the end of the year for shortstop Buck Herzog and catcher Grover Hartley.

Bescher, who left Cincinnati with career totals of 11 homers, 219 RBIs, 496 runs scored, 736 hits, 125 doubles, 53 triples, and 320 stolen bases, a .262 batting average, a .365 on-base percentage, and a .356 slugging percentage, ended up spending just one year in New York, batting .270, scoring 82 runs, and stealing 36 bases for the Giants in 1914, before differences with manager John McGraw caused him to move on to St. Louis. After three years with the Cardinals, Bescher ended his major-league career as a backup with the Cleveland Indians in 1918. Over parts of 11 big-league seasons, Bescher hit 28 homers, knocked in 345 runs, scored 749 times, collected 1,171 hits, 190 doubles, and 74 triples, stole 428 bases, batted .258, compiled an on-base percentage of .353, and posted a slugging percentage of .351.

Although Bescher continued to play in the minor leagues for several more years, he eventually returned to his hometown of London, where he worked as an oil inspector for the state of Ohio. Bescher also managed the Eagles Lodge, earning a reputation during Prohibition as a talented manufacturer of home brew. Bescher lived until November 29, 1942, when an oncoming train slammed into his car, killing him and a female passenger. Bescher was 58 years old at the time of his passing.

REDS CAREER HIGHLIGHTS

Best Season

Bescher played his best ball for the Reds in 1912, when he earned a fifth-place finish in the NL MVP voting by batting .281, posting an on-base percentage of .381 and a slugging percentage of .396, and leading the league with 120 runs scored and 67 stolen bases.

Memorable Moments/Greatest Performances

Bescher contributed to a lopsided 9–3 victory over the Phillies on September 2, 1909, by collecting four hits, driving in two runs, and scoring twice.

Bescher proved to be a thorn in the side of the Phillies again on May 10, 1910, going 4-for-5 with a homer, double, and three runs scored during an 8–6 Reds win.

Bescher had a hand in all four runs the Reds scored during a 4–2 win over the Pirates on July 30, 1910, going 3-for-4 with a homer, double, two RBIs, and two runs scored.

Bescher helped lead the Reds to an 18–8 rout of the Boston Rustlers (Braves) on May 12, 1911, by going 5-for-7 with a double, triple, and three runs scored.

Bescher used his exceptional speed and baserunning ability to lead the Reds to a 3–1 victory over the Phillies on August 6, 1911. After stretching a single into a double and subsequently stealing home earlier in the contest, Bescher tallied the game's final run in the bottom of the eighth inning when he scored all the way from first on a sacrifice bunt.

Bescher contributed to a 10–4 win over the Dodgers on September 10, 1912, by hitting safely four times, stealing a base, driving in two runs, and scoring three times.

Bescher nearly hit for the cycle on July 1, 1913, when he scored twice and knocked in four runs with a single, double, and triple during an 11–4 win over the Cardinals.

Notable Achievements

- Scored more than 100 runs twice.
- Finished in double digits in triples four times.
- Surpassed 30 doubles once.
- Stole more than 50 bases four times, swiping more than 70 bags twice.
- Drew more than 100 walks once.
- Led NL in runs scored once, stolen bases four times, and walks once.
- Finished second in NL in runs scored once.
- Holds Reds post-19th-century single-season record for most stolen bases (81 in 1911).
- Ranks seventh in franchise history with 320 stolen bases.
- Finished fifth in 1912 NL Chalmers Award (MVP) voting.

45

IVAL GOODMAN

One of the National League's better outfielders for much of the 1930s, Ival Goodman spent eight seasons in Cincinnati, proving to be a key contributor to teams that won two pennants and one World Series. A solid hitter, Goodman batted over .300 and surpassed 30 homers, 90 RBIs, and 100 runs scored once each, while also posting an OPS over .900 twice and finishing in double digits in triples on five separate occasions. An excellent defender as well, Goodman led all NL right fielders in putouts three times and fielding percentage twice, with his strong all-around play earning him two All-Star nominations.

Born in Northview, Missouri, on July 23, 1908, Ival Richard Goodman grew up with his three sisters in Poteau, Oklahoma, after moving there with his family as a toddler. Developing into an outstanding athlete during his teenage years, Goodman starred in football, basketball, and track in high school, posting a personal-best time of 10 seconds flat in the 100-yard dash. Although Goodman's high school did not field a baseball team, he competed in his favorite sport as a member of the town team, continuing to do so after rejecting several college scholarship offers and accepting a job with a local electric company.

Discovered by a pro scout at the age of 20, Goodman left his job and signed with the Shawnee (Oklahoma) Robins of the Class C Western Association, for whom he batted .275 in 1930. Goodman subsequently split the next two seasons between the Fort Smith (Arkansas) Twins and the Bartlesville (Oklahoma) Bronchos, performing especially well at Bartlesville, where he batted .320 and led the Western Association with 22 homers, 23 triples, and 120 RBIs in 1932.

Signed by the Cardinals following the conclusion of the 1932 campaign, Goodman received high praise at the time from St. Louis scout, Charley Barrett, who said, "Goodman has everything it takes to make a great ballplayer—a fine arm, speed, and hitting power. He was the best-looking outfielder I saw in the minor leagues last season."

Ival Goodman earned consecutive All-Star nominations in 1938 and 1939.

After inking his deal with the Cardinals, Goodman spent the next two years advancing through their farm system, before being purchased by the Reds for $25,000 on November 3, 1934. Arriving in Cincinnati a few months shy of his 27th birthday, Goodman immediately laid claim to the Reds' starting right field job, which he retained for the next six years. Performing well in his first big-league season, Goodman batted .269, posted an OPS of .743, finished first on the team with 12 homers, 72 RBIs, 86 runs scored, and 14 stolen bases, topped the senior circuit with 18 triples, and led all NL right fielders in putouts.

Goodman subsequently got off to a slow start in 1936, when, after making a conscious effort to hit the ball to all fields, he found himself batting just .206 on May 29. But after conferring with manager Charlie Dressen, Goodman recaptured his natural left-handed swing, allowing him to finish the season with a batting average of .284, an OPS of .823, 17 homers, 71 RBIs, 81 runs scored, and a league-leading 14 triples.

Expressing the value he placed on his starting right fielder at the end of the year, Dressen said, "Every manager I talked to wanted to get Goodman, but I didn't pay much attention to their offers. He's one of my best ballplayers."

After seeing his numbers fall off slightly to 12 homers, 55 RBIs, 86 runs scored, a .273 batting average, and an OPS of .775 in 1937, Goodman reached the apex of his career the next two seasons. Gaining All-Star recognition in both 1938 and 1939, Goodman batted .292, finished second in the NL with 30 homers, and placed near the top of the league rankings with 92 RBIs, 103 runs scored, 303 total bases, a .533 slugging percentage, and an OPS of .901 in the first of those campaigns, before hitting seven homers, driving in 84 runs, scoring 85 times, and ranking among the circuit leaders with a .323 batting average, a .401 on-base percentage, a .515 slugging percentage, an OPS of .916, 37 doubles, and 16 triples in the second, despite missing a month of action with a dislocated shoulder he suffered when diving for a ball in the All-Star Game.

Typically hitting third in the Reds lineup, just ahead of right-handed batters Frank McCormick and Ernie Lombardi, the left-handed-swinging Goodman, who stood 5'11" and weighed close to 175 pounds, pulled the ball mostly to the right side of the field his first few years in the league, although he began hitting more to left after injuring his shoulder in 1939. Known more as a gap hitter than a pure slugger despite his 30 homers in 1938, Goodman hit the fastball particularly well, with former Giants pitcher Harry Gumbert recalling that when he threw him his heater "it sounded like Big Bertha was going off."

An outstanding defensive outfielder, Goodman drew praise for his exceptional work in right from the *Sporting News*, which noted that, despite playing his home ballpark's difficult sun field, he rarely lost track of a flyball. Goodman also covered a great deal of territory and possessed a strong throwing arm, twice throwing out as many as 16 runners on the basepaths. Extremely popular with his teammates as well, Goodman earned their respect by going about his job in workmanlike fashion, rarely drawing attention to himself with any on- or off-field theatrics.

Goodman remained the Reds' starting right fielder for one more year, hitting 12 homers, driving in 63 runs, scoring 78 times, batting .258, and posting an OPS of .724 in 1940, before appearing in a total of only 129 games over the course of the next two seasons due to injury. With Goodman having knocked in only 15 runs and batted just .243 for them in 1942, the Reds sold him to the Chicago Cubs at the end of the year, thereby ending his eight-year stint in Cincinnati.

Goodman, who, as a member of the Reds, hit 91 homers, knocked in 464 runs, scored 554 times, collected 995 hits, 170 doubles, and 79 triples, stole 45 bases, batted .279, compiled an on-base percentage of .349, and posted a slugging percentage of .448, ended up spending most of the next two seasons in Chicago, batting .320 for the Cubs in a part-time role in 1943, before suffering a career-ending injury during the latter stages of the ensuing campaign when he crashed into a wall chasing a flyball against the Cardinals at Sportsman's Park.

Following his playing days, Goodman spent four years managing in the minor leagues, serving as skipper for three different teams in the farm systems of the Cubs, Cleveland Indians, and Pittsburgh Pirates. Experiencing very little success, Goodman became a part-time scout for the Cubs, while also working as a salesman for the Rinaldi Chemical Company. After retiring to private life, Goodman lived until November 25, 1984, when he died in Jewish Hospital in Cincinnati at the age of 76 from what was described as an intestinal disorder.

REDS CAREER HIGHLIGHTS

Best Season

Although Goodman compiled a higher batting average (.323), on-base percentage (.401), and OPS (.916) the following season, he posted the best overall numbers of his career in 1938, when he earned the first of his back-to-back All-Star nominations and his lone top-20 finish in the NL MVP voting by batting .292 and ranking among the league leaders with 30 homers, 92 RBIs, 103 runs scored, 303 total bases, a slugging percentage of .533, and an OPS of .901.

Memorable Moments/Greatest Performances

Goodman proved to be a huge factor in a 12-inning, 8–4 win over the Cubs on April 21, 1935, driving in five runs with a homer and triple, with his two-run three-bagger in the top of the 12th breaking the game open.

Goodman led the Reds to a 10–9 win over the Phillies on June 27, 1936, by homering twice and knocking in four runs.

Goodman provided most of the offensive firepower during a 4–1 win over the Giants at New York's Polo Grounds on May 31, 1938, knocking in three runs with a pair of homers.

Goodman homered off Hall of Fame southpaw Carl Hubbell during an 11–2 rout of the Giants on June 4, 1938, finishing the game with three hits, five RBIs, and two runs scored.

Goodman gave the Reds a dramatic 7–6 victory over the Cubs on April 28, 1939, when he homered with two men aboard in the bottom of the ninth inning.

Goodman delivered the big blow of a 7–2 win over the Phillies on May 17, 1940, when he homered with two men out and the bases loaded in the top of the 11th inning.

Notable Achievements

- Hit 30 home runs in 1938.
- Scored more than 100 runs once.
- Batted over .300 once.
- Compiled on-base percentage over .400 once.
- Posted slugging percentage over .500 twice.
- Posted OPS over .900 twice.
- Finished in double digits in triples five times.
- Topped 30 doubles once.
- Led NL in triples twice.
- Finished second in NL in home runs once and triples once.
- Led NL right fielders in putouts three times and fielding percentage twice.
- Ranks eighth in franchise history with 79 triples.
- Two-time NL champion (1939 and 1940).
- 1940 world champion.
- Two-time NL All-Star selection (1938 and 1939).

46

JAKE DAUBERT

The National League's finest all-around first baseman for much of the Dead Ball Era, Jake Daubert excelled both at the bat and in the field for 15 big-league seasons, six of which he spent in Cincinnati. An excellent contact hitter with occasional power, the left-handed-swinging Daubert had most of his finest seasons in Brooklyn, batting over .300 seven times for the Dodgers, en route to winning a pair of batting titles and one league MVP award. Nevertheless, Daubert proved that he still had a lot left after he arrived in Cincinnati in 1919, batting over .300 three times for the Reds, while also amassing more than 200 hits once and finishing in double digits in triples on five separate occasions. Outstanding with the glove as well, Daubert annually ranked among the top players at his position in putouts, assists, double plays turned, and fielding percentage, with his stellar all-around play earning him seven selections to *Baseball Magazine*'s All-American Team and a place in both the Dodgers and Reds Halls of Fame.

Born in Shamokin, Pennsylvania, on April 17, 1884, Jacob Ellsworth Daubert quit school at the age of 11 to join his father and two older brothers in the local coal mines, where he became a breaker boy who separated slate and other impurities from the coal. Not wishing to experience the same fate as his brother Calvin, who lost his life while working in the mines, Daubert left his job in 1906 to play for a semipro baseball team in Lykens, Pennsylvania. Daubert continued to compete semiprofessionally until late in 1907, when he signed with a minor-league team located in Marion, Ohio. Daubert subsequently split the next two seasons between Toledo of the American Association and Nashville and Memphis of the Southern Association, before the Dodgers purchased his contract from Memphis.

Finally making his major-league debut on April 14, 1910, three days before he celebrated his 26th birthday, Daubert performed fairly well as a rookie, batting .264, driving in 50 runs, scoring 67 times, stealing 23 bases, and finishing among the NL leaders with eight home runs and 15 triples. Daubert followed that up with two more solid seasons, earning a pair of

Jake Daubert proved to be the NL's finest all-around first baseman for much of the Dead Ball Era.

top-10 finishes in the voting for the Chalmers Award by compiling batting averages of .307 and .308, while also totaling 170 runs scored, 24 triples, and 61 stolen bases. Daubert subsequently won the NL batting title in both 1913 and 1914, with his career-high mark of .350 in the first of those campaigns earning him league MVP honors.

Although the 5'10", 160-pound Daubert displayed little power at the plate, he possessed a solid line-drive swing that enabled him to consistently rank among the NL leaders in batting average. Known for his tremendous bat control, Daubert, who spent most of his career hitting either second or third in his team's lineup, rarely struck out and proved to be one of the game's best bunters, with his 392 sacrifice hits representing the second-highest total in MLB history.

In discussing Daubert's ability to move runners along, Casey Stengel said, "Jake Daubert was as good a bunter as I ever saw. He used to put a reverse twist on it like a pool ball. It would hit the ground and—oops—here it is coming back."

An excellent baserunner as well, Daubert stole more than 20 bases six times and placed in the league's top five in runs scored on three separate occasions.

In addition to the contributions he made on offense, Daubert excelled in the field, with *Baseball Magazine* comparing him favorably to Hal Chase, widely considered the greatest defensive first baseman of the Dead Ball Era, when it wrote in 1913, "Jake Daubert is easily one of the greatest infielders Baseball has ever seen. Flashing and sensational like Chase, he is, unlike Chase, never erratic, never prone to sudden error, never sulky or indifferent in his play."

Meanwhile author Robert W. Creamer wrote in his book, *Stengel: His Life and Times*, "Daubert's reputation reflected baseball thinking: His high batting average year after year dazzled people. He looked good at bat, and he looked good in the field. He had quick hands, could bunt amazingly well, and very seldom made an error. But he had little power at bat and little range in the field. No one noticed. He was Brooklyn's captain, and its star."

Daubert continued to perform well for the Dodgers for four more years, batting over .300 another three times from 1915 to 1918, while also topping the senior circuit with 15 triples in the last of the campaigns. However, when the shortening of the 1918 season to 126 games due to the nation's involvement in World War I prompted team owners to prorate player salaries, Daubert, who had been one of the founding members of the Players' Fraternity, maintained that Dodgers owner Charles Ebbets owed him the remainder of his salary since he had signed a multiyear contract with the team. After suing Ebbets for the balance of his pay, Daubert ended up recovering most of his losses in an out-of-court settlement. But Ebbets had the final say, exacting a measure of revenge against Daubert by trading him to the Reds for outfielder Tommy Griffith.

Named team captain immediately upon his arrival in Cincinnati, the 35-year-old Daubert helped lead the Reds to their first NL pennant and world championship in 1919 by batting .276 and placing near the top of the league rankings with 79 runs scored and 12 triples. Although the Reds failed to return to the World Series in any of the next five seasons, the advent of the Live Ball Era allowed Daubert to compile some of the most impressive offensive numbers of his career. In addition to batting over .300 three times, Daubert scored more than 90 runs twice, collected more than 200 hits once, and surpassed 10 triples four straight times. Particularly outstanding in 1922, Daubert ranked among the NL leaders in seven different offensive categories, including batting average (.336), OPS (.886), runs scored (114), hits (205), and triples (22).

Crediting his outstanding performance at such an advanced age to his years in the coal mines, Daubert wrote in an article that appeared in *Baseball Magazine*, "Whatever you can say against it, breaking rock and shoveling coal in the dark certainly does harden a fellow's muscles. "

Daubert also benefited greatly from the cerebral approach he took to his craft, with his son, George, telling the *New York Post* many years later, "He lived baseball. After every game, he played the damn game over six times. He was a student of the game. He would study the game. When dad was playing, he carried a little black book, and he would write in there the eccentric movements of a pitcher. If he was going to throw a fastball, he may do some little thing to tip him off. He watched those little things."

Unfortunately, Daubert had to leave the Reds toward the tail end of the 1924 campaign after falling ill during a road trip to New York. Subsequently diagnosed with appendicitis and gallstones, Daubert also suffered from frequent headaches and a lack of sleep after being hit in the head by a pitch earlier in the season. After having an appendectomy performed by Cincinnati's team doctor on October 2, Daubert failed to make a full recovery, passing away one week later, on October 9, 1924, at only 40 years of age. Although doctors initially cited "exhaustion, resulting in indigestion" as the immediate cause of death, it later surfaced that Daubert suffered from a hereditary blood disorder called hemolytic spherocytosis that contributed to his death, and to that of his son years later.

The life and playing career of Jake Daubert ended with him having hit 56 home runs, driven in 722 runs, scored 1,117 times, collected 2,326 hits, 250 doubles, and 165 triples, stolen 251 bases, batted .303, compiled a .360 on-base percentage, and posted a .401 slugging percentage. During his time in Cincinnati, Daubert hit 23 homers, knocked in 307 runs, scored 469 times, amassed 939 hits, 112 doubles, and 78 triples, stole 64 bases, batted .301, compiled an on-base percentage of .352, and posted a slugging percentage of .409.

One of the most well-liked and respected players of his era, Daubert became a particular favorite of sportswriters, who enjoyed conversing with him on a wide variety of subjects beyond the game. Nevertheless, he never came close to gaining induction into the Baseball Hall of Fame, failing to garner more than 1.3 percent of the votes in any election in which his name appeared on the ballot.

REDS CAREER HIGHLIGHTS

Best Season

Daubert had easily his finest all-around season for the Reds in 1922, when, in addition to batting .336 and leading the NL with 22 triples, he established career-high marks with 12 homers, 66 RBIs, 114 runs scored, 205 hits, 300 total bases, a slugging percentage of .492, and an OPS of .886, while also leading all NL first basemen in putouts, double plays turned, and fielding percentage.

Memorable Moments/Greatest Performances

Daubert helped lead the Reds to an 8–7 win over the Pirates on July 28, 1919, by going 5-for-5 at the plate with one RBI and one run scored.

Daubert contributed to a 10–3 victory over the Boston Braves on September 18, 1921, by going 4-for-4 with a homer, double, and three RBIs.

Daubert hit safely in 22 straight games from April 21 to May 14, 1922, going a combined 32-for-77 (.416), with two homers, three triples, three doubles, 15 walks, just one strikeout, nine RBIs, and 25 runs scored.

Daubert led the Reds to a lopsided 9–3 victory over the Phillies on July 9, 1922, by going 4-for-4 with a homer, stolen base, and four RBIs.

Daubert went a perfect 5-for-5 at the plate during a 9–0 rout of the Braves on August 27, 1922, driving in two runs, scoring twice, and stealing a base.

Daubert contributed to an 8–3 win over the Phillies on August 20, 1923, by going 4-for-5 with a homer, two RBIs, and four runs scored.

Notable Achievements

- Batted over .300 three times.
- Scored more than 100 runs once.

- Surpassed 200 hits once.
- Finished in double digits in triples five times, surpassing 20 three-baggers once.
- Led NL in triples once, sacrifice hits once, and games played once.
- Finished second in NL in runs scored once.
- Finished third in NL in runs scored once and triples once.
- Led NL first basemen in putouts once, double plays turned once, and fielding percentage once.
- Ranks second in MLB history with 392 sacrifice hits.
- Ranks among Reds career leaders in sacrifice hits (2nd) and triples (9th).
- 1919 NL champion.
- 1919 world champion.

47

CHRIS SABO

A beloved figure in Cincinnati, Chris Sabo won the affection of the hometown fans with his grit, hustle, unassuming nature, and unique look that featured a flattop haircut and wraparound protective eyeglasses commonly known as Rec Specs. A solid all-around player, Sabo, who spent parts of seven seasons in the Queen City, hit more than 20 home runs three times, batted over .300 once, and swiped more than 20 bases twice, while also leading all NL third basemen in fielding percentage twice and double plays turned once. The 1988 NL Rookie of the Year, Sabo also earned three All-Star nominations during his time in Cincinnati, with one of those coming in 1990, when he helped lead the Reds to their last world championship.

Born in Detroit, Michigan, on January 19, 1962, Christopher Andrew Sabo grew up in the city's Rosedale Park district, just three blocks from Willie Horton, a member of the 1968 world champion Detroit Tigers. The son of a plumber and a waitress, Sabo developed into a three-sport star at Detroit Catholic Central High School, excelling in baseball, hockey, and golf. A two-time All-State selection on the diamond, Sabo also played goalie on two national championship 17-and-under teams, before enrolling at the University of Michigan after turning down an offer to sign with the Montreal Expos, who selected him in the 30th round of the 1980 MLB Draft. In explaining his decision, Sabo later said, "I always wanted to go to Michigan; that was always my dream."

A three-year starter for the Wolverines at third base, Sabo gained First-Team All-America recognition from both the *Sporting News* and *Baseball America* in his final season, when future Reds teammate Barry Larkin joined him on the left side of the Michigan infield. Selected by the Reds in the second round of the 1983 MLB Draft, with the 30th overall pick, Sabo subsequently spent five long years advancing through the Cincinnati farm system, failing to post overly impressive numbers at any stop, before finally being promoted to the parent club in 1988 after Buddy Bell—the previous

Chris Sabo earned NL Rookie of the Year honors in 1988.
Courtesy of George A. Kitrinos

year's starter at third—sustained an injury during spring training. After replacing Bell at the hot corner, Sabo went on to start 131 games for the Reds in his first big-league season, earning NL All-Star and Rookie of the Year honors by hitting 11 homers, driving in 44 runs, scoring 74 times, batting .271, posting an OPS of .728, and ranking among the league leaders with 40 doubles and 46 stolen bases.

Quickly emerging as a personal favorite of Reds manager Pete Rose, who nicknamed him "Spuds" due to what he perceived to be his resemblance to a bull terrier character named Spuds MacKenzie that appeared in Bud Light commercials, Sabo received praise from his skipper, who said, "He reminds me of me when I was that age—the way he plays the game, I mean. He can't wait to get to offense. He can't wait to get to defense, and, after the game, he's probably mad 'cause he's got to wait 'til tomorrow to play again."

Injured for much of 1989, Sabo appeared in just 82 games and garnered only 304 official at-bats, limiting him to just six homers, 29 RBIs, and a .260 batting average. Far more productive in 1990, Sabo helped the Reds capture the NL pennant by hitting 25 homers, driving in 71 runs, scoring 95 times, stealing 25 bases, batting .270, compiling an OPS of .819, and leading all players at his position in fielding percentage, with his strong all-around play earning him his second All-Star selection and a 13th-place finish in the league MVP voting. Sabo then helped the Reds record a stunning four-game sweep of the heavily favored Oakland Athletics in the World Series by going 9-for-16 (.563), with two homers, five RBIs, and an OPS of 1.611. Sabo followed that up by posting the best overall numbers of his career in 1991, gaining All-Star recognition for the third and final time by hitting 26 homers, knocking in 88 runs, scoring 91 times, stealing 19 bases, batting .301, and compiling an OPS of .859.

More of a line-drive hitter than a slugger, the right-handed-swinging Sabo, who stood 5'11" and weighed 185 pounds, drove the ball well to both outfield gaps, although he also possessed the ability to reach the seats, surpassing 20 homers on three separate occasions. Extremely aggressive at the plate, Sabo drew more than 50 bases on balls just once his entire career, enabling him to compile an on-base percentage that exceeded .350 only twice. Nevertheless, he used his good speed and superior baserunning ability to score more than 90 runs twice and average 26 stolen bases over the course of his first four seasons.

In addition to gaining the approval of his manager, Sabo endeared himself to the fans of Cincinnati with his blue-collar mentality and willingness to work hard, with team historian Greg Rhodes suggesting, "I think there was a connection between him and the fans that was sort of immediate. When people first saw him, they didn't know what to expect, but they loved what they saw. His personality as it came out in quotes and stories, he just seemed like a down-to-earth guy."

Pete Rose expressed similar sentiments when he said, "I know for a long time he played, he drove the same car. He wasn't a material type of guy—he just wanted to play ball. That's why I liked him."

Rose added, "He probably reminded the city of me. When you play hard every day, don't mind getting dirty, and don't walk around like a big shot, this blue-collar town will like you. He played hard every day, and he got pissed at guys that didn't. . . . He had all the ingredients of a good player—you wish every player played like him."

Meanwhile, former Reds teammate Hal Morris, who recalled Sabo playing through an unpublicized broken hand, stated, "I think he was a great teammate and a great player—probably underrated even though he made All-Star games and was Rookie of the Year. His knee gave him problems in the middle of his career, but he was a rare blend of speed and power."

Plagued by an ankle injury that limited him to just 96 games, Sabo finished the 1992 season with only 12 homers, 43 RBIs, 42 runs scored, a .244 batting average, and an OPS of .723. Rebounding somewhat the following year, Sabo hit 21 homers, knocked in 82 runs, and scored 86 times, although he struck out a career-high 105 times, batted just .259, and posted a rather mediocre OPS of .755.

A free agent at the end of 1993, Sabo signed with the Baltimore Orioles, with whom he spent one injury-marred season, before splitting the following year between the Chicago White Sox and St. Louis Cardinals. Choosing to return to Cincinnati when he became a free agent again after the 1995 season, Sabo spent the ensuing campaign serving the Reds as a backup, before announcing his retirement at the end of the year with career totals of 116 homers, 426 RBIs, 494 runs scored, 898 hits, 214 doubles, 17 triples, and 120 stolen bases, a .268 batting average, a .326 on-base percentage, and a .445 slugging percentage. During his time in Cincinnati, Sabo hit 104 homers, knocked in 373 runs, scored 443 times, collected 812 hits, 193 doubles, and 14 triples, stole 116 bases, batted .270, compiled an on-base percentage of .328, and posted a slugging percentage of .447.

Following his retirement as an active player, Sabo spent several years coaching in the Reds' minor-league system and serving as an assistant coach for the University of Cincinnati, before being named head baseball coach at the University of Akron in 2018, a position he held until 2022. An avid golfer and a popular figure at Reds reunion events, Sabo now lives with his wife, Susan, in Sarasota, Florida.

In discussing his Reds legacy, Sabo, who gained induction into the team's Hall of Fame in 2010, said, "I just played baseball. I played as hard as I could. I didn't play any different when I was 30 years old than I did when I was 10. To be perfectly honest, it doesn't matter if people liked me or hated me. A third of the people like you, a third hate you, and a third don't give a crap. That's how I live my life."

Meanwhile, Greg Rhodes summed up Sabo's place in franchise history by saying, "I think he's one of the most distinctive personalities to ever play for the Reds. He's one of a handful of guys that people tend to remember from decade to decade. As time goes on, guys start to fade in memory. I think Sabo will always be a part of the Reds story."

REDS CAREER HIGHLIGHTS

Best Season

Sabo posted the best numbers of his career in 1991, when he earned the last of his three All-Star nominations by ranking in the league's top 10 in eight different offensive categories, including home runs (26), runs scored (91), doubles (35), hits (175), batting average (.301), slugging percentage (.505), and OPS (.859).

Memorable Moments/Greatest Performances

Sabo tied a record for NL third basemen in a nine-inning game by collecting 11 assists during an 8–1 win over the Cardinals in just his second big-league start on April 7, 1988.

Sabo helped lead the Reds to a 3–2 victory over the Giants on June 18, 1988, by going 4-for-4 at the plate with a homer, triple, two doubles, and two runs scored.

Sabo contributed to a 19–6 rout of the Montreal Expos on May 1, 1989, by going 4-for-6 with a double, stolen base, four RBIs, and four runs scored.

Sabo hit two homers in one game for the first time in his career during a 5–2 win over the Braves on April 13, 1990, reaching the seats twice with the bases empty.

Sabo came up big for the Reds in Game 3 of the 1990 World Series, helping them build a commanding 3–0 Series lead by knocking in three runs with a pair of homers during an 8–3 win over the A's.

Sabo led the Reds to a 7–3 victory over the Expos on June 21, 1991, by homering twice and driving in three runs.

Sabo contributed to a lopsided 15–5 victory over the Cubs on April 24, 1993, by going 4-for-5 with a homer, two doubles, five RBIs, and three runs scored, setting the tone for the blowout win with a first-inning grand slam.

Notable Achievements

- Hit more than 20 home runs three times.
- Batted over .300 once.
- Posted slugging percentage over .500 once.
- Surpassed 30 doubles four times, topping 40 two-baggers once.
- Stole more than 20 bases twice, swiping more than 40 bags once.
- Finished third in NL in hits once and doubles twice.
- Led NL third basemen in fielding percentage twice and double plays turned once.
- 1990 division champion.
- 1990 NL champion.
- 1990 world champion.
- 1988 NL Rookie of the Year.
- Two-time NL Player of the Week.
- Three-time NL All-Star selection (1988, 1990, and 1991).

48

GARY NOLAN

Plagued by arm problems throughout his career, Gary Nolan never quite lived up to the huge expectations that surrounded him when he first arrived in Cincinnati in 1967. Nevertheless, Nolan proved to be one of the NL's better pitchers during his time in the Queen City, winning at least 15 games four times and compiling an ERA under 3.00 on three separate occasions, en route to earning one All-Star selection and one top-five finish in the Cy Young voting. A major contributor to Reds teams that won four pennants and two World Series, Nolan helped anchor the pitching staffs of those squads, before ultimately succumbing to the arm woes that brought his career to a premature end.

Born in Herlong, California, on May 27, 1948, Gary Lynn Nolan moved with his family at an early age some 100 miles southwest, to the city of Oroville, an old Gold Rush town situated in the foothills of the Sierra Nevada. Developing into a standout pitcher at Oroville High School, Nolan, who later said, "When I was a kid, baseball was my life," performed so well on the mound that scouts came from miles away to watch him pitch. A member of the varsity squad his final three seasons, Nolan earned All-League honors his senior year while serving as team captain. Maintaining an extremely busy schedule year-round, Nolan spent his summers playing American Legion baseball and holding down two jobs—one at a gas station and the other at the Butte County Public Works Department.

Selected by the Reds in the first round of the 1966 MLB Amateur Draft, with the 13th overall pick, Nolan signed with them right out of high school for $40,000. Subsequently assigned to Sioux Falls (South Dakota) in the Northern League, Nolan dominated the competition at the A level to such a degree, going 7–3 with a 1.82 ERA and 163 strikeouts in 104 innings of work, that he found himself in Cincinnati by the start of the ensuing campaign.

Joining the Reds' starting rotation at the tender age of 18, Nolan did an excellent job in his first big-league season, earning a third-place finish in

Gary Nolan won at least 15 games for the Reds four times.

the NL Rookie of the Year voting by compiling a record of 14–8, throwing 226⅔ innings and eight complete games, finishing second in the league with five shutouts, and placing fourth in the circuit with a 2.58 ERA and 206 strikeouts. Hoping to build upon his outstanding rookie season, Nolan arrived at spring training in 1968 ready to take the next step. However, he experienced a major setback when he strained his right shoulder after throwing just two pitches in the second inning of his first preseason start.

Subsequently sent to Tampa in the Class A Florida State League to help restore the strength in his pitching arm, Nolan ended up spending the next two months in Florida pitching in pain, before being recalled by the

Reds in mid-May. Despite his sore arm, Nolan acquitted himself extremely well the rest of the year, going 9–4 with a 2.40 ERA and 111 strikeouts in 150 innings pitched.

Unfortunately, Nolan hurt himself again early in 1969, when he pulled a muscle in his right forearm while delivering a pitch to Hank Aaron in just his second start of the regular season. But Nolan's injury and subsequent three-month stint with Cincinnati's minor-league affiliate in Indianapolis proved to be a blessing in disguise in many ways.

An extremely hard thrower when he first arrived in the Queen City, Nolan who stood 6'2" and weighed close to 200 pounds, depended primarily on his overpowering fastball to navigate his way through opposing lineups during the early stages of his career. However, with the help of Indianapolis manager Vern Rapp and Reds minor-league instructor Scott Breeden, Nolan developed an outstanding changeup that he incorporated into his repertoire of pitches following his return to Cincinnati. Rejoining the Reds in early August, Nolan won seven of his final 12 decisions, to finish the year with a record of 8–8 and an ERA of 3.56.

Armed with his new weapon, Nolan helped lead the Reds to the NL pennant in 1970 by compiling a record of 18–7, an ERA of 3.27, and a WHIP of 1.285, while also striking out 181 batters in 250⅔ innings pitched. Although Nolan won just 12 of his 27 decisions the following year, he performed well for a Reds team that finished four games under .500, posting an ERA of 3.16 and a WHIP of 1.091, tossing a career-high nine complete games, and registering 146 strikeouts in 244⅔ innings pitched.

Nolan subsequently got off to a tremendous start in 1972, garnering his lone All-Star nomination by winning 13 games by the break. However, discomfort in his neck and shoulder forced him to miss much of the season's second half. Nevertheless, Nolan ended up earning a fifth-place finish in the NL Cy Young voting by finishing the year with a record of 15–5, an ERA of 1.99, and a WHIP of 1.006.

Unfortunately, Nolan missed virtually all of the next two seasons after undergoing surgery to remove a calcium spur from his right shoulder. But while Dr. Frank Jobe, who performed the operation, told him, "I have no idea how you pitched in that sort of pain. You must have been in agony," Nolan found his mettle being questioned by the organization and several of his teammates, recalling, "The hardest part was that many people, including some of my teammates, didn't think there was anything the matter with me. That was one of the reasons I moved out of Cincinnati and sold our home after the 1972 season. Back in Oroville, people didn't doubt my word."

Identifying Sparky Anderson as one of his biggest doubters, Nolan remembered his manager telling him repeatedly, "Pitchers have to throw in pain. Bob Gibson says every pitch he's ever thrown cut through him like a knife. You gotta pitch with pain, kid."

After appearing in only two games with the Reds the previous two seasons, a healthy Nolan rejoined them in 1975. Although no longer blessed with the tremendous speed he once had on his fastball, Nolan compensated for his diminished velocity by depending more on his outstanding changeup and superior control. Taking his regular turn in the starting rotation in both 1975 and 1976, Nolan helped the Reds capture consecutive NL pennants and world championships by posting identical 15–9 records, while also throwing more than 200 innings each year and compiling ERAs of 3.16 and 3.46. But Nolan's arm problems returned in 1977, prompting the Reds to trade him to the California Angels for minor-league infielder Craig Hendrickson midway through the campaign.

Nolan, who left Cincinnati having compiled an overall record of 110–67, an ERA of 3.02, and a WHIP of 1.138, thrown 45 complete games and 14 shutouts, and struck out 1,035 batters in 1,656⅓ innings pitched, ending up appearing in only five games with the Angels, losing all three of his decisions, before being released at the end of the year and subsequently announcing his retirement two months shy of his 30th birthday.

Recalling how his major-league career ended, Nolan said, "I saw Dr. Frank Jobe while out in California, but I pretty much knew I was done. All of a sudden, my career was over."

Following his playing days, Nolan moved to Las Vegas, where he spent several years working as a blackjack dealer at the Golden Nugget Casino, before becoming an executive credit host for guests of hotels owned by Steve Wynn. During that time, Nolan disassociated himself from baseball and the Reds, never wearing his championship rings and choosing not to attend the festivities when he gained induction into the team's Hall of Fame in 1983.

When asked by Cincinnati sportswriter John Erardi in 1986 if he had fond memories of his years with the Reds, Nolan stated that he enjoyed pitching and the relationships he formed with his teammates and the people of Cincinnati. However, he added, "The Reds organization left a bad taste in my mouth by not believing my arm was hurt and thinking it was probably in my head. I know they did, and they know I did."

Nolan continued, "I was blessed. I played in the big leagues. I was fortunate. But I have learned to separate my baseball life and my life in Las Vegas. Most people in the casino probably don't even know I played ball."

Some 20 years later, Nolan re-embraced his playing career and the Reds after visiting the team's Hall of Fame during a trip to Cincinnati. Shown his HOF plaque by museum curator Chris Eckes, Nolan formed a new relationship with the Reds organization that has led to him attending several Hall of Fame induction ceremonies. Now 76 years of age, Nolan, who moved back to Oroville in 2003, has spent the last several years donating his time to numerous charitable causes and civic organizations, including Special Needs for Kids. He also coaches and helps prepare Oroville High School pitchers for college ball.

REDS CAREER HIGHLIGHTS

Best Season

Nolan performed brilliantly for the Reds as a rookie in 1967, winning 14 games, compiling an ERA of 2.58, and recording a career-high 206 strikeouts. He had another outstanding season in 1970, when he helped the Reds capture the NL pennant by posting 18 victories, compiling an ERA of 3.27, registering 181 strikeouts, and throwing 250⅔ innings. But Nolan pitched the best ball of his career in 1972, when he earned his lone All-Star selection and a fifth-place finish in the NL Cy Young voting by compiling a record of 15–5 and ranking among the league leaders with an ERA of 1.99 and a WHIP of 1.006.

Memorable Moments/Greatest Performances

Nolan tossed the first shutout of his career on May 14, 1967, when he yielded five hits, issued two walks, and struck out nine batters during a 1–0 victory over the Phillies.

Although he did not figure in the decision, Nolan recorded a career-high 15 strikeouts over the first 7⅔ innings of a 4–3 loss to the Giants on June 7, 1967, fanning the great Willie Mays four straight times. Praising Nolan for his performance afterward, Mays said, "Nobody's ever done that to me before."

Nolan shut out the Mets on just five hits on June 13, 1967, also walking two batters and recording nine strikeouts during a 6–0 Reds win.

Nolan outdueled Larry Jaster of the Cardinals on July 4, 1967, allowing just three hits and two walks during a 1–0 shutout of the eventual world champions.

Nolan yielded just three hits and two walks during a 10–0 shutout of the Braves on June 5, 1968.

In addition to allowing just four hits and recording six strikeouts during a 5–0 shutout of the Giants on June 29, 1968, Nolan helped his own cause by driving in three runs with the only home run of his career.

Nolan tossed a three-hit shutout against the Phillies on August 10, 1969, walking no one and striking out five batters during a lopsided 10–0 victory.

Nolan allowed just three walks and a pair of harmless singles by right fielder Willie Crawford during a 4–0 shutout of the Dodgers on April 7, 1970.

Nolan earned a 3–0 victory over the hard-hitting Pirates in Game 1 of the 1970 NLCS by working nine scoreless frames during which he allowed eight hits, walked four batters, and recorded six strikeouts, before turning the game over to the bullpen after the Reds erupted for three runs in the top of the 10th inning.

Nolan yielded just two hits and two walks during a 6–0 shutout of the Montreal Expos on May 28, 1975.

Notable Achievements

- Won at least 15 games four times.
- Posted winning percentage over .700 three times.
- Compiled ERA under 3.00 three times, finishing with mark under 2.00 once.
- Struck out more than 200 batters once.
- Threw more than 200 innings five times, tossing more than 250 frames once.
- Led NL pitchers with .750 winning percentage in 1972.
- Finished second in NL in ERA once and shutouts once.
- Ranks among Reds career leaders in winning percentage (7th), WHIP (4th), and strikeouts (10th).
- Five-time division champion (1970, 1972, 1973, 1975, and 1976).
- Four-time NL champion (1970, 1972, 1975, and 1976).
- Two-time world champion (1975 and 1976).
- 1972 NL All-Star selection.

49

LEO CÁRDENAS

One of the last Cuban-born players to defect to the United States before the borders closed, Leo Cárdenas spent parts of nine seasons in Cincinnati, starting for the Reds at shortstop in seven of those. A solid hitter, Cárdenas batted over .300, slugged 20 homers, and knocked in more than 80 runs once each, in helping the Reds capture one NL pennant and seriously contend for the league championship two other times. A good defender as well, Cárdenas acquired the nickname "Mr. Automatic" for his reliability in the field, with his strong all-around play earning him four All-Star nominations before he departed for Minnesota following the conclusion of the 1968 campaign.

Born in Matanzas, Cuba, on December 17, 1938, Leonardo Lazaro Cárdenas grew up with his 14 siblings on the northern shore of the island, some 56 miles east of Havana. After spending his formative years developing his baseball skills on the local sandlots, Cárdenas began his pro career in 1956 with the Tucson Cowboys of the Arizona-Mexico League, for whom he hit 23 homers, knocked in 78 runs, scored 127 times, and batted .316. Scouted and signed by the Reds for $500 the following year, Cárdenas spent the next two seasons manning shortstop for Cincinnati's Class A affiliate in Savannah, Georgia, committing a total of 67 errors in the field, while posting batting averages of .255 and .267. Returning to his homeland in 1959, Cárdenas made only 14 miscues at shortstop, hit 13 homers, and batted .254 with the Triple-A Havana Sugar Kings of the International League. While in Havana, though, Cárdenas experienced a scary moment when overly exuberant supporters of Fidel Castro inadvertently shot him while firing off rifles in the grandstand during a celebration of the 26th of July Movement.

After Cárdenas spent the first few months of the ensuing campaign in the minors, the Reds called him up in late July to fill in for an injured Roy McMillan. Starting 43 games at shortstop the rest of the year, the 21-year-old Cárdenas homered once, knocked in 12 runs, and batted .232, in just

Leo Cárdenas earned All-Star honors four times as a member of the Reds.

over 150 total plate appearances. Although Cárdenas subsequently assumed a backup role for the Reds during their NL championship season of 1961, he solidified his place as the team's shortstop of the future by hitting five homers, driving in 24 runs, batting .308, and posting an OPS of .838, in just under 200 official at-bats.

Displacing Eddie Kasko as the starter at short in 1962, Cárdenas performed extremely well in his first season as an everyday player, hitting

10 homers, driving in 60 runs, scoring 77 times, batting .294, and compiling an OPS of .752, while also ranking among the league's top players at his position in putouts, assists, and fielding percentage. While Cárdenas continued to excel with the glove in 1963, leading all NL shortstops in fielding percentage, he struggled at the plate, hitting seven homers, knocking in 48 runs, batting just .235, and posting an OPS of only .595. However, he rebounded somewhat the following year, gaining All-Star recognition for the first of three straight times by hitting nine homers, driving in 69 runs, batting .251, and compiling an OPS of .656. Even better the next two seasons, Cárdenas hit 11 homers, knocked in 57 runs, scored 65 times, batted .287, posted an OPS of .786, and earned Gold Glove honors in 1965, before batting .255, compiling an OPS of .728, and establishing career-high marks with 20 homers and 81 RBIs in 1966.

One of the better offensive shortstops in either league, the right-handed-hitting Cárdenas possessed more power at the plate than most other players who manned his position, finishing in double digits in home runs on six separate occasions over the course of his career, including three times as a member of the Reds. Typically hitting out of either the seventh or eighth spot in Cincinnati's lineup, Cárdenas proved to be a solid RBI man as well, knocking in at least 60 runs three times while wearing a Reds uniform. Equally adept in the field, Cárdenas, whose long arms and slender 5'11", 160-pound frame gave him a spiderlike appearance, used his good range, soft hands, and strong throwing arm to lead all NL shortstops in putouts three times, fielding percentage twice, and double plays turned once.

Extremely superstitious, Cárdenas also became known for his neurotic behavior and unusual idiosyncrasies that included showering in his uniform to ward off evil spirits. Knowing that Cárdenas feared the letter "x," opposing players often scratched it in the dirt near his position to scare him. Cárdenas's teammates also shared in the fun, occasionally placing a chicken feather near second base since they knew that he ascribed supernatural powers to them. And, while in the middle of a particularly long batting slump, Cárdenas locked his bats in the trunk of his car, vowing not to let them out until they "got better."

Injured for much of 1967, Cárdenas appeared in only 108 games, limiting him to just two homers, 21 RBIs, and a .256 batting average. Healthy for most of the ensuing campaign, Cárdenas gained All-Star recognition despite finishing the year with just seven homers, 41 RBIs, and a .235 batting average. Coming off two subpar seasons during which he spent much of his time feuding with Reds manager Dave Bristol, Cárdenas expected the team to leave him unprotected in the 1968 expansion draft. However, rather than giving him away for nothing, the Reds traded him to the Minnesota Twins for pitcher Jim Merritt on November 21, 1968.

Cárdenas, who left Cincinnati with career totals of 72 homers, 413 RBIs, 415 runs scored, 1,058 hits, 182 doubles, 35 triples, and 26 stolen bases, a .261 batting average, a .313 on-base percentage, and a .377 slugging percentage, ended up spending three extremely productive years in Minnesota, helping the Twins win a pair of AL West titles. Particularly outstanding in 1969 and 1971, Cárdenas earned a 12th-place finish in the AL MVP voting in the first of those campaigns by hitting 10 homers, driving in 70 runs, batting .280, and leading all league shortstops in putouts, assists, and double plays turned, before garnering All-Star honors for the fifth and final time by hitting 18 homers, knocking in 75 runs, and batting .264 in the second.

Dealt to the California Angels at the end of 1971, Cárdenas spent the 1972 season starting at shortstop for his new team, before assuming a backup role with the Cleveland Indians and Texas Rangers the next three seasons. Choosing to announce his retirement after being released by the Rangers just prior to the start of the 1976 campaign, Cárdenas ended his major-league career with 118 homers, 689 RBIs, 662 runs scored, 1,725 hits, 285 doubles, 49 triples, 39 stolen bases, a .257 batting average, a .311 on-base percentage, and a .367 slugging percentage.

Following his playing days, Cárdenas, who, despite fathering eight children with two American wives, never got around to applying for American citizenship, ran afoul of the law in 1998, when he received a sentence of three months in jail and five years' probation for felony assault after shattering the windows of a car occupied by his wife and a male coworker and breaking the man's arm with a bat. Cárdenas, who is 86 years old as of this writing, currently lives in Cincinnati and makes regular appearances at the Reds Hall of Fame and Great American Ball Park.

REDS CAREER HIGHLIGHTS

Best Season

Cárdenas performed well for the Reds in both 1962 and 1966, batting .294 and scoring a career-high 77 runs in the first of those campaigns, before establishing career-best marks in homers (20) and RBIs (81) in the second. But Cárdenas had his finest all-around season in Cincinnati in 1965, when he gained All-Star recognition for the second of three straight times by hitting 11 homers, knocking in 57 runs, collecting a career-high 11 triples, batting .287, and posting an OPS of .786, while also earning Gold Glove honors by leading all NL shortstops in putouts and double plays turned.

Memorable Moments/Greatest Performances

Cárdenas contributed to a 12–4 win over the Mets on May 6, 1964, by going 4-for-5 at the plate, with a homer, double, and four RBIs.

Cárdenas homered twice in one game for the first time in his career during an 8–4 win over the Mets on June 16, 1965, reaching the seats twice with no one on base against starter Al Jackson.

After hitting safely in two of his four previous trips to the plate, Cárdenas gave the Reds a 7–6 win over the Dodgers on July 7, 1965, when he hit a two-out solo home run off reliever Bob Miller in the bottom of the ninth inning.

Cárdenas delivered the only run of a 1–0 victory over the Cubs on August 19, 1965, when he homered with no one aboard in the top of the 10th inning, making a winner out of Jim Maloney, who held Chicago's lineup hitless.

Cárdenas starred during a doubleheader split with the Cubs on June 5, 1966, going 3-for-4 with two homers and five RBIs in leading Reds to an 8–3 win in Game 1, before going 3-for-4 with two homers and three RBIs during a 9–5 loss in Game 2.

Notable Achievements

- Batted over .300 once.
- Hit 20 home runs in 1966.
- Surpassed 10 triples once.
- Surpassed 30 doubles twice.
- Led NL shortstops in putouts three times, fielding percentage twice, and double plays turned once.
- 1961 NL champion.
- 1965 Gold Glove Award winner.
- Four-time NL All-Star selection (1964, 1965, 1966, and 1968).

50

MARIO SOTO

A hard-throwing right-hander who possessed a blazing fastball and knee-buckling changeup, Mario Soto proved to be one of the NL's best pitchers from 1980 to 1984, averaging 208 strikeouts per season and allowing fewer hits per nine innings pitched than any other starter in the big leagues. The winner of at least 17 games twice, Soto also compiled an ERA under 3.00, struck out more than 200 batters, and threw more than 250 innings three times each, en route to earning three All-Star selections and one runner-up finish in the Cy Young voting. Nevertheless, Soto, who experienced arm and shoulder problems that brought his career to a premature end, will always be remembered more than anything for his explosive temper that caused him to become involved in several altercations during his time in Cincinnati.

Born in Baní, Dominican Republic, on July 12, 1956, Mario Melvin Soto grew up with limited means with his two siblings some 35 miles southwest of the nation's capital, Santo Domingo. Raised by his mother, who supported the family by working as a laundress after separating from her husband, Soto developed a strong sense of responsibility at an early age, recalling, "We used to go down to the river at 6 in the morning, baskets of laundry on our heads, and not come back until the evening."

Forced to quit school at the age of 14, Soto took a full-time job as a construction worker, developing into a skilled mason before long. Meanwhile, Soto, who grew up idolizing fellow Dominican Juan Marichal, spent most of his spare time playing baseball on the local sandlots, starting out as a catcher, before transitioning to the mound at 17 years of age because, in his own words, "I couldn't run, and I couldn't hit."

Drawing interest from one major-league scout, Soto remembered, "Once a scout came to me at work and said he wanted to see me play, but I told him, 'Not unless you pay me what I'm making in construction.' I was making $7.50 a day for 12 hours' work."

Mario Soto ranks second in franchise history in career strikeouts.

Soto became far more receptive, though, when, some two months after he began pitching, he received an offer of $1,000 to sign with the Reds after Johnny Sierra, a bird-dog scout for the team, recommended him to fellow scout George Zuraw. Recalling his initial reaction to Soto, Zuraw stated years later, "Frankly, I wasn't impressed. We signed him strictly on a projection basis. I'd be lying to you if I said I thought he would be great."

Arriving in the United States shortly thereafter, Soto experienced difficulties acclimating himself to his new environment. Unable to speak any English, Soto contemplated quitting and returning home on several occasions, before finally deciding to stay the course. But he ended up missing almost two full seasons after breaking his elbow at the Reds' minor-league spring camp in 1974. Fully recovered by the start of the 1976 campaign, Soto discarded his curveball, which caused the injury to his elbow, and relied almost exclusively on his fastball to compile a record of 13–7 and lead the Class A Florida State League with a 1.87 ERA, 197 innings pitched, and 124 strikeouts. Extremely impressed with Soto's performance, Tampa general manager Mike Moore described him as "one of the best players ever to go through (the Reds') organization."

Promoted to Triple-A Indianapolis the following year, Soto won 11 of his 16 decisions, prompting the Reds to summon him to the big leagues in late July. Still only 21 years old, Soto struggled in his first trial with the parent club, going just 2–6 with a 5.34 ERA the rest of the year, earning him a return trip to the minors. Plagued by injury and control problems the next two seasons, Soto spent much of his time shuttling back and forth between Cincinnati and Indianapolis, before joining the Reds for good in 1980 after being converted into a reliever the previous year.

Working exclusively out of the bullpen the first half of 1980, Soto performed erratically, losing all three of his decisions and compiling an ERA of 4.99. But after joining the starting rotation at midseason, he became a different pitcher, earning a fifth-place finish in the NL Cy Young voting by compiling an overall record of 10–8 and ranking among the league leaders with an ERA of 3.07, a WHIP of 1.103, and 182 strikeouts. Described as the "sleeper of the staff" by Ray Buck of the *Cincinnati Enquirer*, Soto also received high praise from Reds pitching coach Bill Fischer, who called him "probably the best pitcher in the National League from July on."

Soto's emergence as one of the finest pitchers in the senior circuit could be attributed directly to the development of his changeup, which gave him the offspeed pitch he needed to complement his fastball. Thrown with the same motion as his mid-90s heater, Soto's changeup arrived at the plate some 10 to 15 mph slower, often freezing batters and resulting in what sportswriter Tim Sullivan called "embarrassing" strikeouts. Taught to him by Scott Breeden, the Reds minor-league roving pitching instructor, the changeup turned Soto into an elite hurler, with Rusty Staub saying, "There's no doubt that his changeup and his off-speed pitches with his fastball make him one of the best pitchers in all of baseball."

Soto, himself, stated, "I get most of my strikeouts with the changeup. That's the pitch that's made the difference for me."

Commenting on Soto's signature pitch, which proved to be equally effective against right-handed and left-handed batters, Reds scout Ray Shore offered, "Velocity is great, but movement on the ball is 90 percent of the battle. Soto throws his changeup with perfect motion . . . but that thing drops right off the table. It's almost like a spitter."

Meanwhile, Reds pitching coach Stan Williams stated, "Mario has one of the best changeups I've ever seen. And I pitched with Johnny Podres and Carl Erskine, who had great ones. They threw theirs differently, sort of like they were pulling down the window shade. Any way you throw it, it keeps the batter guessing."

Building upon the success he experienced the previous year, Soto performed well again during the strike-interrupted 1981 campaign, compiling a record of 12–9 and an ERA of 3.29, while placing near the top of the league rankings with 151 strikeouts, three shutouts, 10 complete games, and 175 innings pitched. Even better in 1982, Soto earned All-Star honors for the first of three straight times by posting a record of 14–13 for a Reds team that finished last in the NL West with only 61 victories, leading all NL hurlers with a WHIP of 1.060, and ranking among the leaders in ERA (2.79), strikeouts (274), innings pitched (257⅔), and complete games (13), with his 274 strikeouts setting a single-season franchise record that still stands.

Although the 6-foot, 170-pound Soto hardly presented an imposing figure on the mound, he demanded the inner half of the plate and never shied away from throwing inside to opposing batters. Soto also occasionally experienced lapses in control, with Reds catcher Joe Nolan saying of his batterymate, "He's just a little bit wild enough to keep batters from digging in."

Unfortunately, Soto also possessed a fiery temperament that sometimes caused him to lose his focus on the mound. Easily distracted by bad pitches, poor calls by umpires, hits, and runners on base, Soto often let his emotions get the best of him, prompting Reds catcher Alex Treviño to say, "He has the tendency to get mad and lose concentration, especially in close games."

Extremely confrontational as well, Soto never backed down from what he perceived to be a challenge to his manhood, displaying that side of his persona during a game against the Phillies on May 31, 1982. Plunked by Philadelphia starter Ron Reed in the sixth inning after hitting two Phillies batters earlier in the contest, Soto set off a bench-clearing brawl by threatening to hurl his bat out to the mound. Although Soto's actions contrasted sharply with what Lonnie Wheeler of the *Cincinnati Enquirer* described as a soft-spoken, loner type of person away from the playing field, they helped cement his reputation as a "loose cannon" that remained with him the rest of his career.

Continuing to excel on the mound in 1983, Soto went 17–13, led all NL hurlers with 18 complete games, and ranked among the leaders with a

2.70 ERA, a WHIP of 1.104, 242 strikeouts, and 273⅔ innings pitched, earning in the process a runner-up finish to Philadelphia's John Denny in the NL Cy Young voting.

Commenting on Soto's brilliant performance, sportswriter Murray Chass wrote, "When Soto gets on the mound, he has the best combination of fastball and changeup in the game today. He is no bully who pushes people around, but an artist who uses the baseball as deftly as if he had a paintbrush in his right hand."

Soto had another huge year in 1984, earning the last of his three All-Star nominations and a sixth-place finish in the Cy Young voting by compiling a record of 18–7, an ERA of 3.53, and a WHIP of 1.129, registering 185 strikeouts, and throwing 237⅓ innings and a league-high 13 complete games. But he provided additional fodder for those journalists who questioned his ability to control his temper when he became involved in two ugly incidents that further sullied his reputation.

The first occurred during a game against the Cubs at Wrigley Field on May 27, when, following a home-run call on a flyball hit toward the left field foul pole by Chicago's Ron Cey, Soto had to be restrained by teammates from attacking third base umpire Steve Rippley. Eventually breaking away from his teammates, Soto rushed into a scrum of players and coaches, forcing him to be tackled by Reds catcher Brad Gulden, who later said, "If he had hit the umpire the way he was coming, he probably wouldn't play another game in his life." Finally isolated from the group, Soto headed toward the dugout, only to be pelted with ice by a fan, which caused him to grab a bat and attempt to climb into the box seats to exact revenge against his assailant.

After being fined $1,000 and suspended by the league for five days, Soto found himself embroiled in controversy again just three starts later, when, following an altercation with Atlanta outfielder Claudell Washington over a pair of brushback pitches, he violently threw the ball into a crowd that had assembled on the mound after both benches emptied. Commenting on Soto's inexcusable act after the game, home plate umpire Lanny Harris said, "When a pitcher fires the ball into the stack and hits an umpire and a coach, I think it is serious."

Once again suspended for five days and fined the larger sum of $5,000, Soto attempted to defend his behavior by saying, "What would you do if someone came into your house and attacked you? Wouldn't you fight back? . . . I do feel bad about what happened. But everybody blows away once in a while. Sometimes you do things and don't remember that you did them. In Chicago, all I wanted to do with the umpires was argue with them. In Atlanta, I was only trying to defend myself. It's only a moment, but people aren't going to let me forget."

Subsequently portrayed in the media as a troublemaker, Soto responded by stating, "I don't care what they say about me. Everybody is entitled to a few mistakes. Nobody is perfect."

In discussing his Reds teammate, Dave Parker said, "Some of his episodes on the field might lead you to believe otherwise, but he's a very nice guy, a leader, and a great competitor."

Meanwhile, Reds manager Vern Rapp urged Soto's critics to view things from the pitcher's perspective, saying, "I wish people knew where Mario comes from, how he had to fight to achieve what he has. He still has to learn self-control, to act like a professional. Mario and I have sat down and talked about this. What he did this year had no malicious intent to it as far as I can see. I think he just became frightened, more than anything else. Somebody was trying to take away his livelihood."

Choosing to take the high road, Claudell Washington stated, "Take nothing away from him. Mario Soto is a great pitcher. He has the best stuff in baseball."

Somewhat less forgiving, Braves catcher Alex Treviño said of his former Reds teammate, "He has a million-dollar arm and a 10-cent head."

Although Soto initially performed well under new Reds manager Pete Rose in 1985, compiling a record of 8–3 and an ERA of 2.48 through the first week of June, the four-man starting rotation instituted by Rose and pitching coach Jim Kaat eventually began to take its toll on him. Despite placing near the top of the league rankings with 214 strikeouts, Soto, who once complained, "Why can't I pitch on five days' rest?," ended up finishing the year just 12–15 with a 3.58 ERA.

Refusing to speak to the press about his slump, Soto isolated himself completely from the media, saying, "When I pitch, this is my career. I have to handle it. I have to work it out myself. I don't have to talk to anyone about it."

Also distancing himself somewhat from his teammates, Soto experienced a marked change in his personality, with Reds beat writer Greg Hoard suggesting, "Somehow, some way, through a series of events and circumstances that only he knows, Soto has become withdrawn where he was once outgoing, and dispirited in performance, where he was formerly a vigorous competitor."

And with the Reds in contention for the NL West title and Soto explaining his failure to make all his scheduled mound appearances the last few weeks of the season by saying, "There's no reason to try to pitch when you're not 100 percent," Hoard wrote, "Soto's legacy for the 1985 season will be that he and no one else lost the Western Division title for the Reds; that he lost heart, lost too many games."

Continuing his boycott of the media in 1986, Soto silently suffered through a horrendous 5–10 campaign that ended mercifully after only 20 starts, when he underwent surgery on his shoulder in late August. Unable to make a full recovery, Soto appeared in just 20 games over the course of the next two seasons, before announcing his retirement shortly after the Reds released him on June 20, 1988.

Soto, who over parts of 12 seasons in Cincinnati, compiled a record of 100–92, posted an ERA of 3.47 and a WHIP of 1.186, threw 72 complete games and 13 shutouts, earned four saves, and struck out 1,449 batters in 1,730⅓ innings pitched, has remained close to the Reds in retirement, serving as a spring-training instructor, scout, and director of the team's Dominican operations. Named a special assistant to the GM in 2009, Soto, who currently resides near his hometown of Baní, in the Dominican Republic, has spent the last several years working closely with the organization's Latin American prospects, serving as a mentor, and helping them transition to a new country, language, and culture.

CAREER HIGHLIGHTS

Best Season

Although Soto posted a better won-lost record in 1984 and struck out more batters in 1982, he had the finest all-around season of his career in 1983, when he earned a runner-up finish in the NL Cy Young voting by finishing second in the league with 17 victories, 242 strikeouts, 273⅔ innings pitched, and a WHIP of 1.104, placing fourth in the circuit with a 2.70 ERA, and leading all NL hurlers with 18 complete games.

Memorable Moments/Greatest Performances

After replacing an ineffective Bruce Berenyi, Soto performed magnificently in a relief role on July 5, 1980, yielding just three hits over 8⅔ scoreless innings, with his brilliant effort allowing the Reds to turn an early 6–0 deficit to the Astros into an 8–6 win.

Soto recorded 15 strikeouts during a complete-game 7–1 victory over the Braves on September 9, 1980, in which he allowed seven hits and one walk.

In addition to yielding just six hits and one walk during a 2–0 shutout of the Mets on June 10, 1981, Soto registered a season-high 12 strikeouts.

Soto dominated New York's lineup again on August 21, 1981, allowing just four hits, issuing one walk, and striking out eight batters during another 2–0 shutout of the Mets.

Soto tossed a one-hitter on October 4, 1981, issuing two walks, recording nine strikeouts, and yielding just a second-inning single by Chris Chambliss during a 3–0 shutout of the Braves.

Soto turned in a pair of superb efforts in May of 1982, striking out 11 batters and allowing just five hits and one walk during a 5–0 shutout of the Pirates on the 7th of the month, before registering 10 strikeouts, issuing no walks, and yielding just four hits during a 2–0 blanking of the Phillies on the 26th.

Soto tossed a complete-game four-hitter on August 17, 1982, issuing no walks and striking out 15 batters during a lopsided 9–2 victory over the Mets.

Soto yielded just three harmless singles, issued two walks, and recorded nine strikeouts during a 6–0 shutout of the Braves on September 13, 1983.

Soto flirted with a no-hitter on May 12, 1984, surrendering just a two-out ninth-inning home run by George Hendrick during a 2–1 win over the Cardinals in which he walked five batters and recorded 12 strikeouts.

Soto hit the only home run of his career during a 4–1 complete-game victory over the Montreal Expos on June 30, 1984, in which he yielded just four hits.

Soto surrendered just two hits, issued four walks, and recorded nine strikeouts during a 1–0 shutout of the Cubs on May 29, 1985.

Notable Achievements:

- Won at least 17 games twice.
- Posted winning percentage over .700 once.
- Compiled ERA under 3.00 three times.
- Struck out more than 200 batters three times.
- Threw 18 complete games in 1983.
- Threw more than 250 innings three times, tossing more than 200 innings one other time.

- Led NL pitchers in WHIP once, complete games twice, and starts once.
- Finished second in NL in wins twice, winning percentage once, WHIP once, strikeouts twice, innings pitched once, and complete games once.
- Holds Reds single-season record for most strikeouts (274 in 1982).
- Ranks among Reds career leaders in strikeouts (2nd) and WHIP (10th).
- 1979 division champion.
- Two-time Reds team MVP (1982 and 1983).
- Finished second in 1983 NL Cy Young voting.
- Three-time NL All-Star selection (1982, 1983, and 1984).

SUMMARY AND HONORABLE MENTIONS (THE NEXT 25)

Having identified the 50 greatest players in Reds history, the time has come to select the best of the best. Based on the rankings contained in this book, the members of the Reds all-time team are listed below. Our squad includes the top player at each position, along with a pitching staff that features a five-man starting rotation, a setup man, and a closer. Our starting lineup also includes a designated hitter. Also listed are the members of the second team, whose relievers were taken from the list of honorable mentions that will soon follow.

FIRST TEAM STARTING LINEUP

Joe Morgan	2B
Pete Rose	LF
Frank Robinson	RF
Johnny Bench	C
Joey Votto	1B
Tony Pérez	3B
Ted Kluszewski	DH
Barry Larkin	SS
Vada Pinson	CF

FIRST TEAM PITCHING STAFF

Bucky Walters	SP
Eppa Rixey	SP
Paul Derringer	SP
Jim Maloney	SP

Don Gullett	SP
John Franco	SU
Aroldis Chapman	CL

SECOND TEAM STARTING LINEUP

Eric Davis	CF
Edd Roush	LF
George Foster	DH
Ernie Lombardi	C
Frank McCormick	1B
Ken Griffey Sr.	RF
Brandon Phillips	2B
Dave Concepción	SS
Heinie Groh	3B

SECOND TEAM PITCHING STAFF

José Rijo	SP
Tom Seaver	SP
Noodles Hahn	SP
Pete Donohue	SP
Johnny Cueto	SP
Pedro Borbón	SU
Clay Carroll	CL

Although I limited my earlier rankings to the top 50 players in Reds history, many other fine players have performed for the fans of Cincinnati through the years, some of whom narrowly missed making the final cut. Following is a list of those players deserving of an honorable mention. These are the men I deemed worthy of being slotted into positions 51 to 75 in the overall rankings. The statistics they compiled during their time in the Queen City and their most notable achievements as members of the Reds are also included.

51—Jay Bruce (OF, 2008–2016)

Reds Numbers: 233 HR, 718 RBIs, 655 Runs Scored, 1,116 Hits, 238 Doubles, 27 Triples, 61 SB, .249 AVG, .319 OBP, .470 SLG, .789 OPS

Notable Achievements

- Hit more than 20 home runs eight times, topping 30 homers three times.
- Knocked in more than 100 runs once.
- Topped 30 doubles three times.
- Posted slugging percentage over .500 twice.
- Hit three home runs in one game vs. Cubs on August 27, 2010.
- Finished second in NL with 109 RBIs in 2013.
- Finished third in NL in home runs twice and doubles once.
- Led NL right fielders in putouts twice and double plays turned once.
- Ranks eighth in franchise history in home runs.
- Two-time division champion (2010 and 2012).
- Five-time NL Player of the Week.
- May 2011 NL Player of the Month.
- Two-time Silver Slugger Award winner (2012 and 2013).
- 2013 NL Wilson Defensive Player of the Year Award winner.
- Finished in top 10 of NL MVP voting twice (2012 and 2013).
- Three-time NL All-Star selection (2011, 2012, and 2016).

52—Clay Carroll (P, 1968–1975)

Reds Numbers: Record: 71–43, .623 Win Pct., 2.73 ERA, 119 Saves, 856 IP, 460 Strikeouts, 1.319 WHIP

Notable Achievements

- Won at least 10 games three times.
- Posted winning percentage over .700 twice.
- Led NL with 37 saves and 65 pitching appearances in 1972.
- Finished second in NL with 17 saves in 1968.
- Compiled ERA under 3.00 six times, posting mark under 2.50 on three occasions.
- Threw more than 100 innings four times.

- Ranks among Reds career leaders in winning percentage (tied for 5th), saves (5th) and pitching appearances (3rd).
- Four-time division champion (1970, 1972, 1973, and 1975).
- Three-time NL champion (1970, 1972, and 1975).
- 1975 world champion.
- Finished fifth in 1972 NL Cy Young voting.
- Two-time NL All-Star selection (1971 and 1972).

53—Ewell Blackwell (P, 1942, 1946–1952)

Reds Numbers: Record: 79–77, .506 Win Pct., 3.32 ERA, 69 CG, 15 Shutouts, 8 Saves, 1,281.1 IP, 819 Strikeouts, 1.288 WHIP

Notable Achievements

- Won more than 20 games once, surpassing 16 victories two other times.
- Posted winning percentage over .700 once.
- Compiled ERA under 3.00 three times, posting mark under 2.50 twice.
- Threw more than 20 complete games once.
- Threw more than 250 innings twice.
- Threw no-hitter vs. Boston Braves on June 18, 1947.
- Led NL pitchers in wins, strikeouts, shutouts, and complete games once each.
- Finished second in NL in ERA twice, WHIP once, strikeouts once, and shutouts once.
- Finished second in 1947 NL MVP voting.
- Six-time NL All-Star selection (1946, 1947, 1948, 1949, 1950, and 1951).
- 1947 *Sporting News* All-Star selection.

54—Dan Driessen (1B, 3B, 1973–1984)

Reds Numbers: 133 HR, 670 RBIs, 661 Runs Scored, 1,277 Hits, 240 Doubles, 23 Triples, 152 SB, .271 AVG, .361 OBP, .416 SLG, .777 OPS

Notable Achievements

- Batted over .300 twice.
- Topped 30 doubles twice.

- Stole more than 20 bases twice.
- Led NL with 93 walks in 1980.
- Led NL first basemen in fielding percentage three times.
- Ranks among Reds career leaders with 678 walks (10th) and 58 sacrifice flies (6th).
- Four-time division champion (1973, 1975, 1976, and 1979).
- Two-time NL champion (1975 and 1976).
- Two-time world champion (1975 and 1976).
- Two-time NL Player of the Week.

55—Reggie Sanders (OF, 1991–1998)

Reds Numbers: 125 HR, 431 RBIs, 499 Runs Scored, 781 Hits, 152 Doubles, 33 Triples, 158 SB, .271 AVG, .353 OBP, .476 SLG, .829 OPS

Notable Achievements:

- Hit at least 20 home runs twice.
- Batted over .300 once (.306 in 1995).
- Posted slugging percentage over .500 twice.
- Posted OPS over .900 once (.975 in 1995).
- Topped 30 doubles once (36 in 1995).
- Stole at least 20 bases five times.
- Hit three home runs in one game vs. Colorado on August 15, 1995.
- 1995 division champion.
- June 4, 1995, NL Player of the Week.
- Finished sixth in 1995 NL MVP voting.
- 1995 NL All-Star selection.
- 1995 *Sporting News* NL All-Star selection.

56—Hal Morris (1B, OF, 1990–1997, 1999–2000)

Reds Numbers: 74 HR, 461 RBIs, 467 Runs Scored, 1,030 Hits, 212 Doubles, 19 Triples, 44 SB, .305 AVG, .362 OBP, .444 SLG, .807 OPS

Notable Achievements:

- Batted over .300 five times, topping the .330 mark twice.
- Topped 30 doubles three times.
- Finished second in NL with .318 batting average in 1991.

- Led NL first basemen with .999 fielding percentage in 1992.
- Two-time division champion (1990 and 1995).
- 1990 NL champion.
- 1990 world champion.
- Three-time NL Player of the Week.
- 1994 Reds team MVP.

57—Bubbles Hargrave (C, 1921–1928)

Reds Numbers: 29 HR, 359 RBIs, 298 Runs Scored, 744 Hits, 146 Doubles, 57 Triples, 27 SB, .314 AVG, .377 OBP, .461 SLG, .838 OPS

Notable Achievements:

- Batted over .300 six times.
- Compiled on-base percentage over .400 twice.
- Posted slugging percentage over .500 three times.
- Posted OPS over .900 twice.
- Finished in double digits in triples twice.
- Led NL with .353 batting average in 1926.
- Led NL catchers in double plays turned once and fielding percentage once.
- Ranks fourth in franchise history in career batting average.
- Finished sixth in 1926 NL MVP voting.

58—Joe Nuxhall (P, 1944, 1952–1960, 1962–1966)

Reds Numbers: Record: 130–109, .544 Win Pct., 3.80 ERA, 82 CG, 20 Shutouts, 18 Saves, 2,169.1 IP, 1,289 Strikeouts, 1.325 WHIP

Notable Achievements

- Won at least 15 games twice.
- Posted winning percentage over .700 three times.
- Compiled ERA under 3.00 twice.
- Threw more than 200 innings three times, tossing more than 250 frames once.
- Led NL with five shutouts in 1955.
- Finished second in NL with 257 innings pitched in 1955.
- Finished third in NL with 17 wins in 1955.

- Ranks among Reds career leaders in wins (9th), strikeouts (3rd), shutouts (10th), innings pitched (6th), pitching appearances (4th), and games started (9th).
- Two-time NL All-Star selection (1955 and 1956).

59—Pedro Borbón (P, 1970–1979)

Reds Numbers: Record: 62–33, .653 Win Pct., 3.32 ERA, 76 Saves, 920.2 IP, 359 Strikeouts, 1.289 WHIP

Notable Achievements

- Won at least 10 games three times.
- Posted winning percentage over .700 three times.
- Compiled ERA under 3.00 twice, posting mark under 2.50 once.
- Posted WHIP under 1.000 once.
- Threw more than 100 innings six times.
- Finished second in NL with 80 pitching appearances in 1973.
- Finished third in NL with 14 saves in 1974.
- Holds franchise record for most pitching appearances (531).
- Ranks among Reds career leaders in winning percentage (3rd) and saves (10th).
- Five-time division champion (1970, 1972, 1973, 1975, and 1976).
- Four-time NL champion (1970, 1972, 1975, and 1976).
- Two-time world champion (1975 and 1976).

60—Red Lucas (P, 1926–1933)

Reds Numbers: Record: 109–99, .524 Win Pct., 3.64 ERA, 158 CG, 18 Shutouts, 6 Saves, 1,768.2 IP, 404 Strikeouts, 1.226 WHIP

Notable Achievements

- Won at least 18 games twice.
- Compiled ERA under 3.00 once.
- Threw more than 20 complete games four times.
- Threw more than 250 innings twice.
- Led NL pitchers in complete games three times, shutouts once, and WHIP once.
- Finished second in NL in wins once, shutouts once, and WHIP once.

- Ranks among Reds career leaders in complete games (10th) and shutouts (tied for 11th).
- Finished sixth in 1929 NL MVP voting.

61—Rube Bressler (OF, 1B, P, 1917–1927)

Reds Numbers: 15 HR, 344 RBIs, 294 Runs Scored, 692 Hits, 90 Doubles, 49 Triples, 37 SB, .311 AVG, .379 OBP, .416 SLG, .795 OPS

Record: 12–9, .571 Win Pct., 2.76 ERA, 12 CG, 1 Shutout, 199 IP, 56 Strikeouts, 1.276 WHIP

Notable Achievements

- Batted over .300 four times, topping the .340 mark three times.
- Compiled on-base percentage over .400 twice.
- Posted OPS over .900 twice.
- Finished in double digits in triples once (13 in 1924).
- Compiled ERA under 2.50 once (2.46 in 1918).
- Ranks among Reds career leaders in batting average (tied for 7th) and on-base percentage (tied for 9th).
- 1919 NL champion.
- 1919 world champion.

62—Bob Purkey (P, 1958–1964)

Reds Numbers: Record: 103–76, .575 Win Pct., 3.49 ERA, 81 CG, 11 Shutouts, 3 Saves, 1,588 IP, 635 Strikeouts, 1.219 WHIP

Notable Achievements

- Won 23 games in 1962.
- Posted 17 victories two other times.
- Compiled ERA under 3.00 once (2.81 in 1962).
- Threw more than 250 innings three times, tossing more than 200 frames two other times.
- Threw at least 17 complete games twice.
- Led NL pitchers with .821 winning percentage in 1962.
- Led NL pitchers in putouts twice, assists once, and double plays turned once.

- Finished second in NL in WHIP once, shutouts once, and innings pitched once.
- 1961 NL champion.
- May 1962 NL Player of the Month.
- Finished third in 1962 Cy Young voting.
- Finished eighth in 1962 NL MVP voting.
- Three-time NL All-Star selection (1958, 1961, and 1962).
- 1962 *Sporting News* NL All-Star selection.

63—Jim O'Toole (P, 1958–1966)

Reds Numbers: Record: 94–81, .537 Win Pct., 3.59 ERA, 57 CG, 17 Shutouts, 4 Saves, 1,561 IP, 1,002 Strikeouts, 1.294 WHIP

Notable Achievements

- Won at least 16 games four times.
- Posted winning percentage over .700 once.
- Compiled ERA under 3.00 twice.
- Threw more than 250 innings twice, tossing more than 200 frames two other times.
- Finished second in NL with 3.10 ERA in 1961.
- Finished third in NL in wins once, winning percentage twice, and shutouts once.
- 1961 NL champion.
- September 1961 NL Player of the Month.
- Finished 10th in 1961 NL MVP voting.
- 1963 NL All-Star selection.

64—Rob Dibble (P, 1988–1993)

Reds Numbers: Record: 26–23, .531 Win Pct., 2.74 ERA, 88 Saves, 450.2 IP, 619 Strikeouts, 1.127 WHIP

Notable Achievements

- Won 10 games in 1989.
- Posted winning percentage over .700 once.
- Saved more than 20 games twice.
- Compiled ERA under 2.00 twice.

- Posted WHIP under 1.000 once.
- Struck out more than 100 batters four times.
- Finished second in NL with 31 saves in 1991.
- Ranks among Reds career leaders in saves (tied for 7th).
- 1990 division champion.
- 1990 NL champion.
- 1990 world champion.
- June 1991 NL Pitcher of the Month.
- 1990 NLCS MVP.
- Two-time NL All-Star selection (1990 and 1991).

65—Eugenio Suarez (3B, SS, 2015–2021)

Reds Numbers: 189 HR, 524 RBIs, 473 Runs Scored, 828 Hits, 144 Doubles, 10 Triples, 25 SB, .253 AVG, .335 OBP, .476 SLG, .811 OPS

Notable Achievements:

- Hit more than 20 home runs five times, topping 30 homers three times and 40 homers once.
- Knocked in more than 100 runs twice.
- Posted slugging percentage over .500 twice.
- Posted OPS over .900 once (.930 in 2019).
- Hit three home runs in one game vs. Pirates on September 5, 2020.
- Finished second in NL with 49 home runs in 2019.
- Led NL third basemen in putouts twice.
- September 2019 NL Player of the Month.
- Two-time Reds team MVP (2018 and 2019).
- 2018 NL All-Star selection.

66—Francisco Cordero (P, 2008–2011)

Reds Numbers: Record: 18–18, .500 Win Pct., 2.96 ERA, 150 Saves, 279.1 IP, 237 Strikeouts, 1.296 WHIP

Notable Achievements:

- Saved more than 30 games four straight times.
- Compiled ERA under 2.50 twice.
- Finished second in NL with 39 saves in 2009.

- Finished third in NL with 40 saves in 2010.
- Ranks second in franchise history in saves.
- 2010 division champion.
- 2009 NL All-Star selection.

67—César Gerónimo (OF, 1972–1980)

Reds Numbers: 44 HR, 344 RBIs, 404 Runs Scored, 869 Hits, 148 Doubles, 43 Triples, 72 SB, .261 AVG, .330 OBP, .371 SLG, .701 OPS

Notable Achievements:

- Batted over .300 once (.307 in 1976).
- Stole more than 20 bases once (22 in 1976).
- Finished second in NL with 11 triples in 1976.
- Led NL outfielders in putouts once and double plays turned once.
- Five-time division champion (1972, 1973, 1975, 1976, and 1979).
- Three-time NL champion (1972, 1975, and 1976).
- Two-time world champion (1975 and 1976).
- Four-time Gold Glove Award winner (1974, 1975, 1976, and 1977).

68—Mike Mitchell (OF, 1907–1912)

Reds Numbers: 19 HR, 420 RBIs, 401 Runs Scored, 892 Hits, 95 Doubles, 88 Triples, 165 SB, .283 AVG, .345 OBP, .387 SLG, .732 OPS

Notable Achievements:

- Batted over .300 once.
- Finished in double digits in triples five times, topping 20 three-baggers once.
- Led NL in triples twice.
- Finished second in NL in RBIs, batting average, slugging percentage, OPS, and triples once each.
- Led NL outfielders with 39 assists in 1907.
- Led NL right fielders in putouts three times and double plays turned twice.
- Ranks seventh in franchise history in triples.

69—Curt Walker (OF, 1924–1930)

Reds Numbers: 43 HR, 482 RBIs, 498 Runs Scored, 1,028 Hits, 152 Doubles, 94 Triples, 69 SB, .303 AVG, .378 OBP, .441 SLG, .819 OPS

Notable Achievements

- Batted over .300 five times.
- Compiled on-base percentage over .400 once.
- Finished in double digits in triples seven times, topping 20 three-baggers once.
- Finished second in NL in triples three times.
- Finished third in NL with 19 stolen bases in 1928.
- Led NL outfielders in fielding percentage once and double plays turned once.
- Led NL right fielders in putouts once and double plays turned three times.
- Ranks among Reds career leaders in triples (6th).

70—Lonny Frey (2B, 1938–1943, 1946)

Reds Numbers: 36 HR, 310 RBIs, 541 Runs Scored, 937 Hits, 158 Doubles, 43 Triples, 68 SB, .265 AVG, .358 OBP, .365 SLG, .723 OPS

Notable Achievements

- Scored 102 runs in 1940.
- Led NL in stolen bases and sacrifice hits once each.
- Led NL second basemen in putouts once, assists once, double plays turned twice, and fielding percentage twice.
- Two-time NL champion (1939 and 1940).
- 1940 world champion.
- Three-time NL All-Star selection (1939, 1941, and 1943).

71—Dick Hoblitzell (1B, 1908–1914)

Reds Numbers: 24 HR, 409 RBIs, 396 Runs Scored, 897 Hits, 132 Doubles, 65 Triples, 127 SB, .283 AVG, .339 OBP, .388 SLG, .727 OPS

Notable Achievements

- Batted over .300 once.
- Finished in double digits in triples four times.
- Topped 30 doubles once.
- Led NL in games played once and at-bats twice.
- Finished second in NL with 180 hits in 1911.
- Finished third in NL with .308 batting average and .782 OPS in 1909.
- Led NL first basemen in double plays turned once.
- Ranks fourth in franchise history with 137 sacrifice hits.

72—Pat Duncan (OF, 1919–1924)

Reds Numbers: 23 HR, 374 RBIs, 361 Runs Scored, 826 Hits, 137 Doubles, 50 Triples, 55 SB, .307 AVG, .355 OBP, .421 SLG, .776 OPS

Notable Achievements

- Batted over .300 three times.
- Finished in double digits in triples three times.
- Finished third in NL with 44 doubles in 1922.
- Led NL outfielders with .993 fielding percentage in 1923.
- Led NL left fielders with 16 assists in 1920.
- Ranks among Reds career leaders in batting average (tied for 10th) and sacrifice hits (9th).
- 1919 NL champion.
- 1919 world champion.

73—Roy McMillan (SS, 1951–1960)

Reds Numbers: 42 HR, 395 RBIs, 497 Runs Scored, 1,074 Hits, 178 Doubles, 29 Triples, 30 SB, .249 AVG, .326 OBP, .332 SLG, .658 OPS

Notable Achievements

- Led NL in sacrifice hits once and games played twice.
- Finished third in NL with 32 doubles in 1952.
- Led NL shortstops in assists three times, putouts twice, double plays turned four times, and fielding percentage three times.
- 1956 Reds team MVP.

- Finished sixth in 1956 NL MVP voting.
- Three-time Gold Glove Award winner (1957, 1958, and 1959).
- Two-time NL All-Star selection (1956 and 1957).

74—Tommy Helms (2B, 3B, 1964–1971)

Reds Numbers: 18 HR, 274 RBIs, 271 Runs Scored, 858 Hits, 145 Doubles, 12 Triples, 23 SB, .269 AVG, .297 OBP, .339 SLG, .635 OPS

Notable Achievements

- Led NL second basemen in putouts once, double plays turned twice, and fielding percentage twice.
- 1970 division champion.
- 1970 NL champion.
- 1966 NL Rookie of the Year.
- Two-time Gold Glove Award winner (1970 and 1971).
- Two-time NL All-Star selection (1967 and 1968).
- 1968 *Sporting News* NL All-Star selection.

75—Deron Johnson (3B, 1B, OF, 1964–1967)

Reds Numbers: 90 HR, 343 RBIs, 269 Runs Scored, 518 Hits, 97 Doubles, 15 Triples, 5 SB, .264 AVG, .316 OBP, .467 SLG, .783 OPS

Notable Achievements

- Hit more than 20 home runs three times, topping 30 homers once.
- Knocked in more than 100 runs once.
- Posted slugging percentage over .500 once (.515 in 1965).
- Topped 30 doubles once.
- Led NL with 130 RBIs in 1965.
- 1965 Reds team MVP.
- Finished fourth in 1965 NL MVP voting.
- 1965 *Sporting News* NL All-Star selection.

GLOSSARY

ABBREVIATIONS AND STATISTICAL TERMS

1B. First baseman.

2B. Second baseman.

3B. Third baseman.

AVG. Batting average. The number of hits divided by the number of at-bats.

BB. Bases on balls (walks).

C. Catcher.

CF. Center fielder.

CG. Complete games pitched.

CL. Closer.

DH. Designated hitter.

ERA. Earned run average. The number of earned runs a pitcher gives up, per nine innings. This does not include runs that score as a result of errors made in the field and is calculated by dividing the number of runs given up by the number of innings pitched and multiplying the result by 9.

HITS. Base hits. Awarded when a runner safely reaches at least first base upon a batted ball, if no error is recorded.

HR. Home runs. Fair ball hit over the fence, or one hit to a spot that allows the batter to circle the bases before the ball is returned to home plate.

IP. Innings pitched.

LF. Left fielder.

OBP. On-base percentage. Hits plus walks plus hit-by-pitches, divided by plate appearances.

OPS. On-base plus slugging (the sum of a player's slugging percentage and on-base percentage).

RBI. Runs batted in. Awarded to the batter when a runner scores upon a safely batted ball, a sacrifice, or a walk.

RF. Right fielder.

RUNS. Runs scored by a player.

SB. Stolen bases.

SHO. Shutouts.

SLG. Slugging percentage. The number of total bases earned by all singles, doubles, triples and home runs, divided by the total number of at-bats.

SO. Strikeouts.

SP. Starting pitcher.

SS. Shortstop.

SU. Setup man.

WHIP. Walks and hits per inning pitched.

WIN PCT. Winning percentage. A pitcher's number of wins divided by his number of total decisions (i.e., wins plus losses).

W-L. Win-loss record.

BIBLIOGRAPHY

BOOKS

Allen, Lee. *The Cincinnati Reds*. Kent, OH: Kent State University Press, 2006.

Armour, Mark. *The Great Eight: The 1975 Cincinnati Reds*. Lincoln: University of Nebraska Press, 2014.

Blair, Rick Van. *Dugout to Foxhole: Interviews with Baseball Players Whose Careers Were Affected by World War II*. Jefferson, NC: McFarland Publishing, 1994.

Creamer, Robert W. *Stengel: His Life and Times*. Lincoln: University of Nebraska Press, 1996.

Luckhaupt, Joel. *100 Things Reds Fans Should Know & Do Before They Die*. Chicago: Triumph Books, 2013.

Shalin, Mike, and Neil Shalin. *Out by a Step: The 100 Best Players Not in the Baseball Hall of Fame*. Lanham, MD: Diamond Communications, Inc., 2002.

WEBSITES

Bio Project, online at SABR.org
(www.sabr.org/bioproj/person)

The Players, online at Baseball-Reference.com
(www.baseball-reference.com/players)

The Teams, online at Baseball-Reference.com
(www.baseball-reference.com/teams)

www.ingramcontent.com/pod-product-compliance
Lightning Source LLC
Chambersburg PA
CBHW061910090125
20103CB00005B/7

9781493085910